THE LAW OF BANKING

The Law of Banking

by
CAMPBELL B. BURNS, M.A., LL.B., PH.D.

Senior Lecturer, The Law School, University of Strathclyde

WILLIAM HODGE & COMPANY LIMITED

GLASGOW

1976

Printed in Great Britain by
William Hodge & Co Ltd, Glasgow

ISBN 0 85279 064 3

PREFACE

It is over a quarter of a century since the last edition of Wallace and McNeil's *Banking Law* and the changes in banking law and practice during that period have rendered that work less valuable to the student of banking and the professional banker. In its original conception the purpose of this book was to provide a text book for the final stage students of the Institute of Bankers in Scotland, while bearing in mind the need of the working banker for the sort of working book which Wallace and McNeil had been.

The choice of subjects was dictated by the syllabus of the Institute of Bankers in Scotland reflecting as it does the considered ideas of the professional, practical banker of those parts of the law which are of most concern to the profession; there could be arguments for other areas of the law to be included, or even for some which appear to be excluded. It struck me that the final arbiters of the content of the book should be the bankers themselves.

In one case it proved that following the syllabus was raising more problems than could be solved by doing so and, following the comments of those bankers who read the manuscript, I decided not to include in this edition any treatment of the Consumer Credit Act 1974. The importance of this Act to the banker will be great but the skeleton of the Act is to be clothed with regulations and until these appear examination of the vague terms of the statute would, in my opinion, have lead to more confusion than elucidation.

The manuscript was read and commented upon by several bankers. I am grateful for the help I had from Mr. J. Russell, Law Secretary of the Clydesdale Bank Ltd., and to Miss Smith and Mr. Davey on his staff whose comments I have incorporated into the final text. I must, however, particularly mention the help of Mr. J. S. H. Allen, Senior Law Secretary of the Royal Bank of Scotland, whose examination of the text and comments upon it went far beyond what could have been expected of any volunteer. The help I had from my friends in banking was great and their encouragement most comforting when it seemed that the work would never be finished. Any worth which the book is found to have can fairly be attributed to them.

The index, Table of Cases and Table of Statutes is the work of Mr. F. McAdams of the Department of Librarianship of this University.

UNIVERSITY OF STRATHCLYDE,   C. B. BURNS,
October 1975.

CONTENTS

PAGE

CHAPTER FOUR

CHAPTER FIVE

PAGE

CHAPTER SIX

CHAPTER SEVEN

CONTENTS

TABLE OF STATUTES

TABLE OF CASES

CHAPTER ONE

BANKER AND CUSTOMER

THE banking contract is not simply defined, comprising as it does the many facets of the relationship between a banker and his customer: when a banker opens an account and thus enters into contractual relations with his customer he is undertaking a relationship in which he may be his customer's debtor or his creditor, his agent, a custodian of his securities or his possessions and a guarantor of his debts through the issue of a cheque card. The responsibilities and the duties of the banker, therefore, vary according to the capacity in which he finds himself at any particular time, while his rights will vary in a similar manner. It is, therefore, perhaps more accurate to refer to the banker's contracts than to the banking contract, the many facets of which virtually disqualify it from single description. When one adds to the more traditional activities associated with banking the services connected with executorship, with the maintenance of company registers, with insurance, and with income tax, all becoming a common part of the business of banks, the argument that within the relationship between a banker and his customer there is not one but several contracts, is strengthened. When, however, a banker is acting as an agent or an executor or an adviser the law which covers such a relationship applies to him as it would to any person acting in a similar capacity; the pecularities of the banker's relationship emerge only when he is acting in the business of banking strictly so-called.

Defining a banker

There is no statutory definition of a banker; for example, the Bills of Exchange Act, (s.2), says a banker includes a body of persons whether incorporated or not who carry on the business of banking while the Bankers' Books Evidence Act 1879 says 'the expression "bank" and "banker" means any person, persons, partnership or company carrying on the business of bankers and having duly made a return to the Commissioners of Inland Revenue and also Savings

1

Banks certified under the Acts relating to Savings Banks and also any Post Office Savings Bank'. In other statutes a man is deemed a banker if the Treasury deems him so, or the Department of Trade recognises him so to be.[1] Thus it seems that the closest that the legislature has come to defining a banker is as someone who carries on the business of banking.

What is, in modern times, the business of banking? The three hall-marks of the banker are the receipt of money on current or deposit accounts, the collection of the proceeds of cheques for customers, and the payment of cheques drawn by customers.[2] Thus in *Bank of Chettinad* v. *Inland Revenue*[3] the Privy Council suggested that a concern is only in banking and is to be treated as a bank if it carries on 'as its principal business the acceptance of deposits of money on current account or otherwise, subject to withdrawal by cheque, draft or order.' Further judicial consideration as to whether a particular business was engaged in banking was given in *United Dominions Trust Ltd.* v. *Kirkwood*.[4] In the Court of Appeal it was clear that the judges were seeking evidence that the company fulfilled the conditions laid down by the Privy Council in *Bank of Chettinad*; those judges, the majority, who were satisfied that the company did maintain current accounts, collected cheques for customers, and honoured cheques drawn on it by customers were prepared to find that the company carried on business as bankers. It must also be said that the reputation of the company in the community, particularly in the banking community, influenced the decision, one judge suggesting that one could not be a banker without a reputation for soundness, stability and probity. The dissentient judge was not prepared to rely on reputation unless backed by performance and he could not identify the three characteristics of a banking business in the circumstances. Thus it might be said that the presence of the three characteristics is of vital importance in ascertaining who is a banker but these should be accompanied by stability soundness and probity.

It should be noted that the Privy Council opinion encompasses the idea that to qualify as a banker, the main business he carries on should include the three characteristics. Thus it might be argued that

---

[1] Companies Act, 1967, s. 123(1).
[2] Paget's Law of Banking; Halsbury's Laws of England.
[3] [1948] A.C. 378 B.C.
[4] [1966] 2Q.B. 431.

if these activities were a minor part, and not the main part, of the activities of a concern, the business might not fall within the definition of a banker. This was held to be the case in *Stafford* v. *Henry*,[5] a decision which might give some concern to departmental stores and co-operative societies which offer banking facilities to their customer. The argument that even where cheque books are issued by such concerns they might not be bankers within the legal meaning can be met, however, merely by the formation of a subsidiary which has as its main business activities which fall within the three characteristics.

It will be appreciated that there are Trustee Savings Banks and similar organisations which clearly fall out with the definition of the law; their legal position is defined by the statutes which create them and regulate their activities.

Defining a customer

The identity of the customer in the banking relationship emerges also from judicial decision; there has been no endeavour to define a customer by statute, although the term appears in certain Acts of Parliament.[6] It is of importance who is a banker's customer from two points of view: a banker owes duties to his customer which are not owed to those who are not customers,[7] and, in certain cases, important protections are offered by statute to the banker acting for a customer[8] which are not available if he is offering services to members of the public who are not customers. However, the decisions as to who is a customer are not entirely clear. Historically, it could be said that a customer was a person who had an account with a banker and some course of dealing with him. This was founded on two cases. In *Matthews* v. *Williams. Brown and Co.*[9] the banker had collected a cheque for a stranger and when it transpired that the cheque had been stolen sought the protection then offered by statute to the banker who received payment on behalf of a customer.[10] The Courts held that a single transaction with someone did not found the banker-customer relationship, the term 'customer' implying a course of dealing. In *Great Western Railway Co.* v. *London and County Banking Co.*[11] where the defendant bank had been in the

---

5 (1850) 12 Ir. Eq. 400.
6 e.g. Bills of Exchange Act 1882, s. 75; Cheques Act 1957, s. 4.
7 e.g. *Lloyds Bank* v. *Bundy*.
8 *infra* p. 194
9. (1894), 10 T.L.R. 386.
10 then 1882 Act, s.2; now Cheques Act 1957, s. 4.
11 [1901] A.C. 414.

habit of collecting cheques for a man and its position in doing so
was under question it was held that to constitute a customer there
must be an account, current or deposit, or some similar relationship.

Neither of these cases nor the proposition they support goes
unqualified. In the case of *Ladbrook and Co.* v. *Todd*[12] a thief,
representing himself as the payee of a stolen cheque, opened an
account with a banker who collected the cheque. The banker's
contention that he collected on behalf of a customer was upheld,[13]
the Court thus adopting the idea that the account was the essential,
identifying feature of the banker customer relationship, not a course
of dealings. The Privy Council followed this view in *Commissioners
of Taxation* v. *English Scottish and Australian Bank*[14] saying: 'A
person whose money has been accepted by the bank on the footing
that they honour cheques up to the amount standing to his credit is a
customer of the bank in the sense of the statute, irrespective if his
connection is of long or short duration. The contrast is not between
the habitué and a newcomer, but between a person for whom the
bank performs a casual service, such as cashing a cheque for a person introduced by one of their own customers, and a person who has
an account of his own at the bank.' Duration, thus, is not of the
essence of the banker customer relationship.

Even the necessity of an account has been questioned. In the case
of *Woods* v. *Martins Bank Ltd.*[15] it was held that the relationship of
banker and customer might exist when no account had been set up.
A man had consulted a bank manager on the investment of funds and
had authorised the bank manager to uplift the funds from a building
society, invest some of the proceeds and retain the balance to await
further instructions. Nearly a month later a current account was
opened. It was held that the plaintiff was a customer. This case
raises some interesting questions as it does not revolve around the
question of statutory protection, being a claim based on negligent
investment advice, and it might have been settled in favour of the
plaintiff on other grounds without discussion of whether or not he was
a customer, particularly so in Scotland.[16]

'But for the purpose of establishing the relationship of banker and

---

12 (1914) 30 T.L.R. 433.
13 he lost the case on other grounds, *infra* p. 28
14 1920 A.C. 683.
15 [1938] 3 All E.R. 116.
16 *infra* p. 26

customer there would appear to be no magic in the actual opening of the account, and when a banker agrees to accept a customer the relationship comes into existence although the account may not be opened until later. In other words the relationship being contractual is subject to the normal rules of contract law, and the making of the contract depends on the acceptance of an offer.'[17]

The question has been raised of whether or not a banker-customer relationship exists while references are being taken up. The answer seems straightforward; if the banker has opened an account and collected a cheque he has a customer and, all things being equal, would be entitled to the statutory protection.

The formation of the banking relationship

The banking relationship comes into being through the consent of both parties, banker and customer, as does any other contract, such consent being adduced from the words, writing, or actions of the parties. The rules regarding the formation of contracts and their validity apply to the banking relationship; it will be based on the full, free and voluntary consent of the parties who must have the necessary legal capacity to enter into it.[18] The law requires no specific form for the formation of the contract, although the customer will usually sign a request which will embody the terms and conditions of the contract. The terms of the contract will be those agreed by the parties, implied from their actions or from the law or usage, and are not capable of unilateral alteration. Thus in *Burnett* v. *Westminster Bank Ltd.*[19] the defendant bank had issued a new cheque book to its customer stating that the cheques in it were to be used only in connection with the account in respect of which the cheque book was issued. A customer disregarded this instruction and subsequently sued the bank for wrongfully debiting an account. It was held that the bank's endeavour to restrict the use of the cheques had not been effective. The banker who wishes to alter the terms on which he holds accounts must bring the new terms to the notice of his customers who in turn must take some action which show that they accept the variation in the terms of the contract. Similarly the customer must heed the terms of the contract and cannot demand an alteration of them or force such alteration on the banker. For

---

[17] Chorley *Law of Banking* 5th. Ed. p. 25.
[18] *infra* p. 30 et seq
[19] [1965] 3 All. E.R. 81.

example, if there is no agreement for overdraft facilities a customer is not entitled to draw cheques which would have the effect of over-drawing his account, or if there are agreed facilities the customer cannot alter the agreed limit merely by drawing cheques which, if debited, would have the effect of increasing the agreed figure. An alteration in the original terms of the contract may be inferred from the actions of the parties; a banker who has allowed a customer to overdraw without express agreement might have difficulty in sub-sequently relying on the absence of such express agreement to claim that the customer was beyond his rights in overdrawing the account.

The termination of the banking relationship

The banking relationship ends when the account is closed, although the obligations and rights arising under it may be altered by the death, bankruptcy, or insanity of the customer, by the arrestment of funds held by the banker, by the registration of Letters of Inhibition, or by the appointment of a receiver on the winding up of a corporate customer. In any of these events the relationship changes and the obligations of the banker change although they are not discharged until the account is closed. It is, of course, plain that when a customer has died no relationship can exist but the banker's obliga-tion to account remains; similarly, if the customer is declared insane or becomes bankrupt his rights in the banking contract change, for he personally has no legal rights to the sums in his account. An arrestment[20] lodged in the hands of a banker alters his obligation to pay on his customer's demand but the relationship continues.

Death of a customer: When a banker receives reliable notice of a customer's death his authority to honour cheques, mandates or orders is revoked.[21] The death of the customer itself does not revoke the banker's authority and payment of a cheque subsequent to the customer's death but before the banker has had a reasonable time to inform himself of the fact will be valid.[22] The notice need not be formal; reliable, indirect information suffices, and if there is any doubt as to the validity of information the banker should take steps to verify it. Sums at credit of a deceased customer should be held until the Confirmation of his executors, Probate, or legal title has

[20] *infra* p. 296
[21] *infra* p. 64
[22] Wallace and McNeill *Banking Law* 8th Ed. p.215.

been produced. If the customer has died in debt to the bank a claim is made against the estate, and notice given to any cautioner.

Mental incapacity: A person who has been legally declared to be mentally disordered has no contractual capacity; his affairs fall into the hands of a tutor-at-law. The banker must take note of the ending of the contractual capacity of his customer and consider his mandate from his customer to be at an end.

More complicated from the point of view of the banker is the position of a customer who has not been legally declared to be mentally disordered but who suffers from mental illness. It is a matter of fact whether at any given time a person has the necessary mental capability to enter into a particular agreement or give a particular instruction. A banker who decides to dishonour a cheque or cheques on the grounds that the customer did not have the mental capacity to give the mandate implied in the cheques could be found to have wrongfully refused to pay. Thus the banker is advised to take the safe course of paying the cheques. 'The consequences, if such action turns out to be unjustified, are far outweighed by the possibility of dishonouring such cheques without foundation.'[24]

The title of a *curator bonis* to the estate of someone adjudged insane and incapable of managing his own affairs is judicial and the banker should be shown a copy of the court order appointing a *curator bonis*.

Bankruptcy, receivership and liquidation: The bankruptcy of a personal customer or the liquidation of a company both have the effect of depriving the usual operators of the bank account of their power to do so and end the right of the banker to accept instructions from them. The title of the trustee in bankruptcy[25] or liquidator[26] to the funds in the account must be exhibited to the banker before payment is made or instructions accepted. Claims, in the case of a debtor balance fall to be made to the trustee or liquidator. A receiver appointed to the property of company may have title to the sums in the company's bank account,[27] if such assets were charged, and if this is the case the receiver, rather than the company's officers, has the right to operate the account. The banker should obtain satisfactory evidence of the proper appointment of the receiver.

---

24 Wallace and MacNeill *op. cit.* p.215.
25 *infra* p. 318
26 *infra* p. 136
27 *infra* p. 132

Closing an account

The banker customer relationship can end by the closing of the account. Either customer or banker may wish to withdraw or the severance may be by mutual consent. In the case of the parties agreeing to terminate their contract there is no difficulty, balances owing to the customer being paid or existing overdrafts cleared.

If the customer decides to end the relationship, he may do so by withdrawing the amount held in the account; in the case of current accounts no notice is required as the sum in a current account is payable on demand. The customer can clear his account by drawing a cheque for the outstanding balance. If in the case of deposit accounts notice by the customer is stipulated in the contract, the banker may insist on the required notice being given.

The banker, however, cannot close an account without giving reasonable notice; the customer must be given time to make such arrangements as are necessary to protect his credit.[28] In *Joachimson* v. *Swiss Bank Corporation*[29] it was said that it was a term of the contract that the bank would not cease to do business except on reasonable notice, the judge suggesting that there should be allowed two or three days to allow cheques in circulation to be presented. But in *Prosperity Ltd.* v. *Lloyds Bank Ltd.*[30] where the bank had given the customer one month's notice to close the account it was held that in the circumstances of the case the notice given was insufficient. The banker requires to take into account all the circumstances and the nature of the account in deciding what reasonable notice would be.

The nature of the banking relationship

The relationship between banker and customer is simply that of debtor and creditor; where money is lodged with a banker the customer becomes the creditor and the banker the debtor in a transaction of loan.[31] Historically there was debate that the banker was a custodian of his customer's money, or a trustee in charge of it, or an agent for the customer, but analysis of the facts of the relationship, particularly the recognition of the banker's acknowledged right to use his customer's money for his own profit, showed the incon-

---

[28] *Buckingham* v. *London and Midland Bank Ltd.* (1895) 12 TLRL 70
[29] [1921] 3 K.B. 110.
[30] (1923), 39 T.L.R. 372.
[31] *Foley* v. *Hill* [1842] 2 H.L. Cas.28.

sistencies of any of these roles with the facts. Two excerpts from judicial opinions illustrate this:

In the case of *Foley* v. *Hill*[31] Lord Cottenham said: 'Money paid into a banker's is money known by the principal to be placed there for the purpose of being under the control of the banker; it is then the banker's money; he is known to deal with it as his own; he makes what profit he can, which profit he retains to himself . . . he has contracted, having received that money to repay to the principal when demanded a sum equivalent to that paid into his hands.' In the case of *Royal Bank of Scotland* v. *Skinner*[32] it was said: 'After some fluctuation of opinion it is now well settled that the relationship of customer and banker is neither a relation of principal and agent nor a relationship of a fiduciary nature, trust or the like, but a simple relation—it may be one sided, or it may be two-sided—of creditor-debtor. The banker is not in the general case the custodian of money. When money is paid in, despite the popular belief, it is simply consumed by the banker, who gives an obligation of an equivalent amount.'

Implicit in the relationship are those obligations arising out of the characteristics of banking other than the receipt of money, the collection of the proceeds of cheques for customers, and the payment of cheques drawn by customers, recognised by the longer description of the banking relationship in *Joachimson* v. *Swiss Banking Corporation*[33] in which Lord Atkin stated: 'The banker undertakes to receive money and collect bills for his customer's account. The proceeds are not to be held in trust for the customer but the bank borrows the proceeds and undertakes to repay them. The promise to repay is to repay at the branch of the bank where the account is kept and during banking hours. It includes a promise to repay any part of the amount due against the written order of the customer addressed to the bank at the branch, and, as such written order may be outstanding in the ordinary course of business for two or three days, it is a term of the contract that the bank will not cease to do business with the customer except on reasonable notice.'

The undertaking of the bank to repay the customer's money depends on the particular terms on which it was received; if into a current account the money is repayable on demand; if into a deposit account or on deposit receipt it will be repayable with interest and on

[32] 1931 S.L.T. 382.
[33] [1921] 3 K.B. 110.

the terms specified in the contract under which the money was lent to the bank. But no matter how, or on what terms, the money is repaid or, through the honouring of the customer's cheques, applied on his direction, the obligation is to repay the customer, an obligation which must be recognised in relation to honouring cheques, forged signatures, pass-books and deposit receipts, the law regarding all of which is founded on this basic obligation.

Other contracts: The banking relationship has been extended by the offering by bankers to their customers of services other than those connected with the receipt and repayment of money and the handling of cheques drawn by or held by the customer. These services commonly include: the collection and distribution of customers' dividends, interest or other payments; the paying of the customer's bills on his direction; the custody of securities, documents and valuables; the issue of letters of credit and traveller's cheques; trade and investments enquiry services; the purchase of stocks and shares and the provision of investment advices and magagement; dealing as intermediary for exchange control purposes and the remittance of payments abroad; acting as guarantors for the customer's obligations, and the collection of bills and documentary credits. There can be added to these services, insurance services, executorship services, share registration services, and computer services.

The duties and responsibilities of the banker and the rights of the customer when such services are used rest on the law which governs any such relationship and are described as appropriate elsewhere in this book.

Banker's charges and commissions: The banker is entitled to charge for his services on terms which will be agreed with his customer, published by him and brought to his customer's attention, or are imported to the contract by usage and custom. In the absence of agreement along these lines he is entitled to a reasonable fee for his services as is any person carrying on a business, reasonableness depending on facts and circumstances.

The duties of a banker

The duties of a banker are to receive money, to collect cheques and bills for his customer, to pay the customer's cheques, and to repay the customer when he is bound to do so. He must also preserve secrecy as to his customer's affairs, not merely while the relationship subsists but even after it has ended. As far as cheques are concerned the nature of the obligations of the banker are discussed elsewhere.[34] In this context will be examined the implications of the obligation to repay as regards money in accounts other than current accounts and the obligations of secrecy.

Secrecy: The relationship between banker and customer is confidential and the banker has a contractual obligation to maintain this confidentiality by not disclosing his customer's business except in the most exceptional circumstances. The circumstances in which the duty of secrecy is not absolute were discussed in *Tournier* v. *National Provincial Bank*[35] although the list given there is not necessarily exhaustive.[36] As outlined in that case the exceptional circumstances are where the banker is compelled to disclose information by law, where there is a public duty to disclose, where the interests of the bank compel disclosure, and where disclosure is made with the customer's consent.

Compulsion by law: A banker can be compelled to give evidence in court and must answer questions put to him. Production of his books and records can be ordered by a court. In this connection valuable privileges are conferred on the banker by the Bankers' Books Evidence Act 1879 which allows copies of bankers' books, rather than the originals, to be produced in Court, and by declaring (s. 3) that the entries are *prima facie* evidence of the matters recorded in the books, allows these copies to speak for themselves in Court rather than having the person responsible for them give evidence as to the content of the books; if the actual books or the presence of a bank official is required the judge will order this if shown special cause.

When an order is requested by a party to a litigation, which will include a criminal prosecution, the Court must be satisfied that the accounts concerned in form or substance are the accounts of a party to the litigation. Such orders are served on the bank which will permit inspection in terms of the order and allow copies to be taken— more usually the bank makes the copies. To gain the protection of the Act, there must be attached to the copy an affidavit which states the following: that the book from which the copy was made was, at the time the copy was made, one of the ordinary books of the bank, that the entries were made in the ordinary course of business of the

34 *infra* p. 180 et seq
35 [1924] 1 K.B. 461.
36 Chorley *op. cit.* p. 17.

bank, that the book in question is in the custody or control of the bank, that the officer making the affidavit has examined the copy with the original and that it is correct.

Other examples of compulsion by law are where the banker is compelled by statute to disclose information for the benefit of the Inland Revenue or the Treasury. Under the Exchange Control Act 1947 the Treasury has power to direct a banker to produce books, accounts or other documents to enable it to obtain information in any case in which it suspects that a person is acting contrary to the regulations or any law made for the purpose of conserving the currency. The power can be used to secure compliance with the law as well as detecting evasions of it.

The Inland Revenue's powers are very extensive. Under the Taxes Management Act 1970 an Inspector of Taxes has the power to request: (a) from persons in receipt of taxable income belonging to others, a return of all such money, value, profits or gains, and a statement of the names and addresses of the persons to whom such belong, and a declaration as to whether every such person is of full age, or a married woman, or a resident in the United Kingdom, or is an incapacitated person. (s. 13); (b) from every person carrying on the business of banking, returns of all interest paid or credited by him during a year specified, the return giving the names and addresses of the person to whom the interest was paid or credited and stating in each case the amount of the interest. Amounts of less than £15 are exempted from this requirement, as are certain amounts due to and from persons not ordinarily resident in the United Kingdom (s. 17); (c) from any registered or inscribed holder of United Kingdom securities, details of income received from such securities on behalf of any other person, together with the relevant names and addresses of each person. (s. 24). Again exceptions are amounts under £15 and those relating to non-residents; and (d) from a nominee shareholder, a statement as to whether or not he is a beneficial owner of the shares of a company and, if not, a statement of the name and address of the person on whose behalf the shares are registered in his name.

Further powers were conferred on the Board of Inland Revenue by the Finance Act, 1975 (Schedule 4, 5) which gives the Board powers to require, by notice in writing, any person to furnish them with such information as the Board may require for the purposes of administering and collecting Capital Transfer Tax.

The Department of Trade has powers under the Companies Acts 1948 and 1967 to require information from bankers. The Department can require any holder of shares in a company to disclose for whom he holds these shares or appoint an inspector to investigate and report on the membership of a company (ss. 172–174; 1948 Act) while, on a wider scale a Department of Trade Inspector appointed to investigate the affairs of a company may require the banker of the company to produce all the documents in their custody or control, attend when summonsed before the inspector, and to give all assistance which he is reasonably able to give (s. 167(1), 1948 Act; s. 39 1967 Act) but no banker can be compelled to give information as to the affairs of any other customer than the company under investigation.

One of the objectives of the Companies Act 1967 was to invest in the Department of Trade a power of swift and informal investigation. Thus under s. 109 the Department is empowered to give direction to a company to produce such books and paper as the direction may specify but this does not apply to bankers unless their customer is the company under investigation (s. 116).

A further inroad into the secret nature of the relationship is to be found in the Consumer Credit Act 1974 (s. 162). This statute provides that a duly authorised officer of the Office of the Director General of Fair Trading or the local weights and measures authority —in Scotland, the regional council—is empowered to enter any premises at all reasonable hours and, if required, on the production of his credentials, in order to ascertain whether any breach of any provision of the Act has been committed and, further, if he has reasonable cause to suspect that a breach has been committed to require any person carrying on, or employed in connection with a business to produce any books or documents relating to it, or where information is recorded other than in a legible form to provide a document containing a legible reproduction of the information. The officer may take copies of any books or documents or may seize and detain them if he has reason to believe they may be required as evidence in proceedings under the Act.

If entry is refused, or if it is likely to be refused, or if giving notice would defeat the object of the entry, a warrant may be granted to the enforcement officer.

Public interest: It is impossible to define the term 'public interest' or describe with any authority when there is a duty to the public to disclose which, while not a legal duty, is so compelling as to justify the banker in breaking his duty of secrecy. For example, in Scotland, there is no duty to report to the authorities that a crime has been committed or that one suspects the commission of an offence or crime. Anyone who does so, or volunteers to answer questions to an investigating police officer does so out of a sense of public responsibility. It would be for a banker to decide where the public interest over-rode his duty of confidentiality, but it is suggested that the banker's duty of confidentiality is very heavy and disclosure of his customer's affairs without legal obligation is a step which would not lightly be taken.

Banker's interest: When the banker's own interests require disclosure of a customer's affairs, disclosure may be made. Thus if a banker wished to sue a customer he may make disclosure of the amount of the indebtedness and the state of the account, or where a cautioner is involved and is being called on he can be told the amount of the overdraft.

Customer's consent: When the customer expressly or impliedly permits the banker to disclose his affairs, or discuss them, the banker may do so. Customers may nominate their banker as persons to whom reference may be made when the customer is seeking credit and in this case there is no difficulty, the consent of the customer is clear. The duties which the banker who gives opinions in these circumstances are not relevant in this context[37] the main question being whether or not the banker should answer enquiries. In the case of express consent the position is clear: outwith such cases the position is not so clear. It may be argued that as it is known that bankers' references are given, incorporating opinions on the standing and trustworthiness of customers, that the customer's consent is implied to such practice. This argument is very strong in the case of trading customers who must know of the practice of giving references and opinions; as far as non-trading customers are concerned the argument is not so strong. Unless the argument that usage and long-established custom have imported an implied consent of the customer to the provision of opinions, the giving of them appears to be unjustified according to the doctrine enunciated in the *Tournier* case.[38]

The banker's duty of secrecy applies to all his knowledge of his

[37] *infra* p. 25 et seq
[38] *supra* p. 11

customer's affairs, not merely to the state of his account, and continues after the relationship between them ends.

The duty to repay

It is a duty of the banker to repay, in terms of the particular contract under which money is left with him, the customer's money. Cheques being dealt with elsewhere,[39] there falls to be examined here deposit accounts, deposit receipts, joint accounts, the combination of accounts, and the status of the pass-book or statement made out by the banker.

Deposit accounts: If money is left with a banker on a deposit account it is repayable in terms of the contract, usually a demand. The banker must take care that the money is paid to the owner of it or his mandatary, otherwise he will be liable to pay or credit the account holder. Withdrawal by the customer is effected by the production of the pass-book and a request for repayment by the customer: any particular rules regarding signatures in the case of accounts not held by individuals must be given effect.

Cheques may be presented for payment into deposit accounts and the banker will collect these. It might be said that he is not, in the circumstances entitled to the statutory protections as collecting banker unless he acted 'without negligence' which prescribes that he should show care in the opening of the account if he anticipates cheques being paid in and acts with caution when a cheque is paid in. There can be no doubt that the holder of a deposit account is a customer.

Deposit receipts: A deposit receipt is an acknowledgement by a banker of the receipt of a sum of money from a named person or persons to be placed on deposit, repayable in the terms of it, normally on demand, on the re-delivery to the banker of the receipt. The relationship of the banker and the depositor is that of debtor and creditor: whether the depositor is a customer of the banker is a matter which has not come before the courts but, particularly, where there has been a course of dealing, bankers treat depositors as customers, even though there is no account in the sense that there are no debit and credit entries.

A deposit receipt is not a negotiable instrument; thus the banker cannot treat an indorsee of it as being entitled to payment on its

[39] *infra* p. 180 et seq

production, such indorsement implying no more than a mandate to uplift the money on behalf of the depositor.[40] The banker need not pay such a third party unless he is satisfied he is carrying out the depositor's instructions. If payment is made other than to the depositor and it transpires that the person to whom it was made had, in fact, no authority the banker will be liable to pay the depositor.[41] In the case of *Wood* v. *Clydesdale Bank Ltd.*[42] the depositor sent from abroad a deposit receipt duly indorsed in favour of his brother together with a letter to the bank authorising payment. Both deposit receipt and letter fell into the hands of a thief who presented them to the bank and received payment. The bank was held liable to pay the depositor. If, however, the depositor caused the loss through his own fraud or negligence he is barred from recovering.[43]

Although a deposit receipt is non-negotiable the obligation contained in it can be transferred by assignation of it, written on or attached to the deposit receipt, duly intimated to the bank.

A deposit receipt is no proof of the ownership of the funds, nor do the terms in which it is taken justify any inference as to the ownership of the funds. But a banker cannot substitute his own knowledge of the true ownership of the funds in defiance of the terms of the deposit receipt. Thus in *Anderson* v. *North of Scotland Bank Ltd.*[44] the bank tried to withhold payment of the sum in a deposit receipt taken in joint names on the ground that they had a claim against one of the parties to whom they believed the money wholly belonged. It was held that they were not justified in so doing but were bound by their obligation to repay either party in terms of the deposit receipt. An exception to this rule occurs when the joint parties are husband and wife and the husband is bankrupt; in such case the bank may withold payment to the wife on the grounds that the wife's funds have become inmixed with the husband's estate.[45]

If the deposit receipt is payable to either party or the survivor then the bank is bound to follow that instruction; if, however, notice is received from either party that payment must not be made without his consent then the banker must take cognisance of that notice and

---

[40] *Barstow* v. *Inglis and Hay* (1857) 20 D. 230.
[41] *Forbes Exr.* v. *Western Bank* (1854) 16 D 807.
[42] 1914 S.C. 397.
[43] *Forbes Exor., supra*
[44] (1901) 4 F. 49.
[45] *infra* p. 322

withhold payment.[46] Again if the banker has issued a deposit receipt in joint names and an arrestment is lodged against the fund as the property of one of the parties he must not pay the funds away to the other party as—on the basis that what appears on the face of the deposit receipt is no evidence of true ownership—the funds may belong, wholly or in part, to the party against whom the arrestment is being used and to pay these away could prejudice the legitimate rights of the creditor. If the other party insists on payment the banker's recourse is to an action of multiple poinding to allow the Court to determine to whom the money should be paid.

Generally, the banker has no duty beyond complying with the terms of the deposit receipt. Thus in the case of *Dickson* v. *National Bank of Scotland*[47] trust funds were placed on consignation receipt the terms of which were that it was repayable on the signature of solicitors who were the law agents to the trust. After the firm had been disolved one of the partners indorsed the receipt in the firm's name and embezzled the money. It was held that the banker had acted properly in encashing the receipt.[48] The banker could assume that the partner was doing an act necessary to wind up the firm's affairs.

A survivorship clause may be intended to effect a donation *mortis causa*. It is no part of the banker to enquire if this is the case; but if he received objections from the executors of the deceased party to the deposit receipt he must take note of it. Such objection would interpel payment.

Consignation receipts: A bank may be offered money on consignation receipt to await the outcome of a dispute, which may or may not be in Court, between parties. The repayment of such money must follow precisely the terms on which it is lodged. If the consignation is judicial, that is ordered by the Court, the order or interlocutor ordering the consignation will specify the terms on which it is to be repaid and these terms must be complied with. If the monies are lodged in the name of the Accountant of Court or the Sheriff-clerk the banker may pay on the instruction of that official but taking a receipt from the recipient of the funds. If the consignation is other than judicial, perhaps by the vendor of property under a right in security of a surplus, the identity of the person to whom it should be

46 Wallace and McNeill *op. cit.* p. 31.
47 1917 S.C. (H.L.) 50.
48 *infra* p. 82

B

paid over and the terms on which it should be paid over are expressed on the receipt. Should any dispute arise as to whom the funds should be paid, the banker can resolve this dispute by the raising of an action of multiple poinding.

Joint accounts: Where an account is opened in joint names the obligation of the banker to repay depends on the terms of the contract. If the signatures of both or all of the parties are required he honours orders signed by all the parties; if one of the joint holders is empowered to sign cheques he can repay on the single signature. Instructions to honour cheques bearing a combination of signatures, say one mandatory signature and one other, or any two out of three, are to be observed.

The death of one party to a joint account will produce consequences which depend on the term of the contract. If the account requires the signature of both or all of the parties, the death of one means that the account cannot be operated. In such case the banker requires to seek exhibition of the Confirmation of the executors of the deceased party or the equivalent such as Probate. If the terms of the contract allow one party to operate the account the death of one party does not stop the operation of the account, the banker being able to honour the signature of the survivor or survivors. If the account is in debit at the time of the death of one of the parties, operations should be stopped, and outstanding cheques returned; otherwise, the rules in *Clayton's Case*[49] could prejudice recourse against the deceased's estate, surviving parties, cautioners and any security held.

A banker is not concerned with the ownership of funds in a joint account, his duty is to repay in terms of the contract. If, however, one of the parties, or the executors of one of the parties, intimates to the banker that the signature of the other, or survivor, should not be honoured as the funds in the account are his or their sole property, the banker is not safe in paying away money after receipt of such notice. In such a case an action of multiple poinding, including the payment of the funds into court, is the banker's safest course. The existence of a survivorship clause does not have the effect of a will.

Combination of accounts: The duty of a banker to repay subsists only while there are funds at the credit of the customer. Where the customer has more than one account the banker will keep these separately but is entitled to mass them to ascertain the customer's

[49] *infra* p. 24

credit balance. Whether notice of this combination must be given to the customer is unclear but where the accounts are of a different nature, say a deposit account and a current account, notice must be given before the accounts are combined.

Set-off: Any creditor has a right to set-off any sums due to him by his debtor against sums due by him to the debtor. The right to do so, also called compensation, is not automatic, but can be pleaded if action is raised for repayment of sums due by the raising of a counter-claim for the amount owing, thus partially or completely extinguishing the claim. There are some conditions attaching to a successful plea of compensation. Principal amongst these is that there must be *concursus debiti et crediti,* and that the debts must be in most cases liquid.

Concursus debiti et crediti means that the party raising the plea of compensation must be debtor and creditor in the same capacity. For example, a banker who owes money to a customer as an executor cannot set-off that sum against the customer's personal overdraft. The debts claimed must be liquid, that is ascertainable. An illiquid claim, unless the amount is instantly verifiable, or a future debt may not be set-off; if, however, the party against whom the claim lies is bankrupt, the other can claim compensation in answer to any action raised on behalf of the bankrupt;[50] otherwise he would be in a position paying out money and receiving back only a dividend.

Contingent debts, that is debts which are due only if certain events occur can be set-off.

Fiduciary claims: If there is a trust expressed or implied by the character in which a customer opens an account the banker must observe this[51] but he has no concern in the way in which money withdrawn from the account is applied as long as he adheres to the contract on which the account was opened. Thus where a second account was opened by a customer newly appointed as an agent for the deposit of the principal's money but the banker was not informed of the reasons for the opening of the second account, it was held that the bank was entitled to set-off the credit balance in this account against the overdraft in the customer's other account.[52] Notice of the

50 *Henderson* v. *Turnbull* 1909 S.C. 510.
51 Re. Gross *ex parte* Kingston (1871) 6 Ch. App. 632.
52 *United Rentals Ltd.* v. *Clydesdale and North of Scotland Bank Ltd.* 1963 S.L.T. (Sh. Ct.) 41.

fiduciary nature of the second account would have bound the banker who would not have been able to set-off.

Lien: A banker has a right of lien, the right to withhold delivery, over all money, bills and negotiable instruments belonging to his customer which are in his possession, the right being exercisable against repayment of sums due to the banker, providing that the securities have come into his possession as a banker, not as a depositary,[53] and that they have come into his hands under a contract which is not inconsistent with the lien. Thus if a customer hands in bills for discount which is refused the banker cannot retain these; nor may be exercise his right of lien over securities left with him for safe custody unless he can show that he granted credit on the strength of holding these securities.[54] In *Robertson's Trustee* v. *Royal Bank of Scotland*[54] it was held that where bearer securities are in the banker's possession there is a presumption that the banker has a lien but such presumption may be rebutted by express contract. There is no lien if the banker has cause to believe that the securities are not the property of the customer, or if he has reasons to believe that they are lodged without the authority of their owner, of if he knows that they are held on trust.[55]

The right of lien does not extend over non-negotiable instruments and it ends when possession is lost. When securities are given up for any purpose the lien is lost.

The right of lien gives the banker the right to withhold delivery of the securities affected by it; it confers on him no right to realise them without Court authority.

The terms on which the banker holds securities is of great importance in deciding whether or not a lien exists; if he acknowledges that he holds them in safe custody there is a presumption that no lien exists, the securities over which the banker has a right of lien should have come into his possession as part of the banking function.

Pass-book: The banker will maintain accounts and the customer will come into possession of copies of these, either through being presented with statements or, in the case of deposit accounts, through the pass-book. Entries in the customer's statement or pass-book

---

[53] *Brandao* v. *Burnett* (1846) 12 Cl. and F. 787.
[54] *Robertson's Tr.* v. *Royal Bank of Scotland* (1890) 18 R. 12.
[55] *National Bank of Scotland* v. *Dickie's Tr.* (1895) 22 R. 12. For the position of stockbrokers see *infra* p.

showing credit entries are *prima facie* evidence of the receipt of the money, a rule which has been extended to pay-in slips,[57] but evidence that the entries are incorrect is competent.[58] Similarly, entries showing money paid to the customer are *prima facie* evidence against the customer when the pass-book has been in his possession and he has not objected.[59]

Two cases illustrate the regard in which the pass-book can be held by the Courts. In *Holt* v. *Markham*[60] the banker credited the customer with more than he was due to be credited and the customer, in reliance upon the statements issued, spent the money. It was held that the banker was barred pleading that the money had been credited under mistake and should be returned. In *Holland* v. *Manchester and Liverpool District Banking Co. Ltd.*[61] an entry had been made in the customer's pass-book and the customer, on the strength of the balance appearing in the pass-book, issued a cheque which was dishonoured. It was held that the customer was entitled to damages for wrongful dishonour of the cheque.

Neither of these cases, turning as they do on the reliance of the customer on the accuracy of his statements, means that the bank is totally bound by the statements it issues, nor is the customer totally bound by accepting without objection an erroneous statement, although if he confirms that he accepts the account as correct, as opposed to merely receiving it and not objecting, the onus passes to him. Thus in the case of *Dickson* v. *Clydesdale Bank Ltd.*[62] a customer who contended that the account had been wrongly debited with two items was held entitled, even after she had signed a confirmation that the account was in order, to sue the bank.

'But the present position of the pass-book is rather uncertain. In England it seems that the mere fact of a customer's pass-book being returned to him by his bankers with entries debited therein of certain cheques passed on his account, which subsequently turn out to have been forgeries, does not preclude the customer, even after the lapse of a considerable time, from setting up the forgery, and that though the pass-book may have been returned to the banker without objection. In Scotland, it has been expressed that there is no rule of law which

---

[57] *Docherty* v. *Royal Bank of Scotland* 1963 S.L.T. Notes 43.
[58] *Couper* v. *National Bnak of Scotland* (1889) 16 R. 412.
[59] *Commercial Bank of Scotland* v. *Rhind* (1860) 3 Macq. 643.
[60] [1923] 1 K.B. 504.
[61] (1909) 25 T.L.R. 386.
[62] 1937 S.L.T. 585.

requires the court to hold that the pass-book must be taken as an accurate record of banking transactions or that the customer is precluded from challenging the transaction.[63]

In *Dickson* v. *Clydesdale Bank Ltd.* it was held that the customer, having signed a confirmation, could not challenge the debit to her account of a forged cheque, but could challenge the debit of a cheque which had been paid to the wrong payee.

The adoption of the pass-book or statement as an accurate record of the state of the account must remain, therefore unclear. It has been suggested that in the case of deposit accounts, where the pass-book is presented with each lodgement or withdrawal, it becomes more in the nature of a stated account and that, taking into account that many deposit account holders are not business people, the banker's position on erroneous entries in deposit account pass-books is weaker than in the case of current accounts.[64]

What is, however, clear is the rule of Scots law that no discharge, however formal, precludes the granter of it from re-opening the question where there has been fraud or mis-representation.

Acceptances

If a banker's customer has accepted a bill of exchange payable at the bank, the banker has a duty to pay the bill if he has instructions to do so and if he holds funds or is willing to meet the bill without holding funds. By directing a bill to his banker the acceptor undertakes to furnish or repay the necessary funds. The extent of the banker's instruction is that the bill should be retired by payment to the proper person and if, for any reason, the banker pays the wrong person he cannot seek re-imbursement from his customer; if, for example, there is a forged indorsement on a bill and the banker pays the holder who has no right to the bill[65] he bears the loss.

An instruction to the banker not to pay a particular bill must be followed but it must be borne in mind that the presentment of a bill acts as an assignation of available funds which the banker must recognise even where he has had no instructions to honour the bill.

The Customer's duties

Insofar as the banking contract places duties on the customer

---

[63] Wallace and MacNeill *op. cit.* p. 9.
[64] Scottish Banking Practice V 3rd. Ed. p. 45.
[65] *infra* p. 159

these tend to have been judicially examined only in so far as the writing of cheques is concerned.[66] Thus in *London Joint Stock Bank* v. *McMillan and Arthur*,[67] Lord Haldane said: 'The customer contracts reciprocally that in drawing his cheques he will draw them in such a form as will enable the banker to fulfil his obligations, and therefore in a form which is clear and free from ambiguity, because the banker as a mandatory has a right to insist on having his mandate in a form which does not leave room for doubt as to what he is called on to do' and in *Joachimson* v. *Swiss Bank Corporation*[68] Lord Atkin stated: 'The customer, on his part, undertakes to exercise reasonable care in executing his written orders so as not to mislead the bank or facilitate forgery.'

The duty of a customer also demands that he should act in such a manner as to avoid loss to his banker by furnishing information whenever he suspects forgery or irregularity.[70]

The Customer as Debtor

A customer has no right to credit from his banker; his right to draw orders on his banker depends on his having available funds and should his account not be in credit the right is extinguished. If, however, by agreement with the banker the customer has a right to overdraw he is entitled to draw orders up to the arranged amount. In such a case the banker becomes creditor in a loan contract. Any such contract depends on its terms but, unless the contrary be the case, it subsists at will and can be terminated by the banker requiring repayment or the customer repaying. No reason need be given where a customer is called on to liquidate his debt[71] although if overdrawing has been permitted against security the banker may be liable in damages, if he, without reasonable notice subsequently refuses to honour a cheque.[72] An agent has no implied authority to overdraw.

When an overdraft is permitted on a joint account the parties are jointly, not jointly and severally, liable; each can be called on, in the absence of express stipulation to the contrary, to pay only a proportionate share of the indebtedness.

---

[66] *infra.* p. 181
[67] [1918] A.C. 777.
[68] [1921] 3 K.B. 110.
[70] *Greenwood* v. *Martins Bank Ltd.* [1933] A.C. 51.
[71] *Johnston* v. *Commercial Bank* (1858) 20 D. 790; *Ritchie* v. *Clydesdale Bank* (1886) 13 R. 866.
[72] Johnston, *supra*; *Buckingham* v. *London and Midland Bank, supra*.

Appropriation of payments: A customer paying money to his banker may expressly or by implication appropriate it to any account he has with the banker. If he has two or more accounts he is at liberty to direct to which the payment is to be applied and the banker must follow this direction. If no appropriation is made the banker is free to appropriate the payment to any account he pleases, to a particular account, to a particular debt which the banker has requested should be paid off, to an unsecured rather than to a secured debt. Once such appropriation has been made and intimated to the debtor it is binding on him, although revocable until then.

Practically the whole law on the subject is to be found in *Clayton's Case, Devaynes* v. *Noble*[73] which states the rules enunciated but also is authority for the rule that in a running account payments in are presumed to be appropriated to payments in the order in which the items occur. Thus where an account is in credit sums paid in are available to met subsequent withdrawals; if the account is in debit sums paid in are to be applied in extinction of the earliest debit items.

In *Devaynes* v. *Noble* a partner in a banking firm, Devaynes, died. At the date of his death the firm owed Noble £1713. Noble continued to bank with the firm until it failed, then owing him in excess of £1713. He sued Devaynes' estate but it was held that the accounts showed that the money due at the date of Devaynes' death had been repaid to Noble by subsequent withdrawals and the amount owing at the date of the firm's failure comprised monies paid in since the date of Devaynes' death for which his estate was not liable. Following upon *Devaynes* v. *Noble*, in the case of *Christie* v. *Royal Bank of Scotland*[74] it was held that the sums due to a bank by a firm at the time a partner died had been extinguished by subsequent payments into the account and a security granted by that partner could not be enforced, while in *Union Bank* v. *National Bank*[75] it was held that a secured debt outstanding when a postponed security was intimated to the banker had been extinguished by the payments into the customer's account of monies after the date of the intimation.

Where it is desired to retain a security or the liability of a party to an outstanding balance in a current account the banker must not

---

[73] (1816) 1 Mer 608.
[74] (1859) 1 D. 745.
[75] (1886) 15 R (H.L.) 1.

allow further withdrawals if he has accepted payments into the account.

The rule in *Clayton's Case* may be rebutted if it can be shown that the parties did not wish it to operate, although it would be unusual for a banker to attempt to rebut it.

A statutory variation to the rule in *Clayton's Case* is to be found in the Consumer Credit Act 1974 (s. 81). Where a debtor is liable to make to the same person payments in respect of two or more agreements regulated by that Act he shall be entitled on making any payment to appropriate the sum paid by him as he wishes between or among the accounts. If he fails to make such appropriation and one or more of the agreements is a hire-purchase agreement, a conditional sale agreement, a consumer hire agreement, or an agreement in relation to which any security is provided, the payment is to be appropriated towards the satisfaction of the sums due under the several agreements respectively in the proportions which those sums bear to each other.

Banker's opinions

The knowledge of his customer's standing, character and business abilities which a banker acquires makes him a suitable referee when opinion is sought on such qualities. No one is duty-bound to give references or opinions; the banker choses to do so as an aid to customers who wish him to do so, and also to facilitate the processes of commerce in which such references play an important part. The position of the banker supplying such references has already been considered in so far as in providing a reference he might be in breach of his duty of secrecy unless the opinion were provided with the express or implied consent of the customer;[76] it is only as a matter of courtesy and not of legal right that such information is asked or given, except at the request of the customer involved.

When, however, a banker decides to write an opinion he must bear in mind that he faces double risk: on the one hand he may be sued by his customer; on the other hand he may be sued by the party to whom the opinion was supplied if he acted in reliance upon it and suffered loss by doing so. These are clearly different issues and should be considered separately.

As far as the customer is concerned the banker should not disclose

[76] *supra* p. 14

facts which a reasonably careful and prudent man of business would
not divulge, and if he does so to his customer's prejudice an action
may lie against the banker. Certainly no figures can be disclosed,
nor anything which would indicate the state of the customer's
account or the extent of his means; such would be a clear breach of
confidentiality.

As far as the third party is concerned the first duty of the banker is
to act honestly. In *Robinson* v. *The National Bank of Scotland*[77] the
representations in the banker's letter upon which the action was
founded were found to be careless, inaccurate and misleading, but as
they were not dishonestly made the banker was not liable; the
relationship between him and the pursuer imposed no duty on the
banker other than to make sure that the information was strictly
accurate.

Nothing in the years since *Robinson* v. *The National Bank of
Scotland* has diminished the duty of honesty, but this case pre-dates
the case of *Donoghue* v. *Stevenson*[78] which is generally accepted to
delineate when one person owes a legal duty of care to another.
Such a duty can be described thus: 'In default of precedent or
analogy the Court may hold that a duty exists where, in its view, a
reasonable person in the defender's position should have foreseen
that conduct by him of the kind in issue would be likely to harm a
person who should reasonably have been contemplated by the
defender as being likely to be affected by such conduct.'[79] That
such a general duty could affect the banker giving an opinion was
discussed in *Hedley Byrne and Co. Ltd.* v. *Heller and Partners*[80] in
which it was established that where an enquiry was made in reliance
upon the banker's special knowledge so that the enquirer expected a
true and faithful reply there does exist such a duty of care, breach of
which will render the banker liable.

Hedley Byrne and Co. Ltd. v. *Heller and Partners* was an English
case and the view of the law expressed in it was considered to be a
fundamental change in English law regarding when a duty was owed;
it, perhaps, represents from the Scottish viewpoint merely an application of the general principle enunciated in *Donoughue* v. *Stevenson* to
the particular situation of the banker answering an enquiry. Two

---

[77] 1916 S.C. (H.L.) 154.
[78] 1932 S.C. (H.L.) 31.
[79] Walker *Principles of Scottish Private Law* p. 1028.
[80] *Hedley Byrne and Co. Ltd.* v. *Heller and Partners* [1964] A.C. 465.

points must be taken into account against the view that the banker answering an enquiry has a duty more burdensome than that stated in *Robinson* v. *The National Bank of Scotland:* (*i*) the broad principle applies only 'in default of precedent', as explained in the quotation from Professor Walker's work, and it might be that *Robinson* is just such a limiting precedent; (*ii*) consideration in the House of Lords in *Hedley Byrne and Co. Ltd.* v. *Heller and Partners* of whether such a duty existed was not strictly necessary to reach the decision in the case, which was decided on other grounds.[81]

Professor Walker does not entertain reservations on this matter: 'A banker giving a financial reference must not only act honestly but, if he knows that the reference is to be or may be acted upon by a third party, must take reasonable care that he does not mislead that third party'.[82]

The duty of the banker to answer honestly and without negligence does not impose on him any duty to make enquiries about his customer; he can rely on the information which he can glean from his own books.[83]

The bankers in *Hedley Byrne and Co. Ltd.* v. *Heller and Partners* were in the end not liable to the enquirer because in each of the two opinions which they had given they had used a form of words which disclaimed liability or responsibility for the statements made and the House of Lords found this the decisive factor. The banker who gives an opinion, therefore, should give it subject to the condition that it is given on the condition that the banker accepts no liability in the matter; if the third party cares to act on the strength of such opinion he has no recourse against the banker, unless—a matter not worth discussing—it is fraudulent.

Investment advice

The historical position that 'it is not within the scope of the business of bankers to seek or make investments generally for their customers'[84] and that investment advice is outwith the scope of banking business altogether[85] clearly does not apply if a banking concern is soliciting the management of funds as part of its business.

[81] *infra*
[82] *op. cit.* p. 904.
[83] Finlayson *Law Lectures for Bankers* p. 268.
[84] *Bishop* v. *Countess of Jersey* (1854) 2 Drew 143, at p. 163.
[85] per *Lord Barker* in *Banbury* v. *Bank of Montreal* [1918] A.C. 626.

In such case the organisation would be liable for the negligence, acts and omissions, of its employees engaged in such activities, just as if it would be liable if the computer services it might also offer were defective and customers who utilised these were occasioned loss. The fact that a bank chooses to offer investment advice, however, does not necessarily make the advising on or managing of investments part of the business of banking. The question must be: Without the offer of such services, is the provision of advice part of the ordinary business of banking, or, to be more specific, if a banker's employee—not specifically authorised in this area— offered negligent advice to a customer, would the banker be liable?

Short of the specific offer by a banker to act in this capacity, the law seems to be that bankers generally have no duty to advise on investments, a view taken in *Woods* v. *Martins Bank Ltd.* [86] but if the banker does hold himself out as offering financial guidance, which will be a matter of fact, then he owes a duty of care to a person who seeks advice and must give that advice with reasonable skill and care. A lack of reasonable care or advice given without reasonable grounds will render the banker liable. [87] If the banker does not hold himself out as an adviser on investment matters his only duty when asked to do so is to advise honesty and to the best of his knowledge and belief.

The decision in *Woods* v. *Martins Banks Ltd.* that the banker owed the customer a duty of care when advising on investments, having shown himself willing do so so, adds little to the law: in the earlier case of *Wilson* v. *United Counties Banks* [88] the defendant bank undertook to look after the business of a customer when he was absent on war service and were held liable for negligent management. What is of interest is whether the modern practices of banks may not have eroded the historical view and that now the provision of such advice might be part of the business of banking and not merely ancillary to it in certain circumstances. It is the practice of banks to suggest through advertising matter that there is available skilled advice in financial matters at any of its branches for anyone caring to consult a bank manager and such claims may have had the effect of moving the boundaries of banking business outwards. If such is the case, then to the duty of honesty owed by anyone giving advice would

---

[86] [1958] 3 All. E.R. 116.
[87] *Dougall* v. *National Bank* (1892) 20 R. 8.
[88] [1920] A.C. 102

require to be added the duties of skill and care when the banker gave advice on investments.

Safe custody

A banker will offer to his customers a facility for the safe-keeping of their valuable possessions, a service for which he may or may not charge. If he does not charge, the banker is a depositary; if he does he is a custodier. The fact that the banker is charging fees or making profits in another connection, e.g. from keeping a credit balance in the customer's account from the proprietor of the deposited items does not mean that the safe keeping is that of a custodier.[89]

The obligations of the depositary and custodier are broadly similar, although the duty of the custodier is more onerous. Either has to show such duty of care as a man of reasonable prudence would show in relation to his own property, but from the custodier there is demanded greater diligence. Neither must use the property nor penetrate any secret it presents, e.g. by unsealing an envelope. The duty is acquitted when the goods are returned undamaged, although if a container is deposited the duty is acquitted when that is returned even though its contents have perished. Accidental loss or destruction of the subject of the deposit does not involve liability; liability will arise only when the custodier or depositary has been at fault. Thus theft by a third party, unless security precautions have not come up to a reasonable standard, will not found liability. Only when there has been a failure in the necessary standard of care demanded in looking after the property can the holder of it be held liable for its loss or damage to it.

Banker's cards

As a service to customers some bankers issue banker's cards which offer to anyone taking a cheque from that customer the guarantee that the cheque—provided that the terms of the card as to signature and amount are met—will be met. The promise of the banker on such a card is binding upon him and he cannot for any reason dishonour a regularly drawn cheque taken on reliance upon that promise.

---

[89] *Giblin* v. *McMullen* (1869) L.R.2 P.C. 317.

CHAPTER TWO

SPECIAL CUSTOMERS

THE capacity of persons or institutions to enter into contractual obligations, the method by which this is done and the consequences of such actions are matters of general application in business transactions and apply also in the banking relationship. Thus the banker must be aware when dealing with customers of any specialities or restrictions upon the legal capacity of any particular customer. In particular, there can be identified as customers in dealing with whom particular care must be taken, young people, companies and corporations, firms, clubs, associations, and other unincorporated bodies, executors and trustees, building societies, and local authorities.

Married women

There is little need now to consider the position of women, married or otherwise, at any length. Limitations upon their contractual capacity are now of historical interest only, and the banker is entitled to treat a lady customer as he would any other person of full age and capacity. One matter which might be taken into account arises out of the English case of *Savory and Co.* v. *Lloyds Bank:*[1] A husband paid cheques payable to his employers into an account in the name of his wife, and the Court held that in opening an account in the name of a married woman the banker should ascertain the nature of her husband's employment and the identity of his employer. The present day relevance of this case might be queried.

Young persons

The age of majority in the United Kingdom for all purposes is 18.[2] After attainment of the 18th birthday a person is an adult, enjoying as well as civil rights, such as the franchise, the full rights in law, including contractual capacity, of an adult. Prior to the 18th birthday a young person's legal capacity depends on age. The law

[1] 1932 2 K.B. 122.
[2] Age of Majority (Scotland) Act 1969.

30

recognises two separate categories of young person, the pupil, and the minor; each has distinct limitations upon his legal capacity.

Pupils

Pupilarity lasts until the age of 12 in the case of girls and until the age of 14 in the case of boys. A pupil has no contractual capacity of any sort and any bargain entered into by a pupil is void. It has been written:[3] 'A pupil has no person in the legal sense of the word. He is incapable of acting or even of consenting.' Any obligations which the law imposes upon a pupil rests on a quasi-contractual or equitable base: for example, he is bound to pay a reasonable price for necessaries sold and delivered to him,[4] while, if money has been lent to him it may be recovered if, and in so far as, it has been expended for the benefit of the pupil, as in the repair of his house.[5]

A pupil will have a guardian who is known as a tutor: the tutor acts for the pupil, protecting his person and managing his estate. The father is the natural guardian of a child while in minority. he is administrator-in-law of the child and as such manages the child's estate. He is entitled to recover sums due to the pupil and to give valid receipts and grant discharges for such payments. Anyone who makes payment of sums due to a child, for example, legacies or dividends, is protected when a discharge or receipt is granted by the tutor. But in certain circumstances, e.g. if aware that the father is insolvent,[6] a person paying money to a pupil has a duty to protect the pupil's interests by requiring the tutor to find caution or refusing to pay except under a Court decree.[7] As administrator-in-law of his child's estate the father is a tutor within the meaning of the Judicial Factors Act, 1849, and a trustee within the meaning of the Trusts (Scotland) Acts 1921 and 1961.[8] These Acts impose on him fiduciary duties in the administration of the child's estate.

If it is necessary in the interests of the child the court may supersede the father's guardianship and appoint a factor *loco tutoris*: apart from this no one else is entitled to act as tutor, with two exceptions; first, anyone who makes a bequest to a pupil may nomi-

---

[3] Erskine *Inst*. I, 7, 14.
[4] Sale of Goods Act 1893, s. 2.
[5] *Scott's Trs*. v. *Scott* (1887) 24 R. 1043.
[6] Gloag and Henderson *Introduction to the Law of Scotland* 7th Ed. p. 694.
[7] *Stevenson's Trs*. v. *Dunbreck* (1861) 4 Macq. 86; *Wardrop* v. *Gosling* (1869) 7 M. 532.
[8] *infra* p. 247

nate a tutor to a child but such a tutor's duties and powers are restricted to the administration of the subject of the bequest and, second, a local authority may by resolution, if the parents have abandoned the child or are otherwise unsuitable, assume all the rights and powers of a parent.[9]

The right of the father at common law to be administrator-at-law of the pupil excludes the mother. By the Guardianship of Infants Act, 1925, the mother on the death of the father is entitled to act as guardian of the child (s. 4(1)). Even while the father has nominated a guardian, the mother may refuse to act with the nominee who must, if he wishes to act, obtain a court order that he should either alone or jointly with the mother (s. 5(3), (4)). If the mother does not refuse to act with the nominee, they act jointly. If no guardian has been appointed by the father, or if the appointed guardian cannot, or will not, act the court may appoint a guardian to act with the mother (s. 4(1)).

A mother may appoint a guardian to act after her death, in which case the father has similar rights to refuse to admit this nominee to act with him (s. 4(2)). Where there are joint guardians they act together: in the event of disagreement between they may apply to the Court for direction (s. 6) and the Court may grant, including, where one of the guardians is a parent, an order as to the custody and maintenance of the child.[10]

A pupil must have a tutor and if he does not, because both parents are dead and there is no nominated tutor, or if the nominated tutor refuses to act, a tutor will be appointed to him. The modern practice is that an officer of the court, known as a factor *loco tutoris*, is appointed. But there is still competent the appointment of the tutor-of-law or tutor-dative. The tutor-of-law is the nearest male relative of the father, over 25 years of age and confirmed in his appointment by the Court. If the nearest male relative of the father does not claim the office within one year or declines to act, any person may apply to the Court of Session for appointment as tutor-dative.

The right of father and mother to act is a natural and legal right. The right of the nominated tutor, the tutor-testamentar, rests on the nomination without further formality. The tutor-of-law and the tutor-dative, together with the factor *loco tutoris,* must be confirmed in their appointment by the Court.

---

[9] Children Act, 1948, ss. 2, 3.
[10] Children and Young Persons (Scotland) Act 1932, s. 73(1).

A tutor may resign, although not father or mother. By the Judicial Factors Act, 1880, (s. 31). the Court is empowered to accept the resignation of a tutor and to appoint a factor in his place. A tutor who fails in his duty, or is unsuitable through mental or physical incapacity or on moral grounds can be, at common law, removed by the Courts, while on similar grounds he can be removed under the Judicial Factors Act, 1880, (ss. 5, 6, 20 and 21) and under the Guardianship of Infants Act, 1886, (s. 6) the Court can remove any testamentary tutor or any tutor appointed or acting by virtue of the Act 'on being satisfied that it is for the welfare' of the pupil and appoint another guardian in his place. The office of tutory terminates when the pupilage ends on the attainment of puberty, or by the death of the tutor or pupil.

Thus it can be seen that in the case of a pupil the banker will deal with the father, whom failing the mother, or with the tutor-of-law or the tutor-dative, bearing in mind the possibility of a tutor appointed to administer particular bequests, and in the case of the decease of one parent joint tutorship.

Dealing with a pupil himself is clearly hazardous and banking facilities of any sort should not be afforded to a pupil. Special provisions are made in law for Trustee Savings Banks which operate in terms of the Trustee Savings Banks Act 1954 to 1964 and for whose benefit there is enacted: 'Where a deposit has been made in a Trustee Savings Bank by or for the benefit of a person under the age of eighteen years of age it shall be lawful for the trustees or managers of the bank to make a payment to that person in respect thereof and his receipt shall be a sufficient discharge notwithstanding his incapacity or disability to act for himself.'[11] The National Savings Bank enjoys a similar protection. In the regulations dealing with it there is a stipulation that 'an application for the withdrawal of money by or in the name of an infant may be made by the infant if of the age of seven years or upwards'. Building Societies are also protected by statute. In the Building Societies Act 1962 (s. 47) there is provision that a receipt to a building society by a minor in respect of payment to him of principal of, or interest on, sums lent to him, is not invalid on the ground that he is of non-age.

Other banks and institutions are not thus favoured and the only safe course of action is to deal only with the tutor.

[11] Trustee Savings Bank Act 1954, s. 23.

C

Minors

Minors are young persons, having achieved puberty, but below the age of 18. They have contractual capacity but of a limited type, the limitations being that should a minor have a curator his contracts must be made with the curator's concurrence and, in any event, his bargains and transactions may be examined and re-opened during his minority and for a period of four years after the attainment of majority, a period known as the *quadriennium utile*. Persons dealing with a minor must, therefore, ascertain if there is a curator, as a contract with a minor is void if it does not have the curator's approval. If there is no curator the minor validly contracts alone subject to the possibility of the contract being set aside. It should be noted that the approval of a curator does not of itself mean the terms of the contract cannot be re-examined.

Curators

At common law the father is the curator of the minor and curatory ends on his death. There is the possibility of other curators: a minor who desires a curator may have one appointed by the Court of Session;[12] if the minor is involved with his curator, or having no curator, at all, in litigation a curator *ad litem* must be appointed by the Court; a father, while in health, that is, not on his death bed, may nominate a curator to assume office on his death; a person may name a curator to a minor for a special purpose, as the administration of a bequest, but such curator's role is confined to advising on the bequest or property; a person who acted as tutor automatically becomes curator at puberty, although the minor can choose a different curator.

The curatorship ends if father or child dies, or when the minor has, with the father's consent, set out on an independent course of life. Curatorship may be ended if the father forfeits it through his conduct. Curatorship over a daughter ends on her marriage.

The distinction between the office of tutor and that of curator is important. The curator has no power of dictation over the minor's person, nor has he the power of management of the estate; in this connection his responsibilities lie in advising, consenting, and concurring with the minor in his management of his affairs. Without such consent the minor does not validly contract, with the probable

---

[12] Administration of Justice (Scotland) Act 1933, s. 12.

exceptions of contracts of service or apprenticeship,[13] and contracts in the course of the trade carried on by the minor.

Quadriennium utile: Any contract made by a minor, including one where the concurrence of a curator was necessary and granted, is voidable during minority and for four years after majority is attained, the period known as the *quadriennium utile.* The grounds on which the transaction may be attacked are minority and lesion, lesion being some considerable injury to the minor's estate. A smaller injury will suffice to constitute lesion where the minor contracted alone than where he had his curator's consent.[14] If such a loss as would constitute lesion be shown, the contract will be set aside. Obvious examples of lesion are gifts, cautionary obligations, and discharges for less than the sum owed. In the case of sale the transaction can be set aside if the terms were not fair, or if the minor has diminished his estate by squandering the proceeds;[15] thus a purchaser from a minor can insist on security for the beneficial investment of the price.[16] Loans to a minor would not be repayable had the loan been mis-spent. There are statutory provisions making it a criminal offence to invite a minor to borrow money by sending documents to him,[17] but such loans are not void.

Defences to a claim for reduction of a contract on the grounds of minority and lesion are; that the terms of the contract were fair, that the minor's estate has not suffered loss, that the minor held himself out to be of full age and was believed on reasonable ground,[18] that the contract was in connection with a trade or business carried out by the minor,[19] and that the minor, in full knowledge of the facts and of his legal rights after attaining his majority, ratified the contract.[20]

From the banker's point of view the lowering of the age of majority from twenty-one to eighteen years of age has greatly eased his responsibilities in dealing with younger customers. In the case of a customer still in minority great caution must be exercised in paying sums due lest allegations of lesion as a result of the transaction

---

[13] *McFeetridge* v. *Stewarts and Lloyds* 1913 S.C. 773.
[14] *Cooper* v. *Cooper's Trs.* (1885) 12 R 473.
[15] *Harkness* v. *Graham* (1833) 11 S. 769.
[16] *Ferguson* v. *Yuille* (1835) 13 s. 886.
[17] Betting and Loans (Infants) Act 1892; Consumer Credit Act 1974, s. 50.
[18] *Wilkie* v. *Dunlop* (1834) 12 s. 506.
[19] *McFeetridge* v. *Stewarts and Lloyds, supra.*
[20] *McGibbon* v. *McGibbon* (1852) 14 D 605.

be brought against the banker. To take an extreme example, a cheque drawn by a minor in favour of a gambling establishment or a book-maker should not be paid; lesion in such a case is obvious. If the banker collects dividends, rents or interest on behalf of a minor the transmission of these to him is generally considered to be safe but clearly if the sums are large the banker must be on his guard. The position is not clearly stated in any authority but in Green's Encyclopediae of the Laws of Scotland it is stated[21] 'the safe rule would be never to pay without the authority of the Court . . . or unless a guardian is appointed to consent in the discharge'.

The concurrence of a curator lessens, but does not remove, the possibility of an action for reduction of the ground of lesion. It is, however, plain that payment to a minor who has a curator without the curator's consent is void, and money thus paid might not be recoverable.

A minor should certainly not be lent money, lest his responsibility to repay be evaded on the grounds of minority and lesion. He can grant guarantees, but these cannot be enforced against him, and guarantees of any indebtedness of a minor by anyone else are worthless[22] on the basis that the ancillary obligation of caution depends on the validity and enforceability of the principal obligation.

Associations of Persons

The law has long recognised that persons will associate together for the accomplishment of particular, common purposes. Perhaps the particular purpose is worship, or recreation, or the pursuit of common protection or common profit. Whatever the purpose may be, the association will be recognised by the law. Broadly, associations will either be incorporated or unincorporated. Among incorporated associations are companies, local authorities, savings banks, building societies and trade unions; while there remain unincorporated most churches, clubs, and all partnerships. The importance of the difference between incorporated and unincorporated associations is vital. When an association is incorporated it is treated in law as a person of full capacity, subject to some restrictions of which persons who deal with the association must be aware, while the

---

21 Vol. X p. 32.
22 *Coutts and Co.* v. *Browne Lecky and ors.* [1946] 2 All. E.R. 207.

unincorporated association does not enjoy this juristic personality, with the exception of Scottish partnerships. Whether any particular association is incorporated or unincorporated is a matter of fact. There is no reason why a congregation or club should not, if found convenient, seek incorporation, while many large business associations, of which the commonest example is professional partnership, remain unincorporated. The banker must know if his customers, not being individuals, form a corporate body or not; and he must know the rules which apply both to incorporated and unincorporated bodies with whom he deals.

Of incorporated associations the commonest, and certainly so in business, is the company, while, also in the business world, the partnership remains a popular means of association, although unincorporated. These associations are discussed in a separate chapter of this work. At this point there fall to be described unincorporated voluntary associations, local authorities, building societies, industrial and provident societies, and trade unions.

Unincorporated Voluntary Associations

Whether a voluntary association is incorporated or unincorporated association is a matter of fact. If incorporated it will normally be a limited company and the rules regarding its administration and relationships with other persons, bank, landlord, or suppliers, are those which apply to any company. If it is not incorporated then it is simply a voluntary association of persons and does not enjoy separate personality in law distinct from the aggregate of its members. Examples are clubs—but not 'clubs' owned by individuals in which the members enjoy, by contract, a right to use premises or facilities but do not participate in management and proprietorship—associations and societies, although some societies are incorporated, for example building and friendly societies may be incorporated. Common types of voluntary associations include churches, but not the Church of Scotland, charities, scientific associations, sporting clubs, and learned societies.

The relationship of the members of a voluntary association amongst themselves is a matter of contract, and generally of no concern to those with whom the association deals. Business on behalf of such an association is carried out by its authorised office bearers, who act as agents for the whole body of the members, and thus, unless they have claimed to have been acting in a personal capacity, office bearers do not incur personal liability on such contracts.

The property of a voluntary association is held by the members jointly, no single member has a separate estate in the association's property, nor any right in respect of possession of it. On a member's death his right in the association property accresces to the others. If the association is wound up any surplus of the joint property may be distributed amongst the members at that time. An exception exists in the case of religious or charitable associations in which the funds or property are held in trust by the members, or trustees if such exist, for the objects of the society. If such organisation is wound up its funds may either be distributed for the furtherance of the society's objectives, or if this be impossible and there is general charitable intent, the court may order a scheme for administration of the funds *cy prés*. If no overriding general charitable intent can be ascertained the funds will be repayable to the subscribers.

If an account is opened in the name of a voluntary association it will require to be operated by nominated officials; the banker must conform with care to the instructions he receives as to the signatories and amounts to be withdrawn. Authority to operate an account does not, of course, confer power to overdraw; such power requires to be specific. The banker should ensure that the operators of the account are authorised in their actions; otherwise by the general law of agency the association may not be bound by their actings. Conversely, agents will not be personally liable to the bank if they are acting within their authority.[23]

The general law of agency also demands that circumstances may put a banker on inquiry in such cases.

When a bank account is opened for a club, association or society, the banker should obtain a copy of the rules or constitution and ascertain from it the powers of committees, councils, or office bearers. An excerpt from the minutes of a meeting of the body, or of an appropriate committee within the terms of the constitution, should also be obtained, such resolution authorising the opening of the account and containing full instructions regarding the powers of the persons who are appointed to operate upon the account, whether they may act singly or jointly and whether the authority is given to individuals or as office bearers. Any such minute should be certified

---

23 *National Bank of Scotland Ltd.* v. *Shaw* 1913 S.C. 133.

by the chairman of the relevant meeting, and the secretary. Changes in the instructions thus received, in the identity of those to operate on the account, and, if relevant, the holders of offices should be obtained in similar minutes. As a matter of practice, an account should be in the name of the association, not in that of a person acting on its behalf, the latter situation producing problems should that person die or wish to conduct a transaction which the banker might find peculiar but be powerless to prevent if the account is a personal one.

If an overdraft is allowed to an association it should be secured over club property or guaranteed by members. A member, as such, is liable to contribute to the club only his agreed subscription; he does not incur liability to the club's creditors unless he has agreed to do so or has acted so as to make himself liable as an agent.[24] The pledging or charging of club assets must be in accordance with the rules.

Friendly Societies

Certain associations or societies are entitled to be registered under the Friendly Societies Act 1974. Assuming that they have seven or more members, have a registered office in Scotland, and prepare rules in accordance with the Second Schedule to the Act, there may register as Friendly Societies associations which have as their purpose the providing by voluntary subscriptions of the members, with or without the aid of donations, for the relief or maintenance of members of the society and their families during sickness or in old age, widowhood, or if orphaned, insurance of all sorts up to certain limits and the relief or maintenance of members in distress. Additionally, societies which exist for the purpose of insurance to any amount against loss of cattle, sheep, lambs, swine, horses and other animals by death from disease or otherwise may register. There may also be registered under the Act societies for any benevolent or charitable purpose, societies which exist, called 'Working Men's Clubs' for purposes of social intercourse, mutual helpfulness, mental and moral improvement and rational recreation, societies called, 'Old People Home Societies', for the purpose of providing homes for the members and others at any age after fifty, and any

24 *Thomson* v. *Victoria Eighty Club* (1905) 13 S.L.T. 399.

other society which the Treasury may authorise as being qualified
for registration under the Act.

The Act makes provision for the registration of branches of any
registered society and provides that every registered society and
branch must have one or more trustees. A trustee may not be the
secretary or treasurer of that society or branch. There are provisions
in the Act regarding the keeping of books, the production of annual
accounts, and the audit of these.

The rules of the society must provide for the appointment of a
committee of management and of trustees.

Despite their registration friendly societies are not incorporated
bodies and deal through their appointed officers and trustees. The
banker who has a friendly society as a customer must therefore
ensure that he is reliably informed, by excerpt minute of a meeting
appointing officers, of the identity of the officers from time to time
while the rules of the society together with any decisions of it will
define the rights and the limits of the rights of the officers.

The property of the society is held by its trustees, whose investment powers are specified in the Act (s. 46); with the consent of the
committee or of a majority of members present at a meeting the
trustees may invest any of the funds of the society or branch in the
National Savings Bank or in any Savings Bank certified under the
Trustee Savings Bank Acts, in the public funds, or in the purchase
of land or the erection or alteration of offices or other buildings on
land, or upon any other security expressly directed by the rules of
the society or branch, or in any investment in which trustees are
from time to time authorised by law to utilise. In connection with
the power to hold land the trustees of a registered society or branch
may, if its rules provide, hold, purchase or take on lease any land
and may sell, exchange, grant heritable security, or lease any such
land and no purchaser, tenant or creditor in any heritable security is
bound to inquire as to the authority for any such transaction,
(s. 53(1)), which offers protection to a banker who may have advanced
money on heritable property. Lending, except on security of heritage
to a friendly society is as difficult as lending to any other unincorporated association. Apart from the reference to granting heritable
securities there is no reference to borrowing powers in the Act,
officers or trustees who borrowed would do so by authority of the
rules or resolutions of the society or branch; in case of difficulty
recouping a loan to a friendly society, except if specific assets were
validly pledged, would not be easy.

Trades Unions

A trade union is defined[25] as an organisation which consists wholly or mainly of workers of one or more descriptions and which includes amongst its principal purposes the regulation of relations between workers of that or those descriptions and employers or employers' associations. A trade union is not to be treated as a body corporate but may make contracts, sue and be sued, be liable for criminal prosecution and the property held in trust for it is liable to diligence or other steps of execution, if a court order is made against it.[26] A trade union cannot register under the Friendly Societies Act 1974, the Industrial and Provident Societies Act 1965 or the Companies Act 1948[27] unless it is a 'special register body'. A special register body is one which registered in the special register set up under the now repealed Industrial Relations Act 1971,[28] which provided for organisations which while not trade unions have a role to play in industrial relations. Only incorporated bodies were eligible to be registered in the special register.

Employers' associations may or may not be incorporated. If they are not they are also capable of making contracts, suing or being sued, are liable for criminal prosecution and their property is liable to diligence.[29]

If an employer's association is incorporated or if a body is a special register body it is treated in every way as having corporate status. A trade union and the unincorporated employer's assocation occupy a special position. All property of such a body must be vested in trustees appointed or changed by a resolution by or on behalf of the body according to its rules. A trade union or unincorporated employer's association must have rules which will cover, amongst other things, the purposes for which and the name in which any property or funds are authorised to be applied or invested, and the appointment or removal of trustees.[30] A trade union or unincorporated employer's association is registered in a register kept by the Registrar of Friendly Societies and will only be so registered if it is a trade union or employer's association within the definitions given in the Trade Unions and Labour Relations Act 1974 and if its rules comply

---

[25] Trade Unions and Labour Relations Act 1974, s.1.
[26] *ibid.* s. 2.
[27] *ibid.* ss. 2, 3.
[28] s. 84.
[29] Trade Union and Industrial Relations Act, 1974, s. 3.
[30] *ibid.* s. 6.

with the statutory requirements. If an organisation is not so registered it is not only an unincorporated organisation but one which does not enjoy the privileges conferred by the statute on trade unions and unincorporated employers' associations which are so registered.

The Trade Union and Labour Relations Act 1974 also demands that a trade union or employer's association must keep proper accounts, records and produce revenue accounts and a balance sheet, which must be audited by a qualified auditor, unless the body is a small one, and which must be submitted to the Registrar annually. These annual returns are available for public inspection. In dealing with a trade union as a customer the banker is entitled to contract with the organisation but he will require to know the details of the officials who operate the account and the extent of their authority. Certified excerpts from the minutes of the union or, where relevant, its governing body, will be sufficient to identify the authorised officers and the scope of their authority. In the case of the union or employer's association trustees deeds of assumption and resignation should be exhibited as evidence of changes in the identity of the trustees.

There is a speciality regarding union property the transfer of which is required to be effected by means of an entry in a register, for example, shares.[31] If there is produced to the keeper of such a register a copy of a deed of assumption or resignation of the trustee which has attached to it a list identifying the securities which the union holds and the deed and list are certified by the president and general secretary of the union or association the keeper of the register, if any security on the list is included in the register he keeps, will make entries in his register giving effect to the changes indicated in the deed.

INCORPORATED ASSOCIATIONS

The essential difference between an incorporated and unincorporated association is that the former is treated in law as a person, has juristic personality or legal entity, while the latter with the exception of Scottish partnerships has not. An unincorporated association is merely the sum of its members and acts through them;

[31] *ibid.* s. 4.

it will, hold its property through trustees. The incorporated association will contract on its own behalf—albeit through agents.

The commonest type of incorporated association is the company, which is treated separately in this book. Others include industrial and provident societies, building societies, local authorities and statutory authorities.

Industrial and Provident Societies

A society for carrying on any industry, business or trade, wholesale or retail, may be registered under the Industrial and Provident Societies Acts 1965 to 1968, if it is a *bona fide* co-operative society, or being conducted for the benefit of the community or there are special reasons why the society should be registered under this Act rather than as a company. The rules of any such society must conform to the Acts and the regulations made under it. Registered under this legislation are co-operative societies, housing trusts, and other societies which exist for the benefit of their members or of the community. They are not non-profit making necessarily, but profits must be applied as is provided in the rules of the society. Such a society is a limited company.

To gain incorporation as an industrial or provident society the association must register with the Assistant Registrar of Friendly Societies whose acknowledgement of registration is conclusive evidence of due registration.[32] Two printed copies of the society's rules, containing provisions as specified in the Act[33] must be presented to the Assistant Registrar. Amongst other matters the rules must provide for entrusting the management of the society's affairs to a committee, for the appointment of that committee, for the holding of meetings, voting thereat, and for the mode of altering or rescinding rules. A society must keep proper books of account and produce accounts in the form demanded by the statute. Provision is made for audit, and for an annual return to the assistant registrar. A society may invest its funds in any security authorised by its rules.

The banker who deals with an industrial or provident society must know the contents of its rules. An account is operated by resolution of the committee of management and copies of such resolution should be obtained. Any changes in the committee or

32 Industrial and Provident Societies Act 1965, s. 2.
33 *ibid*. Sched. 1.

those entitled to operate on the account must be intimated to the banker and certified copies of relevant resolutions must be obtained by the banker.

Lenders to an industrial or provident society must ensure that such lending is within the registered rules of the society and a certified copy of a resolution authorising overdraft or other borrowing by the society must be obtained by the bank.

An industrial or provident society may grant floating charges to secure its borrowing.[34]

Building Societies

A building society is a society existing for the purpose of raising by the subscription of members a fund for making advances to members out of the funds of the society on the security of lands or buildings.[35] A building society may be incorporated or unincorporated, but few unincorporated building societies remain. All societies formed since 1874 have to incorporate under the Building Societies Act. Very few societies remain which are not incorporated; such are not governed by the Building Societies Act 1962 in which the existing law regarding building societies was consolidated.

A building society is registered with the Assistant Registrar of Friendly Societies who must approve *inter alia* its rules, which must contain matters required by the Building Societies Act 1962 (s. 4) but may contain other matters so long as they are consistent with the general law and with the Act.[36] Any changes in the rules must be specially resolved by the society, registered with the Assistant Resgistrar (s. 17) and must be consistent with the constitution of the society.[37]

Two types of building societies can be formed, permanent societies and terminating societies, i.e. those whose rules specify dates or circumstances in which they are to be terminated. There is a difference between the borrowing powers of each type. A permanent society may borrow up to two-thirds of the amount for the time being secured to the society by mortgages from its members (s. 39(2)) while a terminating society has its borrowing power restricted to

---

[34] Companies (Receivers and Floating Charges) (Scotland) Act 1972.
[35] Building Societies Act 1962, s. 1(1).
[36] *Murray* v. *Scott* (1884) App. Cas. 519; *Cullerne* v. *London etc. Building Society* (1890) 25 Q.B.D. 485.
[37] *Bradbury* v. *Wild* [1893. 1 Ch. 377.

whichever is the greater of (a) two-thirds of the amount for the time being secured to the society by mortgages from its members or (b) twelve months' subscription on the shares of the members for the time being.

A building society's directors must be satisfied that the adequacy of any security is assessed by themselves or by a competent person and that such assessment is made only after obtaining a report from a competent and prudent independent person. A society may accept additional security but only as specified in the statutes, but such would not be taken into account in computing the limits of its borrowing outlined in the Act. Records of advances, showing the value of them and the security must be kept.

The funds available to a building society for lending to members include not only the subscription of members but also deposits solicited from the public. Such sums are taken into account in computing the borrowing limits of any society. A power to borrow money must be contained within the rules of the society.

Administration of a building society is prescribed by the Act, which prescribes rules for books, accounts, audit, and an annual report by the directors on the state of the society's affairs, and annual return.[38] An Annual General Meeting must be held.

A society may invest surplus funds only as authorised by the Act, or keep them in current account with an authorised bank.[39]

The relations of the banker and the building society may cover either or both of account holder or borrower. If the first is the case, the opening and operation of the account must be in accordance with the rules of the society, with the statutes under which it operates, and with resolutions of the governing body of the society pertinent to the account.

If the society is a borrower the onus of discovering if the society has borrowing power or has exceeded its borrowing is on the lender;[40] the borrowing power will be stated in the rules together with any restrictions on these. The statutory restrictions must also be adhered to; if they are not the directors are personally liable for any excess borrowed. The loan must be for the purposes of the society.[41]

---

[38] Building Societies Act 1962, ss. 76–91.
[39] ibid. ss. 58–61.
[40] Sun Permanent Building Society v. Western Suburbia B.S. 1921 2 Ch. 438.
[41] Building Societies Act 1962, s. 39.

A building society may offer security for loans made to it but only where express powers to do so are contained in its rules.

Local Authorities

By the Local Government (Scotland) Act 1973 there were created nine regional authorities to be known as Regional Councils to provide certain local authority services within the nine regions into which mainland Scotland was divided by the Act. Within each region there were created districts which fall under the government of district councils who are entrusted within the district for which each is responsible with the discharge of other local government functions. There are fifty-three such district councils. In addition there are three island area authorities for Shetland, Orkney and the Western Islands, which acquit within these areas most of the functions of local government. Specific arrangements are made in the Act for the audit of local government accounts but there is little guidance or instruction to the local authority on the detailed management of their finances or financial arrangement. Every local authority is to have a general fund into which all sums received by or on behalf of the authority must be paid,[42] while all money borrowed by a local authority must be shown in a loans fund which is part of the general fund of the authority.[43] Local authorities are charged to make arrangements for the proper administration of their financial affairs and must secure that the proper officer of the authority has responsibility for the administration of those affairs.

The banker who has a local authority as a customer must ensure that the instructions he receives are those of the authority. As with all customers, instructions as to how cheques are to be drawn are to be followed and should rest on a resolution of the authority itself a certified copy of which should be procured by the banker. Any changes in the identity of the relevant officers, or councillors, should be intimated to the banker.

A local authority is prohibited from incurring capital expenses, defined as any expenses which are to be charged to a capital or borrowing account or which, being of a capital nature, are to be met otherwise than out of revenue unless the local authority has the consent of the Secretary of State for Scotland. This direct method of

[42] Local Government (Scotland) Act 1973, s. 93.
[43] Local Government /(Scotland) Act 1975, Sched. 3, par a12.

control of local authority expenditure replaces control through consent to borrow which was previously required.

Borrowing by local authorities is controlled by the rules in Schedule 3 of the Local Government (Scotland) Act 1975, a consolidated code for borrowing. The Schedule authorises borrowing for any of the following purposes; for acquiring any land which the authority have power to acquire, for erecting any building which the authority have power to erect, for the execution of any permanent work or the provision of any plant or the doing of any other thing which the authority have power to execute, provide or do and which involves expenses of a capital nature, and for any other purpose for which the authority is authorised under any enactment to borrow. Additionally a local authority may borrow such sums as are required to meet other expenses which the local authority considers should be met by borrowing and repayments spread over a term of years, and the authorities may also borrow sums as are necessary to provide working capital or meet any other expenses required for the purposes of any public utility undertaking carried on by the authority. The power to borrow to finance a public utility undertaking is restricted to a sum which does not exceed an amount representing one half of the gross revenue of that undertaking for the immediately preceding financial hear and is to be repaid as soon as is reasonably practical and in any event within two years. Borrowing in excess of that limit or repayment over a longer period requires the consent of the Secretary of State for Scotland. A local authority which is exercising borrowing powers under statutory authority may raise the money by mortgage, overdraft, by the issue of stocks and bonds or bills, from the Public Works Loan Commissioners or by any other means approved by the Secretary of State with the consent of the Treasury.

Schedule 3 also makes provision for temporary loans or overdrafts from a bank of any sums which the local authorities may temporarily require for the purposes of defraying expenses pending the receipt of revenues receivable by them in respect of the year in which those expenses are chargeable and for the purpose of raising the loan in exercise of any statutory borrowing power. Such expenditure may also be met by the issue of bills although the aggregate amount outstanding on bills issued shall not exceed a proportion of the local authority's estimated gross income from the rates as may be prescribed by the Treasury or if no such restriction is made a sum equal to one-fifth of the authority's estimated gross income. In any event a local authority shall not borrow by the issue of bills any year during which the authority's estimated gross income does not exceed £3million.

All money borrowed under any statutory borrowing power by a local authority shall be secured on the whole funds, rates and revenues of the authority and not otherwise and all money borrowed by a local authority and by whatever method shall be deemed to have the same charge and security and shall rank *pari passu*.

A person lending money to a local authority shall not be bound to inquire whether the borrowing of the money is legal or regular or whether the money raised was properly applied, and shall not be prejudiced by any illegality or irregularity, or by the misapplication or non-application of any of that money.

Statutory Authorities

Most important public authorities, British Rail and the Forestry Commission being two examples, are incorporated under the statute which sets them up. Their contractual powers rest on these statutes but, as with any other incorporated body, they act through agents, their officials and officers. The banker who deals with such a corporation treats it as he would any corporation, taking care that his instructions as to the powers of particular officers, say to sign cheques, are clear and are followed. The borrowing capacity of the public corporation is restricted by statute and should the matter arise note should be taken of any such restriction although it seems inconceivable that a public corporation would exceed its powers or, if this were inadvertently done, would seek to deny liability.

Charter Corporations

Some organisations, for example colleges, foundations, universities, and some companies rely for their corporate status on a Charter. The powers of the organisation and the method of administering it can be deduced from the Charter. While in questions as to the regularity of the relationship between banker and the officials of such an organisation the banker has to have regard to the Charter as well as to his agreed instructions from the organisation as to cheques, lending, and other facilities.

Solicitors

Under the Solicitors (Scotland) Account Rules practising solicitors must maintain a client account or accounts, such an account being defined as a current, deposit or savings account at a bank in the title of which account the word 'client', 'trustee', 'trust', or other fiduciary term appears and it includes an account or deposit receipt for a client whose name is specified in the title of the account concerned. Into such an account a solicitor must pay without delay all sums in excess of fifty pounds held for or received from or on behalf of a client, unless the sum is received in the form of cash which is paid without delay in cash in the ordinary course of business to the client or a third party on his behalf, or if in the form of a cheque or draft which is indorsed over in the ordinary course of business of the client or to someone on his behalf.

A solicitor must ensure that at all times the sum at the credit of the client account, or where there are more such accounts than one the total of the sums that the credit of that account or those accounts shall not be less than the total of the client's money held by the solicitor. If however an individual client account is kept specially for a client who has given written authority to overdraw an overdraft on such a client account is not to be taken into account for the purpose of ascertaining whether the correct sum appears in the client account or accounts.

With the exception provided for an overdraft on an individual client account with the written authority of the individual client, no overdraft should be allowed on a solicitor's client account while the Solicitors (Scotland) Act 1949 provides that a balance at credit of a client account cannot be offset against any indebtedness of the solicitor to the bank. There can therefore be no question of allowing compensating interests between a client account and other accounts in the name of a solicitor.

Under the Solicitors (Scotland) Act 1965 there is provision that on the death of a solicitor who immediately before his death was practising as a solicitor in his own name or as a sole solicitor in a firm name the right to operate or otherwise deal with a client account in the name of the solicitor or his firm vests in the Law Society of Scotland to the exclusion of any personal representative of such solicitor and shall be exercisable from the death of the solicitor. The banker with the customer who is a sole practitioner should therefore await the instructions of the Law Society of Scotland as to the operation of any such client account or accounts should the customer die.

D

Stockbrokers

Stockbrokers sometimes negotiate loans with their own banker to enable their clients to buy shares and for the shares to be taken by the banker in security fo such advances. The shares are transferred direct from seller to the bank's nominee and the transaction is covered by standing arrangements between the stockbroker and the bank, the banker treating the stockbroker as his customer. Questions may arise as to the validity of the security and as to what advances it secures for it might be argued that it secures the specific advance made at the time the pledge was made or that the security may be held against the whole indebtedness of the stockbroker to the bank. The answer to these problems may be found in the circumstances surrounding a particular transaction, or in the general law regarding agents and their powers. A banker generally assumes that where a stockbroker applies to him for an advance he is acting on behalf of a client and if the transaction is based on that understanding which might be founded on a general course of business or actual knowledge the security is good against repayment of the specific advances made only. A stockbroker requires the consent of his client to pledge securities, but such consent may be assumed by the fact that the broker is in possession of the shares or can pledge them; a third party acting in good faith and with reasonable caution can assume that the broker has in these circumstances authority to pledge the shares against specific advances. Even if the stockbroker acted without express authority or beyond his actual authority the banker may retain the shares against repayment of the specific advance in connection with which they were pledged in a question with the true owner. If, however, this is the case it is clear the bank cannot argue that it holds the shares against the whole indebtedness of the stockbroker; that would indicate that the bank did not recognise the qualification or the title of the broker and wish to treat him as owner of the shares which runs contrary to the assumption that he is an agent with powers to effect pledges.

The banker's right to retain shares against their true owner depends on his having acted in good faith. In the case of *London Joint Stock Bank* v. *Simons*[44] Lord Herschell said: 'I apprehend that when a person whose honesty there is no reason to doubt offers negotiable securities to a banker or any other person, the only consideration

[44] [1892] A.C. 201.

likely to engage his attention is whether the security is sufficient to justify the advance required, and I do not think the law lays on him the obligation of making any enquiry into the title of the person whom he finds in possession of them: of course if there is anything to arouse suspicion, to lead to a doubt whether the person purporting to transfer them is justified in entry into the contemplated transaction, the case would be different. The existence of such suspicion and doubt would be inconsistent with good faith.'

Thus, if the banker has any reason to doubt the rights of the broker to bind his client to a pledge of the shares he is put on inquiry and should take steps to ascertain the actual extent of the stockbroker's authority. Failure to do so could mean that the banker could not treat the pledge as complete and thus would be unable to retain the shares against a claim by their owner, even for the amount of specific advances.

Despite the fact that the banker assumes and is entitled to assume, that a broker pledging shares does so on behalf of a client, he need not assume that the proceeds from a sale of shares is not the broker's own money. Thus where the proceeds of such sale is paid into the broker's account the banker is entitled to use it to reduce the broker's overdraft and there is no duty to inquire as to the real ownership of the money. If however the banker has actual knowledge that any such money is paid in fraud of a third person's right, the banker cannot plead a right to retain the money.[45]

---

[45] *Thomson and Ors (Dunlop's Trs.)* v. *Clydesdale Bank* (1893) 20 R. (H.L.) 59.

CHAPTER THREE

AGENCY

AGENCY is a relationship between two parties, one of whom, the principal, empowers the other, the agent, to act for him and undertakes to be bound by the agent's acts as if they were his own. The task of the agent is to make contracts on behalf of the principal with third parties under an authority which may be expressed or implied. From the point of view of the banker agency has a double importance; the banker may have to deal with agents and, in certain circumstances, the banker may be an agent. An agent has been defined as 'a person having express or implied power to act on behalf of another party who is called the principal',[1] a definition which neatly describes a relationship between the commoner types of agent, for example, the solicitor acting on behalf of his client. It also, however, covers other cases where the agency is not so obvious, for example, where it is part of an employee's job to enter into contracts—the shop assistant is a good example—or where there is a partnership where each partner has power to deal on behalf of the firm.[2] Directors of a company are agents for the company, a wife is agent for her husband in domestic affairs. No matter if the relationship springs from usage, as is the case in the domestic agency of a wife, or express contract, which will be the case in the appointment of someone to act as an agent, the same principles apply.

Mandate

When an agent acts without remuneration, the contract relationship between him and his principal is more properly called mandate, the agent being called a mandatary, the principal being called the mandant. The principles of mandate are nearly identical with those of agency; where they vary is noted below at the appropriate places.

When a mandate is constituted in writing the document is known

---

[1] Bowstead *Agency* p. 1.
[2] see *infra* p. 74

as a Factory and Commission but more usually it is a Power of Attorney.

Constitution

The relationship of agency may be constituted by express contract —which need not be in writing, even if the contract is to last over a year.[3] Secondly, it may be implied from the actings of the parties. Thirdly, the relationship may be constituted by the one party ratifying prior actings of the other and thus investing the other restrospectively with an authority which he pretended to but did not possess. Finally, the agency may arise through necessity.

Where the agency is constituted by an express contract or instruction, then the terms of that contract or instruction strictly delimit the authority of the agent.

Agency will be implied where the circumstances would indicate that an agency exists, e.g., the manager of a shop is presumed to have the power to contract on behalf of the owner, a wife living with her husband is presumed to be his agent for the purchase of necessary items for the family. Alternatively, the actings of the parties may have implied an authority which in fact was not intended. An example of this is to be found in the case of *International Sponge Importers* v. *Watt*.[4] In this case a traveller who for many years had sold sponges was in the habit of inducing his customers to pay him by cheque made out to him personally, in spite of the fact that the company sent out invoices with directions for payment on them. A customer in good faith paid the traveller on several occasions without challenge by the traveller's principal. When the agent embezzled the payment, the principal raised an action for payment against the customer but it was held that the customer was entitled to assume from the prior dealings with the agent that his authority extended to his receiving payments.

Ratification arises where there has been no agency or where an agent has acted beyond his powers. Then, by ratifying a contract made by the agent, his alleged principal may bind himself to it. The ratification may be expressed or implied from the conduct of the principal.[5] Where such a contract has been ratified the principal assumes liability from its formation. Before ratification can take

[3] *Pickin* v. *Hawkes* (1872) 5 R. 676.
[4] 1911 S.C. (H.L.) 57.
[5] *Ballantine* v. *Stevenson* (1881) 8 R.959; *Barnetson* v. *Peterson* (1902) 5 F.86

place several conditions must be satisfied: the agent must have contracted ostensibly as an agent for the ratifier; the alleged principal or ratifier must have existed at the time of the formation of the contract, e.g. a newly formed company *cannot* ratify contracts made for it by its promoters before its incorporation; the ratifier must have had capacity at the time of the contract's formation;[6] the ratifier must have knowledge of all material facts or have waived such knowledge; lastly, where the contract had to be formed within a certain time or before a certain event, then the ratification must also be within that time or before that event.[7] Agency of necessity—an English term—'seems undistinguishable from the principle of *negotiorum gestio*.'[8] *Negotiorum gestio* is the management of the affairs of a person who is not in a position to manage them himself, e.g. because he is absent, of non-age, or is mentally disordered. The action will be taken without prior authority but on the assumption that such an authority would have been given had the party for whom the action is taken been aware of the need for action, or in a position to give authority. The person who takes action is entitled to the rights and privileges, and suffers the obligations of, an agent. It should be noted that no one is under any obligation to provide services, however obvious the need for these might be.

Capacity

In agency capacity twice arises as a possible difficulty. Firstly, if there is a contract of agency between principal and agent, both parties must have the necessary capacity for the formation of the contract. There need not, however, be a contract between principal and agent: a father may send his son into a shop to buy a bottle of lemonade and there is no contract between father and son although they are principal and agent.[9] The question of capacity arises again in the contracts formed by the agent for his principal. In these cases the capacity which is relevant is that of the principal. A principal cannot extend his own capacity through the employment of an agent whose personal capacity is greater, nor will he suffer any restriction through employing an agent of limited capacity. If an adult is acting as agent for a minor, he can contract with third parties only

---

[6] *Boston Deep Sea Fishing Co.* v. *Farnham* [1957] 3 All E.R. 204.
[7] *Goodall* v. *Bilsland* 1909 S.C. 1152.
[8] Gloag and Henderson *op. cit.* p. 253.
[9] Gow *op cit.* p. 516.

to the extent that the minor himself could do so. If the situation is reversed and the agent is of non-age, he can act to full extent although his personal liability is restricted to that of a minor in the event of a third party suing for breach of warranty of authority.

Rights of an agent

The agent's rights are: to be paid, to be reimbursed for any expenses he incurs and indemnified against liability to third parties arising out of the agency, and a right of lien over the goods of his principal which may be in his possession to fortify claims he may have against his principal.

Remuneration: In the absence of express agreement as to payment of the agent—and the agreement with his principal may provide for salary, commission, brokerage, fees or any combination of these—he is entitled, if he makes his living in this way, to be paid at the customary rate for the services which he provides, or in any case at a reasonable rate. It is possible to have a gratuitous agency, when the term 'mandate' is generally used, and the agent is known as 'mandatory', the principal as 'mandant'. Payment is due to the agent who fulfils his duties, and whether or not he has done so is a question of construction of the agreement or the terms of his agency. Thus in the cases of *Trollope and Sons* v. *Martyn Bros.*,[10] *Dudley Bros.* v. *Barnet*[11] and *Bennet* v. *Millet*[12] commission was held to be due to the agents who had produced clients willing to buy on the agreed terms although the principals refused to sell, while in *Luxor Ltd.* v. *Cooper*[13] in similar circumstances the agent was found not to be due his commission because his agency was in terms that he was to be paid on completion of the sale. The terms of the agency are then of vital importance in ascertaining whether commission is due to the agent or not.

A second point of difficulty regarding the payment of commission may be in determining whether the event or transaction which would have been commission-earning for the agent was actually engineered by him. Though the actual business done may not be directly due to the agent, he may be entitled to commission if he was the means of bringing the parties into relationship with each other.

[10] [1934] 2 K.B. 436.
[11] 1937 S.C. 632.
[12] [1948] 2 All E.R. 929.
[13] [1941] A.C. 108.

Thus in *Walker Donald and Co.* v. *Birrell*[14] a customer was introduced by a shipbroker to a shipbuilder. Their negotiations were fruitless but at a later date the customer placed an order for another vessel, and the agent was held entitled to commission. Yet in the case of *Tribe* v. *Taylor*[15] where an agent had to find a purchaser for a business or someone willing to introduce capital into it for a commission at five per cent on the capital, the agent was paid on capital introduced but when later the lender and the erstwhile principal went into partnership and the lender put up further sums, the agent was found not entitled to commission on these.

Relief: Properly incurred expenses of the agent must be met by the principal, who must also relieve his agent of any liability which he incurs in the discharge of his duties. This right of relief is exemplified in *Stevenson and Sons* v. *Duncan and Others*[16] where a principal refused to implement a contract and his agent was held liable to a claim of damages by the third party. The agent sued the principal and was held entitled to be indemnified by the principal against this claim.

Lien: An agent has a lien over his principal's goods properly in his possession. He can retain any such goods against payment of his commission, or his outlays, or against any claim for indemnity he may have.[17] The extent of the lien—which does not infer a right to sell—depends on usage or custom in any particular type of agency. The right depends on possession and is lost if the agent parts with the property.

The duties of the agent

The duties of the agent are to carry out his instructions, to do so personally, to show the required standard of care in his transactinos, to account, and to act in the interests of his principal.

To carry out instructions: Assuming no illegality or supervening impossibility, any agent must do what he has undertaken to do. In the absence of precise instructions he must act in the best interests of his principal, or according to usage or any previous course of dealing he may have had. He should carry out his duties personally, a term which includes his clerks and servants—there is a presumption

[14] (1883) 11 5 369.
[15] (1876) 1 C.D.D. 505.
[16] (1842) 5 D. 167.
[17] *Glendinning* v. *Hope* 1911 S.C. (H.L.) 73.

that he will do so,[18] expressed in the maxim *delegatis non potest delegare*. This presumption is 'almost eaten up by exceptions'[19] but certainly applies where there is any element of *delectus personae* in the appointment, as there so often is. Authority to delegate may be express, or implied by usage or by the nature of the employment. Where it is clear either expressly or by usage, e.g. in the case of an architect employing a surveyor,[20] that there is authority to delegate, the sub-agent to whom the task has been delegated will assume all the liabilities and duties of an agent in any question with the principal,[21] and the principal becomes liable to the sub-agent as if he himself had made the appointment.[22]

To show care: An agent must show such care and diligence as an agent in his position would normally exercise.[23] A mandatary must show such diligence as a man of common prudence employs in his own affairs, while the agent who professes a special skill must show the skill expected of a reasonably competent and careful person in his particular trade and employment.

To keep accounts: An agent must keep proper accounts of his transactions for his principal and must account to his principal at proper times. When he remits money to his principal he must follow his instructions. If he does not, any loss falls on him.[24] In the absence of instructions he remits through a bank or according to usage.

To act in the interests of the principal: Agency is a fiduciary relationship and the agent, as occupant of a position of trust, must not utilise for his own benefit any advantage he gains through his position. His reward for acting is his remuneration. Nor must his own interests conflict with those of his principal. Thus he must not buy, without disclosure, that which he has to sell for his principal,[25] under pain of having to account for any profit he makes or returning the goods if he has not resold them.

Any profits or secret benefits that the agent derives through his agency may properly be recovered by the principal to whom they belong, unless he knows of the practice and has raised no objection.

18 *Robertson* v. *Beatson* 9108 S.C. 921.
19 Gow *op. cit.* p. 530.
20 *Black* v. *Cornelius* (1879) 6 R. 581.
21 *De Bussche* v. *Alt* [1878] 8 Ch. 286.
22 Gloag and Henderson *op. cit.* p. 258.
23 Bell's *Princs.* s. 221.
24 *Warwicke* v. *Noakes* (1790) 3 R.R. 653.
25 *Graham* v. *Paton* (1917) S.C. 203.

Two cases illustrate these points. In the case of *Boston Fishing Co.* v. *Ansell*[26] the managing director of a company, its agent, ordered some fishing smacks, and unknown to the company received from the builders a commission. He was ordered to pay the commission to the company. In *Morrison* v. *Thomson*[27] a broker employed to buy a ship negotiated with the agent for the vendor for payment to him of part of the vendor's agent's commission—which depended on the price. He was ordered to account to his principal for this money. The principal who seeks to recover such a benefit from the dishonest agent need not show that he has suffered any loss; it is sufficient to prove that the agent has made a profit beyond his agreed remuneration.

Such secret commissions have to be obtained by the agent with the connivance of the third party, as was in the case *Boston Fishing Co.* v. *Ansell*. If this is the case, the principal may repudiate his contract with the third party and sue the third party for damages, as such a corruption of an agent is a civil wrong.[28] He may also dismiss the agent, withhold from him his ordinary commission for the transaction and recover the secret commission from him.

Apart from the consequences at civil law of the offering or acceptance of secret commissions, it is a criminal offence under the Prevention of Corruption Acts, 1906–16, for an agent to accept or solicit or agree to accept or obtain any gift or consideration as a inducement or reward for doing or forbearing to do something in relation to his principal's affairs or for showing favour or disfavour to anyone in relation to his principal's business. The person who offers or provides the gift or consideration is also guilty of an offence.

Relations between agent, principal and third party
In the ideal situation the contract formed by an agent is between his principal and the third party. He himself will obtain no rights and incur no liabilities under it. He cannot however escape liability to a third party for his own negligence, misrepresentation or fraud, whether these were authorised by his principal or not, or whether or not he has bound his principal. Yet the principal may remain liable for the loss caused through the wrongful acts of the agent.

26 [1888] 39 Ch. 339.
27 [1874] L.R. 9 Q.B. 480.
28 *Mayor of Salford* v. *Lever* [1891] I Q.B. 168.

Thus in the case of *Lloyd* v. *Grace, Smith and Co.*,[29] a solicitor who had given his clerk a general authority to conduct the conveyancing business of the firm was found liable in damages to a client who had been fraudulently induced by the clerk to make over to him personally some properties in the belief that these were to be sold and the proceeds re-invested.

The agent's success in forming a binding contract between a third party and his principal will depend largely on his having remained within his authority. If he has acted within his authority he will bind his principal; if he exceeds it he will not and will be liable to the disappointed third party in damages.[30] It is, however, necessary to appreciate that the actual authority given to him by the principal may not coincide with the authority which a third party might be entitled to assume the agent to possess. The rule is that an agent will bind his principal if the contract he makes is within this second area of authority, what is called his ostensible authority.

The actual or real authority of an agent is the authority conferred on him by his principal. Its extent is a question of fact and in any question between the agent and the principal the actual authority is what matters. The ostensible authority of an agent is that which a third party might reasonably believe him to have because of prior dealing with him, because of usage, or because the law recognises agents of his type to be invested with authority of a certain extent. The contracts of an agent which fall within the scope of his ostensible authority—although beyond the bounds of his actual authority—will bind his principal. If the third party has notice that the agent is acting beyond the scope of his actual authority then the principal will not be bound. Two cases illustrate these points. In the case of *Watteau* v. *Fenwick*[31] the manager and licensee of a beerhouse was forbidden to buy cigars on credit. Despite this prohibition he did so and his principal was held to be liable to pay for the cigars, it being within the authority usually confided to such a person to buy such goods on credit. In *Reckitt* v. *Barnett and Co.*[32] an agent who had authority to draw cheques paid a private debt of his own with a cheque drawn as agent. His principal was held entitled to recover

29 [1912· A.C. 716.
30 *Walker* v. *Smith* (1906) 8 F. 619.
31 [1893] 1 Q.B. 346.
32 [1929] A.C. 176.

the value of the cheque as the third party should have realised that the agent was in excess of his authority.

Assuming that an agent acting outwith his actual authority has formed a contract binding his principal, his principal may sue him for breach of contract.

Where he has made a contract with a third party which is discovered not to be binding on his principal because he has acted beyond his authority, he will be liable to the third party, as an agent is held to warrant or guarantee to parties with whom he deals that he does have authority.

Apart from the question of authority, either actual or ostensible, the agent's liability on his contracts will depend largely on how he contracts. He may contract disclosing the fact that he is an agent, he may disclose his agency but conceal the identity of his principal or he may choose to contract as if he were principal, that is without disclosing that he is an agent. The liability of the agent on the contract will vary according to whichever of these three methods he chooses to adopt.

Agent for disclosed principal: Where the agent has chosen to disclose his agency and the identity of his principal, he will incur, normally, no liability,[33] the contract being between his principal and the third party. Exceptions to the rule are where the agent has accepted liability,[34] and where his liability is implied by trade custom.

Agent for an undisclosed principal: The agent who contracts as an agent to the knowledge of the third party but without telling the third party for whom he is acting poses a problem. It would appear as a general rule that such an agent is to be treated as a party to the contract.[35] If he buys he is liable for the price; if he sells unascertained goods he must deliver. But if he sells ascertained goods or in certain other circumstances he must also deliver. There is little Scottish authority in this situation but there is an inclination to presume that the third party would have been unwilling to contract with someone unknown, with the result that an intention that the agent was to be personally liable will be more readily inferred in construing the contract, or that trade usage or custom makes the

---

[33] *Stone and Rolfe* v. *Kimber Coal Co.* 1926 S.C. (H.L.) 45.
[34] *Lindsay* v. *Craig* 1919 S.C. 139.
[35] Gloag and Henderson *op. cit.* p. 260-1.

agent liable in any event, or if he does not name his principal within a certain or reasonable time.[36]

Contracts ostensibly as principal: If the agent contracts ostensibly as principal, both agent and principal are liable on the contract. The third party may sue either the principal or the agent, electing which to hold liable, an election which once made is binding on the third party. Naturally the acts which would amount to election must follow his knowledge that there is a principal.[37] Once this fact comes to his knowledge he must elect, for the liability of the erstwhile concealed principal and that of the agent are alternatives, the choice of the third party to hold one liable discharging the other. What amounts to election by the third party is a question of fact.

Both principal and agent can sue on the contract, but any rights which the third party may have against the agent are pleadable against the principal as if the principal were an assignee of the agent.

It is to be noted that, as far as liability is concerned, the idea of alternative liability outlined here is adopted by some writers as being applicable also where the agent has disclosed his agency but concealed his principal.[38]

Where principal non-existent: The agent who contracts for a principal who has no contractual capacity or who does not exist is liable on the contract. Thus a contract made on behalf of a club,[39] and a promissory note signed on behalf of a congregation unable to be so bound,[40] were both held to be the liability of their makers as contracting parties. Liability on contracts made on behalf of companies not yet incorporated must be assumed by their makers.[41] Ratification in such cases is not competent.[42]

Mercantile agents

A mercantile agent is 'one who in the customary course of his business as an agent has authority either to sell goods or to consign goods for the purposes of sale or to buy goods or to raise money on the security of goods'.[43] The Factors Act, 1889, and the Factors

---

[36] Gow *op. cit.* p. 528.
[37] *Stevenson* v. *Campbell* (1836) 14 S. 562; *Craig and Co.* v. *Blackater* 1923 S.C. 472. *Laidley* v. *Griffin* 1969 S.L.T. 278.
[38] See Lillie *op. cit.* p. 79.
[39] *Thomson* v. *Victoria Eighty Club* (1905) 43 S.L.R. 628.
[40] *McMeeking* v. *Easton* (1889) 16 R. 363.
[41] *Kelner* v. *Baxter* (1886) LR. 2 C.R. 174, European Community Act 1973, s.9.
[42] *Infra.* p. 100
[43] Factors Act 1889, s.1(1).

(Scotland) Act, 1890 which extends its provisions to Scotland, give to such an agent extensive powers and confer on those dealing with him a peculiar security. The position is that where a mercantile agent has in his possession with the consent of the owner goods or the document of title to goods, any sale, pledge or disposition of the goods by him when acting in the ordinary course of his business shall be valid as if he had the express authority of the principal to make the same; provided that the person taking under the disposition acts in good faith and without notice that the agent lacks the authority. It will be seen that any mercantile agent has a wide ostensible authority gained not from usage but by statute. Thus anyone dealing with a mercantile agent as purchaser or lender may do so without fear that the transaction will be invalidated for lack of authority.

One exception to the rule is where the pledge of the goods is in respect of a debt already owed by the agent.[44] Then the pledgee must recognise the superior right of the true owner of the goods, but in giving them up is entitled to any commissions due to the agent by the principal as the agent's right over the goods included his right of lien.

A mercantile agent whose customers have the benefit of the protection offered by the Factors Acts must have possession of the goods. A broker, who is normally simply an intermediary without possession, is not a mercantile agent and his authority will depend on usage, e.g. the stockbroker carries out his business according to the rules of the Stock Exchange. Normally a broker, as an agent, is not personally liable on his contracts unless usage or his agreement with his principal makes him so.

Del credere agent

An agent may contract with his principal to guarantee the performance of the third party in any contract he procures. If this is the case he is said to be a *del credere* agent or to act *del credere*. In return for this caution which he offers to his principal he will normally be paid a higher rate of commission.

Agents for a foreign principal

There is English authority for the proposition that an agent for a

---

[44] *Ibid.*, s. 4.

foreign principal will be personally liable on his contracts but that he can remove this presumption by proving that he is an authorised agent.[45] In Scotland the position would appear to be that if the agent is selling he incurs no liability simply because his principal is foreign; if he is buying them it is a question of proof whether or not he guaranteed the price.[46]

Termination of agency

If there is a contract of agency it will terminate by any of the methods by which contracts terminate. Specially the relationship of agency terminates by acts of the parties and by operation of the law.

The parties may end the agency by mutual agreement or by either of them withdrawing from it. Mutual agreement poses no particular problem; it is a matter of fact whether both have agreed but, where the withdrawal is unilateral, certain rules fall to be observed.

By the parties

Termination by the principal: The principal may recall the agency at any time either expressly or by the appointment of a new agent to do the same job.[47] This, however, assumes that there was no fixed term for the agency. Such a term, if agreed at the outset, must be observed and unjustifiable dismissal of the agent before its expiry will render the principal liable in damages. The termination must not prejudice the agent; he is entitled to be paid any monies due to him, and the obligation of relief owed to him by the principal will continue to cover any liabilities, even those not exigible until after the withdrawal. He must be allowed to complete transactions in which he is engaged and, if he is an agent with an interest (procurator *in rem suam*), the agency is irrevocable except on cause shown. Thus, in a case where brokers had become shareholders in a ship on condition of being appointed sole chartering brokers, their agency was held not to be revocable at will,[48] while in an underwriting contract in connection with the issue of shares in a company

---

[45] *Miller Gibb and Co.* v. *Smith* [1917] 2 K.B. 141; *Holt and Moseley (London) Ltd.* v. *Sir Charles Cunningham and Partners* (1949) L1. L.R. 141; *Cox* v. *Sewell* [1960] 1 Lloyd's Rep. 417.
[46] *Millar* v. *Mitchell* (1860) 22 D. 833; *Bennett* v. *Inveresk Paper Co.* (1891) 18 R. 975; *Girvan Roper and Co.* v. *Monteith* (1895) 23 R. 129.
[47] *Patten* v. *Carruthers* (1770) 2 Paton 238.
[48] *Galbraith and Muirhead* v. *"Arethusa" Ship Co. Ltd.* (1896) 23 R 1011.

a director was authorised to apply for the shares for the underwriters if they themselves, did not apply, and his agency was held not to be terminable.[49]

Withdrawal by agent: The agent may withdraw from the agency at any time but not in the middle of a transaction nor to the prejudice of the principal, otherwise he will be liable in damages.

Operation of Law

The relationship of agency ends when its object is accomplished or its term expires, the achievement of its objects becomes impossible or by death, bankruptcy or mental disorder.

Death: The death of either agent or principal ends the agency. If the principal dies and the agent is unaware of this he continues to bind the estate of his principal.[50] He may also complete transactions pending when the principal died.

Bankruptcy: Bankruptcy of the principal has the same effect as his death, and the same considerations apply regarding knowledge and continuation by the agent. The agent's bankruptcy need not affect the agency. The reverse is the case in mandate.[51]

Mental disorder: The mental disorder of the agent ends the agency, while the effect of the mental disorder of the principal is the same as that of death or bankruptcy. Insanity of the mandant, at least of a short duration, does not revoke a mandatary's authority.[52]

Notification of termination of an agency

When an agency has ended, except through death or bankruptcy which are public facts, the principal should give notice of the fact to the public. If a partnership is involved, such notice is obligatory.[53] If notice is not given, the agent will continue to have ostensible authority and his principal may be bound by his, possibly malicious, acts. To protect himself, therefore, the principal should give specific notice to parties who have had dealings with the agent[54] and should advertise the fact to the public at large.

---

49 *Premier Briquette Co.* v. *Gray* 1922 S.C. 329.
50 *Campbell* v. *Anderson* (1829) 3 W and Sh. 384.
51 Bell *Comm* L, 525; *MacKenzie* v. *Campbell* (1894) 21 R. 904.
52 *Wink* v. *Mortimer* (1849) 11 D. 995.
53 Partnership Act, 1890, s. 36.
54 Bell *Princs,* s. 228; *North of Scotland Bank* v. *Behn Moller and Co.* (1881) 8 R.423.

The banker as an agent

In many ways a banker will have to act as an agent for his customer; examples are: the arrangement of insurances, purchasing and selling stocks and shares, paying accounts and effecting standing orders. Above all the banker is the agent of his customer when he pays or collects cheques. From what has been written it is obvious that the only proper course of conduct for an agent is to ascertain the precise nature of his instructions and to carry these out to the letter. It need hardly be said that the banker is accountable to his customer and must render accounts.

Insurance business: A traditional part of the business of the Scottish banker has been the arrangement of insurance on behalf of his customer, a facet of the business which is of recent date much encouraged. This involves advising the customer of his insurance needs and arranging with insurance companies to provide the necessary insurances. Insurance companies pay commissions to professional people who thus introduce business and, in fact, refer to these people, be they insurance brokers, solicitors, accountants or bankers, as agents. It is undeniable that the banker who acts thus is an agent for the insurance company; he effects contracts between the company and third parties and is remunerated by the company for his efforts. Further for the duration of the insurance he may collect the renewals premiums and be paid a commission for rendering that service to the company also. This is quite straightforward and the normal rules of agency apply to this relationship with an importance exception—that the banker will act as an agent for many insurance companies which are in competition with each other; only the knowledge that this is so, and such knowledge is customary as is the practice, permits this situation. Normally an agent could not act for competitors and observe the fiduciary rules of agency.

What is not, however, straightforward is the relationship between the banker and his customer. If someone is approached by an insurance salesman or broker he will negotiate with him at arm's length, and having been advised and persuaded by such person to contract with a particular company for a particular type of policy would have little recourse if disappointed in the arrangements, short of these having been based on misrepresentation or some other factor which would affect the validity of the contract. Such a proposition is certainly the law if the insurance was arranged by a salesman of the company; it may be questioned if it had been arranged by an independent broker, particularly if there is a relationship between broker and client which could entitle the client to assume he was being given skilled advice.

As far as the banker is concerned, there can be no question that the customer is entitled to expect skilled advice on the merits of different insurances. The banker who is giving advice to a customer on the choice of insurance cover must proceed with caution. Albeit that commission will be earned if the customer is persuaded to insure, that does not mean that the banker is free to look on himself as no more than the agent of the insurance company; he is first and foremost a banker who is providing this service for this customer, and the customer is entitled to expect skilled advice given with care.

Stocks and shares: Customers may find it convenient to initiate their Stock Exchange transactions with their banker. The actual purchase or sale is effected by a member of the Stock Exchange on the instructions of the banker, commission being split between the banker and the stockbroker. The banker is acting as an agent for his customer, delegating the execution of the customer's order to the stockbroker. Once again, the question of the duty of care of the banker arises, should he advise the customer on a transaction. The practice of bankers is merely to suggest, usually on the recommendation of a stockbroker, investments suitable to meet the particular needs of the customer; the choice of a particular stock and the descision to purchase is left to the customer. This practice reflects the caution which is necessary in such circumstances where a customer may have reason to regret a particular purchase or the timing of a particular sale. It has already been generally noted[55] how a banker may incur liability for advice he gives. Investment advice falls into this area and must be given with great caution.

Standing orders: A customer may request his bank to pay on his behalf, and debit his account with the amounts, periodic payments such as subscriptions, insurance premiums, hire purchase instalments and mortgage payments. Such a request is a mandate to the bank to act on the customer's behalf in these matters. If such instructions are taken the banker as agent for the customer must fulfil them precisely; failure to make payments may give an impression that a customer cannot meet his obligations, an impression that could

[55] *supra* p. 25 et seq.

damage his reputation.[56] A bank may attempt to disclaim responsibility for such failure by, say, disclaimer printed on the form authorising the payment. If such disclaimer is adequately brought to the customer's attention it is effective.

TRANSACTIONS WITH AGENTS

Where there is a banking relationship with a person or body who transacts through agents the banker should ascertain the precise nature of the authority of the agent, mandatary or factor. An example of the precautions necessary is the necessity of familiarisation by the banker of the rules of a society, or the Memorandum and Articles of a Company, which is a customer. Where the customer is, however, a firm the banker is entitled to rely on the principle that a partner binds the firm in the ordinary course of its business. Obviously the principles of ostensible authority apply to dealings between an agent and a banker but, equally obviously, no ostensible authority will allow an agent to operate a bank account; only a specific authority will cover that.

Powers of attorney: Formal deeds, known as powers of attorney, are frequently used to constitute or evidence the constitution of an agency. This is particularly so when someone is devolving to an agent the management of his whole or a substantial part of his affairs if, for example, he is elderly, infirm, or going abroad for a lengthy period. When a power of attorney is granted the limits of the authority of the agent are contained in it and its terms must be strictly construed.[57] An attorney is not entitled to the benefit of any doubt as to the extent of his powers, and is certainly not entitled to act in any way not expressly authorised by the deed.[58] For example, there must be express powers to borrow if the principal is to be bound to the loan.

The banker must, therefore, acquaint himself with the extent of the powers contained in such a deed as these affect the banking relationship: thereafter, he must transact with the attorney only in these matters in which the attorney is authorised. In case of dispute the banker should be able to prove the terms of the deed and that the disputed transactions lie within these terms. The best method of

---

[56] an analogy with a mistaken dishonouring of a cheque is not out of place.
[57] *Goodall* v. *Bilsland* 1909 S.C. 1152.
[58] Alternative name for a Power of Attorney is Factory and Commission.

proving the content of the deed is by reference to it, but the original will not normally be available for retention by the bank. A copy will prove the content of the deed and may be obtained either through the registration of the original in the Books of Council and Session or the Books of the Sheriff Court or under the terms of the Powers of Attorney Act 1971. In the former cases an extract of the entry in the Court books is proof of the terms of the deed thus registered. Under the Powers of Attorney Act 1971 the contents of an instrument creating a power of attorney may be proved by means of a copy which (a) is a reproduction of the original made with a photographic or other device for reproducing documents in facsimile and (b) contains a certificate or certificates signed by the donor of the power, or by a solicitor or stockbroker, and is a certificate to the effect that the copy is a true and complete copy of the original. If the original consists of two or more pages a certificate at the end of each page of the copy must state that it is a true and complete copy of the corresponding page of the original.

Procurations: A procuration is a form of document nominating someone to act as procurator or attorney for the grantor of it. A banker must accept it at its face value and note and give effect to the powers—and any limitations to these—which it contains. The terms of a procuration can be proved by the original, an extract of the entry if the document has been registered, or by a copy certified as a true copy by a notary public.

Mandate: The least formal of the methods of creating a delegation to deal with a bank, the mandate, is addressed to the bank, the original being retained by the banker, and requests and authorises the banker to recognise the power of the mandatary in transacting with the bank on behalf of the grantor of the mandate. As with more formal documents the terms of the mandate must be strictly adhered to; power to deal with one aspect of the grantor's affairs does not imply power to deal with others.

A mandate, which should be signed before witnesses, may be granted by any customer. When the account is a joint account all the account holders must sign the mandate if the mandatary is to operate the account, although any one can delegate by mandate his right to sign with the others. An account which is operated by a majority of parties does not follow this rule; the mandate authorising a mandatary to sign on behalf of one of the parties requires the signature of all the account holders.

CHAPTER FOUR

PARTNERSHIP

PARTNERSHIP is described by Bell[1] as 'a voluntary association of two or more persons for the acquisition of gain or profit; with a contribution for that end, of stipulated shares of goods, money, skill and industry; accompanied by an unlimited mandate or power to each partner to bind the company'.

Association between men in commerce comes early in the development of business; in a community, the benefits to be derived from mutual help and co-operation are attractive. The law will recognise such association and provide for the adjustment of the relationships which such association involves.

In Scotland the main body of the law concerning partnerships will be found in the Partnership Act, 1890, a codifying statute which made little change in the common law and, in fact, declares that the rules of common law prevail except so far as they are inconsistent with the express provisions of the Act (s. 46). The other principal Acts concerning the relationship of partnership are the Limited Partnerships Act, 1907, and the Registration of Business Names Act, 1916.

References in this chapter to 'the Act' or to particular sections are references to the Partnership Act, 1890 unless otherwise indicated.

Definition

Partnership is defined in the Act (s. 1) as 'the relation which subsists between persons carrying on a business in common with a view of profit'. The word 'business' is to include (s. 45) 'every trade occupation or profession'.

The relationship of partnership is mercantile. Men can associate for other purposes, e.g., the formation of a club or church. Only when their aim is a business profit are they partners.

Joint adventure: The term joint adventure is used to describe a

[1] Commentaries, II, 499.

partnership constituted for one particular transaction. There is no distinction drawn between joint adventures and more permanent partnerships, the rights and liabilities of the associates being substantially the same. A joint adventure ends automatically on the completion of the single transaction for which it was constituted.

Number of partners: The minimum number of partners is two: it is inherent in the idea of partnership that there is association.

Formerly, the maximum number of partners was prescribed by the Companies Act 1948 as twenty in the case of any business other than banking, and ten where the business was a banking partnership.[2] By sections 119 and 120 of the Companies Act 1967 partnerships formed for the purpose of carrying on business as solicitors, accountants and as members of recognised stock exchanges have had all limits removed from them and banking partnerships may now consist of a maximum of twenty partners. The Department of Trade and Industry is also granted power by s. 120 to remove from any other form of partnership, the limit of twenty partners laid down by the 1948 Act.

Constitution of partnership

The contract of partnership demands no special form. It may be oral or in writing, or it may be inferred from the relationships of the parties or the circumstances of the case. It is usual for a partnership to be founded upon written agreement which, although not essential, has the advantages of providing permanent record of the rights of the parties to the agreement amongst themselves. Sharing in the profits of a business is *prima facie* evidence that a partnership exists (s. 2) but not conclusive evidence.[3] What is important is the intention of the parties—whether they intended to create a partnership, although this intent may be inferred by law from the whole evidence. Whether a partnership exists or not will be of importance to a creditor who is endeavouring to hold one man liable for a debt incurred by an association. If the man denies being a partner the whole circumstances will require to be examined to establish whether he would appear to have been a partner. Certain guides are provided by the Act (s. 2) to help to determine the existence of the relationship. These are (*a*) that a person may receive payment of a

---

[2] Sections 429 and 434.
[3] *Cox* v. *Hickman* (1860) 8 H.L.C. 268.

debt by instalments out of a firm's profits without becoming liable as a partner; (*b*) that a servant or agent of a person engaged in business may be paid by receiving a share of the profits without becoming liable as a partner; (*c*) that the widow or child of a deceased partner may draw an annuity which represents a share of the profits made in the business without becoming liable as a partner; (*d*) that a person may lend money to another to engage in business stipulating for a rate of interest varying with the profits or for a share in the profits without becoming a partner—although such a contract must be in writing and signed by the parties; (*e*) that a person may sell the goodwill in a business receiving in payment a share of profits by way of annuity or otherwise without becoming liable as a partner.

Such a lender or vendor as is described in these last two cases is a postponed creditor[4] should the borrowers or purchasers become bankrupt.

Similarly, specifically excepted from the relationship of partnership are joint tenants or joint owners of property or those who share in the gross returns of property. To render anyone who falls into any of the categories mentioned liable as a partner will require evidence beyond that demonstrating the pecuniary relationship. Intention to create a partnership, be the intention express or inferred from the facts, is paramount.

Holding out: A person who is not a partner in a business may, by his behaviour, render himself liable as if he were a partner for the debts of the business. If, by words or conduct, he represents himself to be a partner or allows himself to be so represented, he is said to be 'holding out' as a partner. In such cases any person who has advanced credit to the business on the faith of the representation may hold the man who is the 'holding out' partner liable for the sum advanced. Such a man is sometimes called a 'nominal partner'.

The Act (s. 14) provides: 'Everyone who by words spoken or written or by conduct represents himself, or who knowingly suffers himself to be represented, as a partner in a particular firm, is liable as a partner to anyone who has, on the faith of any such representation, given credit to the firm, whether the representation has or has not been made or communicated to the person so giving credit by

---

4 *Infra* p. 322

or with the knowledge of the apparent partner making the representation or suffering it to be made.'

The liability incurred by the apparent partner is only to a creditor
who has given credit on the faith of the representation. If the
creditor knows that the apparent partner is not, in fact, a member of
the partnership, he has no claim. Further, the claim is restricted to
creditors of this class; a trustee in the sequestration of the firm cannot
sue a party 'holding out'.[5]

Anyone who holds out takes the risk of his representations being
circulated. But if the representation is made without his knowledge
he will not be liable. Anyone who is being held out as a partner may
obtain interdict to prevent the circulation of the representation.

A holder-out by his conduct does not become a partner, nor can
he be made to become one. A partnership which holds out as a
partner someone who is not a partner will, however, be liable for
debts contracted by the apparent partner.

The holder-out who has to pay a business debt may seek relief
against the partnership.

Firm and firm-name

Persons who have entered into partnership with one another are
collectively called a firm and the name under which their business
is carried on is called the firm-name (s. 4).

In Scotland the firm is a legal person distinct from the partners of
whom it is composed (s. 4(2)). The fact that the firm is a separate
legal person is important in questions relating to actions and
diligences, in ranking in bankruptcy, and in the question of compensation. A partner cannot be sued directly for a firm debt; a
debtor to a firm cannot plead compensation on a debt due by an individual partner, nor can a partner sued for a private debt plead compensation on a debt due to the firm. A partner suing for a private
debt may be met, however, with a plea of compensation on a debt due
by the firm, while the firm sued may plead compensation on a debt
due to a partner. The principle underlying these rules is that a
partner is not a creditor in debts due to the firm but is a debtor in
debts due by the firm.[6]

---

[5] *Mann* v. *Sinclair* (1869) 6 R. 1078.
[6] Gloag and Henderson *op. cit.* p. 150.

In bankruptcy the firm's creditors must rank first against the firm's estate.

A firm can sue and be sued. It normally sues in its own name although an action in the name of all the partners which indicates that it is for a firm debt is competent. If the firm-name is descriptive, e.g. Glasgow Drapery Company, it is necessary in legal proceedings to add to the name the names of three individual partners, if there are so many. This rule does not apply in the Sheriff Court.[7] Where the name is social, i.e. comprising the names of individuals, the firm may sue or be sued in that name. It is immaterial what the names of the partners may be. The firm is not, however, a corporation as an incorporated body is; it has been described as a 'quasi corporation possessing many but not all of the privileges which law confers upon a duly constituted corporation'.[8] A firm cannot hold heritable property, the title of which must be taken in the name of trustees for the firm,[9] but it is capable of holding a lease.[10] Further, it is constituted, and may be terminated, by consent, and terminates by the death or bankruptcy of one of its partners.

It may also be dissolved at the option of the other partners if any partner allows his share of the partnership property to be charged for his separate debt (s. 33(2)).

Registration of business names

A firm which carries on business is required by the Registration of Business Names Act, 1916 to register the name under which it trades unless the name consists only of the true surnames of the partners who are individuals without any additions other than the true Christian names or the initials of such Christian names of the partners.

The particulars which must be registered are: the business name, the general nature of the business, the principal place of business, the name or names of the individual or individuals who are using the business name, and particulars as to former names, nationality and the usual residence and any other occupation. and the corporate names of all partners who are corporations. The date of the commencement of the business must also be stated and the registration

[7] Sheriff Courts Act, 1907 and 1913.
[8] *Forsyth* v. *Howe* (1834) 13 S 42, 47.
[9] Bell, *Princ.* 357; *Kelly's Trs.* v. *Moncrieff's Tr.* 1920 S.C. 461.
[10] *Cooke's Circus Building Co.* v. *Welding* (1894) 21 R. 339.

must be effected within fourteen days of that date. Changes in these particulars must also be registered within fourteen days of their taking place.

Where a corporation uses a business name it must register its corporate name and registered office.

When registration has taken place the firm or individual is issued with a certificate which must be exhibited in a conspicuous place at the firm's principal place of business.

Also demanded by the 1916 Act is publication of the names of the persons or corporations using a business name. In the case of a partnership the names of the partners, or their initials and surnames, and any former Christian names or surnames, and the nationality if not British, of the partners must appear on all business letters, trade catalogues, circulars, or show cards. Where a corporation is involved the corporate name must appear. Failure in publication involves penalties.

Failure in registration where this is required not only involves liability to fines but also a disability to enforce any contract, either in the business name or otherwise unless the Court will grant relief. The grounds on which the Court will grant relief are that the failure was accidental or inadvertent, or that it is just and equitable to do so.

Liability of a partner

Every partner of a firm is liable jointly and severally for the debts of the firm (s. 9). Further, the liability of a partner is normally unlimited; he is liable to his last penny to the firm's creditors if the firm does not meet its debts.

Partners can be held liable only when the debt has been constituted against the firm; the creditor must sue the firm first. If the firm has been dissolved all the partners within the jurisdiction must be sued together.

A partner who meets a firm debt has a right of relief against his co-partners (s. 4) and may call on them to contribute a share, according to their contract, to his loss, a provision which is for his benefit alone and does not affect the right of the firm's creditors to collect payment from a partner personally.

A partner retiring from a firm remains liable for the debts of the firm incurred while he was a partner. The fact that his erstwhile partners have agreed to indemnify him against claims does not affect his liability, for, unless the creditor is a party to such an arrangement, it will be of no avail to him in avoiding liability. The consent of the creditor may be express, or inferred from a course of dealing between the creditor and the firm as newly consituted (s. 170). Such an inference is not easily established. An indemnity is, of course, of value to the retired partner in recovering any such sums he has to pay. The possibility of continuing liability of a retired partner and its evasion has already been considered.[11]

A new partner admitted to an existing firm does not thereby become liable to the creditors for anything done before he became a partner (s. 17). This rule is not absolute. The presumption raised by it may be displaced by the facts and circumstances. Where the whole assets are handed over to a new partnership and the business is continued as before, the presumption is that the liabilities are taken over with the assets and the new partner will be liable. This presumption can be rebutted if the new partner paid into the firm a sum as capital while the other partners contributed their share of the going business.[12]

Limited partnership

The Limited Partnerships Act, 1907 permits the creation of partnerships in which some of the partners may limit their liability for firm debts. Such limited partnerships are rare as the same effect can be achieved on the part of all the associates by the formation of a private company under the Companies Acts.

To constitute a limited partnership there must be one or more persons, called general partners, whose liability for the firm's obligations is without limit, and one or more limited partners, persons who on entering the partnership contribute money or assets valued at a stated amount and whose liability does not exceed that amount.

To obtain this limited liability the partnership must be registered with the Registrar of Companies who is the Registrar under the Limited Partnerships Act. An application for registration states the firm's name, the general nature and place of business, the name of each partner, the terms of the partnership, the date of commencement, and a statement that the partnership is limited and which are the limited partners.[13] It is a curious feature of the statute that it

[11] *Supra* p. 74
[12] *Thomson and Balfour* v. *Boag and Son,* 1936 S.C. 2.
[13] Limited Partnership Act, 1907, s. 8.

contains no provision for publicising the fact of the limited liability where this has been obtained.

To maintain the limitation of his liability a limited partner must take no part in the management of the firm. If he does so he assumes full liability for debts incurred while he intervenes.[14] He may, however, inspect the books, and advise and consult with the general partners on the state and prospects of the business.

A limited partnership is not dissolved by the death, lunacy or bankruptcy of the limited partner unless his share cannot be realised except by dissolution. Nor is the limited partner entitled to dissolve the firm by giving notice.

The limited partner cannot withdraw his contribution while the firm continues. If he does so he is still liable to its full amount and can be called on to contribute to that amount.

The limited partner may assign his interest in the firm with the consent of the general partners, notice of which must be given in the *Gazette*.[15]

The general partners can introduce new partners without the limited partner's consent unless there is express prohibition. If the firm is dissolved the dissolution is carried out by the general partners unless the Court orders otherwise.

Relations of partners

The relationship of the partners amongst or between themselves, their rights and their liabilities, is to be determined by agreement. The agreement which founds the partnership may be express or implied and in any terms that suit the parties. Only where on any specific point the agreement is silent do the rules provided in the Act (s. 24) apply.

These rules, applying only in the absence of agreement, are:

1. All partners are entitled to share equally in the capital and profits of the business and must contribute equally towards all losses.

2. The firm must indemnify every partner in respect of payments made and personal liabilities incurred by him in the ordinary and proper conduct of the firm's business or for the preservation of the firm's property.

[14] *Ibid.*, s. 6.
[15] *Ibid.*, s. 6, 10.

3. A partner who makes an advance or payment to the firm beyond the amount of capital he has agreed to subscribe is entitled to interest at the rate of 5 % per annum from the date of the advance or payment.

4. A partner is not entitled to interest on the capital subscribed by him before the ascertainment of profits.

5. Every partner may take part in the management of the partnership business and has a right of access to the partnership books together with a right to inspect and copy them. The books must be kept at the principal place of business of the firm.

6. No partner has a right to remuneration for acting in the partnership business. The reward for acting for the partnership is in the share of profits due to the partner.

7. Differences arising as to ordinary matters may be decided by a majority of the partners. Specifically requiring the consent of all partners are the introduction of a new partner and a change in the nature of the partnership business; nor can a partner be expelled by majority decision (s. 25).

These statutory rules, or any agreed provision to supplant them, do not affect the basic nature of a partnership, that it is a contract *uberimae fidei*, one in which the parties must act towards each other with complete honesty.

That a partnership demands the utmost disclosure of material facts and circumstances by the parties to it, not only when it is being formed but throughout its continuance, means that a partner is entitled to place the utmost confidence in his fellow partners. This rule of common law, which has been interpreted to mean that a partner is not entitled to use information he gains as a partner for his own benefit and that he may not, even if entitled to do so, dissolve the firm in order to secure for himself a contract which the firm was about to obtain,[16] has been reflected in certain particulars by the Act.

Thus, a partner must account to the firm for any benefit derived by him without the consent of the others from any transaction concerning the partnership, or from any use by him of the firm property, name or business connections (s. 29); he must account for and pay over to the firm all profits he might make from any business of a

[16] *McNiven* v. *Peffers* (1868) 7 M 181.

competing nature which he carries on without the consent of his partners (s. 30); he must render full accounts to his partners (s. 28).

These are, however, supplementary to the generality that a partner must act with scrupulous honesty and without any concealment towards his fellow partners.

The authority of a partner

In dealings with the public every partner is an agent for the firm and for the other partners for the purposes of the partnership business. His acts in the ordinary course of business, and his signing the firm name, bind the firm. The extent of this authority to act as an agent for the firm depends on the nature of the firm business[17] but normally will extend to receiving payment and granting discharges,[18] borrowing money,[17] and undertaking financial transactions generally.[19]

This implied agency does not extend to unusual acts, such as borrowing money at a 40% rate of interest[20] or to acts which are known to be in the private interests of the partner.[21] Nor will the firm be bound when the party with whom the contract is made knows that the partner has no authority or that his authority is limited. Thus if a banker has had sight of a contract of co-partnery and is aware of restrictions upon the authority of any partner he must take care not to deal outwith these restrictions. As with any other agent, the partner warrants his authority[22] and will be liable to a third party when he contracts with him, and the firm is not bound for lack of authority.[23]

Acts which are outwith the normal scope of the ordinary business of the firm will not bind the firm. Thus a partner cannot bind a firm to submit a claim to arbitration.

A firm is liable for the wrongful acts or omissions of its partners acting in the ordinary course of business. The Act (s. 11) states that when a partner, acting within his apparent authority, receives money

---

[17] *Bryan* v. *Butters Bros.* (1892) 19 R. 490.
[18] *Nicoll* v. *Reid* (1878) 6 R 216.
[19] Walker *op. cit.* p. 352.
[20] *Patterson Bros.* v. *Gladstone* (1891) 18 R. 403.
[21] *Walker* v. *Smith* (1906) 8 F. 619.
[22] *New Mining Syndicate* v. *Chalmers* 1912 S.C. 126; *Clydesdale Bank* v. *Paul* (1877) 4 R. 626.
[23] *Fortune* v. *Young* 1918 S.C. 1.

or property from a third party and misapplies it, or when a firm receives money or property from a third party and it is misapplied by a partner, the firm will be liable. Further, a firm may be liable at common law, on the grounds that it received gratuitously the benefit of a wrongful act of a partner.

An admission by a partner is evidence against the firm (s. 15), while representations made by a partner in the course of business bind the firm. A banker who has a firm as a customer would normally be entitled to treat each partner as having authority to bind the firm in the normal course of its business, subject to his knowledge of its affairs. Within this rule there are areas of difficulty and thus it is prudent to take from all the partners of a firm, precise instructions, over their signatures, on the authority of the individual partners together with specimen signatures. If, despite this precaution, any doubt remains as to the ability of an individual partner to bind his firm in any transaction or, if any circumstance of a particular transaction causes the banker to question the propriety of it, then such a transaction should proceed only on the specific instructions and, if authorised, by the signatures of all the partners. A guarantee granted by a firm would be over the signature of all the partners.

Partnership property

Partnership property is all property, rights and interests in property originally brought into the partnership stock, or acquired on account of the firm or for the purposes and in the course of the firm's business. Such property must be held and applied by the partners exclusively for the purposes of the partnership (s. 20). If property has been bought with money belonging to the firm it is deemed to have been bought on account of the firm.

Land or buildings cannot be held in the name of a firm. The title to such property is taken in the name of the partners or of some of them or of some other person in trust for the firm.

The nature of the interest of the individual partner in the partnership property is that of a claim against the firm. His is a *pro indiviso* right; he cannot claim exclusive right to any particular portion of the property. His claim to a share of the partnership property on the dissolution of the firm is an incorporeal moveable right; it can be assigned or attached by creditors and is moveable in the succession of the partner, even if the partnership property is exclusively land or buildings.

Assignation of partnership

Although a partner may assign his interets in the partnership property or his future income from the business he cannot assign his partnership to the point of making the assignee a partner (s. 31). If a partner does assign his interest he remains a partner; his assignee acquires none of the rights of a partner, e.g. he has no right to inspect the books. His right is to receive whatever share of the profits is due to the cedent as brought out in accounts acceptable to the partners, including the cedent. On dissolution he should receive whatever share of the assets is due to the cedent.

Sometimes there is, in a partnership agreement, a right to nominate a partner by will. Such a nomination must be express in the testamentary document;[24] a sole heir could not claim to become a partner without express provision in the will as well as in the partnership agreement.

The reason for this bar on assignability is that the contract of co-partnery is a relationship of a highly personal nature. Like all contracts where *delectus personae* exists delegation to a third party is impossible.

Termination of partnership

A partnership may terminate at the end of a fixed term, by rescission, by agreement, by the achievement of its object if set up for a single adventure, by notice by any of the partners where no fixed time was stipulated, by the death or bankruptcy of a partner, by the business of the firm becoming unlawful, and by the Court. It may also be dissolved at the option of the other partners if any partner allows his share of the partnership property to be charged for his separate debt (s. 33(2)). Some of these require explanation.

Expiration of fixed term: When a partnership was agreed upon for a fixed period of time, it ends with the expiry of that term (s. 32(a)). If, however, after the expiry of the term the business is carried on by the partners without further express agreement the partnership will be deemed to continue on the terms and conditions agreed for the fixed term. This process is known as tacit relocation.

The partnership, after the term of expiry has passed, is known as a partnership at will, that is one which has been entered into for an undefined time. Any provision of the original agreement which is

---

[24] *Thomson* v. *Thomson* 1962 S.C. (H.L.) 28.

inconsistent with a partnership at will, will be ignored, e.g., a right dependent on the giving of three months' notice before expiry will fall as there is no point of time from which the three months might be calculated.[25]

Rescission: A partnership, like any other contract, may be rescinded on proof of its having been induced by error, fraud, or, since it is a contract *uberrimae fidei,* concealment of material facts.

By agreement: As with any contract the partnership may be terminated by the agreement of the partners to do so.

By performance: A partnership constituted for a single adventure or transaction terminates when that object is achieved or completed (s. 32).

By notice: Where the partnership is at will, either because no fixed term was stipulated or because a fixed-term partnership has been continued by tacit relocation, any partner is entitled to dissolve the partnership by giving notice to the others that he intends to do so. Such a notice has the effect of terminating the contract either at the date of dissolution mentioned in it or, if no date be mentioned, at the date of the communication of the notice (s. 32).

Dissolution by the Court: The Act (s. 35) provides for the dissolution of a partnership by the Court. An application by any partner for dissolution of his partnership may be granted by the Court if made on the following grounds:,

1. That a partner is of permanently unsound mind.
2. That a partner is permanently incapable of performing his part under the partnership contract.
3. That a partner, other than the partner suing, has been guilty of such conduct as, regard being had to the nature of the business, is calculated prejudicially to affect the carrying on of the business.
4. Where a partner, other than the partner suing, wilfully or persistently commits a breach of the partnership agreement, or otherwise so conducts himself in matters relating to the partnership business that it is not reasonably practical for the other partners to carry on the business in partnership with him.
5. When the business of the partnership can be carried on only at a loss.

[25] *Neilson* v. *Mossend Iron Co.* (1886) 13 R. (H.L.) 50.

F

6.   Whenever, in any case, circumstances have arisen which render it just and equitable that the partnership be dissolved.

Effects of dissolution

When the partnership has been dissolved the general authority of the partners to bind the firm is ended, although each partner is still entitled to act and bind the firm for the purpose of winding up the partnership affairs and completing transactions unfinished at the date of dissolution. The extent of this authority is shown by the case of *Dickson* v. *National Bank.*[26] A firm of solicitors deposited with a bank on consignation receipt a sum of money belonging to a trust, the receipt bearing that the money was to be repayable on the signature of the firm. Some years after the firm had been dissolved one of the former partners endorsed the receipt in the firm's name, uplifted and embezzled the money. The bank was held justified in accepting the signature and paying the money as it was within the authority of the partner to uplift the money to wind up the partnership affairs.

The winding-up process is primarily the business of the partners although there is provision for the winding-up to be done by the Court (s. 39) if any partner or the representative of any partner applies for this. Winding-up by a judicial factor will not be readily granted by the Court but, at common law, this may be done to protect the partnership property until dissolution where there is substantial disagreement between the partners, if all the partners have died, or surviving partners are incapable or unfit to carry out the dissolution.[27] If a partner has been guilty of misconduct,[28] or if there is danger that a partner may not obtain his due rights on dissolution,[29] a judicial factor may be appointed. A petition to the Court for the appointment of a judicial factor must seek sequestration of the firm's assets.

Carrying on business: If after dissolution the business is carried on by the remaining members of the firm without settling up the share of the deceased or retired partner, the outgoing partner, or his representatives, is entitled to claim from the firm such share of the profits as is attributable to the use of his share of the partnership

26 1917 S.C. (H.L.) 50.
27 Walker *op. cit.* p. 367.
28 *MacPherson* v. *Richmond* (1869) S.L.R. 348.
29 *Allan* v. *Gronmeyer* (1891) 18 R. 784.

assets or 5% interest on the amount of his share. The choice between the remedies is the claimant's.

Winding-up

The winding-up of the firm is designed to collect and realise its assets and to distribute the cash among those entitled to it. If the partnership agreement is silent on the question of settlement amongst the partners, the following rules (s. 44) apply:

1. All losses, including loss of capital, are paid first out of profits, next out of capital, and lastly, if necessary, by each partner in the proportion in which he was entitled to share profits.

2. The assets are applied (1) in paying the debts and liabilities of the firm to persons who are not partners in it; (2) in paying to each partner advances made by him beyond his agreed capital contribution; (3) in repaying to each partner his share of capital; (4) the balance, if any, is divided among the partners in the proportion in which profits are divisible.

CHAPTER FIVE

COMPANY LAW

THE registered company in its modern form represents an endeavour by the law to mould and add to the general law regarding associations a legal vehicle, or type of organisation, which will encourage and facilitate the association of persons who are in pursuit of a common object. It is commonly felt that partnership, particularly in regard to the inability of the partners to limit or restrict their liability to contribute to the partnership debts, is not the most attractive form of legal association, and although it has advantages, of which privacy in its affairs is one, over the registered company as a legal form, the advantages of the latter are considered to outweigh the disadvantages of incorporation.

A registered company is a company registered under the Companies Acts. Once thus incorporated it represents an organisation which by a mixture of contract and legal regulation controls the rights and liabilities of its membership in questions both with the company and amongst themselves and, further, which enjoys in questions with those outside the organisation a defined legal status.

The law regarding companies is largely to be found in statutes, the principal ones in force being the Companies Acts 1948 and 1967 and the Companies (Floating Charges and Receivers) (Scotland) Act 1972. These Acts have from time to time been interpreted and explained by the Courts thus giving rise to a body of case law on the subject.

Corporate personality

A distinctive feature of the registered company is that in common with other incorporated associations it enjoys corporate personality. Alternatively called juristic personality, or legal entity, corporate personality means that the company is recognised in law as a separate person from its members; thus only the company has rights or liabilities under its contracts; it owns its own property; it is not affected by the death, bankruptcy, or mental disorder of any member or by changes in its membership. This doctrine was summed up in the leading case of *Salomon* v. *Salomon & Co. Ltd.*[1] by Lord Macnaughton:

'The company is at law a different person altogether from the subscribers to the memorandum, and though it may be that after incorporation the business is precisely the same as it was before, and that the same persons are manager, and the same hands receive the profits, the company is not in law the agent of the subscriber or the trustee for them. Nor are the subscribers liable, in any shape or form, except to the extent and in the manner provided by the Act.'

This principle of separate corporate personality is of the greatest importance in company law. It means, amongst other things, that those who lend, or sell on credit, to a company can look for payment only to the company and not beyond it to its members. The principle has been applied in every area of law: thus the managing director of a company, even if he owns all the shares but one, cannot lawfully pay cheques payable to the company into his own bank account or draw cheques for his own purposes upon the company's account;[2] the largest shareholders in a company, whose losses could be considerable if the property were destroyed, cannot legally insure the company's property, the right to do so being that of the company as proprietor of the property.[3]

A strict application of the doctrine of corporate personality, of course, leads to the conclusion that those associated with a company will personally incur no liability for the company's debts; a person is not liable for the debts of someone else. This logical conclusion has been, as noted by Lord Macnaughton in the extract quoted above, tempered by statute.[4]

Occasionally the principle of legal personality—what has been called 'the veil of incorporation'—will be disregarded. Thus by statute a member can in certain limited circumstances become liable for company debts,[5] while the ownership of the shares of the company or its constitution may be examined to determine if it is a subsidiary of another company.[6] Various taxing statutes ignore the

---

[1] 1897 A.C. 22.
[2] *A. L. Underwood Ltd.* v. *Bank of Liverpool and Martins Ltd.* 1924 1 K.B. 775.
[3] *Macaura* v. *Northern Assurance Co. Ltd.* 1925 A.C. 619.
[4] *infra* p. 86
[5] 1948 Act; s. 31.
[6] *ibid* s. 154.

fact of incorporation in defining liability for tax and the incidence of tax liability amongst company and membership. The Courts have, from time to time, also lifted the veil of incorporation when it has seemed right to do so. Thus when a company has been used to avoid legal liability the device has been ineffective. Thus in *Gilford Motor Co. Ltd.* v. *Horne*[7] a former employee was restrained by contract from soliciting his employer's customers. He set up a company which sent out circulars to the customers and was held that this constituted a breach of the ex-employee's contract, while in *Re Bugle Press Ltd.*[8] the Court looked into the identity of the owners of the shares in a company and decided that a certain company's actions were improper. Where the corporate device is thus used as a mask for the activities of natural persons or other companies the veil of incorporation will not necessarily disguise impropriety of purpose and will not necessarily protect the perpetrators from the Courts.

Limited liability

The strict application of the theory of corporate personality leads to the conclusion that the members of a company are not liable for company debts. In mitigation of this there is provided by the Companies Act 1948 provision that members will suffer, in most cases, a measure of liability to contribute towards the company's liabilities; the extent of this liability depends on the constitution of the particular company and the method chosen by the incorporators to adjust the liability. Companies registered under the Companies Acts can for this purpose be classified thus: companies in which the liability of the members is limited by shares, those in which the liability of members is limited by guarantee, and unlimited liability companies.[9]

There is the provision in the Companies Act 1948 (s. 202) for the liability of the directors, the manager, or the managing director of a company to be unlimited. This must be provided for in the Memorandum of Association of the company and in any proposal for election or appointment of such a person must state that this is the case and notice of this must be given to any person about to be appointed of this fact by the promoters of the company, or by the

[7] 1933 Ch. 953 (C.A.).
[8] 1961 Ch. 270 (C.A.).
[9] 1948 Act; s. 1 (2).

directors of the company, its managers, or company secretary. Such provision is, in practice very rare.

Liability limited by shares: A company limited by shares is one in which the liability of a member to contribute to the company's assets is met when the member has accounted to the company for the value of the shares he owns. Once he has paid for, or otherwise provided consideration for, these shares he has no further liability; if any amount remains unpaid on shares the owner remains liable to account to the company for that amount.

Guarantee companies: A guarantee company is one in which the liability of the members is limited to the amount which they respectively agree to contribute to the assets of the company if it is wound up. The constitution of such a company[10] must state that each member so agrees and specifies the amount which each member is liable to contribute. A guarantee company may or may not have a share capital; whether it has or not it must register Articles of Association[11] the form of which will depend on whether there is, or is not, a share capital. These Articles must state the number of members with which the company is to be registered, thus giving persons dealing with the company some idea of what the guarantees are worth. If there is a share capital the company must make an annual return[12] like any other company; otherwise a guarantee company makes an abridged form of return.[13]

Unlimited companies: A company may be registered as an unlimited company, in which case there is no limit on the liability of a member to contribute to the company's debts. It is possible to re-register such a company as a limited liability company[14] and to re-register a limited company as an unlimited one.[15] The advantage of an unlimited company is that, as the members do not enjoy the privilege of limited liability, the company is allowed to maintain a degree of secrecy about its affairs; for example, it need not file its annual accounts for public inspection.[16] The unlimited company is not common.

---

[10] s. 2(3).
[11] s. 6.
[12] *infra* p. 110
[13] s. 125.
[14] 1967 Act; s. 44.
[15] s. 43.
[16] *infra* p. 110

Loss of limited liability: The privilege of limited liability may be lost in two ways.

By the Companies Act 1948, s. 31, where a company carries on business for more than six months with fewer than the statutory minimum number of members (seven for a public company, two for a private company)[17] every person who is a member during the time that the business is carried on after the end of the six month period and who knows that the business is being so carried on is personally liable for the whole debts contracted by the company during that time.

By section 332 it is provided that in the winding up of a company if it appears that the business has been carried on with intention to defraud creditors or for any fraudulent purpose the Court may decide that any persons who are knowingly parties to the fraudulent trading shall be personally responsible for all or any of the company's debts as the Court might direct. If a company carries on business and incurs debts when to the knowledge of the directors there is no reasonable prospect of the company being able to pay them, it can be said that there is an intent to defraud creditors,[18] but the section, of course, goes wider than directors and would cover anyone who took part in or was concerned in fraudulent trading.

Public and private companies

Another method of classification of companies is into public and private companies. The statutes tend to be written as if the normal company is a public company and, exceptionally, some companies are private. This is not the case; the majority of companies are private companies, only the minority being public.

A private company is a company which by its Articles of Association (1) restricts the right to transfer its shares; (2) limits the number of members to 50, excluding members who are employees of the company and members who were members when they were employees of the company and who have continued to be members after their employment ended, two or more persons who hold one or more shares in the company jointly being treated as a single member; and (3) prohibits any invitation to the public to subscribe for any of the company's shares or debentures.

---

[17] 1948 Act; s. 1.
[18] Re Wm. C. Leitch Bros. Ltd. 1932 2 Ch. 71.

By section 1 of the Companies Act 1948 the minimum number of members of a private company is two.

A company which does not have the foregoing restrictions in its Articles is a public company.

The restriction on transferability of shares may take any form the draftsmen of the Articles care to adopt; commonly, there is a restriction on members transferring shares without first offering them to other members, but most common of all is simply to vest in the directors a right to refuse transfer of the shares at their discretion. The prohibition on inviting public subscription does not mean that outside finance cannot be sought by a private company; it means that it cannot be sought by way of invitation to the public at large; private solicitation of individuals, institutions or banks is permitted.

The statutes make many concessions of a technical nature to a private company, e.g. a private company can commence business immediately on incorporation, without first having to procure a certificate entitling the company to commence business, nominally called a trading certificate;[19] a private company need not hold a statutory meeting or send a statutory report to its members (s. 130);[20] a private company need have only one director whereas a public company must have at least two (s. 176) and, although a private company must not issue a prospectus it need not register a statement in lieu of a prospectus.[21] However in important respects, e.g., the necessity to employ qualified auditors and the publication of annual accounts, concessions to private companies have been reduced.

Annual certificates: A private company must send with its annual return to the Registrar of Companies a certificate signed both by a director and by the secretary that the company has not since the date of the last return issued any invitation to the public to subscribe for shares or debentures of the company, and, if the number of members exceeds fifty, a certificate that the excess consists wholly of persons employed or formerly employed by the company.

Conversion into public company: If a private company alters its Articles so that they no longer include the provision which constitutes it a private company it becomes a public company and must deliver to the Registrar of Companies a statement in lieu of prospectus. If

19 *infra* p. 91
20 *infra* p. 111
21 *infra* p. 102

it is desired to form a public company the company is usually incorporated as a private company and later converted into a public company.

If a private company fails to comply with any of the identifying characteristics of a private company it loses the privileges of a private company.

Incorporation of a company

A company is incorporated under the Companies Acts by the issue by the Registrar of Companies of a Certificate of Incorporation. Such certificate certifies that the company is incorporated and, in the case of a limited company, that the company is limited.[22] Such a certificate is conclusive evidence that all the requirements of the Act in respect of registration and matters precedent and incidental thereto have been complied with, and that the association is a company authorised to be registered and duly registered (s. 15(1)), a provision which prevents attack on the validity of a company's registration.

To procure the Certificate of Incorporation the promoters of a company must deliver to the Registrar of Companies certain documents and pay the required fees and stamp duties. The documents are: a Memorandum of Association, Articles of Association,[23] a statement of the nominal capital, and a statutory declaration by a solicitor engaged in the formation of the company or by a person named in the Articles as a director or secretary of the company that all the requirements of the Acts in respect of registration have been complied with. If the company is a public company with share capital a list of the persons who have consented to be directors must also be filed.

A company can only be formed for a lawful purpose (s.1(1)) and the Registrar may decline to register it if this is not so; he may also decline to register it if the papers are not in order or if the requirements of the Acts are not complied with. Registration fees must also be paid as they are prescribed from time to time and stamp duty is attracted by the Memorandum of Association, the Articles, and by the statement of nominal capital.

Not required at this stage, but normally sent to the Registrar, are

22 *supra* p. 87
23 *infra* p. 98

notice of the address of the registered office and a return in the form prescribed by the Act containing particulars of the directors and secretary of the company. If the company is a public company there is also filed, the written consent of persons who are nominated as directors and, if they have not subscribed the Memorandum for shares, their written undertaking to take up such shares.

The effect of the issue of the Certificate of Incorporation is to enable a private company to commence business. A public company must comply with further requirements before this is the case. Such a company must file a statutory declaration that when a prospectus has been issued to the public to subscribe for shares the minimum number of shares stated in the prospectus as having to be disposed of have been allotted and paid for in cash, that every director has paid on his shares a proportion equal to the proportion payable on application and allotment on the shares offered to the public, and that no money is liable to be repaid to any applicant for shares because the company has failed to apply for or to obtain permission for the shares to be dealt in on a stock exchange.[24] Where the company has not issued a prospectus the declaration by the secretary is to the effect that the directors have paid on their shares a proportion equal to the proportion payable by the other allottees on application and allotment on the shares payable in cash, and there accompanies such declaration a statement in lieu of prospectus in statutory form.

When the statute has been complied with in these respects the Registrar issues a certificate (called the Trading Certificate) which is conclusive evidence that the company is entitled to commence business.

Memorandum of Association

Every company must have a Memorandum of Association and this must be registered before incorporation with the Registrar of Companies. The content of this document is prescribed by the Companies Act 1948 (s. 2) and it should be in the form, according to the character of the company, set out in the First Schedule to the Act or as near thereto as circumstances permit.

The Memorandum of Association is signed by the founding members of the company, two in the case of a private company,

---

[24] 1948 Act; s. 109.

and seven in the case of a public company, before at least one witness who must attest the signatures (s. 3). A subscriber must write opposite his name the number of shares he has agreed to take (s. 2) which must be not less than one.

Content: The Memorandum of Association contains five clauses. These are:

1. The name of the company, with 'limited' as the last word of the name of a company limited by shares or by guarantee.
2. Whether the registered office of the company is to be situated in England or Scotland.
3. The objects of the company.
4. That the liability of the members is limited, if the company is limited by shares or by guarantee.
5. In the case of a limited company having a share capital, the amount of share capital with which the company proposes to be registered and the division thereof into shares of a fixed amount.

The Memorandum concludes with a declaration that the subscribers wish to be formed into a company in pursuance of the Memorandum of Association and that they agree to take the number of shares set opposite their respective names.

The name of a company: The statutory requirements regarding the name of a company are not extensive. If the company is a limited company the last word of the name must be 'limited' which forms a part of the name and which must not be dropped. Every company must paint or affix its name outside every premises in which business is carried on, engrave its name on its seal, and mention its name in all business letters, notices and other official publications and in all bills of exchange, promissory notes, endorsements, cheques and orders for money or goods, invoices receipts and letters of credit.

In certain cases the Department of Trade may license a company to change its name so as to omit the word limited; the conditions in which such licence will be granted—and it will not be granted to an ordinary commercial company—are stipulated in the Act (s. 19).

A company may change its name by special resolution and with the approval of the Department of Trade (s. 18(1)) or it may be directed by the Department of Trade to change its name. If such direction is given, on the grounds that through inadvertence or otherwise the company is registered with a name too like that of a previously registered company, within six months of the registration of the name the company must comply. If more than six months have passed but the Department of Trade consider that a name gives so misleading an indication of the nature of the company's activities as to be likely to cause harm to the public a similar direction may be given. Such direction can be protested to the courts on application to set it aside (1967 Act s. 46).

Apart from these provisions the most sweeping of the statutory provisions regarding names is that which provides that no company can be registered by a name which in the opinion of the Department of Trade is 'misleading' (s. 17). The discretion of the Department in this matter is unlimited and although notes for guidance are issued by the Department these do not have the force of law. Anyone proposing to register a company or to change the name of a company should enquire the attitude of the Department of Trade to the proposed name before incurring expense.

The fact that a name is acceptable to the Department of Trade or is registered does not offer any protection against attack on the right to use the name at common law. If there is a common law objection to the use of a name, for example, on the grounds that it would confuse the public, such objection can be sustained in the Courts despite the fact that the name is registered.

Companies may take advantage of the Registration of Business Names Act 1916.[25]

The registered office: Every company must have a registered office and the location of it and any change in that location must be notified to the Registrar (s. 107). The address is not given in the Memorandum; what is stated there is whether the registered office is to be situated in Scotland or, alternatively, in England or Wales, a statement which fixes the nationality and domicile of the company. Once established domicile cannot be changed.

The purpose of having a registered office is to permit the public to know where the company can be found, where communications and notices may be sent and where documents can be served on the company. There is no requirement that the company should carry on any of its business in its registered office; frequently companies do not and the registered office, or official address, is to be found in an accountant's or solicitor's office.

Further, certain of the company's registers, books and documents

[25] *supra* p. 73

should be kept at the registered office, but in many cases these may be kept elsewhere if the work is done on them elsewhere. Thus if the company's registers are maintained by a bank, the register of members, the register of directors' interests, the register of substantial shareholders' interests, and the register of debenture holders may all be kept at the bank, notice of this being given to the Registrar. The main point is that the location of those documents to which the public should have access should be known.

The Objects Clause: The third clause of the Memorandum of Association sets out the objects the attainment of which is the purpose of setting up the company. Whether the statement is concise and brief or prolix is a matter of choice for the promoters of the company but the basic rule is the same—a company may legitimately do what is necessary to achieve its objects and activities which fall outwith this category are outwith the powers of the company. This is known as the doctrine of *ultra vires* and is of great importance to shareholders in a company and to those who deal with the company.

From the point of view of the shareholder the doctrine can be used to restrain the officers of the company from risking the company's assets in activities which were not in the contemplation of the investors when the company was set up and to enable officers who cause the company losses through such activities to be held liable to compensate the company. The other application of the doctrine is of importance to those dealing with the company who can find that contracts with the company are void because they fell outwith the permitted area of the company's activities. Thus in the case of *Introductions Limited* v. *National Provincial Bank*[26] a bank which lent money to a company knowing that it was to be applied to a purpose which turned out not to be within the permitted area of activity of the company as laid out in its objects clause was held not to be entitled to recover the loan. There are many cases in which people have been found not entitled to payment, repayment, or damages because the contracts they entered with companies were held *ultra vires* the companies with which they dealt and thus void. It does not matter that the party who contracted had not read the relevant documents; the law applied a doctrine of constructive

[26] 1970 Ch. 199.

notice, which assumed that such knowledge was in the possession of people who deal with companies.

The law in this area has been radically altered by s. 9 of the European Communities Act 1972. This states that where a person deals with a company in good faith in a transaction decided upon by the directors the transaction will be deemed to be one within the capacity of the company and that the powers of the directors to bind the company shall be deemed free of any limitation under the memorandum or articles of the company. A party to a transaction is not bound to inquire as to the capacity of the company to enter into the transaction or as to any limitation on the powers of the directors. The party transacting with the company is deemed to have been acting in good faith unless the contrary is proved. The significance of this change in the law is great. In the case of *Introductions Ltd.* v. *National Provincial Bank*[27] the lenders would have been presumed to have been acting in good faith and unless it could have been shown that they actually knew of the *ultra vires* character of the activity they were financing they would have been entitled to recover their loan. Even when one does have knowledge of the company's objects one might honestly fail to appreciate that a proposed transaction fell outwith the boundaries of the company's permitted objects and would, in such case, still be acting in good faith and be entitled to the protection of these provisions. It is important that the transaction be decided upon by the directors.

As far as the relations of the company and its shareholders are concerned the European Communities Act changes nothing. If a company were to lose money through an *ultra vires* transaction the directors could still be held liable for breach of duty and a shareholder can still seek to restrain a company from any such activity.

Bankers contemplating lending to a company have usually been careful to check that the loans were being applied to *ultra vires* activities and normally requested their corporate customers to supply copies of their Memorandum of Association for examination: in any event the doctrine of constructive notice applied.

The impact of the European Communities Act in these circumstances is debateable. On the one hand, it can be argued that examination of the objects clause is now dangerous; to refrain from doing so

[27] *supra* p. 94

could leave the banker in a stronger position to take advantage of the change in the law. On the other hand, to discontinue a long-established practice simply to take advantage of a change in the law, it could be said, destroys the element of good faith which must be present if the section is to operate. Until the section has been interpreted judicially prudence might demand that the banker should, as ever, acquaint himself with the terms of his corporate customers' Memoranda of Association and deal with his customers within the boundaries dictated by these.

It is common for a company to include in the objects clause a range of what can be identified as powers, rather than objects. The company's objects are the purposes it exists to achieve; powers are methods and devices it may use in the achievement of its purposes. For example, the power to borrow money is not an object of a company.[28] Whether powers are extensively stated or not in the Memorandum of Association can be of importance. The Courts have long taken the view that a company has implied powers to do all things necessary to achieve its objects or which are reasonably incidental to or consequential upon attainment of the company's objects. In the case of doubt as to the legitimacy of any activity however, a power should be included in the Memorandum.

Since 1948 a company has been able, by special resolution, to change the objects clause of its Memorandum without further formality (s. 5). The alterations authorised by the Act are as would enable the company to carry on its business more economically or efficiently, to attain its main purpose by a new or improved means, to enlarge or change the local area of its operations, to carry on some business which under existing circumstances could conveniently or advantageously be combined with the company's business, to restrict or abandon any of the objects specified in the Memorandum, to sell or dispose of the whole or any part of the undertaking of the company, and to amalgamate with any other company or body of persons. If a special resolution of the company has been passed to change the objects of the company any dissenting member has a right within 21 days to apply to the Court which may on considering the application disallow the change, modify it or permit it, making such arrangements as the Court considers equitable to preserve the interests of the dissenting member.

---

[28] *Introductions Ltd.* v. *National Provincial Bank, supra* p. 94

If a change has been effected in the objects of a company not within the scope of the Act no objection to the legitimacy of that change may be made after twenty-one days of the change.

Changes in the objects of the company, as with changes in any other part of the Memorandum of Association, are notifiable to the Registrar.

Liability clause: This clause states, if the company is a limited liability company that the liability of the members is limited.

Share capital: The fifth clause states the share capital of the company and its division into shares of a fixed amount, e.g. £1,000 divided into one thousand shares of £1. The figure stated is the 'nominal' or 'authorised' or 'registered' capital of the company and represents the number of shares which the company may issue; it does not represent the money which the company may raise by the issue of these shares as the shares may be issued for a sum far in excess of their face value, that is issued at a premium.

The nominal capital may be increased (s. 61), or decreased (s. 66), by resolution of the company, but if it is to be decreased Court confirmation of the resolution is required. Other alterations, such as altering the face value of the shares, or converting shares into stock, may also be carried out by resolution of the company.

A company need not issue all of the shares comprising its nominal capital. If it chooses to issue only some, the nominal capital becomes divided into issued capital and unissued capital. Similarly shares issued may not be paid for in full by their holders; if they are, they are referred to as paid up; if not, they are partly paid shares and the balance between what has been paid and the nominal value of the shares remains due to the company. This balance is said to be 'on call' and the company can, subject to its constitution as to the proportion which may be deemed due at any time, call on its shareholders to pay this balance and sue for it if it is not paid. If the company is in liquidation any restrictions on the right of the company to call for the balance do not apply. It is possible for a company to deny itself the right to call for the balance, thus creating a fund known as reserve capital, (s. 60); the liability of the individual shareholder to pay is thus postponed but revives should the company go into liquidation. Any cancellation of the right of the company to call for the balance is a reduction of share capital and requires Court confirmation (s. 66).

While a company may issue its shares for more than their nominal

value, the excess being known as a share premium, it must not issue
them, without Court permission, at a discount, for the original
capital sum received by the company in cash would be less than the
accounts might indicate.

The division of the nominal capital into shares lays the foundation
for much of the adjustment of the rights of the members of the company amongst themselves. The extent of their entitlement to participate in the company's profits, their influence on its management, and
the extent of their right to share in the company's capital will depend,
subject to any special restrictions within particular companies, on
the number of shares each member holds.

Articles of association

The Articles of Association of a company have been described as
the rules of indoor management of the company. In the Articles are
to be found the details of the relationship between the company, its
shareholders, and the directors. With the Memorandum the
Articles constitute a contract amongst these parties (s. 20) and rights
and privileges created in this contract can be vindicated in Court.

In the case of companies limited by shares Articles may be
registered with the Memorandum of Association; in the cases of
guarantee companies and unlimited companies Articles must be
registered (s. 6). All private companies will register Articles as their
classification as private companies depends on their Articles making
the provisions which identify them as private companies.[29]

In the First Schedule to the 1948 Act there are model sets of
Articles for companies (Table A) and Articles registered may adopt
these regulations. If no Articles are registered the regulations in
Table A apply; if Articles are registered Table A still applies in so
far as it is not excluded or modified by the registered Articles.

In questions which might arise regarding the regularity of the
management of the company amongst its members or, for example,
between a member and the company, the contractual nature of the
Articles means that the contents of the Articles rule any such dispute.
If, for example, the directors of a company may not borrow, or
borrow above a certain sum, without the approval of the members, a
failure to gain this approval would be a breach of duty by the directors. The banker, however, would seldom be involved in the rights

[29] *supra* p. 88

and wrongs of such a dispute; rather his concern in dealing with the directors would be the regularity of the transaction with which he is involved. In most circumstances he need not concern himself unduly. Firstly, he may depend on the rule in the case of *Royal British Bank* v. *Turquand*[30] which states that an outsider dealing with a company is entitled to assume, unless he knows otherwise, that the resolutions necessary to authorise a transaction have been passed. Thus in *Mahony* v. *East Holyford Mining Co.*[31] the persons who sign the Articles of a company, and who under the Articles were entitled to appoint directors, treated some of themselves as directors and these persons purported to sign cheques as directors. The Articles provided that cheques should be signed as directed by the Board. The 'Secretary' informed the company's bank that the 'Board' had resolved that cheques should be signed by two of three named directors and countersigned by the Secretary. It was held that the bank was entitled to honour the cheques and the company was bound by them although the necessary appointments had not been made.

Secondly, under Section 9 of the European Communities Act 1972 the powers of the directors to bind the company are deemed free of any limitation under the Memorandum or Articles.

Thirdly, a banker can rely on the apparent authority of certain officers of the company.[32] This has two qualifications: (1) knowledge of any limitation of authority destroys any presumption of ostensible authority of a particular officer, and (2) under no circumstances can a banker assume that a particular officer of a company has ostensible authority to sign cheques; cheques are only properly signed by the company's officers, and in the manner, notified to the banker as having this power.

Promoters

The promoter of a company is 'one who undertakes to form a company with reference to a given project and who set it going, and who takes the necessary steps to accomplish this purpose'.[33] There is excepted from this definition any person who merely acts as the servant or agent of a promoter: a solicitor or accountant who acts

---

30 (1855) 5 E. and B. 248.
31 (1875) L.R. 7 H.L. 869.
32 *supra* p. 59
33 Per Cockburn J. in *Twycross* v. *Grant* (1877) S C.P.D. 469 at p. 541.

professionally in the formation of a company is not a promoter.[34]

It is important to identify promoters of a company as the law invests promoters with fiduciary duties in questions with the company he sets up. He is not an agent for the embryonic company; one cannot be an agent for a non-existent principal. Nor is he a trustee. Nevertheless, from the moment he acts with the company in mind he has a duty to disclose to the company—either to an independent Board of Directors[35] or to intended shareholders[36]—any profits he is making out of the promotion. A failure to make such disclosure renders the promoter liable to the company to account for the profits he has made.

Pre-incorporation contracts: When a promoter has entered into a contract, apparently on behalf of a company not yet formed, the company cannot be held liable on the contract, nor can it sue on the contract. The legal basis of this is that before incorporation the company has no legal capacity and that nothing can be done by an agent which cannot be done by a company. Those who contract in such circumstances, finding themselves without remedy against the company, may now under Section 9 of the European Communities Act 1972 hold the person with whom the contract was made liable on the contract, unless the contract infers an agreement to the contrary.

Prospectuses

It is now rare for a company to be formed as a public company and to proceed to offer its shares to the public for sale. More common is for a private company with trading experience and published accounts to become a public company and offer its shares to the public. However, whenever in the history of a company there is an offer to the public to subscribe for shares or debentures in the company that company must issue a document called a prospectus. A prospectus is 'any prospectus, notice, circular, advertisement, or other invitation, offering to the public for subscription or purchase any shares or debentures of a company' (s. 455), a definition which is of importance as any document which falls within its scope must comply with and conform to very stringent demands from the law regarding its content, the registration of it with the Registrar, and

---

[34] *Re Great Wheal Polgooth Ltd.* (1883) 53 L.J.Ch. 42.
[35] *Erlanger* v. *New Sombrero Phosphate Co.* (1878) 3 App. Cas. 1218 (P.C.).
[36] *Lagunas Nitrate Co.* v. *Lagunas Syndicate* 1899 2 Ch. 392 (C.A.)'

the mechanics of its issue, while there are visited on those responsible for the issue of a prospectus considerable liabilities, both civil and criminal, if it is irregular in its form or content.

The Companies Act 1948 (s. 38(1) and the Fourth Schedule) prescribes the content of any prospectus. Broadly, the aim of the provisions is to ensure that a prospective investor has before him the information necessary to enable him to make an informed decision as to whether or not to invest in a company's shares or debentures. Thus the prospective investor will be informed about the identity of the directors, and any benefit they will get from their directorship, any profit being made by the promoters of the company, the amount of capital required by the company to be subscribed, the company's financial record in the past, the company's obligations under important contracts which it has entered into, and for commission and preliminary expenses, and the voting and dividend rights of each class of share. The information supplied must be supplemented by an auditor's report dealing with the profits or losses in each of the five financial years immediately preceding the issue of the prospectus, or, if the company has been carrying on business for less than five years, the years for which its accounts have been made up. If the proceeds of the issue of shares are to be applied in the purchase of a business there must be a report by named accountants upon the state of that business and if the proceeds of the shares sold under the prospectus are to apply to the acquisition of shares in another company there must be an accountant's report on that other company. If any prospectus includes a statement by an expert—defined as including an engineer, valuer, accountant or any other person whose profession gives authority to a statement made by him—that expert must have consented to the inclusion of his statement in the prospectus.

A failure to comply with the statutory requirements renders those responsible for its issue liable in damages to any person who takes shares on the faith of the prospectus and suffers damage by reason of the contravention. Those responsible for the issue of a prospectus which does not comply with the Act are liable to fines.

If a prospectus contains misrepresentations, anyone who takes shares on the strength of it may rescind his bargain with the company and sue both company and those responsible for the misrepresentation for damages. Under the Act (s. 43) any investor who cannot prove that a person responsible for issuing a prospectus acted fraudulently can sue for compensation as the statute makes such a person *prima facie* liable to those who subscribed on the faith of the prospectus for the loss they sustain. The Act provides certain defences against such a claim, both for the experts, who can be held liable with the promoters and directors, and for the promoters and directors themselves. Criminal liability, also falls on those who authorise the issue of a prospectus which is misleading, although in this case the liability of the experts is, as in the case of a claim for compensation under s. 43, limited to cases where the misleading statement is contained in their own reports or statements.

The civil and criminal liabilities which may follow on the issue of an irregular prospectus fall on those who authorised its issue, a category which includes professional advisers as well as the company's officers. Where the prospectus is issued by an institution such as a merchant bank, which has bought the shares and is offering them to the public, a process known as public placing, the officers of the company remain liable, but the institution is also liable if it does not ensure the regularity of the prospectus.

Statement in lieu of prospectus

Any company, other than a private company, which has a share capital but does not issue a prospectus on its formation, or which has issued a prospectus but has not proceeded to allot any of the shares offered to the public cannot make a first allotment of shares until a statement in lieu of prospectus has been delivered to the Registrar. The form of such a statement in lieu of prospectus is set out in the Fifth Schedule to the Act and it must contain practically the same information as a prospectus (s. 48). The purpose of the statute in demanding the filing of a statement in lieu of prospectus is to ensure that where a prospectus is not being issued but the shares may nevertheless find their way on to a public market potential investors will have or have access to, the information required, to enable them to make an informed decision as to the worth of the shares.

Prevention of Fraud (Investments) Act 1958

This statute is designed to help further in the maintenance of a regular and honest securities market.

Under the Act dealing in any securities, a term which includes shares, stock, debentures, debenture stock, bonds and rights in interest in any shares, is prohibited except in the case of persons licensed by the Department of Trade under the Act, or those persons who do not require a licence.

Persons not requiring a licence are stockbrokers and members of recognised associations of dealers and securities, the Bank of England, any statutory or municipal corporation, exempted dealers, or any person acting in the capacity of manager or trustee under a unit trust scheme authorised by the Department of Trade.

It is an offence for any person other than those specified to distribute circulars which invite persons to acquire, dispose of, subscribe for or underwrite securities unless the circular is a prospectus complying with the Companies Act. In the case of a corporation incorporated in Great Britain but which is not a registered company any such circular must contain the information required by section 417 of the Companies Act, 1948.

Most banks are exempted dealers in securities in terms of the statute, while those which are not hold licences.

By the Act (section 13 as amended by the Protection of Depositors Act 1963 s. 21) a person who by any statement, promise or forecast which he knows to be misleading, false or deceptive, or by any dishonest concealment of material facts or by the reckless making of any statement, promise or forecast which is misleading, false or deceptive, induces or attempts to induce another person to enter into or offer to enter into any agreement for acquiring disposing of subscribing for or underwriting securities is liable to seven years' imprisonment.

Protection of Depositors Act 1963

This Act sets out to penalise fraudulent inducement to the public to invest on deposit and to restrict and regulate the issue of advertisements for deposits.

It prohibits the issue of an advertisement inviting the public to deposit money, the term deposit meaning a loan of money at interest or repayable at a premium but not including for example a loan to a company or other corporate body involving the issue of debentures or other securities.

Excepted from the Act are advertisements in respect of (1) investments within Schedule 1 of the Trustee Investments Act 1961; (2) deposits with a bank or discount company, or a building society, friendly society or industrial or provident society; or (3) deposits with a company incorporated in or having the established place of business in Great Britain, providing that the advertisement complies with regulations made by the Department of Trade as to the content of the advertisement and any accounts required to be deposited with the Department of Trade under the statute have been deposited.

The Department of Trade has power to exempt other bodies from the effects of the Act, a power which is used to exempt charities, deposits at a low rate of interest, deposits in connection with an employer's saving or profit sharing scheme, and deposits with insurance companies.

It is a criminal offence to induce by fraud anyone to deposit money.

The obligations of incorporation

It is a matter of public concern that the affairs of registered companies are regularly conducted, and that their administration and policies should be organised to prevent, as far as possible, abuse of the privileges of incorporation which might lead to injury to the community. Two classes of person in particular require protection from potential abuse of these privileges, the shareholders and the creditors of any company, while potential shareholders or creditors will also benefit from regulation of any misuse of the system. Traditionally in the United Kingdom the main weapon of the law in regulation of companies has been the theory of disclosure. Based on the ideas that those in charge of companies will be careful not to abuse their positions if their administration is subject to public scrutiny and that there is a legitimate public interest in the affairs of companies the members of which enjoy limited liability, the theory of disclosure has shaped the law to demand that companies maintain certain registers and records, keep books and produce audited accounts and reports, the content of which will be put into the public knowledge. The obligations thus placed on companies ensure that information regarding the affairs of a company is available to the shareholders of it, actual and potential, and its creditors, actual and potential.

Statutory registers

It is a matter of public concern who owns a company, who directs its affairs and certain particulars regarding its director and their relationships with the company, and to what extent the company's property is charged in favour of creditors. A company is obliged to maintain registers, available for public inspection, which will disclose such information.

Register of members: Every company must maintain a register of members (1948 Act, s. 110) and if the membership is in excess of fifty, an index to the register. Register and index should be kept at the company's registered office unless the work of maintaining it is done elsewhere when it may be kept at that place, notice of this having been given to the Registrar.

The register of members must show the names and addresses of the members, the number of shares held by each and the distinguishing number of such shares, if apt, the date at which such person was entered in the register as a member, and the date at which he ceased to be a member.

A person becomes a member of a company (1) by signing the Memorandum of Association in which case he is deemed to have agreed to become a member and on the registration of the company will be entered as a member in its Register of Members (1948 Act, s. 26); (2) in the case of a newly incorporated public company, directors who have signed and delivered to the Registrar of Companies, an undertaking to take and pay for their qualification shares are in the same position as if they had signed a Memorandum for the shares (1948 Act, s. 181(2)); and (3) by agreeing to be a member and having his name entered in the company's Register of Members. Entry in the register is the touchstone of membership, the register and not the share certificate being the document of title to the shares, the share certificate being merely an acknowledgement that the name of the person mentioned is duly recorded in the register.[37]

If there are errors in the register the power to rectify it is vested in the Court. If the name of a person is, without sufficient cause, entered in or omitted from the register, or if default is made or unnecessary delay takes place in entering on the register the fact of any person having ceased to be a member the person aggrieved, any member of the company, or the company itself may apply to the Court for an order to rectify the mistake or omission.

'Unnecessary delay' would be the lapse of the period of two months specified in the Act (s. 78) for giving a transferee of shares notice of the company's refusal to register a transfer.

[37] Per Lord Sands in *Inland Revenue* v. *Wilson* 1928 S.C. (H.L.) 42.

The register of members is open for inspection during business hours—a charge not exceeding 10p may be levied on non-members who wish to inspect the register while the company is bound to furnish, on payment a copy of any part of the register to any person who requires it.

A company may, on giving notice by advertisement in a newspaper circulating in the district in which its registered office is situated, close the register for any time or times not exceeding thirty days in each year.

Substantial shareholdings: Where a company has a stock exchange quotation as regards any part of its capital, a person who becomes interested in ten per cent or more of the share capital carrying votes in all circumstances at general meetings must notify the company of this fact, and the number of shares in which he is interested within fourteen days of his being in this position (1967 Act, s. 33). A decrease in his holdings taking him below the ten per cent limit also requires notification. The company must maintain a register in which such intimation is shown, the register to be kept at the registered office or where the register of members is kept (1967 Act, s. 34), and the public has access to such a register on similar terms as it has access to the register of members.

Register of directors and secretaries: A company must keep at its registered office a register of its directors and secretaries. This register will show the names of the directors and any former names, address, nationality and business occupation, together with particulars of any other directorship held by him. The register is open to inspection by members without fee and by others on payment, (1948 Act, s. 200). Within fourteen days of any change in the directors or secretaries of a company notification of this must be sent to the Registrar of Companies.

Directors' shareholdings: A director of a company must give the company written notice of his interests in shares in or debentures of the company or its subsidiary, holding company or co-subsidiary. Such notice must be given within fourteen days after the interest is acquired. An interest in shares or debentures is not excluded by reason of its remoteness or the manner in which it arises or that the exercise of a right conferred by ownership is or may be subject to restraint. In addition directors must notify the interests of their spouses or children under the age of majority in the company's securities.

A company must keep a register in which the information furnished by its directors under these provisions is recorded and access to that register is available on the same terms and conditions as to the register of members.

In addition a company must keep for inspection by its members at its registered office or place where the register of members is kept or at its principal place of business a copy of each director's contract of service or a memorandum setting out the terms of the contract of service if it is not in writing.

Register of charges: Every company must keep at its registered office a register of all charges, fixed and floating, which affect its property. The register must show a short description of the property charged, the amount of the charge, and the names of the persons entitled thereto except in the case of bearer securities (1948 Act, s.104(I)). In addition every company must keep a copy of every instrument creating a charge shown in this register, these copies and also the company's register of charges being open to the inspection of any creditor or member of the company without fee for at least two hours each day during business hours. The register of charges is open for public inspection on payment of a fee.

Books, Accounts and Reports

Books of Account: Every company must keep proper books of account with respect to all money received and expended by the company and the matters in respect of which the receipt and expenditure takes place, all sales and purchases by the company, and the assets and liabilities of the company.

A company is not keeping proper books of account unless they are such as to give a true and fair view of the state of the company's affairs and explain its transactions. Books of account are to be kept at the company's registered office or in such other place as the directors think fit. They are not open to inspection by the public but are open to inspection by the directors, whose right of access to the books has been upheld by the Courts. Shareholders do not generally have a right of inspection unless this is conferred on them by the Articles of Association.

Accounts: Not later than eighteen months after its incorporation and subsequently once in every calendar year the directors of a company must lay before the company in general meeting a profit and loss account made up to not more than nine months before the general meeting, but not more than twelve months when the company has interests abroad, or, in the case of a company not trading for a profit, an income and expenditure account. There must also be laid before the company in general meeting a balance sheet as at the date to which the profit and loss account is made. The content of both profit and loss account and balance sheet must conform to the Eighth Schedule of the 1948 Act as amended by the 1967 Act and additionally must show the amount of any loans to any officer of the company during the financial year or outstanding at the end of the year, made guaranteed or secured by the company or any subsidiary of it, the amount of the directors' emoluments, as prescribed by section 196 of the 1948 Act and section 6 of the 1967 Act, including any particulars of directors' emoluments on which the right to receive has been waived (1967 Act, s.7), and particulars of salaries of employees exceeding £10,000 per year.

The accounts as prepared must be laid before the Annual General Meeting of the company. The balance sheet must be signed by two directors, or if there is only one director as might be the case if the company is a private company by that director. There must be annexed or attached to the balance sheet the profit and loss account, as approved by the directors before the balance sheet is signed, any group accounts, so far as they are not incorporated in the balance sheet or profit and loss account, the auditors' report (s. 156) and the directors' report (s. 157).

The accounts which are to be laid before the company in general meeting together with the annexed documents must be sent to every member of the company and to every debenture holder at least twenty-one days before the date of the meeting.

Group accounts: Where a company has subsidiaries group accounts must be laid before the Annual General Meeting when its own balance sheet and profit and loss account are produced. The exception to this rule is where the directors are of the opinion that such accounts are impracticable or would be of no real value to the members in view of the insignificant amounts involved or would involve expense or delay out of proportion to their value to members, or if the result would be misleading or harmful to the business of the company or its subsidiaries, or if the business of the holding company and that of the subsidiary are so different that they cannot be treated as a single undertaking. If it is claimed that the result would be harmful or that the businesses are different the obligation to produce group accounts can only be dispensed with by approval of the Department of Trade.

A company is a subsidiary of another company if (1) the other company is a member of it and controls the composition of its board, i.e. if by the exercise of power without the consent of any other person it can appoint or remove all or the majority of the directors; or (2) if more than half of the equity share capital is held by the other company; or (3) if the first-mentioned company is a subsidiary of any company which is that other's subsidiary. For the purposes of the production of group accounts a company is deemed to be the wholly owned subsidiary of another if it has no members except that other company and that other company's wholly owned subsidiaries and its or their nominees.

Group accounts usually comprise a consolidated balance sheet and a consolidated profit and loss account for the company and its subsidiaries. They must give a true and fair view of the state of affairs and profit and loss of the holding company and the subsidiaries dealt with as a whole and to enable this to be done the directors of the holding company, unless there are good reasons to the contrary, have to arrange that the financial year of each subsidiary coincides with that of the holding company. There are particular provisions in the Eighth Schedule dictating the form and content of consolidated accounts.

Banking companies: If a company satisfies the Department of Trade that it should be treated as a banking company there are modifications to the Eighth Schedule of which it may take advantage. They may, for example, make undisclosed transfers to and from reserves before arriving at published profits, although they are required to disclose their true profits and reserves to the Bank of England and to the Department of Trade. Behind this privilege is the idea that full disclosure of the fluctuation in the value of their investments or disclosure of periodic losses might lead to a loss of confidence on the part of depositors and the general public. There are similar provisions applying to shipping companies and insurance companies.

Directors' report: When the company's accounts are produced to the membership there must accompany them a report of the directors laying out information as prescribed by the Companies Act 1967 (ss. 16 to 23). Included in the report will be a description of the principal activities of the company during the year, an attribution of

turnover to businesses of different classes which the company may
carry on, the average number of employees in each week of the year,
certain particulars of political or charitable gifts, and, particulars of
exports. In the main the directors' report contains information
which would not be suitable for inclusion in the company's accounts.
It is narrative in form and has the purpose of supplementing the
accounts and giving further information to the membership, and
eventually to the public.

Audit: Every company must appoint an auditor, whose qualifications to act as auditor must have been recognised by the Department
of Trade and who must not be an officer or servant of the company, a
partner or employee of an officer or servant of the company, or a
body corporate. Once appointed an auditor enjoys privileges within
the company which enable him to carry out his duty and protections
against his arbitrary removal from his position. His remuneration is
fixed by the company in general meeting. The duty of the auditors
is to report to the members on the accounts examined by them. Their
report must be read before the company in general meeting and is
open to inspection by any member. To prepare the report the
auditors must carry out those investigations which will enable them
to form an opinion as to whether proper books of account have been
kept by the company and whether the accounts are in agreement
with the books of account. If they think that this is not the case they
must state this fact in their report; similarly if they fail to obtain all
the information and explanations which they feel they should have
they must state that fact in their report.

Annual return: Within forty-two days after the holding of the
Annual General Meeting a company must submit to the Registrar
of Companies a copy of the Annual Return, the content of which is
prescribed by the Sixth Schedule to the 1948 Act. Included in the
annual return are the address of the registered office, the location of
the registers of members and debenture holders if not kept at the
registered office, a summary of the share capital and debentures of
the company, the amount of indebtedness of the company and a list
of present and past members; the particulars of the directors and
secretaries of the company must also be included. Annexed to the
annual return as submitted to the Registrar are the profit and loss
account and balance sheet of the company, a certified copy of the
auditors' report, and a copy of the directors' report. Excluded
from the obligation to annex a balance sheet and the associated

documents to the annual return are unlimited companies, while private companies must send with the annual return a certificate that the company still conforms to the identifying features of a private company.

Company meetings: Every company must hold an Annual General Meeting, with an interval of not more than fifteen months between one Annual General Meeting and the next. The business of the Annual General Meeting is the declaration of any dividend, the consideration of the accounts, balance sheets and reports of the directors and auditors, the election of directors in place of those retiring, and the appointment of and the fixing of the remuneration of the auditors together with any other business which may appear on the Agenda. If default is made in holding the meeting the Department of Trade may call or direct the calling of a meeting.

Apart from statutory meetings, which are held by public limited companies which have been incorporated as public companies, which are rare, and which have as their purpose the review of matters regarding the formation of the company and the issue of its shares, any other meeting of a company is known as an Extraordinary General Meeting. An Extraordinary General Meeting may be called by the directors of a company of their own accord or because they have received a requisition from the membership demanding that such a meeting be held. The directors must give effect to such a requisition.

Every company must keep Minutes of all proceedings of general meetings and the Minute books must be kept at the registered office open to the inspection of members.

Resolutions: The decisions of a company taken in general meeting are generally binding upon the company when they are supported by a simple majority of those present at the meeting and entitled to vote. Such a resolution is known as an ordinary resolution and the votes of members absent from the meeting, even when they have appointed a proxy, are not counted, for unless the company's constitution provides otherwise proxy votes are only counted when a poll of the meeting is taken. A person holding a proxy has a right to demand such a poll.

Items for the decision of the company in general meeting are designated by the Act, and sometimes by the constitution of an individual company as being capable of being passed only by extraordinary or special resolution.

An extraordinary resolution is a resolution passed by at least a three-fourths majority of the votes of members entitled to vote and voting in person or, where allowed, by proxy, at a general meeting of the company of which notice specifying the intention to propose the resolution as an extraordinary resolution has been given. For example an extraordinary resolution is the competent resolution when the company is deciding that it cannot by reason of it liabilities continue its business and that it is advisable to wind up (1948 Act, s. 278).

A special resolution is defined as a resolution passed by a majority of at least three-fourths of the votes of the members entitled to vote and voting in person or, where allowed by proxy, at a general meeting of the company of which at least twenty-one days' notice specifying the intention to propose the resolution as a special resolution has been given. Most of the important resolutions regarding a company, e.g. a resolution to change the objects for which the company is set up, are designated by law or by the constitution of companies as being special resolutions.

Section 136 of the 1948 Act invests the members of any company entitled to attend and vote at a company meeting with the right to appoint another person to attend and vote as his proxy. If the company is a private company the proxy may speak at the meeting but not in the case of a public company. A proxy does not require to be himself a member of the company. He is appointed by an instrument in writing and every notice calling a meeting must state clearly the right of the members to appoint a proxy.

The company's shares

There are no limits in law as to the type or nature of the shares which a company may issue to its members. It therefore is impossible to do more than generalise about the characteristics of specific kinds of shares, even those which are in common use by companies. The terms and conditions upon which a member of a company holds his shares is a matter of contract between himself, the company, and the other members, the contract being based on the Memorandum and Articles of Association of the company and any specific contract, which must be in accordance with the principles stated in the constitution of the company, under which the shares were issued. Thus, it is possible that in one company shareholders are allowed to vote, while in another the right to vote is denied to shareholders of all but a few shares. The rights which attach to any particular shares require particular examination and as a company is not bound to issue all its shares with the same rights, but may confer different rights on different classes of shares, it cannot be assumed that all shareholders in a particular company enjoy the same rights. Even the name by which a class of shares is called gives only an indication of the rights attaching to it any particular company.

Stock: When a company has issued as fully paid all the shares of a particular class it may convert these shares into stock. The advantage of converting shares into stock used to be that the work caused by the fact that each share had a separate number was obviated but now, where all the shares of a particular class are issued and are fully paid, there is no need to maintain the separate numbering of shares (1948 Act, s. 74). From the point of view of a member of the company there is no practical difference in whether he holds stock or shares, his rights will be unaffected and his influence in the company and his right to participate in distributions from it will be calculated in exactly the same way.

Share certificates: Every company must complete share certificates and have them ready for delivery within two months after allotment or after the date on which a transfer is lodged for registration. The certificate is a formal statement by the company that the person therein named is the holder of a number of shares in the company specified in the certificate. Although *prima facie* evidence of the title of the person named in it to the shares the share certificate is not a document of title as the register of members is. A share certificate is not a negotiable instrument but merely facilitates dealings with the shares, whether by way of sale or pledging in security.

The statement in the share certificate as to the ownership of shares and whether or not these shares are fully paid is binding on the company and anyone who relies on such a share certificate and is a loser thereby can pursue the company to compensate the company for his losses. This means that great care must be taken in issuing share certificates.

Stock transfer: When it is desired to transfer shares in a company the company must not register such a transfer unless a 'proper instrument of transfer' has been delivered to the company (1948 Act, s. 75). The form of the transfer may be prescribed by the Articles but it is not a proper instrument of transfer unless it is such a document as will attract stamp duty. Despite the possibility that the Articles of a company may prescribe a form of transfer the common form is that prescribed by the Stock Transfer Act 1963. The form prescribed in this Act can be used for any fully paid up registered securities issued by a company limited by shares, the term resgistered securities meaning transferable securities the holders of which are entered in a register, and includes shares, stock, debentures, debentures stock, loan stock, bonds and units of a unit trust scheme (s. 4). The form set out in Schedule One to the Stock Transfer Act 1963 is signed—it need not be attested—by the transferor and handed with the relevant certificate to the transferee who presents it to the company with a request that such entries be made in the register as are necessary to give effect to the transfer. Where a stock transfer has been executed for the purpose of a stock exchange transaction particulars of the transferee may be inserted in the transfer or, if there are several transferees, supplied by separate instruments in the form set out in the Second Schedule to the 1963 Act, called brokers transfers. The brokers transfer form identifies the stock transfer signed by the transferor and shows the identity of the transferee, or transferees where the original holding has been broken up.

By the use of the stock transfer form and, if relevant brokers transfers, a holding may be transferred to a single purchaser or to several. If there are several purchasers the broker who sells will transmit the relevant forms and share certificate to the company; if there is one transferee he will forward the share certificate and the stock transfer form. Assuming that the transfer documents are properly stamped and the registration fee paid to the company the company must within two months after the transfer is lodged either issue a new share certificate or share certificates in accordance with the transfers or, where the directors are exercising a power to refuse registration, send the transferees notice of their refusal.

Certification of transfers: If the holder of shares desires to sell only some of his holding he will not wish to deliver the share certificate in respect of his whole holding when he makes the transfer. To permit a partial sale, or to facilitate a sale to several purchasers when the transaction is not a stock exchange transaction and brokers certificates cannot be used, the procedure known as certification of transfers can be used. The seller executes the transfer and sends it with the share certificate to the company the secretary of which indorses on the transfer the words 'certificate lodged' or similar words and returns the transfer so certificated to the transferor. The certification of a transfer in this way is a representation by the company to any person acting on the faith of the certification that there have been produced to the company such documents as show a *prima facie* title to the shares in the transferor; it is not a representation that the transferor has title (s. 79(1)). A company which fraudulently or negligently makes a false certification of this sort will be liable in damages to a person who acts on the faith of it to his loss. A certification is deemed to be made by the company if it is made by a person authorised to issue certificated transfers on the company's behalf and if it is signed by a person authorised to certificate transfers on the company's behalf.

When a transfer is certificated the company destroys the original share certificate and issues new certificates.

Forged transfers: A forged transfer is a nullity; thus if a company has acted upon a forged transfer presented to it for registration and removed the name of the true owner of the shares from the register it can be compelled to replace that name. A company can claim indemnity from the person who sent the forged transfer for registration if it has sustained loss through acting upon it.

Normally on receipt of a transfer form a company will inform the shareholder whose name appears as transferor that it has received a transfer form thus giving him an opportunity to protest to the company that he has not in fact signed such a transfer.

Transmission of shares: A transmission of shares occurs on the death or the bankruptcy of a member or if the member is a company if it is liquidated. If a shareholder has died the shares vest in his executor and the confirmation should be produced to the company. If a member's assets have been sequestrated his trustee in bankruptcy will produce his act and warrant to the company as evidence of his right either to be registered himself as a member or to transfer the shares without being registered.

Debentures

While the debentures of a company can be transferred and transmitted in the same way as its shares it is important to note that debentures and shares are quite different. A share by its nature represents the interest of the member of a company and is a measure of his liability to the company and his interest in it; a debenture is simply an acknowledgement by the company that it has borrowed money from the debenture holder. A debenture holder is not a member of the company, his rights being to repayment of the sum lent to the company in accordance with the contract between the company and the lender. The rights of a debenture holder will be contained in the contract; these rights vary from company to company but what does not vary is the character of the debenture which is no more than an acknowledgement of the loan and gives the holder of it no rights of membership, or ownership of, the company.

Forfeiture of shares

Where shares are not fully paid and a member has neglected or refused to pay a call or an instalment the directors of the company may, if expressly authorised by the articles to do so, order forfeiture of these shares. A forfeiture must be used for the benefit of the company as a whole and in good faith and any irregularity in the procedure followed in carrying it out will render it null. Forfeiture for non-payment of debts other than those due arising out of partly paid shares, is invalid, and, similarly, any article which authorises the forfeiture of shares for any reason other than neglect to pay on calls is invalid.

When shares have been forfeited they may be sold or reissued by the company according to the provisions of the articles. If this is done the purchaser of the reissued shares becomes liable for the payment of all future calls, including the one on account of which the forfeiture has been made.

When shares are forfeited the former owner of the shares has no further liability on the shares unless such liability is preserved in the articles.

As an alternative to forfeiture the company has a right to sue when calls are not made.

Share warrant

A share warrant is a warrant issued by a company under seal stating that the bearer of the warrant is entitled to the shares specified in the warrant (1948 Act, s. 83). Only public companies limited by shares can issue share warrants and only if the shares are fully paid and there is authority to issue share warrants in the Articles. When a company issues a share warrant it strikes out of the register of members the name of the holder of the shares and enters the fact that a warrant has been issued. Thereafter the annual return of the company must show the total amount of shares for which share warrants are outstanding and the total amount of share warrants issued and surrendered since the last annual return.

The bearer of a share warrant is entitled to the shares specified in the warrant which is a negotiable instrument so that the title to the shares is transferred by delivery of the warrant.

Treasury consent is necessary for the issue of a share warrant and they must be deposited with an authorised depository. For these reasons the issue of share warrants is not common.

Bearer debentures

A company may issue debentures expressed as payable to bearer which are also negotiable instruments. The title to bearer debentures is transferred by delivery and once again Treasury consent is necessary and the debentures must be deposited with an authorised depository. When interest is due on a bearer debenture, or a dividend is due if a share warrant has been issued, the payment will be made by the company to the person who presents to the company the appropriate coupon which is attached to the warrant or the bearer debenture.

Directors

The directors of a company are those officers of it to whom is entrusted the day-to-day management of its affairs. 'The directors are a body to whom is delegated the duty of managing the general affairs of the company'.[38] Responsibility for a company's affairs is divided; to the company in general meeting are reserved certain powers, such as changing the objects of the company and, usually, the appointment of the directors; while the management of the company is vested in its directors under the duty of accounting and reporting to the membership in meeting. Neither body can usurp the function of the other, although the ultimate power in the company lies with the membership through its power of appointment and dismissal of directors, the latter being a power which any company can exercise by ordinary resolution, except in the case of a director of a private company appointed for life before 1945, and which cannot be diminished by any provision in the Articles of the company or by any contract.

Every public company registered after 1929 must have at least

[38] *Re City Equitable Fire Insurance Co.* 1925 Ch. 407.

two directors; private companies and public companies registered before 1929 must have one. The number of directors, their tenure of office and the manner of their appointment are regulated by the Articles of Association, although first directors are often appointed by being named in the Articles. A company may or may not require by its Articles that a director holds shares; if there is provision for such a share qualification it must be heeded by the directors.

A person who has been disqualified as a director by a Court may not be appointed as a director, while undischarged bankrupts cannot act as directors, a provision usually supplemented in the Articles of companies by the declaration that an undischarged bankrupt cannot be appointed a director and that any director who becomes bankrupt is automatically disqualified. There are provisions which make persons over seventy ineligible as directors of public companies, but these can be avoided by provisions in the Articles or by resolution of the company.

Directors of a company must supply the company with information regarding their shareholdings in the company[39] and are prohibited from dealing in options in their company's shares.

Directors' duties: The duties of a director are divisible into two categories, his fiduciary duties and his duties of skill and care. Both types of duty are owed to the company, not to individual shareholders. Thus if there is a breach of a director's duty only the company can sue him for damages.

The fiduciary nature of part of the duties of directors has led to discussion of whether or not directors are trustees:

'It is sometimes said that directors are trustees. If this means no more than that directors in the performance of their duties stand in a fiduciary relationship to the company, the statement is true enough. But if the statement is meant to be an indication by way of analogy of what those duties are, it appears to me to be wholly misleading.'[40]

In fact a director would not be carrying out his duty to the company if he did not acquiesce in ventures which trustees must never do; the property which directors control is vested in the company while the property of a trust is vested in the trustees. The fiduciary duty of directors is more akin to the fiduciary duty of agents; they should act in the company's affairs with honesty, bearing in mind the best

---

[39] 1967 Act; s. 27(1)(b).
[40] Per Romer J. in *Re. City Equitable Fire Insurance Co. supra* p. 117.

interests of the company, and without regard to personal profit through their office. Strictly, the directors of a company have no claim for remuneration for their services unless this is authorised by the articles of the company or is contractually based in connection with some other service which the director provides for the company. What, however, the directors must not do is make profits for themselves by virtue of their office; one who does so will be liable to account to the company, even where he can show that the company itself lost nothing.[41] A director who has an interest in a contract a company is making must declare that interest; otherwise, he is in breach of his duty.

Where a director has acted in breach of his fiduciary duty he may be relieved of his liability if a majority of the members of the company in general meeting, aware of the full facts, decide to waive the breach. The director concerned may himself vote on such a resolution provided that there is no fraud on the minority. Thus in *Cook* v. *Deek*[43] directors who had negotiated for a contract as if it were for the company but took it in their own names voted as holders of three-quarters of the shares in the company that the company had no interest in the contract. The Court held that their actions constituted a fraud on the minority and the resolution of the company was ineffective.

Alongside the common law there are ranged statutory provisions affecting the fiduciary duties of directors. A company may not by its Articles, or by contract, exempt a director from liability for negligence, default, breach of duty or breach of trust (1948 Act, s.205), although it may indemnify a director against his costs if he successfully defends any action, civil or criminal, arising out of alleged breach of duty. Further, in any proceedings for negligence, default, breach of duty or breach of trust against a director a court may relieve that director from liability on such terms as it thinks fit if it appears that the director has acted honestly and reasonably. Reasonable behaviour is a question of fact, which will be decided with regard to all the circumstances, including those connected with the appointment of the director (1948 Act, s.448). If relief is granted by a Court the company may, if so empowered by its Articles, indemnify the director against his costs.

---

41 *Regal (Hastings) Ltd.* v. *Gulliver* 1942 1 All E.R. 378.
42 *North West Transportation Co.* v. *Beatty* (1887) 12 App Cas 589 (P.C.).
43 1916 A.C. 554 (P.C.).

A director who is in any way interested financially in a contract or a proposed contract entered into or being considered by the company is under a statutory duty (1948 Act, s. 199) to disclose his interest to the board of directors, although such contracts are valid only if permitted by the Articles of the company or affirmed by the company in general meeting.

Companies may not make loans to their directors, or guarantee or provide security for a loan made to a director by another person, unless the company is a subsidiary company and the director is its holding company, or the ordinary business of the company includes the lending of money or the giving of guarantees, and the loan or guarantee is made or given in the ordinary course of business, or the loan is made to provide funds to enable the director to meet expenditure incurred by him for the purposes of the company, or to enable him to perform his duties properly. If a loan is made in the last case the company in general meeting must approve the loan or guarantee and, if it does not do so at or before the next annual general meeting the loan must be repaid or the security discharged within six months after such meeting (1948 Act, s. 190). Particulars of loans and guarantees which fall under this provision must be shown in the accounts.

No company may make to a director any payment by way of payment for loss of office or in consideration of his retirement unless the prior approval of the company in general meeting is obtained for such payment after disclosure of the intention to make such a payment to all the members. (1948 Act, s. 191). Similarly, no one who is making a take-over bid for a company may make payment to a director of that company unless the particulars of that payment have been disclosed to the members (1948 Act, s. 192), while the director in such a situation has a duty to ensure that particulars of any such payment are included in the documents issued to the shareholders.

Further to ensure that the relationship between the directors and the company are as open as possible provision is made (1948 Act, s. 196; 1967 Act, ss. 6, 7) that particulars of the payments and benefits made to or made available to directors be published in the company accounts.

All of these provisions are designed to strengthen and supplement the generality of the common law regarding the fiduciary relation of the director to the company.

As far as the director's duty of care is concerned the law is much more lenient. The most comprehensive review of the scope of this is to be found in the judgement of Romer, J. in *Re. City Equitable Fire Insurance Co. Ltd.* in which the judge made the following proposition: A director need not exhibit in the performance of his duties a greater degree of skill than may reasonably be expected of someone of his knowledge and experience, nor is the director called on to give his continuous attention to the affairs of the company, his duties being performed at board meeting—which he need not attend, though he should when he is resaonably able to do so—while he is entitled to trust the company officials are acting honestly, unless he has grounds to believe that they are not.

These duties are not onerous and are more apt for the part-time director or non-executive director who used to be more common than he now is. It is possible that if an executive director of a company were sued the Courts would hold that he owed much more strenuous duties of care and skill to the company.

The company secretary

A company must have a secretary who can be an individual, a Scottish firm, or a corporation, but who may not be the sole director of the company (1948 Act, ss. 177, 178). Joint secretaries are competent (1948 Act, s. 200(3)).

In the English case of *Panorama Developments (Guildford) Ltd.* v. *Fidelis Furnishing Fabrics Ltd.*[44] the secretary of a company in modern times was described as chief administrative officer of the company with ostensible authority to bind the company in contracts within the day-to-day running of the firm. This judgement, which reflects the practices of many modern companies, contrasts with the judgements in older cases in which the role of the company secretary was considered more circumscribed; in one case[45] the company secretary's duties were considered to be 'of a limited and somewhat humble character'. It is, nevertheless, possible to reconcile the modern and the older cases if it is appreciated that the secretary's ostensible authority to bind the company is limited to those contracts which could be said to be within the area of the administration of the company. In the *Panorama* case the contracts under consideration were for the hire of cars; the company was held liable.

---

[44] 1971 2 Q.B. 711.
[45] *George Whitchurch Ltd.* v. *Cavanagh* (1902) A.C. 117.

Another case in which the authority of the secretary is clear is in the issue of share certificates. A company cannot deny the import of share certificates issued by its secretary; he is the proper official of the company to perform this function. The company will not, however be bound if the certificates are forged.

Beyond these cases the authority of the company secretary is limited; he cannot bind the company in contract, except to the extent stated; he cannot borrow money on behalf of the company;[46] he cannot commence legal proceedings on his own authority.[47] Nor can he register transfers or strike a name from the company registers without the authority of the directors.

The nature and the scope of the duties of a company's secretary depends on the internal arrangements of the company which will delineate his authority and powers, but persons dealing with the company secretary outwith administrative matters should beware the limits of the authority of the company secretary in the absence of specific instructions of the directors.

The company secretary is an officer of the company and thus suffers the same restrictions as to loans from the company as directors and cannot be relieved of liability for breach of duty by contract or under the articles.[48]

The protection of minorities

As the decisions of importance in a company are taken in general meeting the possibility that a minority of the membership of the company will be disappointed in or disapprove of certain decisions is always present. No member can complain that his view is not accepted; it is a known incident of the process of running a company, implied in the law and contained in the contract upon which company membership is based, that the majority view prevails. This does not mean, however, that the minority must reconcile themselves to acceptance of the wish of the majority in every case, or that the majority may do as they like with their power. The case of *Cook* v. *Deeks*,[50] already mentioned, is a case in point; the majority of the votes cast at the general meeting of the company were in favour of a resolution which would have allowed the directors, who

---

[46] Re. Cleadon Trust Ltd. 1939 Ch. 286 (C.A.).
[47] *Daimler Co. Ltd.* v. *Continental Tyre Co. Ltd.* 1916 A.C. 307.
[48] 1948 Act; s. 205.
[50] *supra* p. 119

controlled the majority of the votes, to divert what should have been company profits to themselves. It was held that the minority could protest the unfairness of that situation, a situation which may arise in any company where the majority of the votes are controlled by the directors.

Any shareholder has a right to demand that the affairs of the company are regularly conducted in accordance with the constitution of the company, and may himself take steps to ensure that this is the case, his right to do so being contractual.[51] Where, however, there is no infringement of his personal, contractual rights his right to take action is more limited. In the case of *Cook* v. *Deeks* no individual shareholder could complain of direct, personal harm; the diversion of the business was harmful to the company, the duties which were breached were owed to the company. In such case the individual shareholder cannot himself sue; action lies at the instance of the company as the person harmed. This rule is known as the rule in *Foss* v. *Harbottle*. It will be appreciated that if harm has been done to a company by those who control the majority of the shares these persons can prevent any action being raised by the company against them. Thus there have been developed exceptions to the rule in *Foss* v. *Harbottle* which allow an individual shareholder to sue on the company's behalf in such circumstances. These exceptions are: Where the action complained of is illegal, or *ultra vires* the company, where the action complained of required the sanction of a special resolution and this had not been obtained, and where what was done was a fraud upon the minority by the controllers of the majority shares. A possible fourth exception is where the interests of justice demand that a shareholder should be allowed to take action.

Such an action is called a derivative action, the right of the shareholder to sue being derived from the company. It is also called a representative action. It must be noted that it is taken on behalf of the company.

The rule in *Foss* v. *Harbottle*, although appearing potentially harsh, is necessary to buttress the principle of majority rule in companies; it also flows logically from the theory of juristic personality. It would be intolerable if any shareholder who felt aggrieved by something which had been done in the name of a majority in a company and had been approved by that majority could initiate

51 1948 Act; s. 20.

Court action which would virtually be judicial review of the merits of the majority decision. Such would be a negation of the principle of majority rule. However, no majority can condone illegity, *ultra vires* actions, or fraud, and the law recognises the right of the minority to take action if attempt is made so to do.

It has been felt that the exceptions to the rule in *Foss* v. *Harbottle* are unnecessarily restrictive, that the majority may in its own interests conduct the affairs of the company in such manner which, while not falling within these exceptions—and the possible exception regarding the demands of justice is not far developed—discriminates against the minority interest. In such cases the minority is powerless at common law to seek remedy. To ease this situation the minority may have recourse to statutory protection.

Statutory protection: A shareholder in a company may petition for the winding up of a company on the grounds that it is just and equitable that the company be wound up (1948 Act, s. 222). The Courts have found it just and equitable to wind up companies on a variety of grounds[52] including complaints from minority shareholders that the conduct of the company is unfair to them. Winding-up of a company is a drastic measure, and may not be in the interests of the minority whose shares could have greater value than the value of the proportion of the assets of the company which would fall to the minority on liquidation. Therefore an alternative remedy to winding-up is provided.

Under s. 210 of the 1948 Act, a Court on the petition of a member, may make such order as it thinks fit where it is persuaded that the affairs of a company are being conducted in a manner oppressive to some part of the member, including the petitioner, and that it is just and equitable that the company be wound up but that so to do so would prejudice the oppressed part of the membership.

Oppression, as interpreted by the Courts, means a course of conduct which is unfair, lacking in probity, or 'harsh, burdensome and wrongful'. Inefficiency or carelessness is not enough, there must be evidence of a course of conduct which endeavours to oppress.

If a Court is convinced that a petition under s. 210 is justified, it may make any order it thinks fit, whether for regulating the future conduct of the company's affairs, or for the purchase of the oppressed minority's shares by any member or by the company.

[52] *infra* p. 135

Department of Trade

There are vested in the Department of Trade powers to help ensure the regular administration of companies. These, usually exercised by the Department in the public interest, fall into three categories: inspection of companies' affairs, investigation of the ownership of companies, and inspection of a company's books and papers.

Inspection: The Department has powers to appoint an inspector to conduct an investigation into the affairs of the company. The function of such an inspector, usually a Queen's Counsel, a Chartered Accountant, or a member of the Department, is to investigate the company's affairs and to report to the Department formally on his findings. Interim reports are allowed. The function of the inspector is investigatory, not judicial, but he must act fairly and give anyone an opportunity to answer any allegations made against him or to answer any criticisms or condemnations which the report might contain before such criticisms are made.[53]

To enable him to carry out his functions the inspector is armed with extensive powers; these include: (1) The power to call for the production of documents by the present and past officers and agents of the company. Included in the term agents are bankers but their duty to disclose information to an inspector is restricted to disclosing information about the company under investigation (1948 Act, s. 175). Apart from this anyone who can be called to produce documents is under a duty to produce these and to render to the inspector all reasonable assistance. Such persons are also examinable on oath; (2) The power to ask a Court to order the appearance before him of any other person than is mentioned above with the power to examine that person on oath; (3) The power to investigate any other body corporate which is or has been related to the company, for example, a holding company, a subsidiary, or a subsidiary of the company's holding company; (3) The power, without making an interim report, of reporting matters which tend to show that an offence has been committed.

The Department must appoint an inspector if the company has resolved by special resolution that its affairs should be subject to investigation or if a Court so orders (1948 Act, s. 165(a)). It may appoint an inspector if requested to do so by two hundred members

---

[53] Re Pergamon Press Ltd. 1971 Ch. 388.

of the company, or by a lesser number who amongst them hold one tenth of the issued shares of the company. An application by members must be supported by evidence that the applicants have good reason to require the investigation (1948 Act, s. 164).

On its own initiative, the Department may appoint inspectors if (1948 Act, s. 165) it appears: that the company's business is being or has been conducted for a fraudulent or unlawful purpose, or in a manner oppressive to some part of its members or that the company was formed for a fraudulent or unlawful purpose; that the promoters or the persons managing the affairs of a company have been guilty of misconduct towards the company or its members; or that the members have not been given reasonable information as to the company's affairs.

When the inspector reports, and a copy of the report must be sent to the company, the Department is empowered: to petition, if it is considered expedient in the public interest, for the winding up of the company on the grounds that it is just and equitable that the company be wound up; to petition for relief on the grounds of oppression of some part of the membership of the company;[54] and to bring any civil proceedings which it considers necessary in the public interest in the name of and on behalf of the company.

An inspector's report may reveal affairs which call for the criminal prosecution of some person; in such case the necessary action will be instituted, in Scotland, by the Lord Advocate.

Ownership of companies: The powers of the department to ascertain the ownership of companies are two-fold. It may appoint an inspector to carry out an investigation; or it may require those with information on this matter to disclose that information.

The Department must appoint an inspector when requested to do so by two hundred members, or members holding not less than one tenth of the issued shares of the company. It may do so when it considers that there is good reason for so doing. The remit of the inspector is to investigate and report on the membership of the company for the purpose of determining the persons who are, or have been, financially interested in the success or failure of the company, or able to control or materially influence its policies.

---

[54] *supra* p. 124

Such an inspector enjoys all the powers of a Department of Trade inspector.

If the Department is of the opinion that it is unnecessary to appoint an inspector although there is good reason to investigate the ownership of any share or debentures in a company it may require information from any person whom it considers to be, or have been, interested in such shares or debentures. It may also require information from any person who acted as an agent of someone interested in such shares, agent in this context including a banker.

Production of documents: Under the Companies Act 1967, the Department of Trade is empowered to require companies, or those in possession of them, to produce for inspection books and papers (s. 109). Any person who denies having the papers must state where they are, as best he can. There are included in this power the power to enter and search under warrant.

Receivership

The appointment of a receiver is one of the remedies open to the holder of a floating charge over some or all of the assets of a company. The power to appoint a receiver was introduced to Scots law by the Companies (Floating Charges and Receivers) (Scotland) Act, 1972, on which the rules in this area largely depend. Before this enactment the holder of a floating charge could enforce his rights against the company's property through the liquidation of the company; now by the appointment of a receiver he may take possession of and realise the security without liquidation. It is possible that, the receiver's job done, the company's fortunes may revive, or that the management of the company's affairs by the receiver may have this effect, and thus liquidation be averted; in practice this is not common and the liquidation of the company following receivership is normal.

The task of the receiver is to take into his possession that part of the property of the company which is attached by the floating charge by virtue of which he is appointed and by the exercise of the powers vested in him,[56] and subject to the restrictions placed upon him,[57] pay out the holders of the floating charge. On his appointment the floating charge attaches to the property then the subject of the

[56] *infra* p. 129
[57] *infra* p. 130

charge and operates as if it were a fixed security over that property (s. 14 (7)).

Appointment of a receiver: A receiver may be appointed either by the holder of a floating charge or by the Courts.[58]

The holder of a floating charge may appoint a receiver when there occurs any event which by the provisions of the floating charge entitles him to make an appointment. He may also make an appointment on the occurrence of any of the following events: (1) the expiry of a period of 21 days after the making of a demand for payment of the whole or any part of the principal sum secured by the charge, without payment having been made; (2) the expiry of a period of two months during which interest due and payable under the charge has been in arrears; (3) the making of a winding up order or the passing of a resolution to wind up the company; or (4) the appointment of a receiver by virtue of any other floating charge created by the company.

The appointment is made by the execution of an instrument of appointment (s. 13) by or on behalf of the holder of the floating charge, the appointment dating from the time of the execution of the instrument. A copy of the instrument of appointment has to be delivered to the registrar of companies by the creditors within seven days of its execution, together with notice in the prescribed form.

The Court may appoint a receiver if any event provided for in the instrument which created the charge as entitling the holder to appoint a receiver has occurred. It may also make an appointment (s. 12(2)), where it is satisfied, on the application of the holder of the charge, that the position of the holder of the charge is likely to be prejudiced if no appointment is made and when (1) a period of 21 days has elapsed after the making of a demand for the repayment of the whole or any part of the principal sum without payment having been made, (2) when two months have expired during which time interest due and payable under the charge has been in arrears, and (3) when an order for the winding up of the company has been made or a resolution for the winding up of the company has been passed.

The appointment is made by interlocutor of the Court, dates from the date of the interlocutor, and is notified to the registrar of companies by the presentment to him, with notice in the prescribed form, of a certified copy of the interlocutor.

---

[58] 1972 Act; s. 11.

Whether a receiver has been appointed by the holder of a floating charge or by the Court does not affect the powers and duties of the receiver; subject to any special limitations or conditions which might arise from the floating charge or from the terms of the appointment by the Court, the powers and duties of the receiver appointed by the holder of a floating charge and one appointed by the Court are identical.

It must be noted that while the power to appoint a receiver would not be taken in floating charges executed prior to the commencement of the Companies (Floating Charges and Receivers) (Scotland) Act, 1972, it is competent for the holder of such a charge to appoint a receiver or seek the appointment of a receiver by the Court (s. 11).

Disqualification: Disqualified from being appointed as receiver are: (1) bodies corporate; (2) undischarged bankrupts; and (3) firms according to the law of Scotland (s. 11(3)).

Notification of appointment: Where a receiver has been appointed, notification of that fact must be given on invoices, orders for goods, and business letters issued by or on behalf of the company, the receiver, or the liquidator (s. 24(1)).

Powers of a receiver: A receiver's powers may derive from the instrument by virtue of which he was appointed or from the Act (s. 15(1)) of from a combination of these, the Act stating that the statutory powers may be exercised by any receiver in so far as these are not inconsistent with any provision contained in the floating charge by virtue of which the appointment was made. Any power within the boundaries of the law may be inserted in a floating charge and generalisations about such powers are not possible. The statutory provisions, however, aim to arm the receiver with a complete set of powers which would enable him to perform his functions. These are: (1) power to take possession of, collect and get in the property from the company or a liquidator thereof or any other person and for that purpose to take such proceedings as may seem to him expedient; (2) power to sell, feu, hire out or otherwise dispose of the property by public roup or private bargain and with or without advertisement; (3) power to borrow money and grant security therefor over the property; (4) power to appoint a solicitor or accountant or other professionally qualified person to assist him in the performance of his functions; (5) power to apply to the Court for directions in connection with the performance of his functions; (6) power to bring or defend any action or other legal proceedings in the name or on behalf of the company; (7) power to refer to arbitration all questions affecting the company; (8) power to effect and maintain insurances in respect of the business and property of the company; (9) power to use the company's seal; (10) power to do all acts and to execute in the name and on behalf of the company any deed, receipt or other document; (11) power to draw, accept, make and endorse any bill of exchange or promissory note in the name or on behalf of the company; (12) power to appoint any agent to do any business which he is unable to do himself or which can more convieniently be done by an agent and power to employ and discharge servants; (13) power to have carried out to the best advantage any work on the property of the company and in general to do such other things as may be necessary for the realisation of the property; (14) power to make any payment which is necessary or incidental to the performance of his functions; (15) power to carry on the company's business so far as he thinks it desirable to do so; (16) power to grant leases, to input and output tenants, and to take on any lease of property required or convenient for the business of the company; (17) power to rank and claim in the bankruptcy, insolvency, sequestration or liquidation of any person or company indebted to the company and to receive dividends and to accede to trust deeds for creditors of any such persons; (18) power to present or defend a petition for the winding up of the company; and (19) power to do all others things incidental to the exercise of the other powers accorded to him by the Act.

Rights of the receiver: The receiver is entitled, within 14 days of the company being notified of his appointment, to receive from the company a statement as to the affairs of the company (s. 25(1)(b)). Such a statement, which is to be submitted by, and verified by the statutory declaration of, one or more of the persons who are at the date of the receiver's appointment directors of the company and by the secretary of the company at that date, (s. 26(1)), must show the particulars of the company's assets, debts and liabilities, the names, residences and occupations of its creditors, the securities held by them and the dates of these and such other information as may be prescribed. The receiver may also call for information from officers and past officers of the company, anyone who has taken part in the formation of the company within a year before the appointment of the receiver, and present and past employees of the company.

Duties of the receiver: The receiver has to submit a copy of the statements he receives to the Registrar of Companies together with any comments he sees fit to make on it. The company and the holder of the floating charge by virtue of which the receiver was appointed are also entitled to a copy of the statement.

Further the receiver must, within two months of the end of the year dating from his appointment, make up accounts showing his receipts and payments during that period. Such accounts must be presented annually if the receivership continues and must also be prepared when the receivership terminates. Entitled to copies of these accounts are the registrar of companies, the company, the holder of the floating charge by virtue of which the receiver was appointed, trustees for debenture holders on whose behalf the receiver was appointed and the debenture holders themselves, and the holders of all other floating charges or fixed securities over the property of the company.

Dealing with a receiver: Any person who 'transacts' with a receiver is exonerated from any duty to enquire as to whether any event has occurred to authorise the receiver to act (s. 15(3)).

Agency of a receiver: A receiver is deemed to be an agent of the company in relation to the property attached by the floating charge by virtue of which he was appointed. Subject to that, however, a receiver is personally liable on any contract entered into by him in the performance of his functions, unless the contract stipulates otherwise, but he is entitled to be indemnified out of the property in respect of which he was appointed against any such liability (s. 17).

A contract entered into by the company prior to the appointment of the receiver shall, subject to its terms, continue in force notwithstanding the appointment. The receiver will not incur liability on such contract by virtue only of his appointment.

Precedence amongst receivers: It may happen that a company has granted more than one floating charge and that receivers have been appointed by virtue of each charge. If this happens that receiver whose charge has priority of ranking is entitled to exercise the statutory powers to the exclusion of any other receiver (s. 16(1)); if the charges rank equally the receivers are deemed to be joint receivers (s. 16(2)) and must act jointly unless their instruments of appointment provide differently.

Where a receiver has been excluded because of the appointment of another whose claim to act is stronger, the powers of the excluded receiver are merely suspended and revive when the prior floating charges ceases to attach to the property, that is when the property is released or the debt has been repaid. A receiver whose powers are thus suspended need not release property from his control until he has received an indemnity from the receiver who supersedes him against the expenses and liabilities which he incurred in the performance of his duties.

Prior rights: While a receiver is empowered to take into his possession the property of the company affected by the charge by virtue of which he is appointed he takes it subject to certain burdens. These are: the rights of any person who has effectually executed diligence on all or any part of the property prior to the appointment of the receiver; and the rights of any person who holds over all or any part of the property of the company a fixed security or floating charge having priority over, or ranking equally with, the floating charge by virtue of which the receiver was appointed.

Preferential payments: If the company to which a receiver is appointed is not in the course of being wound up he must recognise as being preferred to the claims of the holder of the floating charge for principal or interest the claims of those creditors whose claims would have been preferred had the company been wound up. There is one modification in the Act (s. 19(1) and (2)) to this: such claims must have been intimated to him or have become known to him within six months of his having advertised for them in the *Edinburgh Gazette*, a rule which allows the receiver to make distribution to the holder of the floating charge without fear that such claims might emerge at some later stage. If payment is made to discharge such claims the amounts involved may be recouped by the receiver out of funds which would otherwise have been available for payment of ordinary creditors.

Distribution of monies: The receiver is charged to pay monies received by him to the holder of the floating charge by virtue of which he was appointed in or towards satisfaction of the debt secured by the floating charge. Such distribution may, however, be made only subject to the following: (1) the rights of the preferential creditors as noted; (2) the rights of the person who holds any fixed security which is over property subject to the floating charge and which ranks prior to or *pari passu* with the floating charge; (3) the rights of persons who have effectually executed diligence on any part of the property which is subject to the floating charge; (4) the rights of creditors in respect of all liabilities, charges and expenses incurred by or on behalf of the receiver; (5) the right of the receiver to be paid and indemnified against expenses and liabilities.

The balance of monies which may be held by a receiver once he has paid off the holder of the floating charge by virtue of which he was appointed is distributed in order to any other receiver, or to the holder of a fixed security over property which was the subject of the floating charge, or to the company or its liquidator.

Burdened property: Where property is burdened and the receiver wishes to sell or dispose of it and cannot procure the necessary consents from those entitled to the benefit of the burden he may approach the Court for authority to sell or dispose of the property free of any such burden. The Court's authority may be given on such terms and conditions as it thinks fit provided that such authority will not be given in the case of a burden prior to the floating charge unless that burden has been met or provided for in full (s. 21).

Cessation of receivership: A receiver appointed by the holder of a floating charge may resign on giving one month's notice to the holders of floating charges over the company's property, the company or its liquidator, and the holders of any fixed security over property which was the subject of the floating charge (s. 22). A receiver appointed by the Court may resign only on such terms and conditions as the Court sees fit.

A receiver who resigns must give notice of this fact to the Registrar of Companies and is entitled to be indemnified out of the charged property against liability for his costs, expenses and charges in the course of his duties. If a receiver is removed by the Court—which he may be on application of the holder of the floating charge on cause shown (s. 22(3))—the notice of his removal is given by the holder of the floating charge.

The necessity of the month's notice is to allow the holder of the floating charge to take steps to protect his position.

When a receiver has resigned and no other receiver has been appointed within one month the floating charge by which the receiver was appointed ceases to attach to the property and again subsists as a floating charge.

Liquidations

The liquidation, or winding up of a company, is the procedure for realising a company's assets, discharging its liabilities and bringing its existence to an end. Winding up may be compulsory, that is ordered by the Court, or voluntary, that is resolved upon by the company itself, but in either case the outcome is the same, the company's assets are distributed according to the law, and its existence is ended.

Compulsory winding up

Compulsory winding up is the winding up of a company by order of the Court. Under s. 222 of the Companies Act 1948 a company may be wound up by order of the Court if:

(a) the company has by special resolution resolved that the company be wound up by the Court;

(b) default is made in delivering the statutory report to the registrar or in the holding of the statutory meeting;

(c) the company does not commence its business within a year of its incorporation or suspends its business for a whole year;

(d) the number of members is reduced, in the case of a private company, below two, or, in the case of any other company, below seven;

(e) the company is unable to pay its debts; or

(f) the court is of the opinion that it is just and equitable that the company be wound up.

To these grounds has been added the additional ground that if there is subsisting a floating charge over property comprised in the company's property and undertaking, and the Court is satisfied that the security of the creditor entitled to the benefit of the floating charge is in jeopardy. This addition, enacted in section 4 of the Companies (Floating Charges and Receivers) (Scotland) Act 1972, entitles the holder of a floating charge to petition for the winding up of a company in addition to his power to appoint, or have appointed a receiver. The security of a creditor is deemed to be in jeopardy if the Court is satisfied that events have occurred or are about to occur which render it unreasonable in the interests of the creditor that the company should retain power to dispose of the property which is the subject of the floating charge.

While the grounds on which a petition for the winding up of a company are in the main self-explanatory there is statutory definition of inability to pay debts and the scope of the 'just and equitable' clause requires some consideration the cases in which is has been invoked.

A company is unable to pay its debts if a creditor to whom is owed a sum in excess of £50 has served in the company at its registered office a demand requiring payment and the company has not within three weeks of the demand made payment or secured payment. If a company has been sued and charged to pay and the charge has expired[59] or if the charge upon an extract registered protest[60] has expired the company is deemed unable to pay its debts. These provisions, which are to be found in section 223 of the Companies Act 1948, remove from doubt when the petition for the winding up is competent on the ground of inability to pay debts, but there is added to them a more general provision that a company will be deemed to be unable to pay its debts when a Court is satisfied that this is the case and in determining the question the Court is directed to take into account the contingent and prospective liabilities of the company.

When considering when it is just and equitable that a company should be wound up the powers of the Court are wide. Examples of cases in which winding up orders have been granted may illustrate the width of these powers. Where the purpose for which the company was set up cannot be achieved it may be wound up;[61] where the company is, as is frequently the case in smaller companies, in reality a partnership, and the management is in deadlock or the 'partners' have lost confidence in each other winding up orders have been granted;[62] oppression of the minority of shareholders will justify the winding up of a company.[63] Whether or not it is at any particular time just and equitable that a company be wound up depends entirely on the facts and circumstances at that time.

Petitioners: Subject to minor restrictions, a winding up petition may be presented by the company itself or by a contributory or by a creditor or creditors, including prospective and contingent creditors, in which cases the Court may require security for costs. If the grounds for the petition are failure to hold the statutory meeting or failure to deliver the statutory report only a shareholder may petition. The Department of Trade may also petition for the winding up of a company when an investigation has shown that its affairs are being conducted fraudulently or oppressively or if the

---

59 *infra* p. 301
60 *infra* p. 170, 171
61 Re Bleriot Aircraft Co. 1916 32 T.L.R. 253.
62 *Loch* v. *John Blackwood Ltd.* 1924 A.C. 783 (P.C.).
63 *supra.* p. 124

persons concerned in its formation or management have been guilty of fraud misfeasance or other misconduct towards its members.

Contributories: The term 'contributory' means every person who is liable to contribute to the assets of the company in the event of its being wound up. Apart from guarantors in guarantee companies, this means holders of partly paid shares and those who disposed of such shares for a period of twelve months after such disposal. The liability of the latter arises only if the registered member does not meet his liability.

Winding up order: The making of the winding up order, which is at the discretion of the Court, operates in favour of all the creditors and contributories of the company. It does not itself affect the company's property but there are restrictions on the free use of that property and its availability to individual creditors which hinge on the commencement of the winding up. The commencement of the winding up in a winding up by the Court is the date at which the petition is presented or, in the relevant case, where the company has resolved that it be wound up by the Court, the date of the resolution. After the commencement of the winding up any disposition of any of the company's property is void and as the winding up is at the date of its commencement equivalent to an arrestment and decree of furthcoming and to an executed and completed poinding no diligence done after the commencement of the winding up is effectual (1948 Act; ss. 227 and 327).

Liquidator: The Court has power to appoint a liquidator, a power which includes power to appoint provisional liquidators. A liquidator is described by the style of 'the official liquidator' of the particular company in which he is appointed and not by his individual name. Once appointed, a liquidator may resign or, on cause shown, be removed by the Court and any vacancy in the position is to be filled by the Court. Joint liquidators may be appointed.

Powers of the liquidator: The powers of the liquidator fall into two categories; those which he may exercise only with the sanction of the Court or committee of inspection if one be appointed, and those which he may exercise without prior sanction. With the previous permission of the Court or committee of inspection a liquidator may: (1) bring or defend any action or other legal proceeding in the name or on behalf of the company; (2) carry on the business of the company so far as may be necessary for the beneficial winding up thereof—although the Court may by order allow him to exercise

either, or both, of these powers without further sanction or inter-
vention of the Court; (3) appoint a solicitor; (4) pay any classes of
creditors in full; (5) compromise all claims or liabilities. Without
the necessity of seeking approval the liquidator may (1) sell the
property of the company by public auction or private bargain; (2) to
do all acts and to execute in the name of the company all deeds
receipts and other documents and for that purpose to use the company seal; (3) to prove, rank, or claim in the bankruptcy, insolvency
or sequestration of any contributory and receive dividends from his
estate; (4) to draw, accept or endorse any bill of exchange or promissory note in the name of the company with the same effect as to
liability as if the bill or note had been drawn accepted or endorsed
by or on behalf of the company in the course of its business; (5) to
raise on the security of the assets of the company any money he
requires; (6) to appoint agents to act for him (6) to do all such other
things as may be necessary for the winding up of the affairs of the
company and for the realisation of its assets.

Subject to general rules, the liquidator in a winding up by the
Court in Scotland has the same powers as a trustee on a bankrupt
estate.[64]

Committee of inspection: When a winding up order has been
made by the Court the liquidator has to summon meetings of the
creditors and contributories to ascertain whether or not application
should be made to the Court for the appointment of a committee
of inspection. If the winding up is on the grounds that the company
is unable to pay its debts no meeting of the contributories need be
called. The appointment is in the hands of the Court and at the
Court's discretion. If such a committee is constituted it comprises
creditors, or their mandatories, and contributories as ordered by
the Court. Its duties are to co-operate with the liquidator in the
administration of the winding up and in Scotland has, in addition
to the powers and duties imposed on it by the company law statutes,
the powers of commissioners in bankruptcy.

Dissolution of the company: When the winding up of the company's
affairs is completed the Court, on the application of the liquidator,
makes an order that the company be dissolved as of the date of the
order and the company is accordingly dissolved.

[64] *infra* Chap. XII

Voluntary winding up

A company may resolve that it be wound up without recourse to the Court. A company may be wound up voluntarily (*a*) when the period, if any, fixed for the duration of the company expires, or in the event, if any, occurs on the occurrence of which the articles provide that the company is to be wound up and the company in general meeting has passed a resolution that the company be wound up voluntarily; (*b*) if the company resolves by special resolution that the company be wound up voluntarily; and (*c*) if the company resolves by extraordinary resolution to the effect that it cannot by reason of its liabilities continue its business and that it is advisable to wind up.

There is an important division in the classes of voluntary liquidation. If the company is solvent then the winding up is known as a members' voluntary winding up; if it is not solvent, and is ceasing business by reason of its liabilities, the winding up is known as a creditors' voluntary winding up. The category into which a voluntary winding up falls is important as in creditors' voluntary winding up the creditors have rights, for example, in the appointent of the liquidator, which are not apt in the case of a members' voluntary winding up.

Members' voluntary winding up: In this case the liquidator is appointed by the members and reports to them. An essential feature of a members' voluntary winding up is the declaration of solvency. This is a declaration by a majority of the directors that they had made a full enquiry into the affairs of the company and that they are of the opinion that the company will be able to pay its debts in full within a period, not exceeding twelve months, stated in the declaration. The declaration must be made within the five weeks' immediately preceding the meeting at which the resolution to wind up is passed and must contain a statement of the company's assets and liabilities at the latest practicable date before the making of the declaration. There are heavy penalties for directors who sign such a declaration recklessly.

Once the declaration has been made and filed with the Registrar of Companies, the winding up commences with the passing of the requisite resolution and the appointment of the liquidator by the company in meeting.

The liquidator must call a meeting of the membership at the end of each year and account to such a meeting for his acts during that year. A final meeting is held when the liquidation is complete and when the fact of the holding of the final meeting is reported to the registrar the company will be removed from the register of companies and thus dissolved three months from the receipt of that return.

Creditors' voluntary winding up: When the statutory declaration of solvency cannot be made the winding up will be a creditors' voluntary winding up. The decision to wind up remains with the company but there must be called a meeting of the creditors on the day, or the next day after, on which the company meeting is held. Creditors are entitled to notice of such a meeting and it should also be advertised in the *Edinburgh Gazette* and two local papers. There is laid before this meeting a full statement of the position of the company's affairs including the estimated amount of the claims. One of the directors of the company is appointed to preside at this meeting. The liquidator appointed by the company must be approved by the creditors at their meeting; if they wish to substitute another for the members' nominee they may do so and their nominee will be liquidator unless the Court, on application by any director member or creditor, directs otherwise.

Another feature of the creditors' voluntary winding up which is not shared by the members' voluntary winding up is the possibility of a committee of inspection. Whether or not there should be such a committee depends on the decision of the creditors; if they decide that one is necessary then there will sit on it an equal number of members and creditors.

The annual meeting and the final meeting which the liquidator has to call in any voluntary liquidation become two; there will be a meeting of the creditors and a meeting of the members and reports and approvals are due from each.

The powers of the liquidator in a voluntary winding up are similar to the powers of the liquidator in a winding up by the Court; those powers which require the sanction of the Court are exercisable with the permission of the committee of inspection or, if there is no committee of inspection, with the permission of the creditors. If the winding up is a members' voluntary winding up those powers are exercised by permission of extraordinary resolution.

Winding up subject to supervision of the Court
When a company has passed a resolution for voluntary winding

up the Court may order that the voluntary winding up shall continue but subject to the supervision of the Court. If such an application is made and an order is made the Court assumes power to supervisit the liquidator and may remove or replace him.

Claims in winding up

Claims by creditors in a winding up are made in the same way as in a bankruptcy and the terms of the Bankruptcy (Scotland) Act 1913 which relate to voting, ranking and payment of dividends are applied.[66]

Equalisation and reduction of diligences

The provisions of the bankruptcy code regarding the equalisation and reduction of diligences apply. A company may be notour bankrupt and the rules regarding equalisation of diligences sixty days before and four months after the constitution of notour bankruptcy apply.[67] The winding up order is itself a completed diligence[68] and all diligences done within sixty days of the commencement of the winding up are equalised with it, that it is reduced.

Fraudulent preferences: Any transaction which would have constituted a fraudulent preference in the sequestration of an individual[69] will be invalid if it takes place within six months of the commencement of the winding up.

Preferential ranking: The list of preferred claims is nearly identical with the list in bankruptcy but there is one exception of great importance to the banker. This is the extension of the right of priority of workers to their payment to those who have made advances to the company to allow payment to be made to workers. In so far as the workers do not have a claim, the lender steps into their shoes. The amount for which preferential ranking may be claimed is limited to sums advanced during the four months preceding the commencement of the winding up and restricted to a maximum of £200 per head. Further, the sums must have been advanced for the purpose of paying wages and payment must have been made.

---

66 *infra* p. 315
67 *infra* p. 311
68 *infra* p. 312
69 *infra* p. 308

CHAPTER SIX

BILLS OF EXCHANGE

A BILL of Exchange is one example of a negotiable instrument, a document which through recognition by statute or common law is virtually equivalent to money. Any negotiable instrument is evidence of a debt due, may be transferred from one party to another by simple delivery or by endorsement and delivery, and confers on a person who takes it in good faith and for value a right to the obligation contained in it, regardless of any defect in title from which his predecessor may have suffered. This characteristic, the practical application of the theory of negotiability, has important consequences. If someone procures a Bill of Exchange by fraud his title to it can be validly challenged by the person defrauded. If, however, the bill then passes into the ownership of another person who takes it for value and in good faith his title is beyond challenge by anyone. Thus the right contained in a bill can be relied upon by such a person. A second characteristic of a negotiable instrument is that the rights contained in it are transferred by its negotiation without the necessity of intimation to the debtor that the creditor's identity has changed, an exception to the normal rule when moveable rights are assigned, that intimation is vital to complete the title of the assignee.

Bills of Exchange were evolved by the necessities of international trade. They were certainly used by Italian Merchants as early as the twelfth century, and probably in use much earlier. They were in use in England by the fourteenth century, while a Scots Act of 1681 recognises that they were in existence in Scotland and extends the rights of holders of them. Their usefulness lay in the fact that they presented a method of settling mercantile accounts without the necessity of transporting money, a hazardous undertaking and this is still the main function of the Bill of Exchange, although they play a growing part in other transactions, notably credit financing. Such other uses are more easily understood, however, after an appreciation of the original purpose has been gained.

141

Illustrations

(1) Assume a Scot owes money to a Frenchman and he himself is owed money by a second Frenchman. Rather than send his creditor money he merely sends him a paper purporting to order his debtor to pay the creditor. Such an order, addressed to the debtor, commanding him to pay the creditor is a bill of exchange in its simplest form. The creditor takes it along to the debtor who obeys the command and thus the Scotsman has paid his debt.

(2) Assume a Scot owes money to a Frenchman but the debt is not due for a year. Then the order to his French debtor will be to pay the sum due, but in a year's time. The French creditor who receives such a document may do one of two things. First, he may put it away in his safe and present it a year later when it is due. Alternatively, he may endeavour to raise money by selling the order to, say, a French bank. The bank may be willing to buy the order but only on the understanding that the French debtor is willing to honour it when it is due. The order, or bill, is then taken to the person to whom it is addressed who acknowledges that he will pay on it. Assuming that he is known as a trustworthy person, the bank will buy the bill for the sum stated on it but at a discount, that is for a sum representing the sum due less interest on that sum for the time until the bank can collect. More formally, the bill is negotiated to the bank who become entitled to the obligation contained in it.

In turn the bank may need money and they may sell the bill once again. Once again the bill is negotiated. The party to whom the bill is thus negotiated will collect in due course. There is no limit to the number of times the order or bill may change hands before payment is due.

The party to whom the order was originally addressed will have signed the bill to signify his willingness to pay when the bill matures, and the original creditor, the bank and any other subsequent owners of the bill may have signed it to negotiate it.

(3) One merchant supplies goods to another on three months' credit. As he delivers the goods he draws an order on his customer ordering him to pay three months thence the price of the goods. The customer signs this bill and the merchant instantly sells the bill thus getting his money immediately. Three months later someone turns up at the customer's premises with the bill and the customer pays on it.

The Bills of Exchange Act 1882

The law relating to Bills of Exchange is governed by the Bills of Exchange Act 1882, which introduce some changes into the existing law but at the same time provided[1] for the retention of certain features of the common law and the law merchant—a term meaning the body of rules which have been evolved by the customs and usages of merchants and traders and have been adopted by judicial decision into the law—except in so far as these rules might be inconsistent with the statute's express provision.

This Act defines a Bill of Exchange:[2] 'a Bill of Exchange is an unconditional order in writing addressed by one person to another, signed by the person giving it, requiring the person to whom it is addressed to pay on demand or at a fixed or determinable future time a sum certain in money to or to the order of a specified person, or to bearer'.

The Parties involved

Applying the statutory definition to the second illustration above, it can be seen that the Scot is making the order, the French debtor is being ordered, while the French creditor is the person specified to receive the money. The bill in the case would look like this:

Glasgow, June 1, 1975.

One year after date pay to the order of J. Berthet
    Twelve thousand francs   12,000 f.

To: T. Blanc,   (sgd) H. McTavish
     Paris

McTavish has drawn the bill and he is known as the 'drawer'. The bill is payable to Berthet (or to his order) and he is known as the 'payee'. It is addressed to, or drawn on, Blanc who is known as the 'drawee'. When he signs it as accepting the obligation to pay contained in it he becomes known as the 'acceptor'.

When Berthet negotiates the bill to his bank he indorses it on the

[1] s. 97(2).
[2] s. 3.

back. He is then an 'indorser', as are subsequent holders of the bill who indorse it. It might be noted that, if the bill is indorsed many times and space on the back becomes limited, a slip of paper, called an 'allonge', may be attached to the bill to carry indorsements.

Characteristics and Functions

Before examining the law involved in detail, it is well to know the main characteristics and functions of the Bill of Exchange. The principal characteristics are:

A. *Evidence of Debt*—a bill evidences that a debt is due. The drawer guarantees that the drawee is due to pay the stated sum and will do so. The drawee when he signs as acceptor acknowledges his obligation to pay. Each indorser guarantees that the sum will be paid and undertakes that if it is not he will pay anyone who loses through non-payment.

B. *Negotiability*—a Bill of Exchange is negotiable. This has two main results: one, that a valid transfer to someone vests in him the right to the obligation contained in the bill without any intimation; two, that a transferee will normally get an absolute title to the bill free of any defects of title from which his predecessors may have suffered.

C. *Assignation*—a bill negotiated assigns, without intimation, the rights it evidences. It is, when presented to the drawee in Scotland, an assignation of funds available to meet it.

The main functions of the bill are:

A. *Transfer of Cash*—As in the first illustration given the use of a bill of exchange as a method of transferring cash obviates the necessity of physical transmission of money.

B. *As an Instrument of Credit*—As in the second and third illustrations the use of bills of exchange provides a ready method of providing credit while avoiding many of the dangers of credit trading. The merchant who takes a bill payable at a future date has a readily saleable asset and an acknowledgement of his due debt which is quickly enforceable should it not be honoured.

Definition and Essentials of a Bill

The statutory definition of a bill of exchange requires little expansion but some points must be noted.

(1) The bill is an *order*. The language of the bill, which need not

be in English,[3] must be imperative.[4] No particular form of words is necessary as long as these are an expression of an order: thus 'credit C or order in cash' was held to be a valid bill.[5] The bill must be in writing though it need not be either holograph or attested, although if the bill is signed not by one of the parties to it but by a notary public, law agent or justice of the peace, as may be, two witnesses must subscribe it also. Print will suffice.[6]

The bill must be signed, the signature being by initials if it can be proved that this method of signing bills was the usual method of signing bills employed by the drawer and that the bill in question was signed by him.[7] However, no document which requires proof to support it can be used to found summary diligence and accordingly summary diligence[8] may not be executed on such a bill.

The signature of a person not only identifies him, it also binds him. Capacity to incur liability as a party to a bill is the same as capacity to contract.[9] If a bill is drawn or endorsed by someone who through non age or is a corporation lacks capacity to incur liability, a person entitled to the bill may still enforce it against, and receive payment from, any other party to it. However, the title of a holder in due course to a bill is not affected by lunacy or drunkenness although complete drunkenness would seem to be a defence against a party to a bill who had a notice that the signature was given in that condition.[10]

In general, however, no one can become a party to a bill of exchange unless his signature[11] appears on it. The Act[12] provides that anyone who signs in a trade or assumed name is liable as if he had signed his own name, and that the signing

---

[3] Re *Marseilles Extension Rlwy.* v. *Land Co.* [1885] 30 Ch. 598.
[4] Thus in *Little* v. *Slackford* [1878] 173 E.R. 1120, 'please to let the bearer have £7 and place to my account and you will oblige your humble servant' held not to be a bill.
[5] *Ellinson* v. *Collingridge* (1850) 9 C.H. 570.
[6] s. 2.
[7] Bell's *Princs.* s. 323.
[8] *infra* p. 171
[9] ss. 53-58.
[10] *Gore* v. *Gibson* (1845) 3 M. and W. 623.
[11] including his signature by procuration, *infra* p. 146.
[12] s. 23.

of the name of a firm is equivalent to the signing of the names
of all the partners of that firm, assuming that the signer has
authority to bind the firm.

Companies become liable on a bill of exchange if it is
signed in the name, or by or on behalf of or on account of,
the company by any person acting under its authority.[13]

Where a bill is signed by someone who adds to his signature
words to indicate that he is an agent or representative, this
is known as signature by procuration. Such is notice that his
authority to sign is limited and that the principal is bound only
if the agent was acting within his authority.[14] Such an addition does not exempt the signer from personal liability if he
has, in fact, no authority[15] but if he has authority which he
misuses for his own purposes his principal will be liable.[16]
Where an agent signs 'per procuration' the taker of the bill
is put on enquiry as to the extent of the agent's authority.

The order must be unconditional. Payment must not
depend on a contingency for 'it would perplex the commercial
transactions of mankind if paper securities of this kind were
issued out into the world encumbered with conditions and
contingencies and if the persons to whom they were offered
in negotiation were obliged to enquire when these uncertain
events would probably be reduced to certainty'.[17] An order
to pay out of a particular fund (as 'out of the money due
from A as soon as your receive it,' or 'out of the money
arising from my reversion when sold') is not unconditional
within the meaning of the Act; but an unqualified order to
pay coupled with an indication of a particular fund out of
which the drawee is to reimburse himself (as, 'which please
charge to my account and credit according to a registered
letter I have addressed to you'[18] or a particular account to
be debited with the amount) or a statement of the transaction which gives rise to the bill, is unconditional. Similarly

13 Companies Act 1948, s. 33.
14 s. 25.
15 s. 26(1).
16 *Union Bank* v. *Makin* (1873) 11 M. 499; *North of Scotland Banking Co.* v.
 Behn (1881) 8 R. 423.
17 Lord Kenyon C.J. in *Carlos* v. *Fancourt* (1874), 5 T.R. 482, at 485.
18 Re Boyse (1886) 33 Ch. D. 612.

the addition of the words 'against cheque' has been held to be unconditional.[19]

The order must be addressed to another person, the drawee, who must be named or otherwise indicated in the bill with reasonable certainty,[20] for example by some official title if not by name. If this were not so the parties holding the bill could not know to whom to apply for payment. If the drawee is not so described, the holder may prove the presentation was made to the person intended. There may be two or more drawees but if they are alternative or in succession the order is not a bill of exchange.[21]

A bill may be drawn payable to the order of the drawer or to the order of the drawee; in other words the drawer and payee or the drawee and payee may be the same person. Where in a bill the drawer and drawee are the same person or where the drawee is a fictitious person or a person not having capacity to contract; the holder may treat the instrument at his option either as a bill or promissory note.[22] Thus, if no one is known to exist answering to the name and description of the drawee the bill is treated as one payable to the bearer. If a name and description are adopted which happen to apply to an existing person but the acceptor does not intend to pay to the actual order of the payee named whom he knows to be, in that connection, fictitious, the bill is also to be treated as payable to bearer.

Time of payment may, or may not be, mentioned in the bill. If it is not, a bill is assumed to be payable on demand; a bill is also payable on demand if it expressly orders payment on demand. Such a bill is called a 'demand bill'. The alternative is to have a 'time bill', that is, one which is payable at a fixed or determined future time. Such a time may be either a date expressly mentioned, e.g. 'on January 1st next' or 'three months from date', or a date to be fixed with reference to an event certain to happen, e.g. 'three months after presentation'. The bill is payable when it matures, either on the fixed date or on the determinable one. Three days of grace

[19] *Glen* v. *Semple* (1901) 3 F. 1134.
[20] s. 6.
[21] s. 6(1).
[22] *Banco de Portugal* v. *Waddell* (1880) L.Q., 5 App. Cas. 161 (H.L.).

were allowed before payment needed to be made,[23] but this is now obsolete.[24]

The order must be for payment to or to the order of a specified person or to bearer. Bills payable to the order of a specified person are called 'order bills' and will be phrased 'pay John Smith or order' and will be payable either to the payee or to someone else as directed by him. A 'bearer bill' is payable to the bearer of it or is one in which the payee is fictitious or non-existent.[25] An instrument which, when issued, does not contain the payee's name may, if a space has been left for the purpose, be converted into a bill by the person in possession filling in a name.[26] A bill made payable to '—— or order', the blank never having been filled in, will be construed as payable to the order of the drawee and is when endorsed by him a valid bill of exchange.[27] But a bill payable to '—— or order' is questionable as a valid document so long as the blank has not been filled in.

The bill should contain a sum certain in money. A sum is certain although it is required to be paid with interest provided that the amount of interest payable is certain or ascertainable by calculation from materials contained in the bill itself. If no rate of interest is stipulated, the rate is presumed to be 5 per cent per annum, or 'legal' interest.[28] Where a bill is expressed to be payable with interest, unless the instrument otherwise provides, interest runs from the date of the bill[29] and if the bill is undated from the issue of it.[30] Where there is no stipulation as to interest interest is payable from the due date of the bill as a due debt.

A sum is also certain in money even if payable by stated instalments.[31]

The sum is also certain when it is to be calculated according to an indicated rate of exchange or at a rate ascertainable

---

[23] s. 14(1).
[24] Banking and Financial Dealings Act 1971, s. 3(2).
[25] s. 7.
[26] s. 20.
[27] *Chamberlain* v. *Young* [1893] 2 Q.B. 206.
[28] *Morgan* v. *Morgan* (1866) 4 M. 321.
[29] Wallace and McNeill *op. cit.* p. 118.
[30] s. 100.
[31] *Carlon* v. *Kenealey* (1843) 12 M. and W. 139.

from the bill. Where no rate of exchange is indicated, the amount payable is calculated according to the rate for sight drafts at the place of payment on the day the bill is payable.[32]

Where the sum payable is expressed in words and also in figures, and there is discrepancy between the two, the sum denoted by the words is the amount payable.[33] The figures may be looked at to explain an ambiguity in the words, but they are not an essential or operative part of a bill.

Inland and Foreign Bills

An inland bill is one which on its face appears to have been drawn and to be payable within the British Islands or to be drawn within the British Islands on some person resident therein.[34] All other bills are foreign bills.

The main difference between inland bills and foreign bills arises if a bill is dishonoured. The holder of a dishonoured foreign bill, if he is to proceed against the drawer and indorsers of it, must protest[35] the bill. The rights of recourse on an inland bill are preserved even if the bill is not protested.

The Relationship and Obligations of the Parties

The rights and liabilities of the parties to a bill may be illustrated by following the progress of a typical bill. The case given in the illustration (2) at the beginning of the chapter illustrates the points.

The drawer: The drawer of a bill of exchange undertakes when he issues it that when it is presented, either for acceptance or for payment, it will be honoured according to its tenor. If it is not accepted when presented for acceptance, or if it is not paid when presented for payment, he undertakes to compensate any party who suffers by its dishonour provided that the requisite steps are taken when the bill is dishonoured.[36] Thus McTavish when he signs the bill and issues it to Berthet, guarantees to Berthet and his successors as owners of the bill that at due date blank will pay and that if the bill

[32] s. 72(4).
[33] s. 9(2).
[34] s. 4.
[35] *infra* p. 170.
[36] s. 55(1).

is presented to him before the due date he will accept it, i.e., signifying by signing the bill that he is willing to pay at the due date.

Issue: Issue of the bill means the first delivery of it complete in form to a person who takes as holder,[37] defined as payee or indorsee of the bill who is in possession of it, or the bearer thereof.[38] Thus Berthet, the payee, is also a holder of the bill.

Delivery: No obligation evidenced by a bill of exchange is complete until the bill has been delivered to the person claiming the obligation is due. The only exception to this is that where an acceptance is written on the bill and the drawee gives notice to, or according to the directions of the person entitled to the bill that he has accepted it, the acceptance then becomes complete and irrevocable. Otherwise there requires to be the transfer of possession, actual or constructive, from one person to another made by or with the authority of the person transferring the instrument. Such delivery, whether from drawer to payee, or from any other party to the bill to be effectual must be made either by or under authority of the party who is claimed to be liable on the bill. A delivery may be shown to have been conditional, or for a special purpose only and not for the purpose of transferring any property in the bill. Behind these provisions lies the idea that the obligation of a party to the bill arises not only out of his signature on the bill, which is essential for the obligation to exist, but the consents envinced by the writing, the delivery of the bill and the intention with which that delivery was made and accepted, such intention, or consent, being the true foundation of the obligation.

Where however a bill is no longer in the possession of a party who has signed it there is a presumption that there has been a valid and unconditional delivery by him which may only be rebutted by proof. But if the bill is in the hands of a holder in due course[39] a valid delivery of the bill by all prior parties is conclusively presumed.[40]

Acceptance: Having decided to sell the bill, but only after having it fortified by acceptance by Blanc, Berthet takes the bill to the bank. Under the Act[41] if authorised by usage or agreement the presentment

[37] s. 2.
[38] s. 2.
[39] *infra* p. 157.
[40] s. 20(2).
[41] ss. 45(8), 49(15).

may be made through the Post Office. Blanc, assuming that he does owe money to McTavish or has an arrangement to accept bills with McTavish, accepts the bill. He will do this by writing his acceptance on the bill and signing it. Blanc now becomes acceptor of the bill and as such incurs liabilities on it. It should be noted that a bill might be accepted before its issue or after, before it is negotiated or after it is negotiated; a bill might never be presented for acceptance, the drawee seeing it for the first time when it is presented for payment.

If however the bill is not a 'time bill', that is payable on a specific date, but a 'demand bill' payable on demand or at a certain period after sight or presentation then presentation for acceptance is necessary to fix the date of maturity of the bill. Alternatively an acceptance of the bill may be expressly stated in the bill to be necessary to render any party to the bill liable to pay on it. In such case presentation for acceptance will require to be made. When a bill is payable elsewhere than at the drawee's residence or place of business it must be presented for acceptance, although this will be excused if the holder has not had time with the exercise of reasonable diligence, to effect the presentation for acceptance before the date for payment.[42] Presentation for acceptance must be made by or on behalf of the holder of the bill to the drawee or to some person authorised to accept or refuse acceptance on his behalf. Subject to the rule that presentation for acceptance should be made at a reasonable hour on a business day,[43] which would be construed as during business hours if the drawee were a merchant or a banker. It should be noted that presentment for acceptance is personal and that it is immaterial where it is made, whereas presentation for payment is local and should be made where the money is—a distinction which may be of importance in deciding whether a holder has used reasonable diligence in presenting a bill for acceptance when that was necessary. Where the drawee is not in business it is a question of fact whether the bill has been presented at a reasonable hour.

Where a bill is drawn on a firm whose business entitles one partner to accept bills in the firm name, presentation to one of the partners is sufficient. Where a bill is drawn on a company presentment must be made to the person authorised by the company to accept bills.[44]

---

[42] s. 39.
[43] Wallace and McNeill *op. cit.* p. 149.
[44] Companies Act 1948, s. 33.

If there are named in a bill two or more drawees, who are not partners, presentment must be made to them all, unless one has authority to accept for all in which case presentment may be made to him alone. Where there are several drawees and the bill is presented for acceptance to one and such acceptance is refused, the bill need not be presented to the others and can be instantly treated as dishonoured.

If the drawee is dead, presentment may be made to his personal representatives; if the drawee is bankrupt, presentment may be made either to him or to his trustee in bankruptcy.

In certain circumstances presentment in accordance with the foregoing rules is excused and a bill may be treated as dishonoured by non-acceptance. If the drawee is dead or bankrupt or has not the capacity to contract by bill, or if the drawee is fictitious presentment for acceptance need not be made; similarly, where, after the exercise of reasonable diligence, presentment cannot be effected, it is excused. The fact however that the holder has reason to believe that the bill, if presented, will be dishonoured does not excuse presentment, nor need the fact that presentment has been irregular, as, for example, where the bill has been presented on a non-business day be fatal to the rights of the holder if acceptance was refused on some ground other than the irregularity, for example that there were no funds available.

Although, in the illustrated case, presentment for acceptance is not strictly necessary, it is advisable, because it binds the drawee to the obligation in the bill, or, if acceptance is refused gives an immediate right to proceed against the drawer. It also has the important effect of attaching funds in the hands of the drawee for payment of the bill when due.

The Bill as an Assignation: When the drawee of a bill has in his hands funds available for the payment thereof, the presentment of the bill to him operates as an assignation of these funds in favour of the holder of the bill. This rule, which does not apply in England, holds even if the bill has been presented for acceptance and that has been refused. Thereafter in any dispute with the drawee himself or any competitor for the funds the holder of the bill may rely on this assignation. The funds are earmarked for him.[45]

In an action against the drawee the bill is used as an assignation

[45] *Watt's Trs.* v. *Pinkey* (1853) 16 D. 279.

and not solely as a bill, the right of the holder to recover being based on the existence of a debt due by the drawee to the drawer, and on the validity of the assignation of that debt to him.

The receipt of a bill payable at a banker's is authority to the banker to pay the bill, and it is the banker's duty to act on the authority and pay accordingly; there is a legal relationship between the banker and the bill holder whose rights must be kept in view.[46] Where a banker has funds in his hands, but insufficient to meet the bill, or where payment of a particular bill has been countermanded—which cannot be validly done by the drawer where the bill was given for valuable consideration—the banker's practice is to transfer the amount standing at the credit of the customer or the amount in the bill to a special account earmarked as against the bill, and to retain the amount until the matter is arranged between the parties or determined by a court.

Where there are several bills belonging to different holders in this position they are preferred as amongst themselves according to the respective dates of presentation to the drawee.

Liability as Acceptor: Liability as acceptor depends on three conditions. The acceptor must be named as drawee or otherwise indicated with reasonable certainty,[47] he must have signed the bill[48] or it must have been signed 'per procuration' and he must have delivered it back to the person presenting it to him or given notice that he is accepting. In the illustration given Blanc accepts the bill and delivers it back to Berthet. This is what is called a general acceptance, although it might have been otherwise.

By accepting a drawee undertakes that he will pay the bill according to the tenor of his acceptance,[49] cannot thereafter deny to a holder in due course that the drawer existed, the genuineness of his signature or his capacity and authority to draw the bill. Nor can he deny the existence of the payee or his capacity to indorse, but he does not guarantee the genuineness or validity of the indorsement. The acceptor, therefore, may refuse to pay on the ground that the payee's signature is forged.

Time for Acceptance: The customary time for acceptance by the drawee is twenty-four hours. When a bill is duly presented for

[46] Wallace and McNeill *op. cit.* p. 163.
[47] s. 41.
[48] s. 17(1).
[49] ss. 17, 19, 44.

acceptance and is not accepted within that time, the person presenting it must treat it as dishonoured by non-acceptance. His failure to do so can prejudice his rights against the parties to the bill against whom he would have had recourse. The drawee may require that the bill be left with him for acceptance but on the lapse of the customary period he must redeliver it accepted or not.

General and Qualified Acceptance: General acceptance is an assent by the drawee or drawees to the order contained in the bill without qualification as to time, place, or amount of payment; a qualified acceptance varies the order of the bill. The drawee may accept the bill subject to a condition, or may accept it partially, for part of the sum only; he may vary the place at which he will pay, or the time at which he will pay.

The holder of a bill faced with a qualified acceptance may refuse to recognise it and treat the bill as dishonoured by non-acceptance. If he does take the qualified acceptance without the consent, express or implied, of the prior parties to the bill against whom he has rights of recourse, he discharges these parties from liability. If the acceptance is a partial acceptance, which would not have the effect of prejudicing the rights of prior parties in any way, they are not discharged.[50]

Negotiation of the Bill

Assuming that Berthet's bill has now been accepted by Blanc, he proceeds to negotiate it to his bank; negotiation need not be to a bank, it could be to any person willing to take the bill. Negotiation is defined as the transferring of the bill so as to make the person to whom it is transferred the holder. Any bill is negotiable unless it contains an express prohibition against negotiation on its face.

The method of negotiation will depend on the character of the bill. A bearer bill is negotiated by delivery alone; an order bill is negotiated by the payee signing it or indorsing it followed by delivery. The indorsement[51] must be written on the bill itself and be signed by, or on behalf of, the indorser; it must be of the whole bill and be to a single indorsee if the indorsee is mentioned. By single indorsee is included the possibility that the sum payable could become due to one or more persons; what cannot be achieved is that the obligation owed in the bill could become due to differing parties individually rather than collectively. An agent having authority, an executor, or a trustee in bankruptcy may negotiate a bill for a named holder but where any person is under an obligation to indorse a bill in such a representative capacity he may indorse it in such terms as to negative personal liability.[52]

In this case Berthet will inscribe on the back of the bill 'pay Bank of Paris' and sign it. Delivered, the bill is thus negotiated to the bank. Such an indorsement is called a *special indorsement*, it specifies to whom or to whose order the bill is to be payable. Other forms of indorsement are the *restrictive indorsement* and the *blank indorsement*.

Restrictive indorsements are recognised to have two forms.[53] The first is where the transferor does not intend the bill to be negotiated further by the indorsee. Such an indorsement would read, in this case, 'pay Bank of Paris only'. The other is where the indorser does not intend to transfer ownership of the bill, but merely to vest the indorsee with the right to collect the bill on his behalf. 'Pay Bank of Paris for collection' or 'Pay Bank of Paris for the Account of Berthet' would be examples of a restrictive indorsement of this second type. The indorsee in this case has the right of the indorser, but cannot transfer the bill unless authorised to do so. If there is such an authorisation, any subsequent transferee takes the bill subject to the restriction. Thus in *Lloyd* v. *Sigourney*[54] where the indorsement ran 'Pay B or Order for my use' and B negotiated to C who collected on the bill C was held liable in payment to the indorser who opposed the restriction.

The third type of indorsement is the blank indorsement. This is where the holder simply signs the bill with no addition to his signature. The effect of this indorsement is to convert the bill into a bearer bill which the transferee can renegotiate by mere delivery without ever signing it himself. If, thereafter, someone comes into possession of it who is nervous of the dangers of having bearer bills in his possession, he reconverts the bill to an order bill by adding above the signature an order to pay himself, and thus the bill becomes an order bill, incapable of further transfer without his signature.

The fact that a person writes his name on the back of a bill and

[52] s. 16.
[53] s. 35.
[54] (1829) 5 Bing. 525; 130 E.R. 1165.

hands it to another does not necessarily constitute him an indorser[55] though it may render him liable as a guarantor.[56] An indorsement written on an *allonge*, that is a slip of paper attached to the bill, or on a 'copy' of a bill issued or negotiated in a country where 'copies' are recognised, is deemed to be written on the bill itself. The transfer of a bill by a separate writing is not an indorsement.

Where a bill purports to be indorsed conditionally,[57] the condition may be disregarded by the payer and payment to the indorsee is valid whether the condition has been fulfilled or not.

Transfer of Bill: Where the holder of a bill payable to his order transfers it for value without indorsing it there is no negotiation. The transfer gives to the transferee such title as the transferor had in the bill but no further rights than those. In addition, however, the transferee acquires the right to have the indorsement of the transferor which he may demand at any time. Unless he has exercised his right to demand negotiation the transferee in such case is subject to any exceptions and objections competent against the transferor. He cannot sue on the bill in his own name nor negotiate it by indorsement. In other words he is not a holder of the bill.

The Indorser's Liability

When Berthet indorses the bill—and any succeeding indorsers are similarly bound—he undertakes the same obligations as the drawer. He undertakes to the indorsee and to succeeding holders of the bill that it will be accepted, if not already accepted, and that it will be paid. If it is dishonoured, the indorsee will compensate any subsequent holder of the bill who loses thereby, or any subsequent indorsee who compensates the holder who finds the bill dishonoured in his hand.[58]

The indorser guarantees the validity of the bill and that he has a good title thereto[59]—he 'backs' the bill and must take responsibility for it. He cannot deny to subsequent parties the genuineness and regularity of the drawer's signature or of any prior indorsements. He is, of course, not responsible for subsequent indorsements; thus

---

[55] *Westacott* v. *Smalley*, 1 C. and E. 124.
[56] *Stagg Mantle* v. *Brodrick* (1895) 12 T.L.R. 12.
[57] s. 11(2).
[58] *McDonald* v. *Nash* [1924] A.C. 625; *National Sales Corporation* v. *Bernard* [1931] 2 K.B. 188; *McCall* v. *Hargreaves* [1932] 2 K.B. 423.
[59] s. 55(2).

he can impugn a subsequent signature as being forged or unauthorised.

Under the Act[60] an indorser can restrict his liability or even negative it by express stipulation on the bill. In a question with the indorsee, he may restrict or qualify his liability without such restriction or qualification appearing on the bill. Such a restriction, if it does not appear on the bill itself, would not be binding upon subsequent holders and, in a dispute with the indorsee, the burden of proving that a restriction or qualification was made would lie on the shoulders of the indorser.[61]

The Indorsee's Position

The Bank of Paris in this case becomes a holder of the bill by the indorsement of Berthet. A holder is defined by the Act[62] as the payee or indorsee of a bill who is in possession of it, or the bearer thereof. In this case, however, the bank is not only a holder but a *holder in due course*.[63]

A *holder in due course* is a holder of a bill who has taken a bill complete and regular on the face of it under the following conditions:

(a) That he became the holder of the bill before it was overdue and without notice that it had previously been dishonoured if such was the fact, and

(b) That he took the bill in good faith and for value, and at the time the bill was negotiated to him he had no notice of any defect in the title of the person who negotiated it.

In particular and to avoid ambiguity, the Act[64] specifies that the title of a person who negotiates a bill is defective when he obtained the bill, or its acceptance, by fraud, duress, or force and fear, or for an illegal consideration, or when he negotiated it in breach of faith or under such circumstances as to amount to fraud.

The importance[65] of being a *holder in due course* is that the *holder in due course* holds the bill free from any defect in the title of and immune from any personal defences, e.g., compensation, which

---

[60] s. 55(2).
[61] for method of proof see Gow *op. cit.* at p. 242.
[62] s. 2.
[63] s. 29(1).
[64] s. 29(2).
[65] s. 38.

may exist among prior parties. He can give a valid discharge of the bill to anyone who pays him and confer on any person, not a party to any fraud or illegality affecting the bill, all his rights as *holder in due course*.[66] He may sue on the bill in his own name.

Every holder of a bill is deemed *prima facie* to be a *holder in due course* but when the issue, acceptance or negotiation of the bill are proved to have been tainted with fraud, duress, illegality, or force and fear, then the holder must prove that he gave value and was acting in good faith.

A party to a bill who takes the bill overdue or not complete and regular on the face of it, or when he knows that it has been dishonoured, or knowing, or with reason to suppose, that his predecessor's title is defective, is not a *holder in due course*, and takes no rights in the bill higher than those possessed by the indorser. He will be known as a *holder not in due course*.

Whether a holder has taken in good faith or not is a matter of interpretation. 'The criterion of good faith is honesty. A thing is deemed to have been done in good faith where it is fact done honestly, whether it is done negligently or not. The question is not whether the holder ought to have suspected but whether he did suspect.'[67]

If one is a holder of a bill he may sue on the bill in his own name and can maintain an action on it in his own name against any or all of the parties liable on the bill unless it can be shown that he holds the bill adversely to the interests of the true owner. He may also proceed with summary diligence or claim in a multiple-ponding or found on the bill as a ground for compensation. If however the bill is payable to a specified person any action on the bill must be raised in the name of that person. A holder who might have sued a party to the bill is entitled to claim against any such party's estate in bankruptcy.

In addition to the rights to sue on the bill of the holder, a *holder in due course* enjoys the important privileges in law noted above.

It must be noted that a *holder not in due course,* whose title to the bill is defective has a power to negotiate the bill to another party who, assuming that he fulfils the specified conditions will become a *holder in due course*.

---

[66] s. 29(3).
[67] Gow *op. cit.* p. 442.

On the death of any holder of a bill his rights in the bill pass to his executors, and on his bankruptcy, if he is the beneficial owner of the bill, his rights pass to his trustee in bankruptcy; but if the holder is not the beneficial owner of the bill as, for example, where he has obtained by fraud, the title does not pass to the trustee.

Overdue Bills: When a bill is overdue[68] it may be transferred but any holder who takes such a bill will not become a *holder in due course*. In normal circumstances when a bill is overdue gives rise to no difficulties, examination of the terms of the bill will indicate the date of its maturity. Where however the bill is a demand bill different factors apply. A bill of exchange payable on demand is ordinarily given with a view to present payment; it must therefore be presented for payment within a reasonable time but what constitutes such reasonable time will vary in the circumstances. In the case of an ordinary cheque—which, of course, is a bill of exchange payable on demand, drawn on a banker—the period permissible is very short, at most a matter of days. Bills of exchange payable on demand are perhaps not quite on the same footing as cheques but it is outwith the ordinary course of business to hold such a document for any protracted period. It is not possible to give guidance as to what would constitute a protracted period; prudence would demand the presentment for payment of a demand bill fairly swiftly. If this is not done the bill will become overdue.

Negotiation to a Party Already Liable on the Bill

It is possible that a bill may be negotiated into the hands of a party to it. If this happens such a party may reissue and further negotiate the bill but he is not entitled to enforce payment of the bill against any intervening party to whom he was previously liable. An exception is that an acceptor who becomes the holder at or after maturity cannot reissue the bill.

Forgery

While dealing with the curative effects of the negotiation of a bill to a holder in due course of defects in title, it is convenient to consider the effect of a forged or unauthorised signature on a bill. 'Subject to the provisions of this Act, where a signature on a bill is forged or placed thereon without the authority of the person whose

[68] ss. 11, 14.

signature it purports to be, the forged or unauthorised signature is wholly inoperative and no right to retain the bill or to give a discharge therefore or to enforce payment against any party thereto can be acquired through or under that signature'.[69]

Any such signature is, therefore, an absolute nullity and this provision forms an important exception to the principle of negotiability. Anyone taking a bill should therefore take steps to check that the signature under which he hopes to derive title is a genuine and authorised signature.

The provisions of the Act which form the exceptions to the rule regarding the nullity of forged or unauthorised signatures include; that the party whose unauthorised signature has been placed on a bill may ratify his unauthorised signature either expressly or by implication and thus may preclude himself from pleading lack of authority;[70] he may 'adopt' his forged signature again expressly or by implication and treat it as his own and then be liable on it;[71] by his conduct he may be barred from disputing the validity of his signature, e.g., where by failing to give notice to the holder of the forgery he has caused the holder loss.[72] Other exceptions are: (a) the safeguard for a banker who in good faith and in the ordinary course of business pays on a forged or unauthorised indorsement on a demand bill drawn on him, or who pays a crossed cheque in accordance with the crossing,[73] (b) the right to treat as a bearer bill any bill the payee in which is a fictitious person, including a real person not intended to receive payment—a holder of such a bill taking it with the name of the payee indorsed on it can enforce it as if it were a bearer bill,[74] (c) the rule which states that, in a question with a holder in due course, an acceptor is precluded from denying the genuineness of the drawer's signature[75] and an indorser from denying the genuineness of the signatures of the drawer and prior indorsers[76]—thus, where there is a forgery on a bill and a holder has to give it up to its true owner, he can sue an indorser who negotiated the bill subsequent to the forgery and that indorser

---

[69] s. 24.
[70] s. 24; *McKenzie* v. *British Linen Co.* (1881) 8 R. (H.L.) 8.
[71] *McKenzie supra*; *Greenwood* v. *Martins Bank* [1933] A.C. 51.
[72] *Imperial Bank of Canada* v. *Bank of Hamilton* [1903] A.C. 49.
[73] ss. 60, 80 and 82; see also Cheques Act 1957 *infra*.
[74] s. 7(3) *Bank of England* v. *Vagliano* [1891] 1 A.C. 109.
[75] s. 54(2)(*b*).
[76] s. 55(2)(*b*).

cannot use the defence that the holder had no right to the bill (d) the rule[77] that a principal is bound by a signature by procuration only to the extent that an agent was acting within his actual authority.

Presentation for Payment

Assuming that the bank as holders in due course do not negotiate this bill further they will present it for payment when it matures. Presentation for payment—which implies a demand for payment—must be made to the acceptor, Blanc, by the bank on the day of maturity. In general terms, presentment must be made by the holder, or some person acting for him and authorised to receive payment on his behalf, at a reasonable hour on a business day at the proper place—the address of the acceptor or the place he has indicated in his acceptance—and to the proper person.

If the presentment is not made on the day of maturity the drawer and the indorsers are discharged not only of all liability on the bill itself[78] but of the debt for which it was granted, at least if they have been prejudiced by the delay. If the bill has been accepted, timeous presentment is not necessary to secure payment from the acceptor, who must pay on his undertaking to do so, but presentment must be made within six months of the due date if summary diligence is to be resorted to.[79]

As has been noted a demand bill must be presented within a reasonable time after its issue if the drawer is to remain liable on it and within a reasonable time after negotiation if the right of recourse against any indorser is to be preserved. What constitutes a reasonable time will depend on the facts of the case, the nature of the bill, and trade custom.

The proper person to make presentment is the holder, that is the bearer of a bill payable to bearer and the payee or indorsee of a bill payable to order but does not include a person holding under a forged indorsement, or by some person authorised to receive payment on behalf of the holder. It should be made to the person designated in the bill as payer, that is either the drawee or acceptor or, if the bill is payable other than at the drawee's residence or place of

[77] s. 25.
[78] s. 45.
[79] infra p. 171; s. 98.

L

business the person to whom the bill directs presentment to be made. Alternatively presentment can be made to some person authorised to pay or refuse payment on behalf of the payer if with the exercise of reasonable diligence such person can be found. Whether an hour is reasonable or not depends on circumstances; a bill domiciled at a bank must be presented during bank hours, at a merchant's place of business, within business hours. If the bill demands presentment at a dwellinghouse it is probable that presentment up until bedtime would suffice.

Presentment is not excused because of the payer's bankruptcy and should be made to the bankrupt and not to his trustee. If the payer is a company in liquidation presentment should be made to the liquidator.

A bill is presented at the proper place where it is presented at the place specified in the bill. If such place be specified presentment to the payer elsewhere is not sufficient although a bill may be presented to a bank sufficiently through a clearing house.[80] If alternative places of payment are specified presentment at one of these is sufficient. Presentment has also taken place if the bill is presented at the specified place of payment although the acceptor has died before maturity or may have left that place. If no place is specified but the address of the drawee or acceptor is given in the bill, presentment has taken place if the bill is presented there and, if no address, is given, the bill should be presented at the drawee's or acceptor's place of business if known and if not at his ordinary residence if known. In any other case presentment may be made to the drawee or acceptor wherever he can be found, or if he cannot be found at his last known place of business or residence. If a bill is presented at the proper place, and after the exercise of reasonable diligence no person authorised to pay or refuse payment can be there found, no further presentment to the drawee or acceptor is required.

If a bill is drawn upon or accepted by two or more persons who are not partners and no place of payment is specified presentment for payment must be made to all of them. A refusal to pay on the part of one of them does not, as in the case of presentment for acceptance, dispense with presentment to the others.

A presentment through the Post Office is sufficient where such is authorised by agreement or by usage.

---

[80] *Boddington* v. *Schlencken* (1833) 4 B. and Ad. 752.

Although generally it is a prerequisite of liability on the part of the prior parties that the holder will present the bill for payment on the due date, delay or non-presentment will be excused in certain circumstances. A delay is excused when it is caused by circumstances outwith the control of the holder and not due to his default, misconduct or negligence. When the cause of the delay ends, presentment must be made with reasonable diligence.

Non-presentment is excused where presentment cannot be effected with reasonable diligence,[81] or where the drawee is fictitious. The drawer cannot insist on presentment as a condition of his liability when the drawee or acceptor is not bound as between himself and the drawer to pay the bill and the drawer has no reason to believe that the bill would be paid.

An indorser for whose benefit an accommodation bill[82] was made or accepted, and who has no reason to expect that it will be paid if presented, cannot insist on presentment. Finally, presentment may be waived expressly or impliedly.

Effect of Payment

Payment by or on behalf of the drawee or acceptor discharges the bill. [83] Thereafter all rights of action on the bill are extinguished and it ceases to be negotiable.

The payment must be in due course, defined by the Act as payment made at or after maturity of the bill to the holder thereof in good faith, and without notice that his title to the bill is defective. To operate as a discharge payment of the bill must be made by or on behalf of the drawee or acceptor. Such payment, which is followed by the holder forthwith delivering up the bill to the payer[84] not only discharges the bill but also all parties to it would have been liable on it. Not extinguished by payment, however, are rights of action which arise out of the bill transaction and which are wholly independent of the bill. Only rights of action on the bill itself are extinguished by its discharge. Thus, if there are joint acceptors and one of them pays, he discharges the bill but retains his right to sue his co-acceptor for his contribution.

---

81 *Cornelius* v. *Banque Franco-Serbe* [1942] 1 K.B. 29.
82 *infra* p. 173.
83 *infra* p. 164.
84 s. 52(4).

Only payment in due course discharges the bill. Payment before maturity does not discharge it. Hence if an acceptor pays on a bill before its due date and it finds its way back into circulation by some means, e.g. by theft, he may be liable to a holder in due course. Payment must be to the holder and by the drawee or acceptor, as party ultimately liable on the bill. Thus if an indorser or the drawer pays on the bill it is not discharged and actions may be raised on it. If the bill is payable to or to the order of a named third party and the drawer pays on it he retains a right of recourse on the bill and may use the bill to enforce payment against the acceptor, but he may not reissue the bill. An indorser who pays on the bill regains all his former rights and may sue the acceptor or any party prior to himself and against whom he has a right of recourse. He may also strike out his own and subsequent indorsements and renegotiate the bill. A bill payable to the drawer's order and paid by him as an indorser may be similarly treated.[85]

One case in which payment by a person other than the drawee or acceptor discharges the bill and the other parties is where an accommodation bill[86] is paid in due course by the party accommodated. His payment, which is that of the original debtor, discharges the bill, no matter in what capacity he is a party to the bill.

Methods of discharge of a bill other than by payment are:

Acceptor Becomes Holder: Where the acceptor becomes holder of the bill in his own right at or after its maturity the bill is discharged.[87] This provision does not apply to an acceptor for honour.[88]

Renunciation or Waiver: The holder of a bill at or after its maturity may renounce his rights against the acceptor. Such a renunciation, if unconditional and absolute, discharges the bill. The renunciation must be in writing, or the bill must be delivered to the acceptor. If the renunciation is in writing it must record the absolute and unconditional renunciation of the holder's rights on the bill—a memorandum made by the holder to the effect that the bill is to be destroyed when it is found is not sufficient although if a letter, expressing an intention to renounce rights in the bill, were in the possession of the acceptor that could prove that a subsequent hand-

---

[85] s. 59(2)(*b*).
[86] *infra* p. 173.
[87] s. 61.
[88] s. 68(5).

ing of the bill to the acceptor was made with the intention that the rights of the holder be waived.

Where there is renunciation its effect is to release the acceptor from all liability on the bill to the holder or to anyone claiming through him.

It is possible that the holder of the bill renounce it conditionally. Where this is done there is no renunciation until the condition is implemented and although the holder may, in such circumstances be barred from enforcing the bill, he is not prevented from negotiating it to a new holder, who is not affected by the disability, which is personal of his predecessor, and may enforce his rights whether the condition be purified or not.

The liability of any party to a bill may also be renounced by the holder before, at, or after, its maturity; but a holder in due course who does not have notice of the renunciation would not be bound by it. When a specific person is released by a holder, the holder also automatically releases all parties subsequent to that person who had a right of recourse against the party thus released. Again a holder in due course who takes the bill after such a waiver is bound by that waiver only if he has notice of it.

Cancellation: A holder may cancel the bill, and if he does so intentionally and on the face of it, the bill is discharged. Similarly any party may be released from liability in the bill by the holder cancelling his signature, which has the effect of discharging that party and also all the parties who had a right of recourse against him.[89] Subsequent holders have notice of the cancellation by inspection of the bill and are bound by it.

A cancellation made unintentionally, or under a mistake, or without the authority of the holder, is inoperative; but where a bill or any signature on it appears to have been cancelled, the burden of proof lies on the party who alleges that the cancellation was made unintentionally, or under a mistake, or without authority.[91]

Material Alteration: A material alteration to a bill or to the acceptance made without the assent of all the parties to the bill avoids the bill except as against the party who made, authorised, or assented to it, and subsequent indorsers; provided that where a bill has been

[89] s. 63(2).
[90] Wallace and McNeill *op. cit.* p. 171.
[91] *Warwick* v. *Roger* (1843) 5 M. and Gr. 340 and 373.

materially altered but the alteration is not apparent, and the bill is
in the hands of a holder in due course, such holder may avail
himself of the bill as if it had not been altered and may enforce payment of it according to its original tenor. An alteration is material
when it alters the business effect of the bill for business purposes,
namely, any alteration of the date, the sum payable, the time of
payment, the place of payment, and where the bill has been accepted
generally, the addition of a place of payment without the acceptor's
assent. Other material alterations are: the substitution of one
drawer for another, an alteration of the name of an indorsee, the
deletion of the acceptor's name and the substitution of another, the
conversion of a joint note into a joint and several one, the addition
of a new obligant on a joint and several note, the alteration of a place
where a bill was drawn so as to convert an inland bill into a foreign
bill.

A mere correction is not a material alteration, nor is the addition
of words which do not alter the effect of the bill as issued.

A bill may be altered before issue although after acceptance. In
such case the acceptor is liable only for the amount of the bill as
expressed when he adhibited his acceptance.

Prescription: By the Bills of Exchange (Scotland) Act 1772 a bill
of exchange ceases to be of force six years after the sum contained
in it became exigible. The effect of this prescription is to bar actions
or diligences founded on the bill; the holder of a bill which has
thus prescribed can collect his money only by proving by writ or oath
that the sum is due.

The prescriptive period runs from the date of maturity of the bill,
fixed date in the case of a time bill or from the expiry of the period
allowed if payable a certain period after sight or demand. In the
case of a demand bill the prescriptive period runs from the date of
the bill.

Under the terms of the Prescription and Limitation (Scotland)
Act, 1973, the obligations under a bill will prescribe after five years.
This has effect from July 25, 1976.

Dishonour of a Bill

In the case illustrated, the life of the bill has been uneventful;
the drawee accepted when asked to do so and paid promptly when
the bill was presented for payment. If he had failed to do either of
these things the bill would have been dishonoured.

A bill may be dishonoured by non-acceptance or by non-payment. *Dishonour by non-acceptance* occurs when the bill has been duly presented for acceptance and acceptance has been refused or cannot be obtained. The bill is also dishonoured by non-acceptance where presentment for acceptance was excused[92] and the bill has not been accepted.

Dishonour by non-payment occurs when a bill has been duly presented for payment and payment has been refused or where presentment for payment is excused and the bill is overdue and unpaid.

By whatever means the bill has been dishonoured the holder acts in the same way. His prime aim is to secure payment on the bill as soon as it appears that the party to whom he was directed to look is not going to pay. He therefore turns to the other parties liable on the bill and exercises his rights against them. His right of recourse against any of the other parties, and how he vindicates it, depends on his taking the appropriate steps on discovering that the bill is dishonoured or can be treated as such.

Notice of Dishonour

When a bill has been dishonoured notice of dishonour must be given to the drawer and to each indorser. Any party not given such notice is discharged from liability on the bill.[93] Notice of dishonour is formal notification[94] of the dishonour of the bill and is designed to alert a party receiving it that he has potential liability to the holder of the bill while preserving the rights of that holder against the parties receiving the notice. It does not matter that an omission to give notice has caused no injury to a party. Two points should be noted: where a bill is dishonoured by non-acceptance and notice of dishonour is not given the rights of a holder in due course subsequent to the omission are not prejudiced by the omission, and secondly where a bill is dishonoured by non-acceptance and due notice of dishonour is given, it is not necessary to give notice of a subsequent dishonour by non-payment unless the bill has in the meantime been accepted.

To be valid and effectual a notice of dishonour will comply with the following rules:

(1) It will be given by or on behalf of the holder, or by or on

---

92 *supra* p. 152
93 s. 48.
94 *Caunt* v. *Thomson* (1849) 18 L.J.C.P. 125.

behalf of an indorser, who at the time of giving it is himself liable on the bill. Notice of dishonour may be given by an agent, authorised to do so, either in his name or in the name of any party entitled to give notice.

(2) The notice may be given in writing or by personal communication, and may be given in any terms which sufficiently identify the bill and intimate that it has been dishonoured by non-acceptance or non-payment, as the case might be. It will intimate that recourse is claimed against the party to whom the notice is given. Whether the bill is sufficiently identified in all the circumstances is a matter of fact; for example, precise details would require to be given to a business house who might be a party to many bills, while fewer details would suffice in the case of individuals. If a written notice is insufficient it may be supplemented and validated by verbal communication.

A written notice need not be signed, while the return of a dishonoured bill to the drawer or indorser is deemed a sufficient notice of dishonour.

(3) The notice may be given as soon as the bill is dishonoured and must be given within a reasonable time thereafter. The time will not be considered reasonable, where the parties reside in the same place, if notice has not been despatched to reach the party the day after the day on which the dishonour took place, or, where the parties live in different places, if notice is not despatched by post on the day after the bill has been dishonoured. Non-business days are excluded in both cases.

(4) Where a party to a bill of exchange receives a notice of dishonour and wishes to preserve his own recourse against prior parties, he has after receipt of the notice of dishonour, the same period of time for giving notice to the prior parties that the holder has after the dishonour.

(5) A notice of dishonour duly addressed and transmitted by post is deemed to have been given, notwithstanding that it is not delivered.

(6) If a holder does not know the address of an indorser, he is entitled to time to make enquiries.

(7) While notice of dishonour should be given to any person against whom the right of recourse of the holder is intended

to be preserved, or to any person against whom the recipient of a notice of dishonour wishes to preserve his right of recourse, it may competently be given to his agent. Whether a particular agent is authorised and competent to receive such notice is a matter of fact: verbal notice given to a solicitor is insufficient, but notice to a businessman's clerk, given at his business premises, is sufficient. Where the drawer or indorser is dead and the party giving notice knows it, the notice should be given to a personal representative if such can can be found with reasonable diligence. It is thought that a notice sent to a drawer or indorser in ignorance of his death is sufficient. Where the drawer or indorser is bankrupt, notice may be given either to him or to his trustee. Where there are two or more drawers or indorsers who are not partners, notice must be given to each of them, unless one of them has authority to receive such notice for the others.

While great emphasis is laid upon the giving of timeous notice of dishonour, delay is excused where it is caused by circumstances beyond the control of the party giving notice, and not imputable to his default, misconduct, or negligence; when the cause of delay ceases to operate the notice must be given with reasonable diligence.

Notice of dishonour is dispensed with when, after the exercise of reasonable diligence it cannot be given to, or does not reach, the party against whom it is sought to serve it. If however before action is taken an address is discovered notice should instantly be served. The right to receive a notice of dishonour may be waived, expressly or impliedly. If waiver is claimed after the omission to give due notice it must have been done with full knowledge of the facts. As regards a drawer notice of dishonour is dispensed with where the drawee is a fictitious person, or a person not having capacity to contract, where the drawer is the person to whom the bill was presented for payment, where the drawee or acceptor is, as between himself and the drawer, under no obligation to accept or pay the bill, and where drawer has countermanded payments.

As regards an indorser notice of dishonour is dispensed with where the drawee is a fictitious person or a person not having capacity to contract and the indorser was aware of that fact at the time he indorsed the bill and where the indorser is the person to whom the bill is presented for payment, e.g., as where he becomes the executor of the acceptor.

Protest: When the bill is, on the face of it, a foreign bill the holder, as well as giving notice of dishonour, must also to preserve his right of recourse protest the bill. A failure to do so discharges the drawer and indorsers.[95] Protest is a formal step, the purpose of which is to provide proof of dishonour acceptable to a foreign court. Inland bills need not be protested only to preserve the right of recourse, but, if summary diligence is to be done, these bills must be protested.

Protest is achieved by first having the bill noted by a notary public. The notary presents the dishonoured bill for acceptance or payment[96] and when refused notes on the bill the date, the fact of non-acceptance or non-payment, his initials and the letters N.P. The bill may be noted for protest the day it is dishonoured or not later than the subsequent business day.[97] The usual memorandum of noting put on a dishonoured bill is:

31/12/75 Pnp (i.e. protest for non-payment) J.S.N.P.

31/12/75 Pnac (i.e. protest for non-acceptance) J.S.N.P.

If a notary cannot be found, a certificate attesting the dishonour may be given by a householder or substantial resident of the place. He does this by signing the certificate in the presence of two witnesses who also sign, and the certificate operates as if it were a formal protest of the bill.[98] It is doubtful whether a householder's certificate will form a warrant for summary diligence.[99]

The protest, a formal notarial certificate attesting the dishonour, is written by the notary. Based on the noting, it may be drawn up by the notary and signed by him at any time after the noting and yet may bear the date of the noting.[1] If summary diligence is to be done, the protest must be drawn up within six months of the noting.[2] The protest must contain a copy of the bill, the name of the person requesting the protest, the place and date of the protest, the reason for protesting the bill, the demand made on the drawee or acceptor and the answer given, or the fact that the drawer or acceptor could not be found.[3]

---

[95] s. 51.
[96] This is not strictly necessary. He may make the protest on the report of a trustworthy person.
[97] Bills of Exchange (Time of Noting) Act 1917.
[98] s. 94.
[99] Hamilton, Bills of Exchange p. 210.
[1] s. 51(4).
[2] Act of 1891, c. 20.
[3] s. 51(7).

A bill which has been protested for non-acceptance may be subsequently protested for non-payment.

Protest for Better Security: Where the acceptor of a bill becomes bankrupt or insolvent, or suspends payment before it matures, the holder may cause the bill to be protested for better security against the prior parties. In such case he has no right of recourse until the date of maturity and then only if refused payment.

Similarly, in Scotland, if during the currency of a bill a party liable on it is threatened with insolvency (*vergens ad inopiam*), the holder may obtain diligence and use inhibitions to prevent the obligant's heritable property being disposed of, or use arrestment to attach his moveable property. In such case a warrant for diligence is granted only when it is alleged that the obligant is threatened with insolvency, an allegation which the person applying for the diligence must prove.

Summary Diligence

One of the popular features of bills of exchange is the speed with which they can be enforced. The holder of a dishonoured bill may raise an ordinary action for payment in a court using the bill as a document of debt. Having obtained a decree of the court, he then does diligence, that is he orders to be carried out for him the procedures by which a court decree is enforced. More rapid and less expensive is the use of summary diligence, a remedy available only in Scotland,[4] whereby diligence can be done without the claim having first been established in court.

The remedy of summary diligence, first introduced in 1681, is open to the holder of a dishonoured bill who has had the bill protested and the protest registered in the Books of Council and Session in Edinburgh or in the books of the Sheriff Court having jurisdiction over the defender. An extract, that is a certified copy, of the protest is obtained and this extract is equivalent to a decree of the court. Diligence can be done upon it by virtue of a warrant for execution indorsed on it. It will be appreciated that the party against whom the diligence is to be done must be within the jurisdiction of the court.

To entitle the holder to use summary diligence, the bill must be on the face of it complete and regular; any irregularity such as alteration or any other defect will render the use of summary diligence

4 s. 98.

incompetent. The liability on the bill of the party against whom summary diligence is to be used must be clear from the face of the bill itself. The bill must have been noted and a protest drawn thereon. The protest must be registered within six months after the date of the bill if the dishonour is by non-acceptance, and within six months of payment being due if the dishonour is by non-payment. Where a bill has been protested for non-acceptance, summary diligence is not competent against the drawee, his liability not having been established on the face of the bill. In the case of bills payable on demand, the period of six months begins to run from the date of the demand.

The warrant to do diligence contained in the extract may be enforced at any time before the prescription period has run on the bill.

Summary diligence cannot be done on a cheque.[5]

Liability of the Parties

The holder of a bill which has been dishonoured looks to the parties to the bill for compensation. Any of the parties can be held liable by virtue of their undertakings and, provided that the holder is a holder in due course and has taken the appropriate steps to preserve his right of recourse, he can proceed against any one he chooses. When the bill has been accepted, the acceptor is the principal debtor, the drawer and indorsers being practically cautioners for him. All are liable in payment to the holder who may recover from any one of them. An indorser who pays may in turn recover from prior indorsers or from the drawer. If the drawer has been compelled to pay he may recover from the acceptor.

When the bill has not been accepted, the primary liability belongs to the drawer. The disappointed holder can go against him or may choose any indorser who has backed the bill. An indorser who pays may turn to prior indorsers or to the drawer. Naturally the holder must bear in mind any restriction on liability which appears on the bill. Such a restriction is commonly placed by a party putting the words 'without recourse' beside his signature. Such a restriction is binding on all parties and naturally will be borne in mind by anyone to whom the bill is offered as it decreases the value of the bill by reducing the number of liable parties.

[5] *Glickman* v. *Linda* 1950 S.C. 18.

The amount which can be claimed when a bill is dishonoured is the amount of the bill, interest thereon from the time of presentment for payment, if the bill is on demand, and from the maturity of the bill in any other case. Where however the claim arises out of dishonour by non-acceptance interest runs only from the date of the maturity of the bill. The expenses of noting, and when protest is necessary and the protest has been extended, the expenses of protest are competently included in the claim.

The expenses of a protest for better security are not claimable.

Accommodation Bills

An accommodation bill is one in which one of the parties has signed a bill as drawer, acceptor or indorser without receiving value for doing so and for the purpose of lending his name to some other person. For example, the drawer of a bill may be indebted to the payee and the acceptor is acting as a cautioner for the timeous repayment of the debt; similarly, an acceptor might be the debtor of the payee and the drawer of the bill be the true cautioner. Suppose Smith wishes to borrow money from Brown. Brown is willing to lend but wants Smith to produce a cautioner and Smith persuades White to act in this capacity. Smith then draws a bill on White in favour of Brown payable at some future time and White accepts the bill, as a favour to Smith, to accommodate him. All three are aware of the arrangement. The principal advantage to Brown of this method of securing White as cautioner as opposed to other methods is that he has a negotiable instrument and if he himself needs money he can discount to some other party before he is entitled in time to collect this debt. He will also be able to use a summary diligence if the bill is not honoured.

Such a bill is known as an accommodation bill, sometimes called a 'wind bill' or a 'kite'; Smith is called the party accommodated, White the accommodation party. The Act provides[7] 'An accommodation party to a bill is a person who has signed a bill as drawer, acceptor or indorser, without receiving value therefor, and for the purpose of lending his name to some other person'.

Accommodation bills differ only slightly from ordinary bills. Any holder who has given value for the bill—this would include the

[7] s. 28.

original lender as well as subsequent holders and transferees who have taken for value but without indorsement[8]—can hold the accommodation party liable, whether he knows the bill to be an accommodation bill or not. Alternatively a holder who does know the true relationship represented by the bill may proceed against the party accommodated and is not barred from this course of action by failure to present the bill for payment,[9] failure to give notice of dishonour,[10] or failure to protest the bill.[11]

Naturally, if the accommodation party does pay on the bill, he can recover from the party accommodated, their true relationship being proved by parole evidence.[12] Accordingly where someone has accepted a bill and it is admitted or proved that the acceptance was given without valuable consideration he can free himself of a claim for relief by a drawer or indorser who has paid the bill by proving that he accepted it for such a person's accommodation.

The ordinary rule that payment by the drawer to a holder does not discharge the holder's claim against the acceptor, does not apply when the bill has been accepted for the accommodation of the drawer.[13]

Referee in Case of Need

The drawer or any indorser of a bill may write on the bill the name of a person to whom a holder may resort if the bill is dishonoured by non-acceptance or non-payment. Such a person is known as a referee in case of need. The holder, his bill dishonoured, need not resort to the referee in case of need unless he chooses to do so.[14] He may go ahead with the ordinary steps to be taken if the bill is dishonoured.

No particular form of words is necessary to appoint the referee in case of need provided that it is clear that such a person is to be resorted to only in case of need, and that he is not drawn upon alternatively or in succession to the drawees. The person who inserts the name of such a referee should specify for whose honour the referee is to accept or to pay. The position of the reference may show by

---

[8] *Hood* v. *Stewart* (1896) 17 R. 749.
[9] s. 46(2)(c).
[10] s. 50(2)(c)
[11] s. 51(g).
[12] s. 100; *McDonald* v. *Whitfield* [1883] A.C. 733.
[13] per Stephen J., *Solomon* v. *David*, 1 C. and E. 83; s. 59.
[14] s. 15.

implication for whose honour it is intended; as where it occurs below the signature of the drawer or of an indorser.

If the holder chooses to use the referee in case of need he must protest the bill before presentation to the referee in case of need.

Acceptor for Honour

When a bill has been protested for dishonour by non-acceptance any person not already a party to the bill can offer to act as acceptor. To do so he requires the consent of the holder and, if permitted, he signs the bill and assumes the liabilities of acceptor. An acceptor for honour is protecting the reputation, the honour, of some party to the bill for whom he acts and in the absence of contrary indication by him it is assumed that he intervenes on the part of the drawer. As well as his liability to the holder, the acceptor assumes liability to all parties subsequently to the party he represents.[15]

The obligation undertaken by the acceptor for honour is that he will pay on the bill provided that it has been presented for payment to the drawee, has been protested for non-payment and is presented to him without delay.

An acceptor for honour may offer his services when a bill has been protested for better security, as well as for non-acceptance.

It is essential that the bill should have been protested for until it has been, no one except the drawee can validly accept it.

Payment for Honour

When a bill has been protested for non-payment any person may intervene and pay for the honour of any party to the bill who is liable on it. Payment for honour must be attested by a notarial act of honour either written on the protest or attached to it. Payment for honour discharges all parties to the bill subsequent to the party for whom the payer intervened. The payer steps into the shoes of the holder, inheriting his rights and duties as regards the person for whose honour he paid and all parties liable to that person.

Where two or more persons offer to pay a bill for the honour of different parties, the person whose payment will discharge most parties to the bill is entitled to be preferred. Thus a payment for the honour of the acceptor is preferable to one for the honour of the

[15] ss. 65, 66.

drawer; and a payment for the honour of the drawer to one for the honour of an indorser, and one for a prior to a later indorser.

The payer for honour, on paying to the holder the amount of the bill and the notarial expenses incidental to its dishonour is entitled to receive both the bill itself and the protest.

If the holder of a bill refuses to receive payment for honour he loses his right of recourse against any party who would have been discharged by such payment.

Bills in a Set

A bill in a set is one bill drawn in duplicate or triplicate, the two or three documents together constituting a set. The reason for drawing bills in a set is to reduce the chance of loss in transit by dispatching each of the, say, three bills in different mails or by different routes to the payee. The bills are numbered and each refers to the others in the set. The first bill is called 'the first of exchange', the second 'the second of exchange' and so on.

The set, as long as each part is numbered and contains reference to the others, is treated as one bill[16] and discharge of the bill is procured by the payment of one of the set; similarly dishonour follows dishonour of one of the set. The obvious drawback of bills in a set is that the different parts will find their way into the hands of different people, and to regulate the relationships which might arise in these cases certain rules are provided in the Act.[17]

These rules are: (a) where the holder of a set indorses more than one part he is liable on each part he indorses as if the parts were separate bills; (b) the acceptance must be written on one part only; the drawee who accepts on more than one part is liable as if the separate parts were separate bills; (c) as between holders of separate parts of the same bill, the true owner is deemed to be the holder in due course whose title was complete first—but any party who accepts or pays on the part first presented to him is not affected by this rule; (d) if an acceptor of a bill in a set pays on a part not bearing his acceptance he will be liable to a holder who presents in due course the part bearing his acceptance.

Foreign bills are frequently drawn in a set; inland bills rarely are.

---

[16] s. 71.
[17] s. 71.

Lost Bills

A holder who loses a bill before it is overdue may ask, and indeed compel, the drawer to give him a bill of the same tenor. But as a condition of the issue of the duplicate bill the holder, if requested, must give security to the drawer to indemnify him against any claims should the lost bill be found and enforced against him,[18] as could be the case if a bearer bill or indorsed order bill were found and negotiated into the hands of a holder in due course.

Inchoate Bills

When a bill is incomplete in any material particular the person who has it may fill in the particular in any way he thinks fit.[19] Negotiated into the hands of a holder in due course, the bill is enforceable according to its tenor.

The most absolute form of inchoate bill is the blank bill. The Act provides[20] 'Where a simple signature on a blank stamped paper is delivered by the signer in order that it may be converted into a bill, it operates as a prima facie authority to fill it up as a complete bill for any amount the stamp will cover, using the signature for that of the drawer, or the acceptor or indorser.' Such a bill, in a question between the original parties, must be filled up within a reasonable time and strictly in accordance with the authority,[21] but if negotiated into the hands of a holder in due course is enforceable by him even if the authority is exceeded[22] or there was delay in filling it out.[23]

Value Received

The expression 'value received' is often found on bills. This expression serves no purpose whatever; its omission has no effect on the validity of the bill.

PROMISSORY NOTES

A promissory note is an unconditional promise in writing made by one person to another, signed by the maker, engaging to pay, on

---

[18] s. 69.
[19] s. 20; *Russell* v. *Banknock Coal Co.* (1897) 24 R. 1009.
[20] s. 20.
[21] s. 22.
[22] s. 84.
[23] s. 85(2).

M

demand, or at a fixed or determinable future time, a sum certain in money to, or to the order of, a specified person or to bearer.[24]

A promissory note must therefore contain a promise—although the word promise need not be used[25]—and may also contain a pledge of collateral security with authority to sell or dispose of it.[26] It must be delivered to the payee or bearer.[27] The obligation must be to a specified person or to bearer.

The drawer of the note is the maker and any other parties to it are indorsers. Under the Act [28] the maker of the note corresponds to the acceptor of a bill of exchange—which means his is the primary liability upon it—and the first indorser is deemed to correspond with the drawer of a bill. The maker's obligation is to pay on the note in the terms in which he issued it; he cannot, for example deny when asked to pay that his payee existed or had capacity to indorse.[29] His liability does not depend upon presentation for payment,[30] although if the note is payable at a particular place it must be presented there to render the maker liable.[31]

The indorser of the note is not liable on it until it has been presented for payment to the maker.[32] Also, if the note is payable on demand, presentation for payment must be made within a reasonable time if the indorser is to remain liable.[33] What constitutes a reasonable time depends on the nature of the note, usage of trade, and the facts of the case.[34] The rules dealing with due presentation, excuse for non-presentation and delay, and with protest are as for bills of exchange.[35]

A note may be drawn by two or more persons. Their liability on it depends on the tenor of the note,[36] but unless there is an indication to the contrary their liability is joint and several. Thus 'I promise to pay . . .' signed by two or more persons imports joint and several

[24] s. 83(1).
[25] Lillie op. cit. p. 217.
[26] s. 83(3).
[27] s. 84.
[28] s. 89(2).
[29] s. 88.
[30] s. 87(1).
[31] s. 87(2).
[32] s. 87(2).
[33] s. 86(2).
[34] s. 86(2).
[35] supra p. 161, 170.
[36] s. 85(1).

liability[37] and 'We promise to pay . . .' has the same meaning.[38]

Promissory notes are negotiable instruments[39] and all the provisions of the Bills of Exchange Act, with necessary modifications, apply to them. Summary diligence can be done on them and prescription applies to them.

IOUs

An IOU is not a promissory note, but merely an acknowledgement of indebtedness, implying an obligation to repay on demand. It is not a negotiable instrument, any assignation of it being achieved by formal deed and intimation to the granter of it. An IOU need not be addressed to any specific person nor does it attract stamp duty; it must, however, be holograph of the granter and be signed by him.

The usefulness of an IOU is as a document of debt which may be used as evidence in any action raised for repayment of the sum contained in it.

[37] s. 85.
[38] s. 97(2); Bell's *Princs.* s. 81.
[39] Act of 1704, 3 and 4 Anne c. 9.

CHAPTER SEVEN

CHEQUES

THE statutory definition of a cheque is: 'A bill of exchange drawn on a banker payable on demand'.[1] Thus cheques share all the characteristics of bills of exchange;[2] for example, they are orders, unconditional and in writing. A cheque must be signed by the drawer, the sum contained in it must be certain and in money, and it must be payable to or to the order of a specified person or to bearer. But in addition to the exhibition of these characteristics the cheque, as opposed to the bill of exchange, (1) must be drawn on a banker, and (2) can only be payable on demand, as opposed to, in the case of ordinary bills, possibly payable on a specified or calculable date.

The law regarding cheques is to be found in Part III of the Bills of Exchange Act, 1882 and the Cheques Act 1957, the two statutes to be construed as one, as interpreted and applied by the courts, and, in addition, in the other parts of the Bills of Exchange Act since all the provisions of that Act[3] which apply to demand bills apply to cheques. Yet a cheque is not merely another species of bill, for there are many specialities arising out of the use of cheques and the relationships involved which distinguish cheques from bills.

The primary feature of a cheque is that it is drawn on a banker,[4] a person or body of persons, whether incorporated or not, who carry on the business of banking.[5] Two consequences flow from this: (1) a cheque does not require to be accepted, and in fact rarely is, as it is intended for payment, not for circulation; (2) a cheque is not really an order to a debtor to pay a third person the whole or any part of a debt owed. Strictly considered—and assuming the customer has a credit balance with the banker—the relationship will bear

[1] Bills of Exchange Act 1882, s. 73.
[2] *supra* p. 141.
[3] s. 73.
[4] *supra* p. 1.
[5] *supra* p. 1.

this interpretation but: 'It is more like an appropriation by the customer, i.e. the drawer to the payee of what is treated as ready money in the hands of the banker, as his agent. Hence the drawer in giving the order to the banker to appropriate to a creditor of the drawer, must be considered as the person primarily liable to pay; that is as the drawer of the cheque he is in reality the acceptor of it as a bill of exchange.'[6]

The Parties to a Cheque: The parties to a cheque are the same as the parties to a bill,[7] the drawee inevitably being a banker. However, neither the payee nor the banker need, in the ordinary course, sign a cheque and thus cannot be considered a party to it in the strict sense of that term. If for any reason either the payee or banker, or any other person, does sign the cheque, then he will become a party in the legal sense and incur the liability of a party to a bill. Anyone who draws a demand bill on a banker is drawing a cheque but, in practice, such bills are drawn by customers of a banker and for the sake of clarity, the drawer will be referred to as the customer, unless he draws the bill in some other capacity.

The Duties of the Customer

A customer in drawing a cheque must take reasonable and ordinary precautions against the unauthorised or forged alteration of the cheque. If he draws it carelessly so that the banker is misled, then the customer, not the banker, is liable for any loss which occurs as a result of the careless drawing of the cheque. Thus in the case of *London Joint Stock Bank* v. *MacMillan and Arthur*[8] a fraudulent clerk made out a cheque for £2 for signature by his employer. He did not write the amount in words and left a space in front of the number '2'. After the cheque was signed he raised the amount to £120, filled in the words accordingly, and obtained the money. The employer endeavoured to sue the bank for £118 claiming that the account had been wrongly debited. The claim did not succeed. In the case Lord Finlay said: 'It is beyond dispute that the customer is bound to exercise reasonable care in drawing a cheque to prevent the bank from being misled. If he draws a cheque in a manner which facilitates fraud, he is guilty of a breach of duty as between

---

[6] Lillie *op. cit.* p. 200.
[7] *supra* p. 143.
[8] 1918 A.C. 777.

himself and the banker, and he will be responsible to the banker for any loss sustained by the banker as a natural and direct consequence of this breach of duty.' A recent case further illustrates this point. In *Lumsden* v. *London Trustee Savings Bank*[9] the plaintiffs had permitted a cashier to draw cheques in such a way as that the cashier could alter the description of the payee after signature so as to enable him to pay the cheques into a bank account he held in a fictitious name. It was held that the plaintiffs were blameworthy and the claim which they made against the bank on sound legal grounds was reduced in value to reflect the fact that their own negligence contributed to the fraud.

It is a matter of opinion what constitutes negligence or carelessness. In the case of *Slingsby* v. *District Bank Ltd.*[10] a space was left by the drawer between the name of the payee and the words 'or order'. A fraudulent solicitor inserted in that space 'per Cumberbitch and Potts' (the name of his firm) and obtained payment of the cheque. It was held in the Court of Appeal that the drawer had not been negligent.

Where a cheque has been altered in some way the question of negligence is one of fact, to be decided only on a view of the cheque together with any evidence available as to the course of dealings between the parties; but it is clear from the decision in *London Joint Stock Bank* v. *MacMillan and Arthur* that the customer does bear a responsibility for what happens to a cheque between his signing it and its being presented.

If there is evidence of alteration on the face of a cheque the banker who pays on such a cheque does so at his own risk.

Forgery: Where the signature of the drawer is forged the bank must not pay on the cheque. By section 23 of the Bills of Exchange Act, 1882 a person cannot be liable as a drawer of a bill unless he signed it in that capacity. By section 24, where a signature is forged such signature is wholly inoperative; the banker cannot debit his customer's account because the cheque is not the customer's order. It does not matter how skilful the forgery might be; a banker has an absolute duty to recognise his customer's signature, and if he makes a mistake he must refund the money to the customer. The only defence open to a banker who has given effect to a forged cheque

---

[9] (1971) Lloyd's Rep. 114.
[10] [1932] I K.B. 544.

and is being asked to repay the money is that the customer is pre-cluded by his own actions from founding an action on the forgery. Thus in the English case of *Greenwood* v. *Martins Bank*[11] a wife had repeatedly forged her husband's signature to cheques. He knew of the forgeries but did not inform the bank. A few months later, following a matrimonial disagreement, the husband threatened to inform the bank of the forgeries and the wife committed suicide. The husband then sued the bank for the return of the monies paid under the forged cheques and it was held that he should not succeed as by his delay, until after his wife's death, he had prevented the bank from suing the wife under the law as it then stood. Thus he was barred from using the forgery against the bank. In the House of Lords it was stated: 'The deliberate abstention from speaking in those circumstances seems to me to amount to a representation to the respondents that the forged cheques were in fact in order, and assuming that detriment to the respondents followed, there were . . . all the elements of estoppel,' (the English term equivalent to personal bar). There is no Scottish case directly in point, although in the case of *McKenzie* v. *British Linen Company*[11a] silence by someone who had been warned that his signature appeared on a bill when that signature was forged was held not to bar him from repudi-ating liability on the bill. The decision in this case, which does not at first glance square with the Greenwood case, may turn on its facts; it must also be borne in mind that the person whose signature was forged in the Scottish case was not a customer of the bank. In *Greenwood* the judge, considering the banker/customer relationship said: 'The banker, if a cheque were presented to him which he rejected as forged, would be under a duty to report that to the customer to enable him to enquire into and protect himself against the circumstance of the forgery. That would involve a corresponding duty on the customer, if he became aware that forged cheques were being presented, to inform the banker in order that the banker might avoid loss in the future.'

Mutilated Cheques: Where there are signs that the cheque has been torn, there is a possibility that the drawer tore it with the intention of destroying it. The banker faced with such evidence that

---

11 [1932] 1 K.B. 371.
11a (1881) 8 R. (H.L.) 8.

he might not be carrying out the wishes of his customer should not
pay such a cheque.

The Duties of the Banker

A banker's first duty to his customer is to honour his cheques up
to the amount standing at his credit or to the limits of an agreed sum
to be drawn by the customer on overdraft. The cheque must be
presented within banking hours and within a reasonable time of its
being drawn.

The penalty for a banker who unjustifiably refuses to honour a
cheque is that he will be liable in damages to his customer for
breach of contract and injury to credit, the damages being made
up of actual loss, if any, incurred in the particular transaction and
compensation for loss of credit or reputation. A person who is in
business is entitled to recover substantial damages without pleading
or proving actual damage but a person who is not a trader is entitled
to recover only nominal damages for the wrongful dishonour of a
cheque unless he can prove actual loss.[12]

The banker's duty to honour cheques depends, of course, on the
customer being in funds; a banker is under no obligation to provide
an overdraft. If he has agreed to do so he cannot refuse to honour
a cheque drawn on the strength of the agreement, but the customer
is not entitled to assume, even if he had overdraft facilities in the
past,[13] that his cheques will be met beyond the actual amount
standing to his credit or the agreed limits of his overdraft facilities.

It is normally no difficult matter to ascertain whether the customer
is in funds or within the agreed limits of his overdraft and the banker
is entitled to a reasonable time to make the necessary entries in his
books; an error in making entries which led to dishonouring
cheques would render the banker liable to the customer if the cheques
should have been met. If a payment for a customer's credit has been
made at a branch other than the one at which the account is maintained, the customer's account is not due to be credited until advice
has been received at his branch of the payment, unless the customer
can show that the credit was not advised promptly.

A customer may keep several current accounts with the same bank,
perhaps at different branches. The banker will keep these accounts

---

[12] *Gibbon's* v. *Westminster Bank* 1939, 55 T.L.R. 888.
[13] *Ritchie* v. *Clydesdale Bank* (1886) 13 R. 866.

separately but is entitled to mass them to ascertain the customer's credit balance.[14] Whether notice of this combination must be given to the customer is unclear but, where the accounts are of a different nature, say a deposit account and a current account, notice must be given before the accounts are combined.[15] The customer who keeps several accounts cannot draw a cheque on one account in reliance on a credit balance in another but he can transfer monies from one account to another. If a banker has been in the habit of honouring cheques relying on the combined balances of two accounts he cannot stop doing so without notice to the customer. The banker who does this is relying on his right of set-off, which is available only when the funds are held in the same right by the customer. Similarly, if accounts are kept at different branches the banker may rely on the balances held in other branches in deciding whether or not to honour a cheque. He need not do this but, if he has been in the practice of doing so, again he must not discontinue this practice without warning his customer.

When the customer has accounts with different branches care must be taken, when cheques are presented, that they are being presented to the correct branch. Thus in the case of *Burnett* v. *Westminster Bank Ltd.*[16] the customer had two accounts with the bank at different branches. Using the cheque book from one branch, but wishing to have the amount of the cheque debited to his account in the other branch the customer altered the name of the paying branch in ink. Later he stopped payment of the cheque, advising this to the branch on whom he had drawn the cheque by altering the printed form. Via the bank's mechanical sorting system the cheque was presented to the branch which had issued the cheque book, the alteration not being noticed, and the cheque was met. The customer claimed that his account had been wrongly debited on the basis that his instructions had not been followed. It was held that the bank had wrongly honoured the cheque and that the instructions on the cheque book cover were not a sufficient alteration of the previous practice and contract between the customer and bank to bind the customer not to alter his cheques. It may be that the use of magnetised cheques is now sufficiently accepted that this case would not be followed.

14 *Garnett* v. *McKewan* (1872) L.R. 8 Ex. 10.
15 *Kirkwood* v. *Clydesdale Bank* 1908 S.C. 20.
16 [1965] 3 All E.R. 81.

A further possible manipulation by the customer is to deposit cash in an overdrawn account to meet specific cheques he has issued. If he does this it must be by arrangement with the banker who is then bound to meet the cheques; in the absence of such special bargain the banker may choose to use the cash to reduce the debit balance and then refuse to honour the cheques. Another possible problem is where a customer has deposited effects, cheques and drafts, in his account and cheques have been presented. The banker must then decide whether to honour or dishonour the cheques while the effects remain uncleared. He has no obligation to honour cheques against uncleared effects but if he has been in the habit of so doing he must give warning to his customer that he will discontinue this practice.

A banker is not entitled to retain his customer's money unless he has a right of set-off against the customer. Set-off may only be exercised where the debt owed by the customer is ascertained and liquid. Thus if there is a dispute between customer and bank as to the liability of the customer to the bank there is no right of set-off. Thus in the case of *King* v. *British Linen Co.*[17] the bank, believing the customer to owe them money, which was disputed by the customer, decided to retain the funds at the customer's credit and dishonour cheques drawn by the customer before notice was given to him of its intention to do so. The bank was held liable in damages for injury to its customer's credit.

Dating of Cheques: A banker should not honour a cheque which is undated, a precaution which reflects the possibility that, although the drawer had made out the cheque, he did not intend to issue it. A cheque is not issued until the drawer parts with it to a third party with the intention that the proceeds shall be paid to or to the order of that person or to bearer according to how the cheque is drawn. Thus if the customer were to deny issue, the banker would have to show that the cheque had been issued. The practice of bankers of not honouring undated cheques was approved in *Griffiths* v. *Dalton*[18] (although the case was decided on other grounds). An undated cheque is, however, valid (s. 3(4)(a)) and any person in lawful possession of a cheque may put on a date, subject to any limitations on his authority to do so (s. 20). In *Griffiths* v. *Dalton* the holder of

17 (1899) 1 F. 928.
18 [1940] 2 K.B. 264.

an undated cheque filled in a date eighteen months after being given an undated cheque, and it was held that the right of a holder to complete an inchoate bill lasted only a limited time and that, in the circumstances of that case, eighteen months was not a reasonable time. A banker has, under section 20, the right to fill in a date but doing so does not protect him from a claim that the cheque had not been issued.

Post-dated Cheques: The honouring of a post-dated cheque before its due date is not fulfilling the customer's mandate and his account cannot be debited with the amount of the cheque until the stated date. Anything—the death, the bankruptcy of the customer, a countermand—which would preclude the honouring of the cheque at its date, would cause loss to the banker who had paid before the date. A post-dated cheque can be negotiated before its date.

Stale Cheques: Like other bills of exchange a cheque prescribes under the sexennial prescription. Like demand bills, however, it should be presented for payment or negotiated within a reasonable time and in any event, even if it has been negotiated from hand to hand within periods which could be reasonable as far as each party is concerned; it must be appreciated that a cheque is drawn with the intention that it should be presented for payment, not endlessly negotiated. Against this background there has arisen a custom of bankers in Scotland to regard cheques which are presented six or more months after their date as 'stale' and to refuse payment without confirmation of the cheque from their customer.

Signatures: The banker is not fulfilling his mandate if he honours cheques signed other than in the style agreed with the customer. Any irregularity in signing, e.g. the signing by fewer trustees than stipulated, should cause the rejection of the cheque. Any loss caused through a failure to reject such a cheque would fall on the banker.

Alterations in a Cheque: The customer's duty to prevent alterations in a cheque has been discussed; a banker should not pay on a cheque on which there appears material alterations unless these have been made with the drawer's assent.

Words and Figures: It is not a requirement of law that the sum in a cheque should be expressed both in words and figures. The only direction of the law in this is contained in section 9(2) of the Act: 'where the sum payable is expressed in words and also in figures, and there is discrepancy between the two, the sum denoted by the words is the amount payable'. There is no legal justification for the practice of rejecting cheques on the grounds that the sum is not stated in words, except perhaps that it is part of the contract between banker and customer that the customer should fill in his cheque in a normal manner, and in a manner which would not facilitate fraud. The ease with which figures can be altered is the reason for the suspicion of bankers of cheques which do not bear the sum in both words and figures.

Many organisations have reached agreement with their bankers to enable the issue of cheques by machine. A banker may require an indemnity in such cases.

Non-transferable Cheques: If the drawer does not wish his cheque to be transferred he may indicate on the face of it that he intends payment to be made only to the stipulated payee. This can be done by the addition of the word 'only' after the payee's name, the alternative instruction 'or order' being deleted by the drawer, or it may be done by writing 'not transferable' on the face of the cheque. A cheque thus drawn must not be honoured by the banker on whom it is drawn if there is any evidence that the cheque has been transferred.

This rule increases the duties of the banker and some banks do not permit the issue of non-transferable cheques.

Lost Cheques: When the holder of a cheque has lost it he does not lose his rights in it against the drawer or any prior party. By the Act[19] he may compel the drawer to give him another cheque in identical terms, provided that he is prepared to indemnify the drawer against any claim which may be made should the lost cheque be found again. Should a lost cheque come into the hands of a person who is a holder in due course, that person will have a valid claim against the drawer and any other prior party to the cheque. The banker on whom such a cheque is drawn is not affected by the losing of the cheque unless he had received, as will usually be the case, a countermand of the lost cheque. If the countermand is valid he must give effect to it. If no countermand has been received he must honour the cheque in the normal course.

Account Payee

Another frequent addition to crossing is that of 'account payee', or 'account payee only'. This addition is a direction to the collecting

[19] s. 69.

banker that the money must be credited only to the account of the named payee.

Cheques as Evidence of Payment

An unindorsed cheque which appears to be paid by the banker on whom it is drawn is evidence of the receipt by the payee of the sum payable by the cheque.[20]

Certified Cheques and Bankers' Drafts

A banker who certifies a cheque certifies simply that at the time of the certification the customer has sufficient funds to meet the cheque. Certification does not amount to acceptance and it has not yet been settled whether the banker would be liable, if the cheque were not met, on the grounds that he represented that it would be.

A banker's draft is an instrument drawn by the banker on himself in favour of a payee nominated by his customer. The advantage to the payee is that he knows that the bank is liable to pay on the draft. The use of drafts has largely superseded that of certified cheques. Drafts are entitled to the statutory privileges of cheques.[21]

Receipts on Cheques

Some customers wish to have a form of receipt from the payee incorporated on their cheques. The legal consequences of this can be important to the banker who is handling a cheque, and these depend on the form which the cheque takes.

If the form of the cheque is: 'Pay . . . or order, on the attached receipt being signed,' or a similar form, the document is not a cheque at all as it is not an unconditional order as required by the statutory definition. The decision in *Bavins Junior and Sims* v. *London and Southwestern Bank*[22] to this effect was based on such a wording as is given would be valid in application to any wording which imposed a clear condition on the bankers concerned in the collection and paying of the cheque. It is normal for the paying banker to take from his customer who wish to issue such cheques an indemnity against loss to himself which indemnity would put him in the same position as if he had paid on a cheque. The collecting banker by virtue of the terms of the Cheques Act, 1957 (ss. 1 and 4) may have the same

[20] Cheques Act 1957, s. 3.
[21] *ibid.* ss. 4(*d*) and 5.
[22] 1 L.B.B.

protection as if these instruments were cheques but it is considered that such protection might be lost should there be evidence of such an instrument having been transferred; thus a collecting banker should handle such instruments only for the named payee.

Instruments of this type are normally identified by having printed on them a bold 'R'.

If the wording on the cheque is an instruction to the holder rather than a condition placed on the paying banker, the unconditional nature of the instrument is not affected, it remains a cheque and the banker's position is protected.

The Third Parties Involved

The obvious third party involved in the transaction is the payee of the cheque. He is entitled, assuming no prohibition on the face of the cheque, to negotiate the cheque thus becoming an indorser and involving an indorsee in the transaction. The indorsee may or may not be a banker.

The principal obligation of the holder of a cheque is to present it for payment within a reasonable time. Undue delay on his part which prejudices the drawer will entitle the drawer to deduct any loss from the amount of the cheque. Thus if a payee delays in presenting a cheque until after the banker suspends payment he will be entitled to recover from the drawer of the cheque not the amount of the cheque but any dividend paid to the drawer on that amount on the bank's liquidation. If the cheque had been presented timeously the sum would have not been in the possession of the bank and the drawer would have been a creditor of the bank for that amount less.

An indorsee similarly should not hold a cheque but in the event of his being refused payment he may, as a holder in due course sue the drawer of the indorser. If payment is refused on a cheque there arises the question of whether or not notice of dishonour to the drawer and prior parties is required. By the Act[23] the drawer of the cheque is entitled to notice of dishonour but such notice is excused in the following cases: (a) where there was between the banker and the drawer no obligation to pay the cheque, e.g. through lack of funds and, (b) where the drawer has countermanded payment.

Otherwise all the rules regarding ordinary demand bills, their

[23] *supra* p. 167.

indorsement, their negotiation, and the rights and duties of the parties apply to cheques.

The right of the payee, or of an indorsee, assuming he acts in good faith, is to receive in due course payment on the cheque. If he does not receive this from the banker on whom the cheque is drawn he has recourse against the drawer or any other party liable on the cheque.

Cheques drawn to impersonal payees or payable to 'wages', or 'cash', are not strictly cheques, not being payable to a 'specified person' as required by the Act. They are however covered by the Cheques Act, 1957.[24]

Where the payee is not correctly described it is a matter of decision for the banker whether to meet the cheque or not. If no payee's name appears then the cheque must not be met as it is not payable to a 'specified person' and thus is not a cheque at all. However, bankers do tend to meet lazily drawn cheques and if it is quite clear to whom the customer intended payment to make the banker is safe in ordering such a cheque. Examples would be cheques payable to 'gas', 'electricity' or 'rates' all cases in which it is clear to which authority the customer intended payment to be made.

Banker as Holder of a Cheque

By section 2 of the Act 'the payee or indorsee of a bill or note who is in possession of it or the bearer thereof' is a holder of a cheque. Thus the banker who is in possession, or is the bearer of a cheque is a holder, the term merely implying possession.

Or more importance is that the banker may be in regard to a particular cheque a holder for value or a holder in due course.[25] A holder for value is the holder of a bill, which includes, of course, a cheque for which value has at any time been given. Thus a banker may be a holder for value of a cheque when he has cashed *for a customer* a cheque drawn on another bank, where the customer has the right to draw against cheques paid into his account or lodged for collection before they are cleared, where a cheque is paid in for the purpose of reducing an advance and where the banker has a lien on the cheque. A banker may also be a holder for value when he has cashed a cheque for a non-customer. In any case the banker who is a holder

24 s. 4.
25 *supra* p. 157.

for value, and more strongly if he is also a holder in due course, may proceed on his own behalf to recoup any losses which occur through the cheques not being met.

Crossed Cheques

A crossing on a cheque is the addition on its face of two parallel transverse lines.

The practice of crossing cheques grew out of the practice of London bankers who in 1775 set up the London Bankers' Clearing House, an establishment to which cheques given to bankers for collection by the customers could be taken and handed to the representatives of the bank on which the cheques were drawn.

To identify the cheques the clerks wrote across them the name of the bank handing them over for payment thus ensuring that a bank dishonouring a cheque would know to which bank it should be returned.

The practice was for bankers to send their cheques to the clearing house on the afternoon of the day after they had been given to them for collection and merchants, discovering this and its import—that they need not provide cash in their own bank until the day after they drew the cheque—began to write a banker's name on the cheque thus ensuring that it would go through the system. From this practice developed the habit of writing not the name of a banker but simply the words 'and company' or 'and co.' usually between two lines on the cheque. Bankers presented with such a cheque for payment would refuse to pay on it unless it was presented to them through a bank, the named bank if the cheque was crossed specially, i.e. with a specific bank named, or any bank if the crossing was general, i.e. without mentioning a particular bank.

This developing practice was statutorily recognised and the rules regarding crossing are now to be found in Acts of Parliament.[26]

As two bankers would be involved, they became termed the paying banker, i.e. the one on whom the cheque was drawn and the collecting banker, i.e. the one presenting for payment.

The General Effect of Crossing: A crossing on a cheque is a direction to the paying banker that he must pay only a banker and to the holder of the cheque that payment will be made only to a bank.

---

[26] 1882 Act ss. 76-81; Cheques Act 1957.

Types of Crossing: Only two types of crossing are recognised. A crossing is general if it is thus:[27]

A special crossing will look like this:[28]

In addition the words 'not negotiable' may be added. The effect of these words—which need not be between the lines—is considered later.

The crossing may be put on a cheque[29] by the drawer, by a holder or by the collecting banker. A general crossing may be altered to a special crossing by a holder or by a collecting banker.

The banker paying a crossed cheque must observe the crossing, paying only another banker and, in the case of a specially crossed cheque only the banker nominated in the special crossing; a failure to observe the crossing will involve the paying banker in liability for loss which may arise due to his not observing the crossing. Such failure will also rob him of the protection which is conferred on the paying banker who pays on a crossed cheque.[30]

If more than one crossing bearing bankers' names appear then the paying banker is bound by section 79 to refuse payment. If he pays

[27] 1882 Act s. 76(1).
[28] *ibid.* s. 76(2).
[29] s. 77.
[30] *infra* p. 194.

N

such a cheque, or if he pays a cheque to one banker which is specially crossed to another he will be liable. An exception to this rule occurs in the case of a cheque crossed by two bankers when one banker is the agent for collection of another. When a bank which is not a member of the clearing house wishes to have cheques collected it will do so via a bank which is a member and on delivering cheques for collection will cross these cheques. The relationship between such bank is that of principal and agent and the crossing stamps may appear on a cheque without offending against section 79.

Protection of the Paying Banker

A paying banker who pays on a crossed cheque in accordance with the crossing and does so in good faith and without negligence is entitled to debit his customer with the amount of the cheque.[31] He has protection against paying the wrong person should the cheque have been stolen or an indorsement on it have been forged.[32] If the banker ignores the crossing he is liable to the true owner of the cheque, except where the crossing has been obliterated or altered clandestinely and this is not apparent on the face of the cheque and the banker has paid in good faith and without negligence. In addition to the valuable protection thus offered the banker has further protections regarding indorsements of cheques.[33]

Protection of the Collecting Banker

The collecting banker's protection depends on the Cheques Act 1957. This Act[34] provides that the banker who collects on a cheque after having credited a customer with the amount of it or who receives payment of a cheque for a customer and subsequently discovers that the customer's title to the cheque was defective does not incur any liability to the true owner by reason only of having received payment of the cheque. This protection which applies both to crossed and uncrossed cheques, depends on two considerations. First, the relationship of banker and customer must exist; the holder of the cheque for whom the bank was collecting must have an account with the bank—a stranger for whom a bank cashes a

[31] s. 80.
[32] infra p. 195.
[33] infra p. 195.
[34] s. 4.

cheque is not a customer.[35] Second, the banker must have acted in good faith and without negligence so that if the circumstances warrant the bank suspecting that his customer is not the true owner the banker will lose the protection conferred by the Act.

According to section 90 'A thing is deemed to be done in good faith within the meaning of the Act, where it is, in fact, done honestly whether it is done negligently or not'. In ascertaining whether a banker is entitled to the benefits of the statutory protections it will be a question of fact whether he has acted in 'good faith', 'in the ordinary course of business' or 'without negligence'.

Further Protection for Bankers

Bankers enjoy further protection from the law regarding indorsements on cheques. These protections cover forged or unauthorised indorsements and irregularly or unindorsed cheques.

When a banker is presented with a cheque drawn on him and pays it in good faith and in the ordinary course of business he is deemed to have paid the cheque in due course, even though indorsements on it were forged or made without authority.[36]

Further the banker who in good faith and in the ordinary course of business pays a cheque drawn on him which is not indorsed or is irregularly indorsed does not in doing so incur any liability by reason only of the absence of indorsement or the irregularity of indorsement and he is deemed to have paid it in due course.[37]

The effect of these provisions does not allow the banker to ignore indorsements. If he does so, he does at his peril and there are certain circumstances, e.g. payment in cash, where failure to obtain an indorsement can prejudice the banker's right to recover.

With instruments which are analogous to cheques, dividend or interest warrants and payable at two or three banking offices, conditional drafts and bankers drafts drawn on themselves which are not cheques in that they cannot satisfy the statutory definition the provisions of the Cheques Act would not apply, save that they are specifically brought within the protection offered by the 1957 Act; but it must be borne in mind that the protection of that Act applies only to instruments which are not indorsed or are irregularly

---

[35] *supra* p. 3 et seq
[36] 1882 Act, s. 60.
[37] Cheques Act 1957, s. 1.

indorsed, not covering instruments which bear forged indorsements for which the banker relies on the parent statute. Thus in dealing with analogous instruments these protections are not apt.

'Without Negligence'

There are no cases in which banker's right to statutory protection has been challenged on the grounds that he did not act 'in good faith'. Cases have arisen as to whether or not the banker was acting for a customer[38] but the main ground of attack on bankers where there has been loss through the use, or misuse, of cheques and analogous instruments has been that the banker did not act 'without negligence'. The burden of proving that he acted 'without negligence' falls on the banker.

There is no statutory definition of negligence; what constitutes negligence can only be deduced from the decided cases, which, although indicative of the views of the courts, are by no means exhaustive of the wide variety of circumstances in which a duty is placed on the banker and he is called on to acquit that duty. Two generalities may be taken as the foundation of the duty of care: (1) the banker who is handling cheques must take reasonable precautions to safeguard the interests of the true owner of the cheque; (2) consequently, he may by circumstances be put on inquiry regarding a particular cheque and, if so, must make reasonable inquiry.

A definition which has been put forward as covering the cases already decided and which merits attention is: 'Negligence may be defined in this context as failure to make inquiry in cases when a reasonably competent cashier would make an inquiry, or, where such an inquiry has been duly made, failure to appreciate that the answer obtained is not a satisfactory one.' But, as was remarked by the judge in *Smith and Baldwin* v. *Barclays Bank Limited*[39] the banker is not a detective; when he has made such inquiries as circumstances would dictate to the prudent banker and has received answers which would satisfy a prudent banker he has acquitted his duty. It is a matter of fact as to what inquiries were called for or what would be sufficient answers. In the case of *Smith and Baldwin* v. *Barclays Bank Limited* it was held that the banker was entitled to rely on the information he had received in answer to his inquiries;

---

[38] e.g. *Woods* v. *Martin's Bank, supra* p. 4.
[39] (1944) Jo. Inst. of Bankers 65, 171.

in the case of *Baker* v. *Barclays Bank Limited*[40] it was held that the banker should not have accepted the explanations he received when he made his inquiries.

Cases in which negligence has been held include:

References: it is negligence not to take up references at the time when account is opened or to fail to check them.[41]

Employer's Cheques: It is negligent for a banker to collect without inquiry cheques payable to or drawn by the customer's employer.[42] A banker should know who a customer's employer is when an account is opened although there is English authority that it is not the bank's duty continually to keep itself up to date as to the identity of the employer's of all its customers.[43]

Company Cheques: The proper place for cheques drawn in favour of a limited company is in the company's account. Thus in *A. L. Underwood Ltd.* v. *Bank of Liverpool and Martins Ltd.*[44] the bank made no inquiries on receiving cheques payable to a company but indorsed by the sole director and chief shareholder and paid into his own account. It was held that the circumstances put the bank on inquiry. In an analogous case, *Hannans Lakeview Central Ltd.* v. *Armstrong & Co.*[45] the collecting bank was held to be negligent in collecting for its customer cheques payable to the company and indorsed by him on its behalf as Secretary. The customer had authority to indorse on behalf of the company but the court held that he had no authority to pay cheques so indorsed to the credit of his personal account.

Partnership Cheques: Cheques payable to a partnership should not be collected without inquiry on behalf of a partner's private account[46] nor is the banker entitled to assume that all is in order if a customer presents for the credit of his own account a cheque drawn on his firm and signed by himself.

Per Pro Cheques: When a customer presents for the credit of his private account cheques drawn by himself per pro someone else the banker is put on inquiry. Thus in *Morison* v. *London*

---

[40] [1955] 2 All E.R. 571.
[41] *Ladbrook* v. *Todd* [1914] All E.R. 1134.
[42] *Savory and Co.* v. *Lloyd's Bank Ltd.* [1932] 2 K.B. 59.
[43] *Orbit Mining and Trading Co.* v. *Westminster Bank Ltd.* [1963] 1 Q.B. 794.
[44] [1924] 1 K.B. 775.
[45] (19600) 16 T.L.R. 236.
[46] *Bevan* v. *National Bank* (1906) 23 T.L.R. 65.

County and Westminster Bank Ltd.[47] the banker was collecting cheques signed per pro by the customer drawn on his employer's account coupled with the knowledge of the banker that the customer was the manager of the employer's affairs was held to be sufficient to put the banker on inquiry. In the case of *Lloyd's Bank Ltd.* v. *Chartered Bank of India, Australia and China*[48] it was held that the suspicions of a banker should have been aroused when the customer was paying into his own account cheques signed by himself and another official on behalf of his own employers. Defendants knew that their customer was an employee of the chartered bank and was transferring large sums of money from the chartered bank to his own account.

Cheques to Official and Trustees: A cheque payable to an official in his official capacity should not be collected on behalf of that official in his private capacity without inquiry. The same rule applies when cheques are drawn to someone in a fiduciary capacity. Nor should the account of a third party be credited with cheques so drawn.

It is negligent to collect a cheque crossed 'account payee' for any account other than that of the payee[49] or to collect cheques not consistent with the payee's station in life[50] or cheques not consistent with the description given of his occupation by the customer at the time of the holding of the account. In the latter two cases questions must be asked if the banker is to escape the charge that he acted negligently.

Termination of Banker's Authority

The Act[51] provides that the duty and authority of the banker to pay a cheque drawn on him is determined, or terminated, by a countermand of payment or by a notice of the customer's death.

Countermand: Countermand is an instruction to the banker not to pay on a cheque which has been issued and may be made by the customer by any means, orally or in writing. Should the countermand have been made otherwise than in formal writing the banker should

---

47 [1914] K.B. 356.
48 [1929] 1 K.B. 40.
49 *House Property Co. of London* v. *London County and Westminster Bank* (1915) T.L.R. 479.
50 see *Lloyd's Bank Lt.* v. *Chartered Bank of India etc. supra.*
51 s. 75.

insist that his instruction be confirmed in writing by the customer. In the case of *Curtice* v. *London City and Midland Bank Ltd.*[52] the House of Lords suggested that they were not satisfied that a banker was bound to act on a telegram countermanding payment.

The responsibility of ensuring that the banker is informed of the intention to countermand the instruction contained in the cheque lies on the customer. Thus in *Curtice* v. *London City and Midland Bank Ltd.* the telegram stopping payment of a cheque lay in the banker's letter-box unnoticed until after the cheque had been paid. It was held that the countermand was not effective until the telegram came into the manager's hands.

To be effective any countermand must sufficiently identify the cheque. Thus in the case of *Westerminster Bank* v. *Hilton*[53] the customer in his countermand gave the wrong number for the cheque which he wished to stop. The cheque was also post-dated, a fact which the customer omitted to mention. The bank paid the cheque on presentation and it was decided that the bank was entitled to assume that the number of the cheque as stated in the telegram was that of the cheque intended to be stopped and as the instructions were not clear so as to render the bank liable for negligence the action against the bank should fail. The right of a drawer to stop payment of a cheque continues up to the last moment when payment must be made or refused by the banker, normally the close of business on the day of presentment of the cheque. If, however, the banker has indicated to the presenter that the cheque has been honoured before that time the cheque is met and countermand thereafter is ineffective.

A countermand by one partner of a cheque signed by another is effective and similarly where there are several signatories required on a cheque a withdrawal required by one signatory of his authority to pay withdraws the banker's mandate to meet the cheque. In the case of a company a countermand by one director or by the secretary of the company is effective to stop payment of a company cheque.

If a cheque has been effectively countermanded and yet the banker has paid it the loss falls on him; he cannot debit his customer's account nor can he look to the person who received the money for repayment, provided that the recipient has acted in good faith.

52 1908 1 K.B. 239.
53 (1926) 43 T.L.R. 124.

Notice of Death: Notice or knowledge of the death of a customer ends the banker's authority to meet cheques, although once again he must retain funds to meet cheques presented to him. In ascertaining what funds are available, the balance of all the customer's accounts must be considered. It is to be noticed that the death of the drawer does not, of itself, operate as a revocation of the banker's authority and payment of a cheque subsequent to the customer's death but before the banker has had reasonable time to inform himself of the death will be valid.

Analogous to the death of the customer are notice of the customer's sequestration,[54] the granting of a Trust Deed by the customer or of his certification. In the last case the banker should not consider his authority to be withdrawn through the mental disorder of a customer until the facts make it obvious that the customer's unsoundness of mind is of the nature as would withdraw the authority; his confinement in a mental hospital or certification, or the appointment of a curator on his estate would justify the banker in refusing to meet cheques.

Arrestment: The receipt of an arrestment which attaches the funds held by the banker also terminates the banker's authority to meet cheques issued by the customer[55] unless he is prepared to allow an overdraft as the customer has lodged funds subsequent to the arrestment to permit payment of cheques.

---

[54] *infra* p. 312.
[55] *infra* p. 296.

CHAPTER EIGHT

THE LAW OF PROPERTY

THE law of property can be described as the area of the law concerned with the legal rights of persons in respect of things, material and immaterial, which can be enforced against the world at large. A layman will use the word property to denote ownership, or, sometimes to describe something which is owned, a common example of which is to describe a man's 'property' meaning something he owns. But in law a man's property is not merely that which he owns but that in which he has a right of property which, while including ownership, also includes other rights such as subsidiary rights in land which fall short of ownership, possession, the rights of a security holder, or limited rights of use or enjoyment. The identifying feature of a property right is that it should be recognised by, and can be defended against the whole world; it is a right *in rem*, a right in something, not a right *in personam*, one which can be vindicated only against a particular person. Thus if a house is sold the purchaser has a right under the contract instantly the bargain is duly made against the seller to complete the bargain and transfer the right of ownership in the house; only however when the transfer is completed has the purchaser a *ius in rem*, sometimes called a real right in the house. Until that time emerges his rights are personal against the seller. The emergence of a real right occurs at an ascertainable point in time, a time which can be of great importance if there is dispute as to the ownership or competition between someone claiming a right in property against the purchaser of it. When the real right is constituted varies with circumstances and with the nature of the property and is dealt with later in this chapter.

Corporeal and Incorporeal Property

The things in which rights of property may be established may or may not have physical existence; for example, a debt may form an important part of a creditor's estate. A classification of the objects of property can be made using that distinction as its basis. Under the heading of material things might be land, buildings, furniture, tools, stock in trade while that capable of ownership without material existence encompasses rights of all descriptions, rights in land, for example, the right of a security holder, debts, copyright, patents or the right of a holder of an insurance policy. The fact of corporeal existence of a particular thing, or the fact of the incorporeal nature of rights, strictly so called, has led to the evolution and development of different rules in the law of property dealing with these different objects of property and, to that extent the distinction is important.

Heritable and Moveable Property

In Scots law another distinction made in classifying the objects of property is between those which are heritable and those which are moveable. This method of classification is of greater importance but co-exists with the previous classification.

Heritable property includes all subjects naturally immoveable, land, minerals in land, trees and crops as they grow upon land, buildings and fixtures attached to a building. Such are corporeal heritable subjects. Heritable property also includes incorporeal rights such as the right of a feudal superior,[1] or the right of a landlord to collect rent, although unpaid arrears of rent are deemed paid and form part of a man's moveable estate.[2]

Moveable in law are things moveable physically, which is a matter of fact. Also included in the classification of moveable property are incorporeal rights not connected with heritable subjects, such as debts and undertakings to pay money including those secured on heritage,[3] shares in companies and government and local authority stocks and loans. Many other intangible rights are moveable.

Whether a particular subject of property is corporeal or incorporeal, heritable or moveable, is of significance in several ways: the legal rights which may exist in relation to it, how it may be acquired or disposed of, how title to it is completed, how diligence is done against it, and the rights of succession in it on the proprietor's death all depend on the nature of the property. For example where goods[4] are sold the right of property in them pass

---

[1] *infra.* p. 212
[2] Wardlaw's Trs. Wardlaw (1880) 7 R. 1070.
[3] Erk. II. 2, 8; Bell *Princs.* 1479.
[4] defined, Sale of Goods Act 1993, s. 64.

when the parties intend it to pass[5] independent of delivery or physical transfer, while a right of property in heritable subjects does not pass until a formal conveyance of it has been executed and delivered to the purchaser and the real right of the person in whose favour that conveyances is drawn does not emerge until the conveyance is registered in the General Register of Sasines, the property registers for Scotland.

Heritable Securities: Where money has been lent and its repayment secured over heritage or where any bond to pay money is secured by a disposition of heritage in security or by any real burden upon heritage such assets were at common law, because of their connection with land, deemed heritable in the succession of the creditor. By statute[6] such assets are deemed to be moveable except when calculating the legal rights of children[7] when they are excluded from aggregation with other moveable property to ascertain the funds available to meet these legal rights.[8]

By the Succession (Scotland) Act, 1964, s. 14, the whole of an estate vests in an executor for the purposes of administration but heritable debts and annuities are payable out of heritable estate in preference to moveable estate.

Real Burdens: A debt payable from and attaching as a burden to land, not necessarily exigible as a personal obligation from the proprietor of that land for the time being, is a real burden. Any such debt, a ground annual, an annual payment due from lands, is an example, is moveable in the creditor's succession. Feu duties and rents, which are not usually real burdens but arise from personal obligations are heritable, although arrears are deemed paid and are moveable.[9]

Fittings and Fixtures: It is a principle of Scots law that anything built on land, affixed to it or planted in it, becomes part of the land. Thus when seeds are sown or paint applied to a building something essentially moveable by its nature becomes part of heritable subjects. This is not merely a matter of curiosity; questions of importance regarding items of great value may arise out of the application of this rule. There can be contest in several circumstances as to whether

---

5 *ibid.* s. 16.
6 Titles to Land Consolidation (Scotland) Act, 1868, s. 117.
7 *Bell's Trs.* v. *Bell* (1884) 12 R. 85.
8 *infra* p. 226.
9 Walker Principles of Scottish Private Law, p. 1156 *et seq.*

a particular piece of property has become part of heritable property by attachment, or accession, or whether the moveable property remains moveable. Such occasions are: where different parties are entitled to succeed to the heritable and moveable elements of an estate, where a purchaser and the seller of heritable property may disagree as to what precisely has been purchased and should thus pass to the buyer, where in a bankruptcy or liquidation, a heritable creditor is asserting his rights to property which the general creditors think is theirs by right, and where there is a dispute between a life renter and a fiar,[10] and where at the expiry of a lease the tenant wishes to take with him things which he has installed which the landlord may claim to be his by right. The extent of the heritage can also be of importance in cases regarding valuation for rateable purposes and concerning the valuation of subjects for security purposes.

In determining whether anything is a heritable fixture or not three criteria are usually applied, the degree of attachment, the purpose of the attachment, and the relationship of the contesting parties.

The question of degree of attachment is usually resolved by consideration of whether the article is so fixed that it cannot be removed without damage to itself or to the heritage,[11] although an answer in favour of removal without damage is not conclusive if the article is substantial and has been in its place for a substantial period[12]— for example machinery attached only by its weight may be a fixture.[13] Articles, such as keys, themselves moveable are fixtures as they are considered to be adapted to be used with particular heritage and would not be as useful elsewhere. This principle applies also to other articles designed for use with particular heritage although the degree of annexation is not high.[14] Moveable items may become heritable or fall to be treated as heritable by declaration of the owner.

The second material question in determining the question of whether a particular piece of moveable property has become heritage or not is that of the purpose of the annexation. Was the article attached so that it might be better enjoyed or for the improvement of the heritage? If the purpose of the attachment was the

---

[10] *infra* p. 240.
[11] Bell's *Princis.*, 1473.
[12] *Christie* v. *Smith's Ex.* 1949 S.C. 572.
[13] *Brand's Tr.* v. *Brand* (1878) 5 R. 607.
[14] *Fisher* v. *Dixon* (1845) 4 Bell 286.

improvement of the heritage then the article would be treated as a fixture and thus not be removeable, having lost its moveable character.

The relationship of the parties in dispute can be of relevance also in adjudicating whether or not a particular article can be removed. In the case of dispute between successors of a common ancestor,[15] or between heritable creditor and general creditor[16] and seller and purchaser[17] the court will generally lean in favour of the article remaining with the heritage. It is competent in the case of sale to provide specifically in the missives for the removal of fixtures, as in any other contract between parties who might be in competition but, in the latter case, for example as between landlord and tenant, the rights of a *bona fide* third party, such as a purchaser of the heritable property or a heritable creditor, will not be effected by this bargain unless the third party was a party to it.

An inference in favour of removal exists where the parties are landlord and tenant, particularly so when the fixtures are made by the tenant for the purposes of his business[18] while articles attached by a life renter can usually be removed when the limited right expires.[19]

Destination: Property of any character may become of another by destination, the determination of the proprietor that this is to be the case, deduced from his actions or declarations. Thus where building materials are brought to a building site for use their character is heritable[20] while books jewels and furniture may be declared to be heritable in succession.[21] This change in character by destination is effective only in succession, not in of the claims of creditors. Any right may be thus changed, personal bonds may be drawn to exclude their aggregation in moveable estate[22] while on the basis that the intention of the proprietor is paramount, land sold but not paid for is moveable in succession[23] and money to be paid for land not yet conveyed to the purchaser is heritable in succession.[24]

---

[13] *Elwes* v. *Maw* (1802) 3 East 38.
[16] *Luke* v. *Smith* (1894) 1 S.L.T. 545.
[17] *Graham* v. *Lamont* (1875) 2 R. 438.
[18] *Dowall* v. *Miln* (1874) 1 R. 1180.
[19] *Fisher* v. *Dixon, supra.*
[20] *Johnstone* v. *Dobie* (1783) Mor. 5443.
[21] *Baillie* v. *Grant* (1859) 21 D. 838.
[22] Titles to Land Consolidation (Scotland) Act 1868, s. 117.
[23] *McAdam's Exor.* v. *Souters* (1904) 7 F. 179.
[24] *Malloch* v. *McLean* (1867) 5 M. 335.

Conversion of this nature may even be constructive through instructions to trustees; if trustees are directed to buy heritage the necessary funds are deemed to be heritable; if they are instructed—not merely permitted—to sell heritage the value of the heritable subjects falls to the moveable estate.

Contracts Relating to Heritage

All contracts relating to heritage belong to the category of contracts known as *obligationes litteris*, those obligations of great importance which demand for their constitution and for proof of their terms and existence probative writing, that is writing which is proof of its own authenticity and content without supporting evidence. The necessity for probative writing to found a valid contract relating to heritage covers offers, acceptances, deeds conveying title to heritage or constituting burdens by way of heritable security or servitudes in heritable subjects. The only exception is a lease for less than one year which may be entered into less formally. Where a contract must be in probative writing it does not exist until the agreement of the parties is in probative writing and the parties to any such agreement may withdraw from it until the probative writing is produced and executed.

A probative writing is one which proves itself in a court, which raises by its form a presumption that it is genuine. Anyone who challenges a probative writing in court must accept the burden of proving it is not genuine.[25] This is the reverse of the normal situation, where a person offering a document as evidence in a court must show it to be genuine by having witnesses identify it. A document becomes probative on account of its form. It may be an attested document, a proven holograph document or a writing *in re mercatoria*.

Attested Documents: An attested document is one which is signed by the party or parties undertaking obligations or granting them and by two witnesses over 14 years of age who know the identity of the subscriber and who have either seen him sign it or have been told by him that he has signed it. After all the signatures have been appended to the document, there is added to it a testing clause, sometimes called a clause of attestation, in which the whole circumstances of the execution of the document are stated, including the

---

[25] *Ferrie* v. *Ferrie's Trs.* (1863) 1 M. 291.

date of the execution and the identities and designations of the witnesses (unless their designations are added to their signatures). Some technical defect in the execution of the document will not invalidate it[26] but this does not excuse the need for two witnesses or for contemporaneous signature.

The law used to demand that an attested document be signed by the parties at the foot of each page, but the Conveyancing and Feudal Reform (Scotland) Act 1970 (s. 44) provides that a probative deed consisting of more than one page, except a will or other testamentary writing, need be signed on the last page only. There is provision[27] for documents to be signed by a notary on behalf of blind persons or those unable to read.

Finally, some statutes lessen the formality in particular cases. Companies documents are deemed to be probative if sealed with the company seal and signed by two of the directors or one director and the secretary of the company without witnesses.[28] While the Merchant Shipping Act 1894 (s. 24), declares that a bill of sale for a ship needs but one witness.

Holograph Writings: A holograph writing is one written throughout, or in its essential or operative parts, by the person signing it. Further a document not in handwriting will be treated as holograph if the subscriber writes the word 'adopted as holograph' above his signature. Writings proved holograph are, in the ordinary course, by custom probative.

Documents in re mecatoria: Documents connected with ordinary commercial transactions will be treated as probative. Such writings as cheques, bills of lading, mandates, procurations, and receipts, if genuine, prove their date and the facts they narrate and record.

A case which illustrates the necessity for probative writing in the creation of contract relating to heritage is that of *Goldston* v. *Young*.[29] In this case one of the parties had written out an offer and acceptance for the sale of a shop. The acceptance he signed himself, while the other party signed the offer. In a dispute between them it was held there was no contract. The acceptance was, being holograph, probative, but the offer was not. In a contract in which the law demands probative writing neither party is bound until the

---

[26] Conveyancing (Scotland) Act 1874, s. 18.
[27] Conveyancing (Scotland) Act 1924, s. 18.
[28] Companies Act 1948, s. 32(4).
[29] (1868) 7 M. 188.

contract is in probative writing. *Locus poenitentiae*, or the right to withdraw, continues until the probative writing is in existence.

Personal Bar

There is one exception to the rule regarding the necessity for probative writing to form a contract, and that is where one of the parties is personally barred from withdrawing from the arrangement because he acted as if he would be bound by it despite the fact that the writings were not probative. The idea of personal bar is that the law demands consistency of action. One cannot act as if one acquiesces in an arrangement and then exploit some formal loophole to escape from its consequences. Personal bar has two aspects, *rei interventus* and homologation.

Rei Interventus: In the case of *rei interventus*, if one party has acted on the strength of the defective contract, altering his position or incurring expense and the actings are either known to the other party or are the inevitable and foreseeable result of the agreement, then the other party is barred from withdrawing from the agreement. Thus in the case of *Grieve* v. *Barr*,[30] where there was an improbative lease of a farm, the action of the tenant in entering and cultivating the farm constituted *rei interventus*, which prevented the landlord from withdrawing from the agreement. Other actings which have been held to constitute *rei interventus* are: advancing money on the strength of a defective undertaking to grant a disposition in security,[31] altering property the subject of the agreement,[32] and payment of the price.[33]

Some points of importance regarding the actings which may constitute *rei interventus* are: they must be material, not unimportant; they must be unequivocally referable to the agreement; they must be subsequent to the agreement, e.g. expenses incurred in anticipation of a contract would not constitute *rei interventus*.

Normally, *rei interventus* acts to perfect an imperfect agreement, e.g. a contract relating to heritage contained in improbative documents. However, the term *rei interventus* has also been applied to the situation where parties have been negotiating a contract and one of them has acted, and been known and allowed to act by the other

[30] 1954 S.C. 414.
[31] *Boyd* v. *Shaw* 1927 S.C. 414.
[32] *Colquhoun* v. *Wilson's Tr.* (1860) 22 D. 1035.
[33] *Foggo* v. *Hill* (1840) 2 D. 1322.

party, on the mistaken assumption that the negotiations had reached the point of agreement. In barring the other party from resiling, the law in fact states that the actings in question are evidence of agreement. In this situation it appears that proof of *rei interventus* is not restricted to writ or oath, even where the contract is one relating to heritage.[34]

Homologation: While in dealing with *rei interventus* it has been seen that the personal bar is against withdrawing or resiling, after the actions of another have taken place, homologation depends on the actions of the person who wants to withdraw. In the same way as a man may be led to believe by the apparent acquiescence of another that a defective agreement is being treated as valid, he may be led to believe this by the positive action of the other. If A and B agree in improbative writing that A sells a house to B and B moves in, digs the garden and commences decoration, his actings will constitute *rei interventus* which will prevent A from resiling. B himself is equally barred for he has homologated the contract. His actings cure the defect in the contract. A tenant who pays rent on the strength of an improbative lease homologates the lease.

A case which illustrates the principles of homologation is *Mitchell* v. *The Stornoway Trs.*[35] There existed an informal agreement for the feuing to Mitchell by the Trustees of an area of ground. Mitchell in reliance upon this agreement made application for building permission to the local Dean of Guild Court. In the process of his application being considered the Trustees, through their factor, assisted the burgh surveyor to whom the plans had been remitted for examination. It was held that by this assistance the Trustees had homologated the agreement. It might also be argued that Mitchell's actions constituted *rei interventus*.

The foregoing consideration of the doctrines of *rei interventus* and homologation is confined to the cases where there is a writing, albeit improbative. The doctrines may also operate to set up a contract where the agreement is not contained in even an informal writing. In this case the existence of the agreement must be proved by writ or oath, and the actings referable to it be used to constitute *rei interventus*. Thus in the case of *Walker* v. *Flint*[36] a tenant was

---

[34] *Errol* v. *Walker* 1966 S.L.T. 159.
[35] 1936 S.C. (H.L.) 56.
[36] (1863) 1 M. 417.

o

trying to deny his landlord's right to evict him. He was claiming that he had reached verbal agreement with the landlord for a three-year lease, and that on the strength of that agreement had erected buildings on the land. He claimed that those operations constituted *rei interventus*, but it was held that the tenant first had to prove that there was an agreement for three years, and this proof might be adduced only by the writ or the oath of the landlord.

Joint Property and Common Property

Where more than one person has a proprietorial interest in property the parties may hold the property jointly or be common proprietors. Whether their interest be joint or common affects the nature of that interest and the rights of the parties.

Joint Property: Where joint property exists the parties have one title to the subjects, their interests are equal and on the death of either the interests of anyone passes to the survivor or survivors. No joint proprietor has a right to dispose of his interest, by will or otherwise, nor to create burdens on it, nor may a joint owner demand a division of the subjects to give him separate title to an identifiable share of it. Examples of joint ownership are ownership by trustees, and ownership by the members of an unincorproated association. Decisions regarding the management of joint property are taken by a majority of the joint proprietors.

Common Property: Common property is possessed undivided by one or more proprietors in common but each has a separate title in a fraction of it. A right of property in common may be sold, disposed of by will or passed on intestacy and can be burdened. No common proprietor has a title to an identifiable part of the subjects but any one is free to call for a division of the subjects and can take action to secure such division or, if division is not possible or would be inequitable, for sale of the subjects and division of the proceeds.

Common property is managed by the unanimous decision of the common proprietors but necessary repairs can be instructed by any single proprietor.

THE FEUDAL SYSTEM

Most of the land in Scotland is held on feudal tenure under the feudal system. Introduced to Scotland in the 11th and 12th centuries, the cardinal feature of the feudal system is that land is held not absolutely but under grant from some other person subject to certain conditions and burdens, but without reversion to that other person while the terms of the grant are being observed. Thus while the identifiable proprietor of land has the physical right of possession and use of the land there will co-exist with his rights in it rights of a different nature, the rights of those under whom he holds the land. The actual physical possession is held by a vassal while the person from whom he holds is the superior. There may be more than one superior as originally feudal estates were granted by the sovereign to vassals who in turn created a feudal relationship with others; as there is no limit on the creation of new feudal relationships there may exist in any piece of land alongside the right of the vassal in possession several other estates each with an interest in the land, each entitled to obligations and returns from the land.

The vassal who enjoys occupation and use of the land may be at the end of a lengthy chain of such interests; he will have a superior to whom he owes duties, but the superior in turn will have a superior, who may or may not be the Crown to whom the chain will ultimately stretch for the sovereign is the ultimate owner of land in so far as rights in it have not been granted to vassals. The superior holding from the Crown is vassal in chief.

Those rights in land which have not been granted to a vassal but which have been reserved and the burdens and obligations created in the grant to a vassal are the estate in land known as the superiority interest or estate, while the rights enjoyed by the vassal, including use and possession of the land but subject to the superiority or superiorities which co-exist with them amount to the state of fee or *dominium utile* in the land. All the simultaneous interests in the land, that of Crown, superiors and vassal have defined interests in the land, the definition being partly as stated by law generally and partly as laid out in the grants relating to the land. Any such interest can be enforced or defended. There is a relationship of tenure between each proprietor and his superior which stretches from the ultimate vassal who enjoys the *dominium utile*, through his superior backwards to the Crown. Included in this relationship will be rights and obligations in and due from the land and belonging to and owned by the various parties.

Allodial land: Where, exceptionally, land is held outright and absolutely, outwith the feudal system it is allodial land. Allodial land includes the Crown's ultimate superiority and superiority rights reserved by the Crown in the land of subjects, the sovereign's own property, land belonging to the sovereign's eldest son as Prince and High Steward of Scotland, and churches, churchyards, manses and glebes. By statute land acquired compulsorily by a local authority is freed from feudal burdens and is thus like allodial land. Also akin to allodial land is land held under the udal system, another form of tenure of land known in Orkney and Shetland only.

Blench holding: Of various other forms of tenure, now obsolete, blench holding is the holding of land in return for services or tributes, usually trivial, designed to acknowledge the rights of the superior. The tribute in blench holding is frequently exigible only on demand. In modern form it is commonly one penny if asked and the form of creation and other incidents of blench holding making it undistinguishable from feudal tenure.

The Dominium Directum

A superiority, or *dominium directum*, is the estate of any feudal land holder who creates a new feudal estate in his lands to be held under him. It comprises the rights in the land not reserved to the crown or any over-superior together with those not conveyed to the vassal and will include the right to collect feu duties, to enforce real burdens imposed on the land by the feudal grant and a reversionary right to the land should the vassal be in breach of the terms of the feudal grant. The estate of superiority can be sold as can be the right to collect feu duties while the other rights of the superior are retained.

Creation: A feudal estate is created by probative deed, common forms being the feu charter, feu disposition and feu contract; the form of the last being bilateral, the feuar being a party to it and thus undertaking liability on it. The personal liability of the feuar where the form is feu charter or feu disposition is accepted by acceptance of the deed.

The foundation writ of the feudal relationship will describe the parties to it, the consideration, whether are valuable or not, and will convey and describe the land. The description of the land will be sufficient to identify it, it may be by name, by boundaries, by reference to a plan or measurements or by reference to a description or plan already recorded in the Register of Sasines. Also included in the clause conveying the land are the burdens and conditions upon which the grant is made and accepted; a further clause will specify the payments due by the vassal. Further clauses of a technical nature are also included in the document creating the feudal relationship.

The grant of the feudal writ invests the vassal with a personal right against a superior; a real right is obtained by the registration of the deed in the General Register of Sasines.

Feu Duty: The most obvious, but not necessarily the most important, incident of the superiority is the right to demand and collect a feu duty. Historically the return to the superior could be in cash or in kind and could encompass casual or periodic payments exigible in certain circumstances. The rendering of services as a return to the superior is now abolished and all returns must be in money and of a fixed amount; prior feu duties not expressed in money had to be converted to money and stipulation for casual payments is no longer competent; where these were included in older grants they have been absorbed into the annual feu duties by increasing it.

Prohibition of New Feu Duties: By the Land Tenure Reform (Scotland) Act 1974 no deed executed after the commencement of that Act may impose a feu duty. If there is a charter of *novodamus* or similar deed changing the feudal burdens on an existing feudal relationship a feu duty may be imposed but it must not represent an increase on the feu duty payable out of the lands. The statute does not prohibit the creation of new feudal estates, it merely prohibits the creation of new monetary feu duties.

Allocation of Feu Duty: Several persons may buy parts of the *dominium utile* from a vassal without his creating a separate feudal estate; for example a tenement property of flats may be sold off into several separate flats. The feu duty continues to be exigible from the land and unless there is some arrangement to the contrary each proprietor of a part is liable jointly and severally with the others for the whole, or *cumulo*, feu duty. The feu duty may be divided, or allocated amongst the separate parts in which case the proprietor of each part is liable for his proportion of the whole feu duty and that direct to the superior. Allocation may be effected by the vassal if he has consent to do so from the superior in the original feudal grant or the superior may subsequently agree to allocation; if such an allocation has taken place the fact is endorsed on the original feudal grant in a memorandum of allocation or a separate memorandum of allocation is recorded in the General Register of Sasines. An allocation may also be granted in a duly recorded charter of *novodamus*, the deed used if there is any variation of the terms of the feudal holding.

An allocation of feu duty may also be forced on the superior by action by the proprietor of lands burdened with an unallocated portion of a *cumulo* feu duty under the Conveyancing and Feudal Reform (Scotland) Act 1970; the proprietor serves notice on the superior or person to whom the feu duty is paid stating that the part of the feu duty apportioned on his property is to be allocated. If no objection is made the notice effects the allocation. Allocation takes effect from the next term of payment occurring not less than three months after service of the notice. If the superior does object to the amount or the portion for which allocation is sought the Lands Tribunal will adjudicate on the proposed allocation and allocate the feu duty by order.

The notice of allocation does not require to be registered.

Redemption of Feu Duties: The vassal, the proprietor of a feu may, redeem his feu duty at any term of Martinmas or Whitsunday. This right does not prejudice any arrangement for redemption made prior to the commencement of the Land Tenure Reform (Scotland) Act 1974 or any other method of redemption which affects the feu.

The redemption is effected by the proprietors giving notice to the superior or his agent in terms stipulated by the Act, not later than the term of redemption and paying to the superior or his agent a sum calculated in terms of the Act. When such notice is given and payment made the feu duty is redeemed, although the other burdens affecting the feu continue in force as if the feu duty were still exigible. On redemption the superior or his agent must give a receipt in form laid down by Act.

The sum required to redeem, the redemption money, is such a sum of money as would, if invested in two and a half per cent consolidated stock at the middle market price at the close of business last preceding the date occurring one month before the term of redemption produce an annual sum equal to the feu duty, and also any amount of feu duty unpaid in respect of the feu, liability for which has accrued up to and including the term of redemption and any interest or other payment exigible in respect of the arrears of feu duty.

A proprietor of land burdened with an unallocated portion of a *cumulo* feu duty may not redeem it unless all the proprietors co-operate in seeking redemption. He may, however, seek allocation as a preliminary step and, that accomplished, force redemption.

On Transfer of Land: When land is transferred for valuable consideration the feu duty must be redeemed. The date of redemption on which the feu duty is deemed to be redeemed is normally the date of entry under missives or under a deed containing a conveyance of feu; if the date of entry was before the date of the obligation or if no obligation existed, the date of the deed containing the conveyance the date of redemption is the date of the obligation or deed. The redemption money is calculated by reference to the middle market price of two and a half per cent consolidated stock at the close of business on the day one month before the date of redemption.

Liable to pay the redemption money to a superior is the person who was proprietor of the feu immediately before the date of the obligation to grant the conveyance or the date of the conveyance if there was no such obligation. After redemption no further payment in respect of feu duty for a period after the date of redemption is due but the feudal relationship continues in force in all other respects.

If the redemption money is not paid to the superior it, together with interest from the date of redemption until the payment, is secured in favour of the superior in the land subject to the feu in the same manner and subject to the same remedies as the feu duty deemed to be redeemed. If the redemption money has not been paid the proprietor of the feu for the time can rid the land of the burden of the unpaid redemption money, interest and any unpaid feu duty by giving notice to the superior in terms of the Act. Two months after the giving of such notice, or after the date of redemption whichever is the later the land ceases to be burdened and no action, for recovery lies against anyone except the proprietor who is liable to pay the redemption money and, in the case of unpaid feu duty a person who is liable for payment of that before the date of redemption.

If the superior on receipt of the notice and before the expiry of the two month period raises an action for recovery of his arrears or redemption money the court may order that the land continue to be burdened and the sums due exigible for a further period which the court considers reasonable to enable the superior to recover. The superior is not, however, entitled to recover at the expense of anyone other than those whose sole liability the sums would have been if the two month period had elapsed unless the court is satisfied that it is not reasonably practical to recover from them. Any court order of this sort or any extension of it must be registered in the General Register of Sasines.

Real Conditions: Apart from the right to the money return represented by the feu duty the superior can enforce in questions with the vassal any conditions which affect the lands. To be a real condition, a burden must appear in the dispositive clause of the deed constituting the feudal relationship and it must be clear that the intention is that the burden is to attach to the lands described in the deed, not merely to affect the original feuar and his heirs; the deed in which the burden is constituted must be registered in the General Register of Sasines. Alternatively the conditions may be laid out in another, recorded, deed and be imported to the feu charter, feu disposition or feu contract by reference to that deed. A real condition must be specific and precise, any ambiguity as to its meaning will be resolved in favour of the feuar while it will be construed strictly to impose the least possible restriction on the use of the land which its terms will bear. Vagueness is fatal to an attempted creation of a real condition.

Conditions which are contrary to the law, inconsistent with the nature of property, contrary to public policy, which serve no purpose or are vexatious will not be enforce.

The superior may enforce the observance of the real conditions while he has both title and interest in the subjects; he may do so by invoking clauses in the deed on which the feudal relationship rests or by using the ordinary remedies provided by the law. He may lose his right to enforce them by express waiver, by a change in the law, or by acquiescence in contravention of the conditions. Where contravention is by a particular proprietor and the superior can be said long to have acquiesced in it the superior loses his right to enforce the conditions against that feuar, while the superior of a district may lose his right to enforce against all the feuars if he has acquiesced in contravention by some of them.

Co-feuars may be entitled to enforce the feudal conditions imposed by a common superior, if it was intended that the particular restriction was intended to benefit co-feuars; for example a terrace of houses may be owned by co-feuars, the restriction on use of the proprietors being designed to uphold the amenity of the terrace and a waiver in such case by the superior in respect of one property would not remove the right of a co-feuar to enforce a feudal condition against his neighbour.

Real conditions affecting a feu may be varied in certain circumstances by the Lands Tribunal, a court set up in Scotland by statute for such purpose. At the instance of a proprietor whose lands are burdened with a land obligation (the statutory term which includes feudal conditions) the Tribunal may alter or vary a land obligation but their jurisdiction to do so is limited by the Act. They may do so if they conclude that the obligation has become unreasonable or inappropriate, that there have been changes in the character of the land affected by the obligation, or because there have been changes in the character of the neighbourhood or because of other circumstances which the tribunal may deem material. Further the Tribunal may act if satisfied that the obligation is unduly burdensome compared with any benefit resulting or which would result from its performance or that the existence of the obligation impedes some reasonable use of the land.

The applicant may use any of these grounds or a combination of them: if he is claiming that the obligation has become unreasonable or inappropriate he should show casual connection between the changes or material facts and the unreasonableness or inappropriateness of the land obligation. No application is competent in respect of an obligation which has been created for the first time in a deed not more than two years before the application.

The power of the Lands Tribunal on such an application is to vary or discharge the obligation but it may add or substitute any provision which it considers reasonable as a result of the variation or discharge; if such addition or substitution is proposed it must be acceptable to the applicant. If the applicant does not find the proposal acceptable the Tribunal may refuse to order variation or discharge of the obligation.

The Tribunal also has power to award compensation to the superior if it is granting a discharge or variation. The amount, payable by the applicant, is the amount that the Tribunal think just under either, but not both, of two headings: (1) A sum to compensate for any substantial loss or disadvantage suffered by the superior in consequence of the discharge or variation of the obligation, or (2) a sum to make up for an effect which the obligation produced when imposed in reducing the consideration then paid for the interest in the land.

If the application is on the ground that the obligation is impeding reasonable use of the ground and the Tribunal is of the opinion that money could not compensate the superior due to exceptional circumstances related to amenity or otherwise the Tribunal may refuse a variation or discharge of the obligation.

The superior may oppose any application and the Tribunal has a discretion to hear any other person who appears to them to be affected by the obligation or by its proposed discharge. This right of audience may extend to neighbours or co-feuars, although in the latter case, if such have a right to enforce the condition they would have a right to oppose the application rather than simply be heard on it at the Tribunal's discretion.

The Tribunal's order is recorded in the General Register of Sasines and the land obligations as varied remain enforceable as if contained in the original grant.

The Superior's Remedies

The superior's enforceable interest fall under two headings: his right to collect his feu duty and his right to enforce the real conditions.

Feu Duty: The feu duty is not merely a personal debt owed by the proprietor of the feu but also a *debitum fundi*, a real debt exigible from the land itself. The means of collection of feu duty reflect this duality of character.

A personal action for payment is competent against the vassal, his liability being for the feu duty during his ownership of the land continuing until a notice of change of ownership in statutory form has been served on the superior. An original vassal may have undertaken a personal obligation to pay feu duties even after ownership has changed and if this be the case, he remains liable.

The remedies which reflect the real nature of the debt are:

Hypothec: this is a latent right in security of the crop and the plenishings of the land; it secures payment of the last or current feu duty only.

Poinding of the Ground: this is an action to attach goods brought on to the land by the vassal, and by his tenants, if their rent is unpaid. The security thus obtained covers all arrears of feu duty unless the vassal has been sequestrated in which case it covers one year's arrears and the feu duty for the current term.

Adjudication: The superior may, as can any heritable creditor, seek to have the land adjudicated to him.[37]

Tinsel of the Feu: The superior may seek tinsel of the feu, a declaration that the feu duty is unpaid and that the land and all on it should revert to him. The declaration, called a declaration of irritancy, may be averted by payment of the arrears; in any event no action of declarator of irritancy can be raised by a superior unless there has been default of payment of the feu duty for the five years preceding the raising of the action. The entitlement to declarator of irritancy may be based on statute or on the terms of the feudal grant but the outstanding arrears cannot be recovered when the declaration of irritancy is obtained. The reversion of the land to the superior voids any security rights granted by the vassals, unless the creditors purge the irritancy, and also voids sub-feus. Anyone whose rights might be affected by tinsel can, by paying the arrears, avert declaration of irritancy which is not deemed final until the court decree is registered in the General Register of Sasines.

Real Conditions: The remedy of the superior who finds a vassal in contravention of any real condition lie in irritancy of the feu or in obtaining interdict in cases where the contravention is active or a decree ordering the vassal to perform his obligation when these call for action which he is neglecting to take.

A declarator of irritancy for contravention is the most competent remedy but can be averted by the vassal's compliance with his obligations.

The Dominium Utile

The estate of the vassal is an estate of proprietorship. A landowner can use his lands as his own except as far as he is restrained from so doing by law or by agreement, which includes the observance of real burdens and conditions; even if these did not arise from the direct agreement of the proprietor his agreement to observe them is inferred from his acceptance of the tenure.

The main burdens of the vassal correspond with the rights of the superior: he must pay the feu duty and observe the feudal conditions. His rights are to use the land subject to the law; all the incidents of ownership are his and, within the law and the

[37] *infra* p. 303.

boundaries of the feudal conditions, he may do with the subjects as he will.

In relation with the world at large the proprietor may take all steps necessary to vindicate his rights against interlopers and others. He is free to sell his interest in the land without interference from the superior who can exercise no control over the selection of the purchaser nor in any way profit from the exchange. The land naturally forms part of the vassal's estate and can be disposed of by him by rule or otherwise and falls to his executors on his death.

Pre-emption: Occasionally there is found in a feudal grant a clause which allows the superior the first opportunity to buy the land should the vassal wish to sell it. The effect of this right has been reduced by statute: by the Conveyancing and Feudal Reform (Scotland) Act 1970 (s, 46) the land need be offered to the superior only once, even if the clause of pre-emption purports to be exercisable on more than one occasion. A refusal by the superior, and non-acceptance within twenty-one days of the offer is deemed by the statute to amount to refusal, cancels the clause entirely.

Planning Considerations: Important restrictions on the use of land by the proprietor of it are imposed by the various planning statutes. Development of the land, with very minor exceptions, requires the consent of the local planning authority; thus the owner of the land is free to use his land only within the boundaries laid down by the planning code. Change of use of any property amounts to development.

If it is desired to develop land, application must be made to the local planning authority whose consent is required before the development may proceed; their adverse decision can be appealed to the Secretary of State. The importance of the existence of the planning code cannot be underestimated; the value of land will depend entirely on the purpose to which it may be put.

THE LAW OF SUCCESSION

The law of succession is the body of rules governing how a person's property is to be distributed on his death to those who succeed in his place. Largely now governed by the Succession (Scotland) Act 1964 (as amended), these rules prescribe how the property is to be divided amongst a person's relatives according to whether he had or had not expressed wishes on the matter and according to the nature of the property, whether heritable or moveable. Outwith that Act, but relevant to this subject, are the powers and duties of the executor to whom is entrusted the function of administering the estate to the point of its distribution amongst those entitled to it.

The property comprised in an estate are all property, assets or rights capable of valuation, liquidation, or conversion into money. In calculating its extent all debts and liabilities must be deducted for any right of succession is postponed to the rights of creditors. The valuation is taken as at the date of death, a fact of some importance in assessing the estate's liability to Government taxes and in the division of property amongst the successors. The valuation at the date of death is not, however, conclusive in assessing the liability of the estate to Government taxes. If there has been a decrease in the value of shares or securities, quoted on the stock exchange, within twelve months after the date of death the value for estate duty purposes will be similarly reduced if the investments are sold. (Finance Act 1973, s. 45.) The whole estate vests in the executor, who will meet out of it all taxes and claims, although in settling these he will have to take into account whether such claims are against the heritable or moveable estate.

Usually the date of death is easily ascertained but in case of disappearance there exists machinery to have death presumed judicially. At common law the court must be presented with evidence sufficient to rebut the presumption that a person will live for a substantial period, stated as 80 to 100 years.[38] By statute[39] there is a modification of the common law situation; a presumption of death may be made if a man has disappeared and not been heard of for seven years or more. A petition may be presented by any person entitled to succeed to any estate on the death of the absentee, or to any estate the transmission of which depends on the death of the absentee, or who is fiar of an estate over which the absentee enjoyed a life rent. A decree on such a petition narrates the fact of disappearance, the date at which the absentee was last known to be alive and that he died at a specified date, or if there is no evidence of a probable date of death, that he died seven years after the date when he was last known to be alive. Such decree allows a petitioner to succeed but not to the exclusion of the absentee, if he turns up within thirteen years of the decree or, if title to the estate

---

[38] Dickson, Evidence para. 116.
[39] Presumption of Life Limitation (Scotland) Act 1891.

is registrable in public registers, within thirteen years of registration; nor does the decree defeat the rights of parties who have better title to the estate than the petitioner and it does not apply to claims under insurance policies—although in practice insurance companies will generally pay on such decree. Thus the common law provisions are not entirely supplanted by the Act.

Testate and Intestate Succession

When a man has directed how his estate is to be disposed of he is said to be testate; if he has not done so he is described as intestate. In the latter case the rules of succession govern the distribution of his estate, or that part of it, if he has left incomplete directions, i.e. died partially testate, the destination of which the deceased has not directed. Where there is a direction, i.e. when the deceased is testate, however, it cannot affect certain rights which by law belong to surviving spouses and issue; these legal rights are not defeasible by Will.

Testate Succession

No one is under any obligation to make a Will, testament or settlement; one may choose to die intestate. If there is any testamentary writing some rules regarding its validity must be borne in mind.

Form: A Will must be in writing and must be subscribed by the testator. Whether it is valid depends on the same rules of law regarding the authentication of deeds, i.e., it should be an attested deed or should be holograph of the testator or adopted as holograph by him. The only exception to this rule is in the case of legacies not exceeding £100 Scots which can be made verbally; such nuncupative or verbal legacies involving such trivial sums form an unimportant exception to this rule.

There are no special form of words required in a Will, any wording which shows testamentary intention will suffice.

A formally drawn Will identifies the testator, the intended beneficiaries, and the extent of the intended benefit; it will include the due date of its execution, name the place it was made and normally ncludes a clause disposing of residual estate. Such a clause is not necessary, as a valid Will may dispose of only part of the estate. Similarly, if part of a Will cannot be given effect, if, for example, a named legatee has died, the Will remains valid. Observations on the usual content of the Will must be general as the rule of law is that, assuming the writing is properly authenticated, a Will is valid if drawn in words which express testamentary intent, which in cases of dispute the courts will decide by considering the wording of the document; such should themselves be capable of indicating intention to make bequests. Even where the wording will bear the interpretation that there could have been testamentary intention, there are possibilities that the grantor of the deed did not intend the document as a Will but as a draft, a personal memorandum or letter of instruction; it will be for the courts to decide on all the circumstances surrounding such a writing which might indicate whether the document was intended as a Will or not.

A Will may be contained in several documents; assuming these each do satisfy the rules of authentication they will be read together in ascertaining the intention of the maker; it is, however, possible that by a valid Will the maker imports to its terms the content of other documents which do not themselves satisfy the rules regarding authentication and such device is effective in incorporating into a Will any document of the sort referred to. The inclusion of such writings must be expressed in an authenticated Will as distinct from those cases where a Will may be held to be supplemented or amended by further authenticated writings which are read with it.

Holograph Wills: If a Will is attested little difficulty regarding its validity on the grounds of adequate authentication will arise. Where a Will is in the writing of the grantor and signed by him, although not written throughout by him but subscribed by him with the addition in his handwriting of words which show he intended the content to be treated as holograph, no witnesses are required to make the Will valid as far as authentication is concerned. Such a holograph document will be treated as a Will by the courts if lodged with affidavits from two persons who knew the handwriting of the grantor to the effect that the writing and signature are his.[40] If there is a dispute as to the genuineness of a holograph Will those who claim it to be a Will and seek to set it up as a Will must prove the genuineness of the writing. Once the handwriting is shown, or held, to be genuine the document will suffice as a Will even to the admission of an interlineation or alteration in it in the handwriting of the subscriber; such alterations, unless authenticated, would not be authentic in an attested deed.

[40] Trusts (Scotland) Act 1961.

Difficulty can arise when an attempt has been made to make a Will by filling in blanks on a form. Such a form will become a Will if it is attested or adopted as holograph by the testator but if he has merely filled in blanks in his handwriting and signed the form there can be room for dispute as to whether or not the document is a holograph Will. It will be treated as a holograph Will if there is in the handwriting of the subscriber sufficient, read without reference to the other parts, to constitute a Will; if testamentary intention can be deduced from those words the intent to make a Will succeeds; if this is not the case the document will have no testamentary effect.

Codicils: Testamentary writings subsequent to a Will which amend, modify, or supplement it are known as codicils. Unlike informal documents which may be expressly incorporated in any Will by declaration within its terms, a codicil must follow the rules of authentication.

Testamentary Capacity

Males above the age of fourteen and females above the age of twelve have testamentary capacity. Persons suffering from mental illness may not have testamentary capacity if the illness is such that at the time of making the Will the testator was unable to appreciate fully what he was doing or the significance of what he was doing. Through such incapacity he might not appreciate the extent of his property or what he was doing with it; either would be fatal to the attempt. Where mental illness is sporadic, the validity of any Will depends on whether it was made in a period of lucidity or not. Similarly Wills made under the influence of drink or drugs where the effect of these was such as to deprive the testator of understanding the nature or the significance of his actings will not be effective.

Challenge to a Will on the grounds of incapacity is open to any person who would benefit by the reduction of the Will.

Reduction of Wills: Apart from challenge to a Will on the basis of the mental incapacity of the testator a Will can be reduced on the grounds of facility and circumvention, force and fear, undue influence, or deception and error.

Facility and circumvention occur when at the time of making the Will the testator was weak in body or mind, although not mentally ill, to an extent that he was open to the influence and persuasion of someone who exploited the testator's facility to his own advantage. A Will made under duress is invalid.

Undue influence arises where there is a relationship which inspires confidence and trust and the testator was influenced improperly by the party in whom he had confidence or trust to make a Will. If a solicitor draws up a Will and is a beneficiary he must show that there was no undue influence, a rule which applies to any other person who stood in a fiduciary capacity to the testator.

If a Will was made by someone deceived, fraudulently, innocently or negligently, as to some matter material to his making of the Will it is reducible. If he was labouring under some error, although self-induced as to a material matter the Will can be avoided.

Revocation: A Will, once, made, may be revoked by the testator at any time. Such revocation may be made expressly by declaration in a later Will, which will normally be effective, although if inconsistent with the rest of the Will in which it appears, as where the later was based on the assumption that an earlier Will would stand, the earlier Will will be effective.

Revocation may also be implied by the making of a later, valid and effectual, Will; if its terms are inconsistent with an earlier testamentary writing, although it is a matter of interpretation whether the inconsistency between the two is such as to imply revocation of the earlier or whether the two are to be read together.

The destruction of a Will will revoke it if deliberately done; when an instruction has been given by the testator to destroy a Will such instruction is held to be equivalent to a Will. The destroyal of a Will can have the effect of reviving an earlier Will which had not been destroyed. When destruction is accidental, done without the testator's authority or accomplished without real intention, for example, when drunk, or insane, or in anger, to revoke the Will stands if its content can be proved. If a Will, known to exist cannot be found on the testator's death, there is a presumption that it has been deliberately destroyed by the testator.

The testator may endeavour to cancel his Will by obliteration. Such obliteration must be authenticated to be valid unless the scoring out is so complete as to render the deed illegible.

There is also the possibility that a Will is reduced if subsequent to making it a child is born to the testator, including an illegitimate child. Based on the idea that the testator would have wished to make provision for such a child, the presumption that the birth reduces the Will is removed if circumstances show it was a testator's intention that the Will should stand. Mere opportunity to alter the Will after the birth is not enough to rebut the presumption in favour of reduction, more positive indication that the testator wished the will to stand is required, although mere declaration by the parent is not enough.

The challenge of any such Will lies at the hand of the child excluded and, if successful, has the effect of reducing the Will as a whole without reviving any earlier Wills which it revoked. Thus the parent's estate is administered and distributed according to the rules of intestacy which will benefit the child.

LEGAL RIGHTS

The whole law of succession, both common law and statutory, was changed by the Succession (Scotland) Act 1964 but there is maintained by that Act the basic idea that a spouse or children cannot be entirely deprived by Will of participation in the distribution of a dead person's estate. Originally capable of excluding the possibility of disinheritance of close relatives, the rules as they now stand may have dubious value if determined effort is made to exclude their applicability; in the absence of elaborate rearrangement of property, designed to achieve this end, the rules do, in effect, restrict the free disposal by will of property.

Ius Relictae and Ius Relicti

The legal right of a spouse, wife (*ius relictae*) or husband (*ius relicti*) is to payment of one-third of the moveable portion of the deceased's net estate at the date of death. If there are no children, or if surviving children have discharged their legal rights, the proportion is one-half.

Legitim: Legitim, also known as the 'bairns' part', is the claim of children and remoter issue to a share in the moveable portion of a parent's estate. It may be claimed from the estate of each parent in turn. The fraction involved—known as the legitim fund—is one-third of the net moveable estate if there is a surviving spouse whether or not he or she claims legal rights, and one-half if there is no surviving spouse or if the spouse has discharged his or her claim. The fund available is the same as that from which the legal rights of a surviving spouse will be met, the net moveable estate of the parent as at the date of death, although heritable bonds, including ground annuals and personal bonds are excluded from the calculation.

Entitled to share in the legitim fund are all the issue of the deceased, including those of earlier marriages, posthumous children, illegitimate children and adopted children, together with the issue of any person who predeceased the parent who would have been entitled to share in the legitim fund. If all claimants are children of the deceased, or if all are grandchildren, they share the fund equally; if there are claimants of both categories the grandchildren share amongst themselves the share which would have fallen to their deceased parent.

Collation: Any person claiming a share of the legitim fund must collate advances made to him, or the proportion appropriate to him of any advances made to the person through whom he is entitled to share in the fund. By collation is meant that the amount of any such advance is added notionally to the legitim fund before its division and the division being made the amount of the advance is deduced from the share falling to the person who enjoyed the advance. By this doctrine equality amongst the children of a deceased parent is achieved. Collation, called collation *inter liberos*, can only be called for from claimants on the fund; if one potential beneficiary of the legitim fund has enjoyed advances but is not claiming on the legitim fund these advances are not taken into account.

Advances must be distinguished from loans which would be due to the estate as a whole and thus be taken into account in calculating the whole moveable estate, not merely in increasing the legitim fund. Advances must also be distinguished from payments made in discharge of a parent's duty to maintain and educate a child or those designed to remunerate a child for services arising out of a contract. Gifts made out of heritable property cannot be the subject of collation as the retention of these by the deceased in his own possession would not have increased the legitim fund in any event, nor can there be a legitimate call for collation where the donor has made it clear, expressly or otherwise, that the recipient's right to legitim was to remain unaffected by the gift. Those benefits which would require to be collated depend on circumstances; they have been held to include advances to set a child up in trade, interests settled on daughters on marriage, and provision made to provide for a child's maintenance till majority and subsequent liferent.

Discharge of Legal Rights: A person entitled to legal rights may waive or discharge these voluntarily and if this is done before the death of the ancestor or spouse the person thus renouncing his rights is treated as dead for the purpose of computing and dividing legal rights. If the discharge is after the death, the shares of the estate due to fall to the other claimants do not increase, the amount renounced falls into the residual part of the estate.

Where the discharge of legal rights is contained in an ante-nuptial settlement, the law used to permit provision to be made to exclude children from claiming their share of the legitim fund and such provision bound the children. The right of a child and of remoter issue to legitim cannot now be excluded by a marriage contract made after September 10, 1964; whatever such contract may provide the descendant has the election between the provisions in his favour in the marriage contract and his legitim.

Satisfaction of Legal Rights: Legal rights may be satisfied by the acceptance of the provisions of the Will in lieu of legal rights. A legatee cannot reject the provisions of a deed and benefit under it; thus if he accepts the testamentary provision he forfeits his claim to legal rights, a principle known as approbate and reprobate, or election. If the Will was executed before the Succession (Scotland) Act 1964, as amended, came into force a claim for legal rights did not automatically mean forfeiture of testamentary provisions, unless there was provision in the will that its provisions were made in full satisfaction of legal rights or that a claim for legal rights would involve forfeiture of the provisions of the deed. If such declaration is not made, legal rights can be claimed and the amount of the testamentary provision is applied or restored to the estate to compensate for what is taken out by way of legal rights and the surplus is available to the spouse or child concerned. This doctrine, known as equitable compensation, will eventually pass from the law as the statutory provisions, giving the beneficiaries a single choice between the alternatives, eventually apply to all testamentary writings. An express provision to the contrary, permitting choice without forfeiture is competent.

If there is a partial intestacy, that is if the testamentary writing does not dispose of the whole estate, a spouse or descendant may take the provisions made in a Will and claim legal rights in the estate which has fallen into intestacy.

Where a spouse or descendant has to elect, he must have full knowledge of the alternative rights; election made in ignorance or under error, or in circumstances not indicative of free choice will not be final. Election need not be immediate, but should be made without unreasonable delay.

Legacies

The legal rights of a spouse and descendants having been taken into account, a testator is free to dispose of the remainder of the estate, 'the dead's part' as he will. Assuming he wishes to gift, either conditionally or outright, rather than to create a trust he will provide legacies or bequests for those he wishes to benefit.

Special Legacies: A special or specific legacy is a gift of a specific object or item of property. Where such legacy is directed the legatee is entitled to the delivery of that item of property. Gifts of an object, or sum from a specific source, are special legacies known as demonstrative. A special legacy may fail if the object of it, or the source, in the case of a demonstrative legacy, had ceased to be the property of the testator at the time of his death. This may happen because the subject of the legacy has been sold, given away or has perished. It is a question of fact whether the property to satisfy a special legacy is still part of the estate or not. If it is not, nothing is due to the legatee.

General Legacies: Legacies which are not special in character are known as general legacies and fall to be satisfied out of any available estate.

Conditional Legacies: A testator is free to attach a condition to a bequest; the legatee to qualify to take the bequest must fulfil that condition, or be deemed to have fulfilled the condition by doing everything in his power to implement it, although failing to do so through no fault of his own.

A condition attached to a legacy may be repugnant and, if so, it is discharged; the legatee is then entitled to receive the bequest unconditionally. Examples of grounds on which conditions have been set aside are: impossibility of fulfilment, illegality or immorality and uncertainty. If the condition cannot be fulfilled or if the meaning of the condition is not certain, or it is conducive to illegal or immoral conduct it will be void. A condition is also void if its fulfilment is against public policy or would be contrary to the accepted customs of the country.

If the condition is repugnant to the gift or its purpose it will not be implemented.

Subject of Legacies

If the subject matter of a bequest is uncertain it cannot be implemented; it is, however, identified sufficiently if the testator's intention be adequately ascertainable from the terms of the testamentary writing.

If the subject matter is burdened, the legacy carries the burden with it, unless a testator has made it clear that the executor should clear the burden; if so, the legatee can demand this be done.

One cannot dispose of other people's property and if a testator has, through error, attempted so to do the bequest fails. If it can be shown that he knows that the subject did not belong to him, the executor should accept the bequest as a direction to purchase the property and do so with a view to transferring it to the beneficiary. The legatee can elect to take in value instead and must do so if the subject cannot be acquired by the executor.

Legatees

The important factor is that the legatee should be sufficiently identified. A precise identification is not necessary as long as a description used is sufficient to indicate the intention of the testator and evidence extrinsic to the deed may be used to help determine who was intended as beneficiary by the testator. If, however, the description is too uncertain the bequest is void.

If members of a group or class are the potential legatees the actual beneficiaries will be those of that class at the date of death of the testator. There can be difficulty in ascertaining who was meant to benefit when descriptive terms, rather than actual names of persons, are used and it is a matter of interpretation which is helped by previously decided cases, who should be included. For example, it has been held that 'family' includes only sons and daughters.

Where there is a bequest to a group of beneficiaries the right to participate in the division of the bequest depends on survival of each member of the group until the testator's death. The Will may provide otherwise, in which case the share of any predeceasing member of the group will not accrue to the others of that group but fall into the residual portion of the estate or intestacy as the case might be. There is a presumption that a bequest to members of a class or group will be divided equally amongst those who survive. Intention in the Will may defeat equal division, while, if the group are relations of different degrees, there is a presumption that division is *per stirpes*, grandchildren, for example, sharing the portion their predeceased parent would have had in an equal division with the testator's other children.

If a potential legatee predeceases the testator the legacy lapses; if a legacy is to an organisation, such as a charity, which has changed its identity the legacy will not lapse unless the change has made the organisation out of a different character. If the bequest was for a purpose which has failed the legacy lapses. When a legacy lapses for any reason the amount of it falls to residue or into intestacy if residual provisions have not been made in the Will.

There is an exception to the rule that the predecease of a legatee will avoid the bequest and that is where it was in favour of a predeceased's descendant, which can include nephews and nieces, if from the Will it appears that the testator was treating them as if they were his own children. In such cases the legacy falls to the issue of such a descendant. The basis of this exception lies in the idea that the testator would have wished to provide for such issue, it can therefore be ignored if he has made separate provision for such issue or in any circumstances which show that the testator did not mean to benefit the issue. If such intention can be shown the principle does not apply.

Residue

The fund which remains after the satisfaction of debts, duties, expenses and payment of any claims for legal rights and legacies is the residue of the estate. The amount of any legacies which have failed or lapsed and the sum of any accretions to the estate fall into the residue fund.

The testator is free to bequeath the residue, subject to the general rules of succession or bequest; if he has not done so, or if his attempt to do so does not succeed, the residue fund is distributed according to the rules of intestate succession.

If the residue has been divided and one of the shares has lapsed, that share falls into intestacy unless the Will directs otherwise.

INTESTATE SUCCESSION

Where a person has died without a Will or other testamentary right, or if his Will is not valid, or makes an incomplete disposal of his estate, the rules of intestate succession are applicable. While maintaining legal rights, *ius relictae* and *ius relicti* and *legitim*, these rules provide rights prior to the legal rights, and may necessarily dispose of the whole estate.

Naturally the first claims on the estate are for the satisfaction of debts and other proper charges and duties. Division of the estate occurs only when these have been met and the amount of these naturally affects the available estate.

Statutory Prior Rights

The creation of the Succession (Scotland) Act 1964 are the prior rights of a surviving spouse when there is intestacy, whole or partial. Designed to protect a spouse, and particularly a widow, prior rights rank as a first claim on an estate, after debts have been met, and may have the effect of exhausting it entirely for the benefit of a spouse, and at the expense of children. They are met out of as much of the estate as is undisposed of by testamentary disposition, a provision which means that if there is a partial intestacy the prior rights can be claimed against the part of the estate which has fallen into intestacy while the disposal of the other part is governed by the Will.

Prior rights fall into two categories; the surviving spouse is entitled to claim both.

Housing Right: This right is to receive the transfer to the surviving spouse of the relevant interest of the deceased in any one dwelling house being the ordinary residence of the surviving spouse. If the house was owned by the deceased the right transferred is that of ownership subject to any burdens; if tenanted, other than under the Rent Restriction Acts, the leasehold interest is transferred. To avoid difficulty the Act declares that 'dwelling house' includes any garden or portion of ground attached to, and usually occupied with, the dwelling house or otherwise required for the amenity or convenience of the house.

The right to the dwelling house is subject to the financial limit of £30,000. If the value of the dwelling house is above this figure, the spouse is entitled to payment of £30,000 from the estate.

Two further cases in which the prior right is satisfied by cash payment of the value of the house, subject to the upper limit of £30,000; firstly, if the deceased was a tenant of subjects which included the dwelling house, say a farm, the landlord cannot be compelled to grant a separate lease of the farmhouse; in such case a financial payment is made. Secondly, if the dwelling house forms the whole or part of subjects which was used by the intestate for carrying on a trade, profession, or occupation, and the value of the estate as a whole would be likely to be substantially diminished if the dwelling house were disposed of otherwise than with the assets of the trade, profession or occupation, the surviving spouse takes the value of the house, subject to the maximum of £30,000.

A point of some importance is that the surviving spouse, not necessarily the deceased, should be ordinarily resident in the dwelling house if the prior housing right is to be claimed.

There can also arise the question of the surviving spouse being ordinarily resident in more than one house, for example, if there are town and country houses. In such case the right of the surviving spouse is to any one of the houses, which can be chosen in the unfettered discretion of the spouse within six months of the deceased's death.

Along with the right of the surviving spouse to the dwelling house there is a right to furniture and plenishings; if two houses are involved the surviving spouse may elect between the furniture and plenishings of either an election which is independent of which house is chosen but which is to be made within six months of the death.

The right to the furniture and plenishings is restricted in financial terms to £8,000; if the contents of any one house exceeds this figure items to that value may be chosen. While furniture and plenishings is a vague phrase, and the statutory definition makes no attempt to define it exhaustively, saying it includes 'garden effects, domestic animals, plate, plated articles, linen, china, glass, books, pictures, prints, articles of household use and consumable stores,' there is excluded 'any article or animal used at the date of death of the intestate for business purposes or money or securities for money or any heirloom'. Heirlooms are articles which have association with the intestate's family of such nature and extent that they ought to pass to some member of that family other than the surviving spouse of the intestate.

The surviving spouse's right to house and furniture are the first items to come out of the deceased spouse's estate.

The effect of these provisions can have the effect of causing a man or woman, who knows them, to consider if his or her spouse might not be better provided for should he or she die intestate, rather than testate.

Monetary Rights: Postponed to the housing right and the right to furniture and plenishing is a monetary right, given to children, if there are any, as well as to the surviving spouse. The right of the surviving spouse is to payment of £8,000 from the estate, if there are no issue, and £4,000 if the deceased left issue.

Legal Rights: The traditional legal rights as preserved in amended form fall to be met once the statutory prior rights have been satisfied. If the latter exhaust the estate they are satisfied by the transfer of the whole estate.

Dead's Part: The part left of the intestate's estate once prior rights and legal rights are met falls to be disposed of according to the next of kin who survive the deceased. The succession opens successively to the following groups of next of kin; (a) children, taking the whole available funds; (b) a parent or parents and brothers or sisters: half to the parent(s), half to the brothers and sisters; (c) brothers or sisters, the whole estate; (d) one or both parents, the whole estate; (e) surviving spouse, the whole estate; (f) uncles or aunts on either paternal or maternal side, the whole estate; (g) grandparent or grandparents, on either side, the whole estate; (h) brothers or sisters of any of the grandparents, the whole estate; (i) ancestors of the intestate, generation by generation successively without distinction between paternal or maternal lines, the brothers and sisters of any ancestors having right before ancestors of the next more remote generation, the whole estate.

Where brothers and sisters of an intestate or of an ancestor of the intestate have right under these provisions to succeed those who are full blood relatives are entitled to succeed in preference to those relatives of half blood.

Where a person, if he had survived an intestate, would have had right, otherwise than as a parent or spouse of the intestate, to any part of the free intestate estate, but has predeceased leaving issue who do survive the intestate, such issue have the same right as their parent would have had had he survived. In all cases where the free intestate estate is falling to a group then the portion of the estate falling to that group is divided equally amongst the members of it if they are all in the same degree of relationship. If children are representing a deceased parent, they divide equally amongst themselves the share which would have fallen to the parent.

The Crown is *ultimus haeres* to any estate to which no person is entitled to succeed in accordance with these rules.

Administration of Estates

Whether succession is testate or intestate the estate will require to be administered. The extent of the estate will be ascertained, it will be ingathered, debts and duties satisfied, and finally, it will fall to be distributed amongst those who, either by testamentary provision, or by law, are entitled to it. This administration is carried out by an executor, a person confirmed in office by the court to carry out these tasks. An executor becomes interim proprietor of the estate but subject to his duties to pay debts due and distribute to those entitled to it. Historically the office is gratuitous but a bank may take fees for its services in such capacity and provision is normally made in the will to permit this. Only exceptionally would a bank act as executor except where nominated by testamentary writing. Executors may be of the following character:

Executor-Nominate: An executor nominate is one who is entitled to act through nomination in a will. Such nomination may be expressed, implied, or made by reference. Also entitled to act as executor-nominate are trustees nominated by the testator and those assumed to act as trustee in a relevant trust or appointed to such a trust by the court. If there is no such nomination, a general disponee, universal legatory, or residual legatee under a will is entitled to the office.

Office as executor cannot be forced on any person and confirmation of a nomination may be refused by the court if litigation is in prospect or if the court were satisfied that the appointment would result in injury to the estate.

Executor-dative: In the case of intestacy or if no nomination were made in a testamentary writing an executor may be appointed by the court on petition. Eligible for appointment as executor-dative are: (1) the surviving spouse, where that spouse's prior rights under the Succession (Scotland) Act 1964 exhaust the whole estate; (2) any universal legatee; (3) next of kin at common law; (4) persons having a right of succession to the free estate of the intestate under the Succession (Scotland) Act 1964. Amongst themselves, such persons are entitled to the appointment in the order in which they would succeed; (5) the issue of such persons as mentioned in the last category; (6) creditors of the deceased; (7) legatees; (8) the procurator fiscal of court or a judicial factor.

When a petition is presented for appointment as executor-dative the petitioner must state in which capacity the appointment is claimed.

Where someone has been appointed executor-dative another may petition to be appointed to act with him; normally the persons and categories listed follow in the order stated. An executor-dative, unlike an executor-nominate, must find caution for his honest management of the estate, and a Bond of Caution must be given up. Cautioners may be insurance companies but personal cautioners are acceptable.

Executor-creditor: Where there is no petition for confirmation a creditor may petition the court for appointment as an executor. While other executors must seek appointment to the whole estate, the executor-creditor needs to seek confirmation only to the amount of his debt, which must be liquid or constituted by decree during the lifetime of the deceased. If the debt was not constituted in the deceased's lifetime a creditor may require next of kin to seek confirmation as executor: if they do so the creditor collects his debt from them, while, if they do not without renouncing the succession they are liable to pay as intromitting with the estate without title. If there is renunciation the creditor may constitute his debt against them as renouncing next-of-kin and then proceed to seek confirmation to allow him to administer the estate to collect what is due to him.

Notice of intention to seek confirmation as executor-creditor must be given in the *Edinburgh Gazette* and a claim to confirmation may be successfully resisted by any creditor with a debt preferable to that of the petitioning creditor. Confirmation as executor-creditor is a form of diligence on the estate and burdens the property with the exception of special legacies. Any other creditor who does diligence within six months of the death of the debtor is entitled to rank equally on the estate with the executor-creditor.

Executor ad omissa: An executor, with the exception of the executor-creditor, is confirmed in the whole estate; if there have been omissions in the original inventory, the executor must lodge a further inventory and obtain an addition to the inventory upon which he was confirmed; such addition is called an eik. An interested party may seek to have an executor compelled to repair any omission or, alternatively to have himself confirmed executor *ad omissa.*

Executor ad non executa: The office of executor does not transmit on the death or incapacity of its holder. If the estate remains unadministered a person entitled to it or interested in it may petition for his appointment as executor *ad non executa*; more common is recourse to the procedures whereby the executor's executor takes over the administration.

Confirmation

The title of an executor to act in that capacity, to take possession of, administer and dispose of the estate is his confirmation. An Executor (nominate or seeking office in some other capacity) petitions the Sheriff Court of the area in which the deceased was domiciled, or if he had no fixed domicile or if that was outwith Scotland, the Sheriff of the Lothians and the granting of such petition is the title to apply to be confirmed as Executor. Only in the special procedure for small estates does the granting of a petition constitute the Confirmation of the Executor. Such petition may be contested but only in so far as the right or fitness of the petitioner to be confirmed.

Inventory: An inventory of the estate to which confirmation is sought accompanies the application for confirmation or, in the small estates procedure, the petition for appointment; such inventory is accompanied by an affidavit that it contains all the estate known to the petitioner. It distinguishes between property in Scotland, that in England and Wales, and that situated elsewhere, and includes a description of heritable property acceptable for the conveyance of heritage. It is accompanied by any testamentary writing on the strength of which appointment is sought. It will be stamped to show that any necessary duties have been paid.

Confirmation: The document granted by the court to the confirmed executor is confirmation of his appointment to that office, his power to act, and vests in the executor, for the purpose of administration, the whole estate, heritable and moveable, as listed in the inventory which is reproduced as part of the confirmation.

Executor's Responsibilities: Executors have the power, privileges and immunities and are subject to the limitations and restrictions which affect gratuitous trustees, although in the case of an executor-nominate these may be varied by the testamentary writing under which he was appointed. The trust which is involved is to administer the estate in accordance with the testator's directions, if there are any, and in accordance with the law, subject to accounting for his actings and transactions.

In ascertaining the extent of the deceased's estate it is a question of fact, the executor being entitled to that estate subject to debts, burdens, obligations due of it. Any representative capacity of the deceased must be recognised. Thus property in which the interest of the deceased was that of executor falls outwith the estate although statutory provision is made to allow an executor to include any such property in an inventory and there transfer it to another executor or trustee, if one is appointed, or even to distribute it, in terms of the original charge to the deceased, to beneficiaries. An executor is not bound to assume this responsibility.

An executor is bound to exercise due diligence in ingathering the estate and is allowed twelve months to accomplish this; he may be liable for interest on losses if debts due remain unrealised after the expiry of the twelve months.

He may sue for the recovery of debts, if the claim is included in the inventory of the estate; although unconfirmed executors may initiate action for recovery of debt they cannot grant effective discharges until confirmed and, therefore, cannot enforce payment until that time. Generally the executor can initiate any action or continue to participate in any current action, or defend any action raised against the estate. The executor may continue the business of the deceased and may tender performance of the deceased's contracts, unless these demand personal service from the deceased. He is personally liable for business losses.

The executor can pursue any action either by continuation or initiation of it where the estate under his control has suffered loss, but he is restricted in actions for purely personal injury to the deceased to those raised by the deceased before his death. The executor is liable for wrongs committed by the deceased in his lifetime.

The liability of the executor to pay the debts of the deceased springs from his taking the estate burdened as it is, but he is not personally liable unless he has acted wrongfully in such a way as to incur liability, for example by paying ordinary debts when preferential debts remain unpaid.

An executor cannot be compelled to pay any debt until six months have elapsed from the date of death of the deceased. This arises from the rule that all creditors who have done diligence within six months of the death, including having themselves confirmed executor-creditors or citing other executor-creditors, against the executor are entitled to rank equally; thus payment before the expiry of this period might exhaust the estate before a late claimant emerges.

The right of a creditor to equal ranking falls on the expiry of a six month period; if at a later time another claim emerges it will be paid if funds are available in the estate. If no funds remain and these have been distributed to beneficiaries the claimant must look to them. The executor's duty is to ascertain the extent of claims and to make provision for these; if he has done this prudently he is entitled after six months to proceed to distribute the estate in terms of the will or according to the law and will be personally immune from liability to later claimants.

The preferential claims, which must be met first, are Crown taxes, the expenses of confirmation, death-bed and funeral expenses, and widow's and family mourning. The distribution of the net estate is then made in the following order: prior rights of the surviving spouse on intestacy, to house, furnishing and plenishing, and financial provisions; claims to legal rights so far as not discharged or satisfied by other provisions; special legacies and general legacies, observing any order or priority of payment prescribed by the testator; residue; and any amount falling into intestacy. Interest is due on a financial provision and on legal rights.

The executor should retain money to meet contingent claims, such as under a guarantee.

In his administration of the estate under his control the executor should act with scrupulous honesty and is bound to be able to account for his transactions with the estate. His duties in regard to investment of funds in his control are not as onerous as those of trustees in a continuing trust and he is not necessarily at fault if he retains funds uninvested in his own hands. If, however, he cannot account for any monies, he is liable, and if he allows the executry funds to become inmixed with his own he can be held liable for interest as the money should have been separately banked. Either creditors or beneficiaries can call an executor to account.

Transfer of Property

Heritage: An executor may transfer heritable property by disposition, his title to do so being the confirmation. If the transfer is in satisfaction of prior rights, legal rights, a claim in intestacy, or a legacy, or to a residuary beneficiary, he may effect the transfer by a docket, attested by two witnesses on the confirmation relating to the property, which docket will identify the heritage being transferred. The title of the transferee then rests on the docketed confirmation.

Where any person has in good faith and for value acquired title to any interest in heritable property which has vested in an executor directly from the executor, or from any person deriving title directly from the executor, the title so acquired is not challengeable on the ground that the confirmation of the executor was reducible or has in fact been reduced, or, in the latter case, that the title should not be transferred by the executor.

Moveable Property: An executor transfers moveable property by delivery, payment, transfer of shares, or assignation as may be appropriate.

Discharge of Executors: When the estate has been administered the executor's office is exhausted. He will normally ask those to whom the estate has been transferred to grant him receipts for property received, and discharge.

LIFERENT AND FEE

It is not uncommon for there to exist, usually as a result of bequest, different interests in particular property through which one person, or a group of persons, enjoys the use and, if any, the revenues of the property during life, but when that interest ends the right to the property vests in another party. This other party has rights in the property during the lifetime of the former, but these do not include use or revenue and must be exercised in such manner as not to disturb the rights of those who enjoy the rights of use. Such an arrangement is known as liferent and fee, the interest of the person who is to enjoy the use being liferent, while the other interest is known as fee.

The less common form of liferent, known as proper liferent, arises when the liferenter is the feudal proprietor of lands, his rights therein being restricted by the concurrent existence of the other estate, and in duration. More common is where the estate in question comprises moveable property or heritable and moveable property both vested in trustees who are directed to make revenue and use available to the liferenter. Where there is such interposition of trustees, and, possibly where moveable property is involved, the liferent is called improper liferent, the position of the liferenter being more akin to that of a beneficiary under a trust than to that of a liferenter in proper liferent. Improper liferent is the more

common, although the principles of proper liferent as to the nature
and extent of the rights of the parties will be identical if the trustees
in a situation creating an improper liferent are merely instructed to
allow a liferent to the liferenter; if they have more specific instructions in the constitution of the trust these must be followed, and it
is possible that these may so vary the traditional relationship between
the liferenter and the other party entitled to the estate on the termination of the use and enjoyment of the liferent that it might be more
proper in the circumstances to consider that the parties are merely
beneficiaries with different entitlements, rather than to consider
them to be liferenter and fiar. In the absence of such instructions
the traditional principles will apply although, when moveable
property is involved, these have had to be adapted and extended.

The Nature of Liferent: The right of liferent is the right to possess,
use, and enjoy the revenues from, an estate during life, subject to not
destroying the substance of it. A liferent need not necessarily be
granted for life, it may terminate before death if there is apt direction
to that effect in the creation of it, on the occurrence of an event, such
as marriage or remarriage of the liferenter.

The Nature of Fee: The right of the fiar is to full ownership of the
estate undiminished by the liferenter's use on the termination of the
liferent.

The Liferenter's Rights

In proper liferent, the liferenter is feudal proprietor of the subjects and has the rights of use, enjoyment and revenue arising from
that ownership. Co-existent with his ownership is the right of the
fiar to the subjects undiminished at the end of the liferent. From
the nature of the two rights, the rights of the liferenter can be deduced.
The general principle is that recurring income and profits belong to
the liferenter, while accretions to the capital value of the estate
belong to the fiar. Thus the liferenter is entitled to feu duties, rents,
royalties, other regular payments, and crops. The proceeds of
thinning timber, normal windfalls and usual cropping fall to the
liferenter. Despite the principle that the estate should not be diminished, the liferenter is entitled to the proceeds of a mineral lease if
it had been productive of income to the creator of the liferent and to
work minerals if the creator had done so.

If the liferent is improper, the trustees will follow these rules,
unless otherwise directed by the truster; they may also have in their

Q

ownership moveable property and the general principle that income enjoyed by the trustee will belong to the liferenter applies. Thus interest payments, dividends on shares, periodic cash distributions, royalties from patents and published works will be passed to the liferenter. Any payment to the estate of a capital nature, repayments, bonus issues of shares, and the proceeds of any sale of assets, belong to the capital account and should be accounted for to the fiar. If for example, shares are sold the price falls to the capital account but a sum which represents any dividend element in the price obtained should be payable to the liferenter.

Wasting assets are treated as productible income for the life-renter although the taking of such profits depreciates the estate.

Rights of the Fiar

The main right of the fiar is to enter into full possession of the estate on the termination of the liferent and to have, in the case of improper liferent, the estate made over to him. In the case of improper liferent, the management of the estate is in the hands of the trustees and they usually have discretion in this area. If the liferent is proper, the fiar has rights in the estate: he may intervene to preserve its integrity, is entitled to fell timber, but subject to recognising the ordinary requirements for wood and shelter of the liferenter, and may work minerals not subject to the liferent but with regard to surface support and the amenity of the estate.

Liabilities

In improper liferent the trustees are liable for the outgoings of the estate as proprietors; whether they deduct the cost from the income of the estate or charge the fiar's interest will depend on the terms of the trust, which failing the traditional rules regarding proper liferent apply. The basic principle is that outgoings of a recurrent nature, e.g. rates, feu duties, maintenance and ordinary repairs, are met by the liferenter, who is bound to maintain the property, wear and tear excepted, in as good order as he got it. A liferenter can be found liable to find caution against the depletion or damage to the estate if there is danger that this might occur. Extraordinary expenditure is met by the fiar.

Creation of a Liferent

Proper liferent is created in writing in terms apt to create it and the title of the liferenter is completed by the recording of the deed, if appropriate, in the General Register of Sasines or of a notice of title based on the deed if it is not itself capable of being recorded.

An improper liferent is created as a trust where there is express provision, or if it can fairly be implied from the words of the truster, that a liferent is intended. Provisions for 'income,' 'interest,' 'rents out of property during their lifetime,' have all been held to found liferent. If the transfer of a particular property to the trustees requires writing, the creation of a trust over that property requires writing. Testamentary intentions require to be in writing. These rules apart, a trust need not be created by writing, but normally it is. Most continuing liferents are created by testamentary writing but can arise through *inter vivos* settlements, such as marriage contracts. Unlike testamentary trusts these need not be in writing, except in so far as writing is necessary to transfer the affected property, but generally they are.

Assignation of Liferents: A proper liferent cannot be assigned so as to put the assignee in the position of the liferenter; individual rights arising out of the liferent may be assigned but only as to give the assignee right to these during the lifetime of the liferenter. No greater right than that enjoyed by a cedent can be created by assignation.

The right of the liferenter in improper liferent can be assigned and the trustees must heed the assignation. Two exceptions to this rule are: first, where the right of beneficiary can be construed as a right of occupancy; then there is no power to the beneficiary to let the subjects. Whether a right of occupancy is bestowed rather than a liferent is a question of interpretation and circumstance. Secondly, where a liferent is declared to be alimentary it cannot be assigned, except, perhaps that part which might be considered excessive.

Alimentary Liferent: Where a liferent is declared to be for the maintenance and support of the liferenter he is not free to assign it, except, perhaps, for that part which is excessive to his needs. The purpose of the creation of an alimentary liferent was to create income for the beneficiary which he could not alienate, pledge, or otherwise interfere with; such a liferent is also beyond the reach of the creditors of the beneficiary except in so far as it may be excessive for his maintenance and support, in which case the excessive portion may be subject to diligence. Such a liferent may be declined before acceptance but it cannot be cancelled, discharged, or waived except in exceptional circumstances.

Under the Trusts (Scotland) Act 1961 (s. 1(4)) there is provision made for a petition to the court which, at its discretion, may authorise any arrangement varying or revoking an alimentary liferent provision and making a new provision in its place, including, if thought fit, new provision for the disposal of the fee or the part thereof burdened with the liferent. The court will do this only after having regard to the alimentary beneficiary's income from all sources, and such other factors as it thinks material. The alimentary beneficiary's consent is required, but if this cannot be procured, e.g. because he is under eighteen, incapacitated or unborn, the court may assent on behalf of such beneficiary.

Termination of a Liferent

A liferent comes to an end when the liferenter dies; if it was hedged with some condition governing its continuation, the fulfilment of that condition ends the liferent. Apart from alimentary liferents a liferent ends by discharge, renunciation, or if the liferent and fee become vested in the same person.

TRUSTS

The concept of a trust embraces the idea that ownership of property is vested in one or more persons not for their personal use but for its administration and use for the achievement of the purposes as the trustees are directed by the trust. Trustees are normally the proprietors of the property in their charge but such proprietorship is qualified by the purposes for which they hold the property which is charged by virtue of its being trust property with burdens preferable to any claim upon it by the trustees or made against them except in their capacity as trustees. Should trust purposes prove impossible to accomplish, or fail to exhaust the property there is a reversionary interest in the available property for the creator of the trust or his executors or assignees; there is no reversion to the trustees themselves in that capacity. Essentially in a trust the outright proprietor of property has transferred the ownership of that property to trustees directing them to hold it for the purposes he indicates in constituting the trust. The person creating a trust is known as the truster, those who administer it, the trustees, and those for whose benefit the trust is set up, the beneficiaries. The position of the truster is best equated in law to that of a donor; that of the trustee to the proprietor of property subject to burdens and conditions as to its administration, use and application, and that of a beneficiary to a person who has rights in property not his own. The rights of the beneficiary may be, but seldom are, exercised against the property as they would be, for example, if the beneficiary had a right to have transferred to him specific items of the trust property; more usually the beneficiary's rights are exercisable against the trustees to ensure that the property is properly administered and the revenues are paid over in accordance with the trust purposes.

Classification of Trusts

Public Trusts and Private Trusts: A public trust is one in which the purpose of the trust is the benefit of the public, or some substantial or identifiable portion of it. In a private trust the benefits of the trust are reserved for private individuals or personae.

Simple and Special Trusts: A simple trust is one in which the trustee holds a property at the instance of the truster but without specific directions as to its application, the property being held pending the instructions of the truster. An example of this sort of trust is the nominee holder of shares in a company. The special trustee is given instructions as to the purposes of the trust.

Express and Implied Trusts: Where the intention to create a trust is explicit the trust is an express trust. If the direction implies that a trust should be created the trust is an implied trust. Included in implied trusts are resulting trusts, those in which the trust purpose have not been declared, or have failed, and constructive trusts, those raised by the operation of law which directs that in certain circumstances a person will hold property in his possession as a trustee and not for his own benefit.

Inter Vivos and Mortis Causa Trusts: A truster may set up a trust during his lifetime and may even act as a trustee if he chooses. He may be a beneficiary of it there being no prohibition on any person enjoying the role simultaneously of truster, trustee and beneficiary, or any combination thereof, bar that a sole trustee cannot be a sole beneficiary. A *mortis causa* trust only becomes operative on the death of the settlor/donor or truster.

Other Trusts: Apart from those who are trustees in trusts proper the law has extended the concept of trust to apply to all who hold or administer property for the benefit of others. Thus tutors, judicial factors, executors, and, as far as not specifically provided for in specific legislation, trustees in bankruptcy are considered bound by the rules relating to trusts.

Constitution of a Trust

Capacity: Any person having legal capacity to dispose of his own property can create a trust over any property over which he has a legal right of disposal. Included in the definition of person are companies, corporations and institutions, or firms. A legal right of disposal can exist where only a limited right exists in property assuming that it is only the limited right which is put in trust and no bar in doing so is implied in the limited right.

Subject Matter: Any property which is capable of transfer or assignation can be made the subject matter of a trust. If the subject matter is not adequately defined or cannot be ascertained from an interpretation of the trust deed the trust will fail through uncertainty.

Form: A *mortis causa* trust can be created only by an authenticated *mortis causa* writing and becomes operative only on the death of the truster, assuming that it remains unrevoked.

An *inter vivos* trust may be created in theory without the necessity of writing. In practice a writing purporting to create a trust will be the foundation of it, and, in law, if writing was necessary to transfer the property intended for the trust, no trust can be created without writing. As with testamentary writings no special form of words is necessary if the intention of the truster to create a trust can be ascertained. If no writing is necessary validly to transfer the property, a trust may be created by a conditional gift or transfer, but it will be a question of interpretation whether the gift was made on such terms as to constitute a trust in the property it comprised or not. Such difficulties are prevented if the trust is express and in writing and for these reasons most trusts are thus formed.

If a writing exists which purports to convey property absolutely to a person and there is a claim that he is a trustee of that property rather than a proprietor such claim will only succeed, if disputed by the holder of the property, by reference to acknowledgement by the holder in writing or on oath that he is a trustee; evidence other than that is not competent.

Trust Purposes and Objects: The trust purposes are the intention of the truster for the application of the trust funds. The objects of the trust are those intended to benefit.

A purpose, if declared, must be sufficiently specified to allow the trustee to give effect to it; if purposes are not so declared the trust fails unless it has been the intention of the truster to give the trustees full discretion in the application of the trust property; in such case, although there are no purposes, the trust may stand.

Similar rules apply to the objects of the trust.

TRUSTEES

Any person who has legal capacity to hold and deal with property may be a trustee, although a minor requires the consent of his curators, if he has one, to assume office, and in acquitting his duties enjoy the privileges of minority. Undischarged bankrupts may act as trustees, as may aliens, but not so to permit them status which as individuals they could not enjoy, such as ownership of a British ship. Corporations who have legal power to do so may be trustees, as may local authorities in public trusts.

There is no limit in the number of persons who may be appointed; it is a matter of construction as to whether each and every person nominated must accept office to constitute the trust; if such be not the case, the acceptance of office by any one of a number of those nominated will constitute the trust.

Nomination as trustee may be made in the trust deed and may be by name, by designation of the holder of a particular office. No one is compelled to accept office as a trustee although in the case of a nomination *ex officio* it may be that the terms of appointment to that office compels acceptance. Usually a nominated trustee is free to decline and incurs no responsibility as trustee until he accepts. A trustee, unless the contrary is expressed, is free to resign although if he is a sole trustee he may not do so unless new trustees have been assumed or appointed by the court. Similarly if all trustees wish to resign they must ensure the continuation of the trust in like manner.

Assumption of Office: If a nominated trustee decides to accept he may do so expressly or his acceptance may be inferred from his performing the duties of a trustee or allowing his name to be used on trust documents. An acceptance of office should be in writing but need not be.

If a nominated trustee does not wish to accept he may disclaim office either expressly or by his actings. A disclaimer, if clear, is final. Delay in accepting is not necessarily disclaimer but if prolonged may infer unwillingness to act.

New Trustees: Under the Trusts (Scotland) Act 1921 (s. 3(*b*)) any trustee or a quorum of trustees have power to assume further trustees unless they are specifically forbidden by the terms of the trust to do so. It is a matter for discretion when such power should be exercised unless there must be a certain number of trustees. The assumption of new trustees is effected by a deed of assumption for which a form is given in the Act, signed by the assuming trustees which acts as a conveyance of the trust property to the trustees as they exist after the assumption. The power of assumption may be exercised by a majority or by a quorum, but all trustees must have notice of the intention to exercise it. If the signatures of a quorum cannot be obtained assumption of new trustees requires the consent of the court, an application being made by the remaining trustees or any beneficiary. If any trustee becomes insane or incapable of action through physical or mental disability or absence from the United Kingdom for six months, the remaining trustees may assume new trustees. Any dispute as to the assumption of new trustees can be referred to the Court of Session.

Any trustee in exercising his power of assumption should take reasonable care to ensure that the new trustees are fit persons; if a trustee is exercising his power of assumption to enable himself to resign he has a special duty in this respect and may be held liable to beneficiaries for any breach of trust if the assumed trustee was not a fit person. Any deadlock as to the assumption of a trustee may be resolved by the Court of Session, which also has powers in special circumstances to forbid the assumption of a new trustee. Assumed trustees have the same powers as nominated trustees, unless the trust deed provides otherwise, and this includes their power, in their turn, to appoint further trustees. An assumed trustee is not personally liable for the administration of his predecessor unless he has acquiesced in it but he is bound to account for his predecessor's administration. When trustees cannot be assumed under any trust deed or when a sole trustee by reason of physical or mental incapacity, absence from the United Kingdom, or disappearance, both for a period of at least six months the Court of Session may on the application of any party interested in the trust estate appoint a trustee will all the powers necessary for the office. More broadly the court has power to appoint new trustees whenever it is necessary for the administration of a trust.

Resignation: By the Trusts (Scotland) Act 1921 (s. 3) a trustee may resign unless the terms of the trust forbid this. A trustee who has accepted any bequest, legacy or annuity given on condition that he became a trustee or a trustee who is remunerated for his services is not free to resign unless the terms of the trust permit this; in the absence of such express permission such a trustee may request court permission to resign which may be granted on such terms as the court may think just, having regard to the interest of the trust. Legacies taken may require to be repaid.

Resignation is entered in the trust's sederunt book and is signed by the resigning trustee and the other trustees. It is immediately effective. Alternative by the resigning trustee may sign a minute of resignation in the form prescribed in Schedule A of the Trusts (Scotland) Act 1921 and register that in the Books of Council and Session and intimate it to the remaining trustees. Such a resignation is effective when intimation to the remaining trustees is complete. If the address of any trustee is unknown intimation may be made edictally through the Keeper of Edictal Citations.

The effect of resignation is to devolve the trust property on the remaining trustees. No conveyance or transfer is needed, although a conveyance may be demanded. Having resigned a former trustee has no future responsibility for the trust or for the actions of his successors. He is entitled to a discharge from both the trustees and the beneficiaries; if such discharge is granted by co-trustees it frees him from liability for acts done after his resignation but probably not from liability for acts done while a trustee. Discharge from the beneficiaries has full effect and, if it cannot be obtained through the incapacity of any beneficiary, the resigning trustee may petition the court to discharge him.

Removal of Trustees: The Court of Session has a common law power for the protection of the beneficiaries and the proper administration of the trust to remove a trustee from office. Such removal will be effective if the trustee is not performing his duties or is acting dishonestly. It is not sufficient ground for removal of a trustee— other remedies being available—that their management of the trust is negligent or that they cannot agree amongst themselves. The court may also remove any person who is a sole trustee and has become insane or incapable of acting by reason of physical or mental disability or by being absent continuously from the United Kingdom for a period of at least six months or having disappeared for the similar period. In such case the court will appoint new trustees.

Without removing the trustees the court may sequestrate the trust estate and appoint a judicial factor to administer it; the trustees being superseded in their administration. Such an appointment can be sought at the instance of a trustee or of a beneficiary. Supersession by a judicial factor can be justified on grounds less than that necessary to justify removal, for example where there is deadlock in administration or where the conduct of trustees seems to make it dangerous to leave the trust in their hands. The factor's appointment by the court may be recalled at any time.

Powers of Trustees

The powers conferred on trustees to enable them to acquit the trust purposes are derived from the trust deed, the common law and from statute. Basically the controlling source of a trustee's powers is the trust deed and the statutory powers are intended to supplement those or even to render the provision of express powers unnecessary. Despite the dominant position of the powers expressed in a trust deed the courts may intervene to assist in the administration and execution of the trust in two ways. Exceptionally the Court of Session under its *nobile officium* may grant further powers to a trustee if the conditions of a trust are making it unworkable, rendering its purposes fruitless or endangering the estate; the court acting under these powers will not extend the powers merely because it would be beneficial to do so. By the Trusts (Scotland) Act 1921 (s. 5) the court may grant authority to trustees to exercise any statutory power even if doing so would be at variance with the terms of the trust if the court is satisfied that it is expedient for the execution of the trust in all the circumstances to permit this. Apart from these two possibilities the court may consider any application by trustees to interpret their powers if they are doubtful as to the extent of these. Under the Administration of Justice (Scotland) Act 1933 (s. 17) trustees or a majority or quorum of them may apply to the court for direction on questions relating to the investment, distribution, management or administration of the trust estate, or as to the exercise of any power vested in or as to the performance of any duty imposed on them. Such petitions may appropriately be presented to aid the trustees faced with a practical difficulty.

Statutory Powers: By the Trusts (Scotland) Act, 1921, as enlarged by the Trustee Investment Act 1961, trustees are invested with a list of general powers which they may exercise where such exercise would not be at variance with the terms or purposes of the trust. The list includes power to realise part of the estate by public auction or private bargain; to feu or lease any part of the heritage; to borrow money on the security of any part of the estate; to appoint factors and law agents and to remunerate them; to compromise claims or submit them to arbitration; and in respect of securities held by the trustees, to concur in any scheme or arrangement for the reconstruction of the company, sale to another company, takeover by another company, amalgamation, or variation of rights, to accept other securities in lieu and to subscribe for or renounce rights issues all as though the trustees were beneficial owners of the security.

Trustees are further empowered, where such act is not at variance with the terms or purpose of the trust to acquire with funds of the trust estate any interest in residential accommodation reasonably required to enable the trustees to provide a suitable residence for occupation by any of the beneficiaries. Normally trustees must invest to produce a return (and in any event there is no right to acquire heritable property as an investment unless specifically authorised to do so by the trust deed), but this provision gives them a limited power to acquire an interest, which may be acquired either by purchase or by lease, for occupation by any beneficiary of the trust without requiring to obtain a rent. By the Trustee Investments Act 1961 (s. 2) the validity of a transaction for the sale of heritage and of any title acquired by the purchaser may not be challenged on the grounds that the sale is at variance with the terms or purposes of the trust.

Investment Powers: One of the responsibilities of trustees is to invest the trust's funds appropriately for the fulfilment of the trust purposes. Difficulties may arise in acquitting this power as the interests of different beneficiaries may not be identical; for example, beneficiaries who are interested in the capital of the trust will be interested in the conservation and growth of that capital, while those interested in income from it may consider different forms of investment to be advantageous from their point of view. Traditionally a great deal of caution was demanded of trustees in their investment policies and a considerable deal of diligence was demanded from them even when exercising powers specifically conferred on them by the trust deed. Only with the specific authority of the trust deed can a trust estate contain bearer investments because of the risk of loss by theft.

The investment powers of trustees will spring from the trust deed, or from the law, or from some combination of both. As it was felt that the traditional forms of investment allowed by law to trustees were much too restrictive it became common for the truster to prescribe wider investment powers than the law permitted. No matter that such powers were contained in the trustee deed the trustees had to use their powers and exercise their discretion wisely and avoid hazard. A trustee must show the same degree of diligence in carrying out his duties as a man of ordinary prudence would exercise in his own affairs. He can, and should, take advice, but the responsibility of decisions in the course of administration remains with him. In one case trustees allowed one investment in their portfolio to fall in value through failure to keep regular watch and were held liable to make good to the beneficiary, notwithstanding a substantial rise in the remainder of the investments under the trustees' management, and in spite of a clause in the trust deed purporting to indemnify them against such claims. The original list of authorised trustee investments is contained in the Trusts (Scotland) Act 1921. By the Trustee Investments Act 1961 there was introduced a new concept of authorised trustee investment, the new powers being in addition to any already granted to trustees: previous powers do not limit the statutory powers but trust deeds signed after this Act was passed may restrict these powers if a trustee so wishes. The purpose of the Act was to allow trustees to invest in a wider range of investments than had previously been authorised but up to a limit of one-half of the trust fund. The Act defines 'narrower range' investments and 'wider range' investments and makes provision for 'special-range property'. The narrower range investments are subdivided into those 'requiring advice' and those 'not requiring advice'; these being defined and listed in the first and second schedules to the Act.

The narrower range investments not requiring advice are broadly those where both the capital and the interest earned are fixed and guaranteed; examples are defence bonds, national savings certificates, National Savings Bank deposits, Trustee Saving Bank deposits and National Development Bonds. The narrower range investments requiring advice are investments normally thought to be safe investments because the funds are guaranteed by some national or local authority but differ from the other category of narrower range investments in that the capital value may fluctuate on the stock-market or the interest payments may vary. Such investments include: British Government Securities, Treasury bills and tax reserve certificates; all securities where the interest payment is guaranteed by the United Kingdom government, fixed interest securities issued by public authorities or nationalised industries in the United Kingdom; fixed interest securities issued by the government of any overseas country within the Commonwealth or by any public or local authority within such a territory, provided the securities are registered in the United Kingdom; certain debentures issued by companies in the United Kingdom, local authority loans of all kinds charged on their revenues; special investment deposits in a Trustee Savings Bank; deposits in a designated building society; mortgages or loans on heritable securities; and feu duties and ground annuals.

The 'wider range investments' are those of a more speculative nature where both capital and income tend to fluctuate and include certain securities issued by United Kingdom companies, shares in designated building societies, and unit trusts approved by the Board of Trade. Those companies whose shares fall within 'wider range investments' are those where (a) the company's total issued and paid up capital is not less than £1 million; and (b) the company in each of the five years immediately preceding the calendar year in which the investment is made, has paid a dividend on all the shares issued by the company of every type (except for shares issued after the last dividend was declared, or shares, which by their terms of issue did not rank for dividend in that year). A company formed to take over another company or acquire the shares in another company is deemed to have paid a dividend for this purpose in any year in which a dividend has been paid by the other company or companies as the case may be.

The narrower range investments, whether or not requiring advice' are always authorised investments for trustees. In the absence of investment powers in the trust deed the wider range investments can only be taken up by trustees who follow the procedure specified in the Trustee Investments Act 1961 (s. 2). Trustees wishing to take advantage of the wider range provisions must make a once and for all division of the trust fund into two parts, which are equal at the time of the division. Thereafter no investments may be transferred from one part of the fund to the other unless (1) the transfer is authorised, or required, by the Act or (2) a compensating transfer of investments of equal value is made. Property falling within the narrow range portion of the trust fund must be invested in narrow range investments only and any property invested in any other way which is, or becomes comprised in that part must be transferred to the wider range part, with a compensating transfer; or alternatively reinvested in narrow range investments as soon as may be.

Where any property accrues to a trust fund after the division has taken place, then (1) if the property accrues to the trustees as holders of investments already comprised in either part of the fund, the accrual will fall to the same part of the fund, for example an issue of bonus shares in respect of an existing holding of shares in the trust; or (2) in any other case the trustees must secure by apportionment of the accruing property, or the transfer of property from one part of the fund to the other, or both, that the value of each part of the fund is increased by the same amount.

Where trustees acquire property in consideration of a money payment, the acquisition of the property is treated as an investment and not an accrual, notwithstanding that the amount of the price paid is less than the value of the property acquired: for example, on taking up a rights issue, an acquisition of equity rights would have to be added to the wider range part, and a compensating transfer made. If the rights were sold, however, this would be treated as an accrual and the proceeds would follow the parent holding.

If apportionments have been carried out allocating proportions of dividend or interest to capital, such portions falling into the capital of the trust are not treated as accruals to be added to the original investment but as acquisitions requiring to be apportioned over the fund.

Where trustees make any payment of cash out of the trust fund they have discretion as to which part makes the payment.

The trustees can carry out their own valuation and division of the trust fund although the Act (s. 5) provides that if a trustee obtains from a person, reasonably believed by him to be qualified to make it, a valuation in writing of the trust fund, such valuation shall be conclusive in determining whether the division of the trust fund or any transfer or apportionment of investments has been properly made.

Special Range Investments: If a truster has given specific instruc-

tions about a particular block of stocks and shares and such cannot
be retained because they could not satisfy the requirements of any
type of authorised investment the truster is deemed by the Act to
have given a special power to his trustees to invest in or to retain
these shares. This covers any investments which the trustees are
authorised to hold under the terms of the trust deed, as distinct
from the various Acts, or which became part of a trust fund in
consequence of the trustee's accepting bonus shares or taking up
rights issues which were based on such investments. Special range
investments of this kind are treated as a separate part of the whole
trust fund and are taken away from the trust fund into a special
category before the valuation and division takes place to determine
the narrower range and wider range portions. If any investment
existing in the narrower range or wider range part of the fund is
converted into a special range investment, it must be carried into the
separate special range fund, as must also any accrual to existing
special range investments. On the other hand, if property within
the special range category is converted to property other than the
authorised special range investment it must be transferred to the
narrower range or to the wider range part of the fund, or apportioned between and any transfer of property from one of these
parts to the other should be made which is necessary to secure that
the value of each of these parts of the fund is increased by the same
amount. If the trustees are charged with the accomplishment of
different trust purposes and utilise certain portions of the trust fund
for each of these purposes, each portion thus identified can be
treated as a separate trust fund and the investment rules applied
separately to it. Under the Act (s. 6) a trustee is charged to have
regard to the need for diversification of the trust investments in so
far as appropriate to the circumstances of the trust and to the suitability to the trust of investments of the description proposed and
of the particular investment proposed within that description.

Before exercising any power of investment the trustees must
obtain and consider proper advice, having regard to diversification
and suitability, such advice to be taken from a person reasonably
believed by the trustee to be qualified by his ability in, and practical
experience of, financial matters.

Apart from the choice of investments, the trustees must keep
their investments under review, and, particularly, a trustee retaining
an investment made in any category requiring advice must determine

at what intervals the circumstances and, in particular, the nature of the investment make it desirable to obtain advice about retaining the investment, and he must obtain and consider such advice accordingly. If one of the trustees is a person reasonably believed by the others to be suitably qualified to give advice then outside advice need not be taken.

The Duties of Trustees: The general duty of a trustee in administering a trust is to exercise the care of a reasonably prudent man. A high standard is set but there is not absolute liability for error or loss nor for error of judgement but good faith, honesty and conduct adequate by the trustees' own judgement do not necessarily equal the duty of care demanded at this standard. The test of whether the requisite standard of care has been reached is objective.

A trustee must retain the control in administration of the trust and must not delegate it or surrender it to fellow trustees or agents. This does not mean that the trustee may not employ persons of skill to advise on technical matters; in fact he should do so. He must not however subordinate his judgement to their advice but must seek to evaluate it and himself take the decisions. Where properly qualified and competent advisers have been employed by the trustee he is not liable for dishonesty or malperformance of duties properly entrusted to them.

A trustee must allow no conflict to arise between his own interest and those of the trust; any benefit or profit which he does receive through being trustee he must account for to the trust and this will include payment or fees unless the truster authorised the charging of these or all the beneficiaries have agreed to a charge being made. No personal profit must be made from the trust and this demands that the trustee should refrain from transacting as an individual with the trust's estate lest there be conflict between the interest of the estate and his personal interest.

Accumulations of Income

There is occasionally in a trust a direction to the trustees to accumulate income and not to pay it out.

By statute[40] there are prescribed six periods which, independently of each other, limit a permissible period of accumulation. Accumu-

[40] Accumulations Acts 1800—1892

lation of income is illegal unless at least one of these periods applies and if a relevant period ceases to apply accumulation becomes illegal. The periods are:

1. The lifetime of the grantor of an *inter vivos* trust deed.
2. Twenty-one years from the death of a testator.
3. The duration of the minority or the respective minorities of any person or persons living or *in utero* at the death of the grantor.
4. The duration of the minority or respective minorities of any person or persons who, under the terms of the deed directing the accumulation, would for the time being, if of full age be entitled to the income directed to be accumulated. This provides for the accumulation during minority but commencing some time after the grantor's death, for example, after the implementing of a prior trust purpose: and in an *inter vivos* trust the accumulation is allowed although the period begins during the life of the grantor and ends after his death notwithstanding (1) above.
5. A term of twenty-one years from the date of the making of the settlement.
6. The duration of the minority or respective minorities of any person living or *in utero* at that date.

In 5 and 6 the accumulation is valid although the periods may begin before and end after the death of the grantor; these last periods are obviously designed to apply the principles of 2 and 3 to *inter vivos* trusts. It is clear that the restrictions operate where income has in fact been accumulated, whether or not there was an actual duty to accumulate, and whether or not the power to accumulate extends to income produced through investments which themselves represent income previously accumulated.

In all cases, income arising after accumulation is forbidden must be paid over to the beneficiaries entitled to it under the trust deed as if accumulation had not been directed; and should it be that there is no provision settling this, the income may fall into intestacy.

R

CHAPTER NINE

RIGHTS IN SECURITY

A LENDER of money relies on the undertaking of his debtor to repay the money. Often he feels it wise to reinforce this obligation in some way, usually by stipulating for the transfer to him of some property in security of the advance so that, should repayment not be made, he can satisfy his claim out of the property.

A right in security 'denotes a right in the creditor upon an event, ordinarily the default of the debtor, to seek satisfaction in so far as possible of the debt out of a specific asset'.[1] Or, 'The term right in security may be read as denoting any right which a creditor may possess for the recovery of his debt in the event of the bankruptcy of his debtor, distinct from and in addition to, the right which he possesses in common with all other creditors of claiming a ranking in the sequestration'.[2] This second definition is wider than the first for it can be read to include any corroborative obligation undertaken by a third party. Such a cautionary obligation whereby a third party undertakes to pay should the debtor default falls outwith the scope of this chapter, except in the case where the third party is reinforcing his personal obligation with a pledge or property.

Security may be created by express contract, by implication of law, or by the use of diligence. No matter how the security is constituted, the ultimate test of its validity arises on the bankruptcy of the debtor when the body of creditors and the security holder are in competition. If the security is good its holder can retain the property against the wishes of the other creditors; if it has not been properly constituted the property over which the alleged security was granted, or is thought to exist, will require to be given over to the trustee on behalf of the creditors as a body, and the creditor, who considered himself secured, will accordingly rank with the other creditors.

Of course, a banker, while bearing in mind that his security, if it is

---

[1] Gow, Op cit. p. 271.
[2] Bell, *Principles*, para 203.

to be relied upon, must be complete and valid against the borrower's creditors in the circumstance of his bankruptcy, may also wish to provide that the security is realisable without the customer's becoming bankrupt. If the banker in the ordinary course of his business wishes to discontinue facilities afforded to a customer he will wish to avail himself of any rights in security that he may possess should the customer prove unable to repay his indebtedness. It is a matter to be dealt with in any particular contract creating rights in security that the banker obtains the power to realise his securities in such circumstances.

The majority of rights in security are created by contract, but there are rights in security which arise through the operation of law and through the use of diligence.[3] Example of rights in security which arise through operation of law include hypothec and lien, the existence of which in any particular property might affect the suitability and worth of that property as a suitable subject for security. These apart, however, the usual method of the creation of a right in security is contractual, but there are specialities of the law which depend on the nature of the subject matter, whether it is heritable or moveable property. In either case, however, the object of the creditor is the same, to achieve a 'real' right in the property to reinforce his 'personal' right against the debtor.

Third party security: There is a distinction to be drawn between security held from the borrower, and security provided by a third party. When the borrower himself pledges security he provides his own property. It is however possible that the security is provided by a third party. It does not matter who is providing the security as far as the constitution of it is concerned; the same principles apply. The entitlement of the lender however to take possession of, or realise the security will require to be stipulated according to the source of the security.

Security over moveable property

Corporeal moveables: The cardinal rule of Scots law as far as security over corporeal moveables is concerned is plain: there is no real right created until the creditor has possession of the goods. The agreement alone will not create a right in security; it must be followed by the delivery of the goods. The principal exception to this

[3] *Infra,* Chap. XI

rule concerns the right of companies to grant floating charges.[4]

The contract whereby corporeal moveables are transferred in security is called pledge. It is a contract by which one places in the hands of his creditor a moveable object, to remain with him in security of a debt or engagement, to be redelivered on payment or satisfaction, and implies mandate, on failure to fulfil the engagement at the stipulated time or on demand, to have the pledge sold by judicial authority.

So long as the goods remain in possession of the borrower or under his control, no pledge has been effected. Delivery is essential to complete the right of the lender. While this principle would, at first sight, seem to debar from forming suitable subjects for security all but the smallest items unless the lender were prepared to warehouse, garage, or store the security subjects, this is not in fact the case, as the delivery required to complete the pledge may be actual, symbolic or constructive.

Actual delivery: This takes place when the goods are transferred into the control of the lender. They may be physically transferred or the total control of them may be transferred. Thus in the case of *West Lothian Oil Company* v. *Mair*[5] barrels in the yard of a company were enclosed by a fence, and the key of its gate was given to a party who advanced money on the security of the barrels. It was held that there had been delivery and the security was completed. In the normal case however there would require to be physical transfer of the goods to complete the security.

Symbolic delivery: This occurs where the security subjects are aboard ship at sea. During that time the title to the goods is the bill of lading, which has been issued at the port of shipment in respect of the goods. Indorsement and delivery of a bill of lading transfers ownership of such goods, and therefore indorsement and delivery of the bill of lading can be used to effect a pledge of the goods. No intimation to any person is necessary that there has been such a transfer.

The lender taking a bill of lading in security, like a purchaser of goods which are at sea, has to ensure that on the face of the documents there is no indication that the shipment is other than regular, that the goods are aboard the ship and in good condition, and that

[4] *Infra*, p. 277
[5] (1892) 20 R 64.

there is no bar to his demanding, if necessary, delivery of the goods to him or to his order at the port of delivery.

Constructive delivery: Constructive delivery may be effected when the goods are in a store belonging to a third party. It is essential that the goods are in a neutral warehouse; that is, one owned or under the control of a third party not in any way identified with the owner of the goods. An order to the neutral store-keeper to deliver to the lender, or the indorsation of the store-keeper's receipt for the goods in favour of the lender, may effect delivery if the following conditions are satisfied: (1) the store-keeper is an independent third party, not a servant or agent of the lender; (2) there is intimation to the storekeeper so that he is aware that he holds on behalf of the lender and that the lender possesses through him; (3) the goods are specifically ascertained and identified.

Warehouse-keepers receipt: When goods are deposited in a warehouse or store the warehouse will acknowledge that the goods are held to the order of the person named and at his disposal, the goods being described by marks or numbers and by quantities. This acknowledgement or receipt is not a document of title and itself confers no title in the goods, either in the person named in the receipt or in any person to whom he may transfer it. Occasionally, but not very usually there is issued by a warehouseman a 'warrant for goods' which is a document of title which passes by indorsement and delivery. The following is the statutory definition of a 'warrant for goods': 'Any document or writing being evidence of the title of any person therein named or his assignees or the holder thereof to the property in any goods, wares or merchandise lying in any warehouse or dock, or upon any wharf, and signed or certified by or on behalf of the person having custody of the goods, wares or merchandise.'[6] In any event it does not matter whether there is proffered as evidence of the existence of goods a warehouseman's receipt or a 'warrant of goods'; a lender taking the goods in security will intimate to the warehouseman that the goods should be held for him and not for their proprietor. In either event the warehouse-keeper's document should be taken into the custody of the lender.

Where the goods are held on receipt by the warehouseman transfer of the right in them is effected by delivery order, defined[7] as 'any

---

[6] Stamp Act 1891, s. 111.
[7] Ibid., s. 69.

document or writing entitling, or intending to entitle any person therein named, or his assigns or the holder thereof, to the delivery of any goods, wares or merchandise of the value of £2.00 or upwards, lying in any dock or port or any warehouse in which the goods are stored or deposited on rent or hire, or upon any wharf, such document or writing being signed by or on behalf of the owner of such goods, wares or merchandise upon the sale or transfer of the property therein'.

The transfer of the goods contained in the receipt and delivery order is not however complete until the delivery order is acknowledged by the store-keeper and a fresh acknowledgement obtained in the name of the lender. Only then is the pledge complete.

Ascertained goods: To be effective the transfer must be of ascertained goods. Under the Sale of Goods Act, 1893 (s. 16) no property in unascertained goods is transferred to the buyer until the goods are ascertained. Normally the warehouseman's receipt and delivery order will specifically identify the goods and this is a sufficient ascertainment and identification of them. It may be however that what is being pledged is part of a larger quantity of goods in the property of the borrower and in such case there must be ascertainment. Thus in the case of *Hayman* v. *McLintock*[8] there were a number of bags of flour in a store with no distinguishing marks. A delivery order for some was intimated and acknowledged by the storekeeper but it was held constructive delivery had not taken place because there was no means of determining which bags were transferred. Setting apart by the store-keeper of goods mentioned in the delivery order from a mass belonging to the borrower will constitute ascertainment, even when done subsequently, when the delivery date will be the date of ascertainment.

Warehouse-keeper's lien: A warehouse-keeper has a general lien, or right of retention, on all goods under his control for any claims which he may have against the owners for, for example, rent, insurance, or other expenses. This lien will form a prior charge on the goods to any being constituted by the pledge of them and the lender should therefore ascertain that there is no such charge and that further dues to the store-keeper are met at the expense of the borrower.

Releasing the security: Where a warrant for goods' is held the

---

[8] 1907 S.C. 936.

security in the property is released by indorsement and delivery of it to the borrower. When the goods are held under warehouse-keeper's receipt the lender must issue the borrower with a delivery order which he will intimate to the store-keeper.

Realisation of the security: As holder of a delivery order or warrant the lender is entitled to sell or otherwise dispose of the goods without the necessity of any further procedure, but this right to sell is limited by the fact that the proceeds of the sale must be accounted for to the borrower for any surplus remaining after the debt has been satisfied.

Security over incorporeal moveable property

A right of any kind may be transferred in security by written assignation followed by intimation to the obligant. Apart from those rights contained in negotiable instruments, intimation of the transfer of a right to the obligant is necessary if a right is to be effectually transferred. Thus, where a policy of insurance was delivered without intimation to the insurance company it was held that no preferential right vested in the transferee [9]

The right obtained by the security holder through the assignation is the right held by the cedent; he is affected by all pleas competent against the cedent. The Transmission of Moveable Property (Scotland) Act 1862 provides that a person's right in a personal bond may be assigned, or a conveyance of moveable estate may be effected, either by a separate writing or by an assignation indorsed on the bond or conveyance itself and forms, both brief and concise, are provided in the schedules annexed to the Act. Such assignation is validly intimated (1) by a notary public delivering a copy thereof certified as correct to the person or persons to whom intimation may in any case be required or (2) by the holder of such assignation, or any person authorised by him, transmitting a copy thereof certified as correct by post to such person. In practice, it is usual to send the principal assignation along with a copy of it to the person entitled to receive the intimation and get him to write his acknowledgement on the principal, the copy being retained by him. The words 'bond' and 'conveyance' in the Act extend to and include personal bonds for payment or performance, bonds of caution, bonds of guarantee, bonds of relief, bonds aids assignations and security of every kind,

---

[9] *Wylie's Ex.* v. *McJarrett* (1901) 4 F. 195.

policies of insurance, protests of bills or promissory notes, dispositions, assignations and other conveyances of moveable or personal
property or effects. Moveable estate extends to all personal debts
and obligations and moveable or personal property or effects of
every kind.

Insurance policies

A common form of security subject is an insurance policy over
the life of the borrower, or possibly over the life of some other
person, usually a cautioner for the borrower. The rights obtained by
the lender, according to the contract, are either the right to the
surrender value of the policy, or the right to collect the proceeds of
the policy on the death of the insured or on the maturity of the
policy, or both of these.

It is essential that the policy is assignable. A life policy is usually
assignable and almost invariably contains a statement to that effect.
If there is a prohibition upon assignation the policy is of no value as
a security unless the insurer is prepared to vary that condition.
Similarly, if the surrender value of the policy is of interest to the
lender, as it will be should the borrower become insolvent, it is
essential that the policy must be by its terms capable of surrender for
cash. If there is a prohibition against surrender then the utility of the
policy as security is limited. The right in security is effected by an
assignation of the policy which will include power to the lender to
collect the proceeds and grant a discharge for the amount, to sell or
surrender the policy, and to do with the policy and the monies
payable under it everything which the assignor himself could have
done before he granted the assignation.

The utility of a policy of insurance as a subject for security depends
upon its validity and enforceability against the insurer. As an
assignee under an assignation takes no higher right in the subject of
the assignation than that possessed by the cedent, any defences
available to the insurance company against the insured will be useful
to them against the lender; therefore the lender must take steps to
ensure that the policy is in force, that the premiums have been paid
and are kept paid to keep the policy in life.

Insurance companies must elect at which of their offices notice of
assignation has to be given and the address of that office is stated on
the policy. Intimation of the assignation is made usually by sending
to the insurance company the assignation and a copy of it, the copy

being retained by the company while the principal is returned indorsed with an acknowledgement.

Where there are other assignations outstanding, the assignations take preference amongst themselves according to the date of their intimation with the insurance company.

Reassigning a policy: When a policy is no longer required as security it may be transferred back to the insured by means of a retrocession, divesting the lender of his title and vesting the insured in his title again, restoring to him the rights which he had in the policy at the time he granted the assignation.

Unassignable policies: There are special provisions regarding policies of insurance under the Married Women's Policies of Assurance (Scotland) Act 1880 which affect the utility of some policies as security subjects. Under this Act (s. 2) a married man may effect a policy on his own life for the benefit of his wife or his children, or for the benefit of his wife and his children. A policy of this kind, which will specifically state that it is drawn under this statute, does not form part of the husband's estate but creates a trust on behalf of the beneficiaries. Such policy cannot therefore be validly assigned to a bank, even with the consent of the beneficiaries.

Stock Exchange securities

When stock exchange securities or similar types of investment are offered to a bank in security for an advance, the completion of the title of the lender depends on the nature of the particular security.

Shares in a company: The mere delivery of the share certificate representing shares in a company offers a lender no security of any sort and further steps must be taken to constitute, or towards the constitution of, a greater right in the shares. The lender may take steps to have himself registered as a member of the company. This is achieved by presenting to the company's registrar the standard form under the Stock Transfer Act 1963 signed by the borrower as owner of the shares transferring the shares to the lender or his nominee. The registrar of the company on receipt of the transfer form will register the lender as the proprietor of the shares. The terms and conditions upon which the lender holds the shares are a matter for agreement between himself and the borrower but this agreement should vest the lender with a power of sale; otherwise, court authority would be required before such sale could be made.

While the lender or his nominee is the registered holder of these shares he will be treated by the company as if he were proprietor; all notices concerning the company's affairs, accounts and reports, will be sent to the lender and he will be entitled to exercise as apparent owner of the shares the usual rights of a shareholder. The lender must see that any benefits accruing to the real owners of the shares, or any information affecting their interest, are passed on to them.

For example, if a new issue or a bonus issue is being offered by the company the lender would require to inform the owner of the shares on receiving notice of this, and act on the instructions of the owner to preserve his position with regard to whatever steps the company is taking.

As an alternative to registration the lender may prefer to take into his possession the share certificate and a duly executed transfer form in respect of it but not to proceed to register this transfer. In this case the lender's security is incomplete and the holder of a subsequent transfer who seeks registration or a trustee in bankruptcy of the borrower may defeat the lender's right in security by procuring registration before the lender does.

Where a bank takes shares in a public company in security from a customer and secures registration of these shares in its own name, or that of its nominee, it will be unusual if these are the only shares in that particular company which the bank holds. Normally the aggregate of the shares pledged by customers, or otherwise held on behalf of customers, will be treated as a single holding in the company concerned. Difficulty can arise when the property is due to be returned to the borrower. It is a basic rule of pledge that what the borrower is entitled to get back is the property which he pledged, not property in substitution for it or property of equivalent value. Thus what should be returned are the actual shares pledged. In *Crerar* v. *The Bank of Scotland*[10a] it was held that only an established course of dealing between the bank and its customer permitted the bank to return an equivalent quantity of shares; had there been no course of dealing the bank would have been in the wrong to deliver an equivalent quantity. Thus a bank should ensure at the inception of the pledge that it has the right to deliver substitute shares of the same denomination if it does not wish to maintain the separate holdings required to permit re-delivery the precise shares pledged.

Shares in a private company are not freely transferable; thus the

10a 1922 S.C. (H.L.) 137

banker who takes these in security cannot demand registration as the holder of these shares and become a member of the company. This reduces the attraction of such shares as security subjects, as does the limited, or sometimes non-existent, market in such shares.

Other securities

Post Office registers: Where government stocks are held on the registers kept at the Post Office register certificates will be issued in respect of an individual's holding. This holding may be transferred on the special form provided and there is no objection to a transfer in security.

British Savings Bonds, National Development Bonds, Defence Bonds: These bonds are registered at the Post Office, the evidence of title of the proprietor being a bond book. These bonds cannot be transferred from their holder by way of security although it is possible to make a purchase of British Savings Bonds direct into the name of a lender, specifically designated with the beneficial owner's name. As the lender is the registered proprietor this is a security. A subsequent transfer of the bonds from the lender to the owner is permitted whenever desired.

Trustee Savings Bank Registers: Holders of stock on a Trustee Savings Bank Register must maintain an account with that particular savings bank and have the interest on the stock credited to that account. A lender who wishes to take security in such stock must, unless he has an account with the particular savings bank in question, arrange to have the stock transferred from that register to the Bank of England or Post Office Register where it may appear with lender as proprietor.

Unit Trusts: The interests of a borrower in a Unit Trust can be transferred in security to a lender on an ordinary stock transfer form.

Security in ships

Under the Merchant Shipping Act, 1894, the property in a British registered ship is divided into sixty-four shares, and not more than sixty-four persons can be registered as owners of a ship, save that up to five persons can be joint owners of any share. Registers are maintained at ports of registry and the particulars regarding the ownership of any registered ship may be ascertained from the register at its port of registration, in which both original ownership and any transmission thereof will be registered. The person or persons appearing on the register as individual or joint owners of a ship, or any share therein, may dispose of or mortgage the ship or share without qualification, and purchasers or lenders on the security of the ship or shares in a ship, so long as they act in good faith, are protected notwithstanding any defect in the title of the transferor, the public being entitled to rely on the entries in the register. Even single shares may be mortgaged or sold.

The mortgaging of a ship is accomplished by the registration with the registrar at the ship's port of registration of an instrument in the form prescribed by the Act.[10] The registrar is bound to register such mortgage and any transmission of it, which may be by death or bankruptcy, as well as by the act of the lender, in which case there is a statutory form of transmission. A transmission has to be authenticated by the transferee. Mortgages have priority amongst themselves according to the dates of their respective registrations. An unregistered mortgage is not invalid, but will be postponed to a registered mortgage, even where the holders of the registered mortgage were aware of the existing of the prior, unregistered charge.

A mortgagee is not deemed to be owner of the ship save so far as is necessary to make it available as security for the debt in the mortgage, and cannot take possession of the ship until there has been default in payment, on the part of the mortgagor, or a breach in his duty in respect of the mortgage by unlawfully impairing the subject of the security. If either be the case, the registered mortgagee has absolute power to dispose of the ship or share in respect of which he is registered, and to grant effectual receipts for the purchase money. Postponed mortgagees cannot, except under the authority of a competent Court, sell a ship or share over which they hold mortgages without the consent of prior mortgagees. In selling the mortgagee is bound to exercise that care and diligence which a prudent man would show in the management of his own affairs, and, if a surplus emerges on sale, must hold that surplus as a trustee for the owner of the ship and for any postponed mortgagees.

A mortgagor also has the power to take possession of a mortgaged ship and to draw its earnings, though he must exercise his operation of the ship with prudence and is liable for its disbursements; he is entitled to remain in possession until his mortgage is paid either by the mortgagor or from the ship's earnings.

[10] s. 24.

Rather than proceeding by way of mortgage, it is possible for a type of security to be taken in a registered ship by the lender having the ownership of the vessel transferred to his name by bill of sale duly registered; the advantages of this procedure over mortgages are minimal while the disadvantage is that the registered proprietor of a ship becomes liable for the risks incidental to the ownership of the vessel, risks which are not of any concern to the registered mortgagee. This method of taking security is rare.

Discharge of a mortgage: On production of a mortgage deed, with a receipt for the mortgage money, duly signed and attested, indorsed on it, the register makes an entry in the register book to the effect that the mortgage has been discharged whereupon the property, if any, which passed to the mortgagee vests in the person in whom, having regard to any intervening acts and circumstances, it would have vested had the mortgage not been granted.[11]

In a question between the mortgagor and the mortgagee, the mortgage is discharged when the debt has been paid or satisfied in other competent manner, even although the discharge has not been executed and registered. Thus there is a certain risk in taking the transfer of a mortgage, as, if the mortgage has been discharged, an assignee of the mortgage will have no rights under it, as the original mortgagee can confer no rights higher than he himself possesses. That the mortgage is still outstanding should be checked with the owner of the ship or share.

Fluctuating advances: Where the advance is to be a fluctuating, rather than a fixed amount, the form of mortgage will reflect this.

Fishing boats: Fishing boats may be registered under the Sea Fishing Boats (Scotland) Act, 1886 and any boat so registered may be made security for a loan or other valuable consideration. Similar rules to those in the case of ships apply.

Security over heritable property

The creation of a valid right in security over lands or buildings depends on the registration of the document creating the right in the Register of Sasines. Until the deed is so registered there is no real right and it is not effective against third parties, e.g. a successor to the lands either by inheritance or subsequent sale.

Unlike moveable property, which must appear to be in the owner-

[11] Ibid. s. 32.

ship of the lender, heritable property, because of the existence and use of the Register of Sasines, can be charged by the lender without his taking physical possession of it and be burdened in his favour so that he has a right in the property for the repayment of the advance.

The standard security: The lender who advanced money on the strength of a heritable security had, at one time, a choice of methods by which his loan could be secured. He could choose an *ex facie* absolute disposition of the security subjects to him, which disposition, when registered, would indicate to anyone examining the Register of Sasines that the lender was in fact proprietor. Alternatively, the lender could choose either a bond and disposition in security or a bond of cash credit and disposition in security. However, a new form of heritable security, the standard security, was introduced by Part II of the Conveyancing and Feudal Reform (Scotland) Act 1970. The provisions of the Act relating to the standard security came into effect on 29th November 1970 and, with certain very minor exceptions, it is now incompetent to create a heritable security other than by the standard security.[12] There are, however, still in existence, securities created by the former methods and, accordingly, these methods cannot yet be treated as having passed out of the realm of practical conveyancing into legal history.

The standard security is, 'a flexible type of security adaptable for use whether the debt is of fixed or uncertain amount or an open-ended obligation or even an obligation *ad factum praestandum'*.[13] [14] The Act defines 'debt' so as to include, apart from obligations *ad facta praestanda*, all loans or advances of money, present or future, of fixed or uncertain amount. Any obligation to pay feu-duty, rent or any other periodic sum payable in respect of land is excluded. The definition of debt in the Act widens the scope of the standard security beyond that of the former methods.

Basically, the standard security comprises a personal obligation, by the debtor to the creditor, to perform the obligation to which the security relates and a grant to the creditor of the interest in the heritage over which the security is to be secured. The personal obligation may, however, be constituted in a separate instrument.

The standard conditions: Schedule 3 of the Act contains what are

---

[12] Conveyancing and Feudal Reform (Scotland) Act 1970, s. 9(3).
[13] and obligation to perform duties.
[14] Halliday, *Conveyancing and Feudal Reform (Scotland) Act 1970*, p. 63.

known as the 'standard conditions', which regulate the maintenance, management and insurance of the security subjects by the debtor; calling-up; default and the rights of the creditor on such default; and the debtor's right of redemption. The conditions may be imported into the security deed by reference to Schedule 3 and accordingly it is unnecessary, where there is no alteration or variation of the conditions, to express them in the deed. The conditions comprise those which would normally be included in a standard security. However, they are not an exhaustive list and the parties may add to, vary or exclude any of them except those relating to sale, foreclosure and the procedure on redemption. Neither may the non-variable conditions be altered indirectly by a variation of the others.

Calling-up: Where the creditor in a standard security intends to require discharge of the debt secured, and failing discharge to exercise his powers of sale, foreclosure, entering into possession and repair, reconstruction and improvement, he may serve a calling-up notice on the debtor and the proprietor where the two are different. The notice calls on the debtor to fulfil his obligation within two months or such longer period as may be stipulated in the notice. However, the period of notice may be shortened or dispensed with by the agreement of the debtor. Where the debt is of an uncertain amount it is necessary to have a certificate, signed by the person authorised to do so in terms of the security, ascertaining the amount due at the time when the calling-up notice is served. However, the creditor may be precluded from calling-up by the terms of the security, e.g. if the obligation is to pay by instalments.

Default: A debtor is held to be in default in three situations:
1. Where a calling-up notice in respect of the security has been served and not complied with.
2. Where there has been a failure to comply with any other requirement arising out of the security. There are two avenues open to the creditor in the second situation. First, he may proceed by way of *notice of default.* Here, the creditor serves a notice on the debtor, and the proprietor of the security subjects where he is not the debtor, calling on the debtor to purge the default. However, a notice of default is competent only where the default complained of is remediable. An obvious example of such a situation would be where there is a condition in the standard security that the debtor must insure the security subjects and this condition has not been complied

with. A person served with a notice of default may, within fourteen days of the service of the notice, object by way of application to the sheriff having jurisdiction over the security subjects. The Court may order the notice to be set aside in whole or in part or may vary or uphold it. The period of notice required is at least one month, during which time the debtor may purge the default. Again, the period of notice may be shortened or dispensed with by the agreement of the parties. It is not competent to serve a notice of default when the default is in respect of non-compliance with a calling-up notice. The remedies available to the creditor on non-compliance with a notice of default are sale, foreclosure and repair, reconstruction and improvement.

Secondly, the creditor may apply to the Court under s. 24 (1) of the Act for a warrant to exercise any of the remedies which he would be entitled to exercise had there been a failure to comply with a calling-up notice. Moreover, the default in this situation need not be remediable.

3. Where the proprietor of the security subjects is insolvent. Note that it is the proprietor's insolvency, not the debtor's, which is important. Although normally the proprietor and the debtor are one and the same, this is not always the case. Insolvency, for this purpose, is defined in detail in the standard conditions. In this case too, the creditor may apply to the Court under s. 24(1) for a warrant to exercise any of the remedies available on default by non-compliance with a calling-up notice.

Remedies on Default: Where the debtor is in default, the creditor may, without prejudice to any other remedy arising from the contract, exercise such of the powers of sale, foreclosure, entering into possession and repair, reconstruction and improvement as are available to him and which he may consider appropriate.

(1) *Sale:* The power of the creditor to sell the security subjects or any part of them, a non-variable condition, is exercisable whenever the debtor is in default. The sale may be concluded either by private bargain or public sale after advertisement and the creditor must take all reasonable steps to ensure that the price at which the security subjects are sold is the best that can reasonably be obtained.[15]

---

[15] 1970 Act, s. 25.

(2) *Foreclosure:* Where the creditor in a standard security has exposed the security subjects for public sale, but not private bargain, at a price not exceeding the amount due under the security or under any security ranking prior to or *pari passu* with it and has failed to find a purchaser for the whole security subjects at that price, or has been able to sell only part of the subjects at a price less than that amount, then he may exercise the power of foreclosure. Foreclosure requires a decree of the Sheriff Court in whose jurisdiction the property is situated. The effect of such a decree is to make the creditor absolute proprietor of the security subjects or such part as has not been sold. The remedy of foreclosure is non-variable.

(3) *Entering into possession:* Before the creditor may enter into possession, an application to the Sheriff Court for a warrant to do so is necessary, except in the case of non-compliance with a calling-up notice.[16] Where a creditor has entered into possession he may receive and recover rents and feu-duties, let the security subjects, and has all the rights of the debtor in relation to the granting of leases or rights of occupation, and management and maintenance of the subjects transferred to him.

(4) *Repair, reconstruction and improvement:* Where the debtor is in default the creditor may effect such repairs and make good such defects as are necessary to maintain the security subjects in good and sufficient repair. Also, the creditor may effect such reconstruction, alteration and improvement on the subjects as would be expected of a prudent proprietor to maintain the market value of the subjects. This right will usually be exercised in preparation for a sale or letting of the security subjects.

Standard Condition 12 makes the debtor personally liable for the whole expenses of the preparation and execution of the standard security and all exprenses of the creditor reasonably incurred in calling-up the security or exercising any power conferred on him by the standard security.

Redemption: Initially, under the 1970 Act, the debtor's right of redemption could not be varied. The debtor or, where the debtor was not the proprietor, the proprietor could redeem his standard security by giving the creditor at least two months' notice of his intention and by paying the whole amount due under the security. However, 'the unfettered power of redemption made loans for

16 Ibid., s. 20(1).

S

fixed periods on heritable securities in Scotland impracticable, with the result that Scottish industrial and commercial concerns were being denied finance on heritable security where the lenders were prepared to make advances which were repayable only on a specified date. Moreover, bodies such as building societies, whose organisation was adapted to comparatively long term lending, were precluded from inserting conditions with regard to early redemption designed to discourage the conversion of a long term loan into short term financial accommodation'.[17] Some change was therefore necessary and this came in the shape of the Standard Securities (Scotland) Act 1971, which now permits variation or exclusion of the right to redeem but enacts that, where the power of redemption still exists, the procedure for redemption laid down in the standard conditions[18] must be followed, and accordingly the debtor must still give the creditor at least two months' notice of his intention to redeem the security. The creditor may, however, waive the necessity for a notice of redemption or agree to a period of notice of less than two months.

The obligations of a security holder

The obligations of a security holder are to exercise ordinary care while the security subjects are in his possession and to return the security subjects to the borrower when the loan is repaid.

In the case of heritage the security holder rarely has physical possession of the subjects; in the case of moveables he is liable for the loss or destruction of the security subjects due to his fault while he has possession. He is not liable for accidental damage. The right of recovery of his loan is not affected by the loss of the subjects, although he is no longer secured, unless tender of the loan has been justifiably made and the return of the subjects wrongfully refused.[19]

The obligation to return the security subjects on repayment of the loan is absolute; the creditor must return the subjects pledged, the exact subjects pledged.

If he is realising the security the creditor must proceed in accordance with his power of sale, be it express or, as in the case of heritable securities, statutory; failure to observe the rules will entitle the purchaser to withdraw from the sale or the debtor to have it reduced.

---

[17] J. M. Halliday, 1971 S.L.T. (news) 197.
[18] Standard Condition No. 11.
[19] *Fraser* v. *Smith* (1899), 1 F. 487.

Towards the debtor the security holder holds a fiduciary position. He must, in selling, have regard for the interest of the debtor. He can be interdicted by the Court from a sale which does not serve these interests, or those of postponed creditors.[20] If he does sell disregarding these interests, an action for damages may lie against him at the instance of the debtor or postponed creditor.

Security rights in leases

Ordinary leases: The tenant's interest in a lease may have value for security purposes, provided that it is assignable. A creditor who takes such as lease in security obtains no preferential right unless he actually enters into possession of the subjects, which not only involves him in liability for the rent, but for performance of the duties of the tenant under the lease. There is no exception to the rule that the creditor must take possession; an assignation of a lease in security not followed by actual possession by the assignee is invalid against other creditors.[21]

Long leases: By the Registration of Leases (Scotland) Act, 1857, as amended by the Land Tenure Reform (Scotland) Act, 1974, a lease of twenty years or upwards of duration may be registered in the General Register of Sasines, and, where there has been recording on behalf of the tenant, the tenant may charge the lease by standard security in the same way as he might charge property which he owned. The standard conditions apply in so far as they are not excluded. It will be noted, of course, that the creditor obtains only the leasehold rights in security and that these, towards the end of the term of a long lease, may be of diminishing value as the lease will revert to the landlord on its expiry.

Securities implied by law

Three rights in security are implied by law; lien, right of retention and hypothec. Lien and the right of retention have already been considered.[22]

Hypothec: In the main the term hypothec denotes a right in security implied by law and not requiring possession, although a hypothec can be created by express agreement with regard to ships;[23]

---

[20] *supra* p. 258
[21] *Cabell* v. *Brock* 1828, 3 W and s. 75.
[22] *supra* p. 20
[23] the creation of express hypothecs in ships is nearly obsolete.

The main hypothecs are those of a superior, a landlord, a solicitor, and certain marine hypothecs.[24]

Both a landlord and a superior, where the land or heritable property is held in feudal tenure, have a hypothec, a right in security over the contents of the subjects, to secure payment of the rent or feu-duty. Covered by such a hypothec is the *invecta et illata*, the contents such as furniture, equipment or stock, including items not belonging to the tenant or vassal such as hired equipment.[25] Not included are money, clothing, tools of trade, property of the tenant's or vassal's family or lodgers, and property only temporarily on the premises.

The hypothec, which secures only one year's rent or feu-duty, must be enforced within three months of the due date of payment and is enforced by a process known as sequestration for rent or feu-duty. This action has the effect of making the right in security concrete over items of the *invecta et illata*. To reinforce his hypothec the landlord or superior can interdict the removal of the *invecta et illata* or obtain an order for their re-installation if they are removed.

A solicitor's hypothec covers outlays by him and is exercisable over expenses to which his client is entitled by the solicitor's taking decree in his own name. The solicitor may petition the Court to charge any property the subject of a Court action in favour of the solicitor for the amount of his expenses.

Relationships between security holders

Where the security subjects are moveable and the security has not been created by floating charge, there will be no question of there being more than one security holder in any particular item; the necessity for delivery to the creditor precludes that. Where there is a floating charge or where the subjects are heritable there may be more than one security holder. How are they treated by law when the borrower is bankrupted or liquidation commences or when one security holder decides to realise his security?

Where a company has created rights in security over its assets and has used the statutory provisions to create two or more floating charges, the charges rank according to the time of their registration unless the instruments provide they are to rank equally. Where there

---

[24] e.g. the hypothec of the seamen over the ship for wages.
[25] *Ditchburn Organisation (Sales) Ltd.* v. *Dundee Corporation* 1971 S.L.T. 218.

is a fixed charge, the right to which has been constituted as a real right before a floating charge has attached to all or any part of the property of a company, the fixed charge has priority over the floating charge.

Where the security right arises by implication of law, such as a superior's or landlord's hypothec, it takes precedence over the floating charge even if instituted after the registration of the floating charge.

Where the security subjects are heritable, the borrower cannot, without the lender's consent, create further securities which might compete with that of the lender but the borrower may grant further securities, these taking precedence according to the dates of their recording in the Register of Sasines

Catholic and secondary securities: The situation may arise that one security holder over heritable subjects has a security over two properties owned by the same debtor while a second security holder has a postponed security over one of the properties. The first security holder is known as the catholic creditor, the second as the secondary creditor. The secondary creditor has little control over the actions of the catholic creditor—he cannot, for example, object to the catholic creditor discharging that part of his security which covers the property not subject to the secondary security.[26] If, however, the catholic security holder realises his debt by selling the property subject to the secondary security he must assign his security over the other property to the secondary bondholder. If both properties are sold by the catholic creditor any balance remaining after satisfying his loan is due to the secondary creditor rather than to general creditors or to a trustee.

If there are secondary creditors interested in both properties, any surplus upon their realisation is apportioned rateably according to the values of the properties between the secondary creditors.

Floating charges

An exception to the rules that moveable property can only be charged when delivered to the creditor and that to create a real right in security in heritable property requires the registration of a standard security, exists in that incorporated companies, whether incorporated under the Companies Acts or otherwise and including

[26] *Morton (Liddell's Curator)* (1871) 10 M. 292.

industrial and provident societies, may charge in security all or any part of their property of any nature by means of a floating charge. A floating charge is simply a document granted by a company in favour of a creditor charging its property, or any part of it, which, when duly executed and registered, has the effect of charging the company's property; should the company be wound up a valid charge will attach to the property then comprising the company's property and undertaking or, as the case might be to part of that property and undertaking, and has effect as if the charge were a fixed security over the property to which the floating charge attaches in respect of the principle of the debt or obligation to which it relates, and any interest due, or to become due, thereon. If a receiver is appointed by the holder of floating charge or by the Court, the floating charge by virtue of which he was appointed attaches on his appointment to the property which is the subject of the charge.

The introduction of floating charges to Scots law in 1961 was effected in recognition of a belief that Scottish companies were at a comparative disadvantage in the matter of borrowing money to their English counterparts; the rules requiring delivery to create a valid security meant that much of the valuable assets of a company, for example, in stock and trade or vehicle fleet, could not, practically, be used to secure borrowings. By the device of floating charge this disadvantage is remedied, although the charge can affect heritable property also, notwithstanding that the instrument creating the charge is not registered in the Register of Sasines.[27] After ten years' experience of the working of the device in Scotland the law was substantially reformed and is now to be found in the Companies (Floating Charges and Receivers) (Scotland) Act 1972. References hereafter to sections are to this Act unless otherwise stated.

Form of a charge: There is no prescribed form of words for the creating of a floating charge; all that is required is that an instrument, bond or other written acknowledgement is executed under the seal of the company which purports to create a floating charge (s. 2 (1)) while execution includes execution by an attorney authorised by the company in writing under seal to execute charges (s. 2 (2)).

Registration of charges: Of vital importance both as to the validity of a charge and as to its relationship with other securities is that it must be registered with the Registrar of Companies. The

---

[27] Companies (Receivers and Floating Charges) (Scotland) Act 1972, s. 3.

schedule to the 1972 Act, by means of amending the Companies Act 1948, prescribes the rules regarding registration. There are added to section 106 of the Companies Act 1948 eleven sections (A-K) which govern registration.

The Registrar of Companies is charged with keeping, with respect to each company, a register of all the charges requiring registration; the register is to show the important details of any charge, the amount secured, the particulars of the property charged, the persons entitled to the charge and, in the case of a floating charge, a statement of any provision of the charge and of any instrument relating to it which prohibits or restricts or regulates the power of the company to grant further securities ranking in priority to, or *pari passu* with, the floating charge, or which varies or otherwise regulates the order of ranking of the floating charge in relation to existing securities (s. 106D, 1948 Act).

Not only floating charges must be registered. Other charges which must be registered are: a charge on land or any interest in land, not including a charge for rent, ground annual, or other periodic sum payable in respect of the land but including a charge created by a heritable security; any security over the uncalled share capital of the company; and any security over incorporeal moveable property of any of the following categories—the book debts of the company, calls made but not paid, goodwill, a patent or licence under a patent, a trade mark, and a copyright or licence under a copyright. Also registrable are securities over a ship or aircraft or any share in a ship. If a registrable charge is not duly registered in terms of the statute it becomes, in a question with the liquidator and any creditor of the company, void as far as the security over the company's property which it covers is concerned. The money secured by a charge not duly registered is immediately repayable.

Duty to register: The company is charged with the duty of sending to the Registrar of Companies for registration the particulars of every charge created by the company and of issues of debentures of a series requiring registration under the Act. Registration may also be effected on the application of any person interested in the charge; if the registration is effected on the application of some person other than the company that person is entitled to recover from the company the amount of any fees paid by him to the Registrar. There are default fines imposed on a company and any officer of it who is in default of the registration provisions.

If a company acquires property which is subject to a charge of a sort that, if it had been created by the company after the acquisition of the property, would have been required to be registered, the company must cause the prescribed particulars of the charge, together with a certified copy of the instrument creating it, to be delivered for registration.

What is required to be registered are the particulars of the charge, together with a certified copy of it.

Certificate of registration: The Registrar has to give a certificate of the registration of a charge registered under the Act, stating the name of the company and of the person first named in the charge, of all the persons entitled to the benefit of it and the amount thereby secured. This certificate is conclusive evidence that the requirements of the Act as to registration have been complied with.

Effect of registration: The effect of registration is to give notice to all concerned, including persons taking fixed securities of the company, that the charge exists and of the terms of it.

Ranking of floating charges: When a floating charge attaches on a company's liquidation to the property it covers it does so subject to the rights of any person who has effectually executed diligence on that property or any part of it, or who holds a fixed security over the property, or any part of it, ranking in priority to the floating charge, or who holds over the property, or any part of it, another floating charge ranking in priority to the floating charge which has attached.

Where there are different securities and charges these rank amongst themselves as follows. First, where there is a fixed security arising by operation of law affecting the property covered by the floating charge, or any part of it, that fixed security shall have priority over the floating charge. Thereafter, where the order of ranking of the floating charge with any other subsisting or future floating charges or fixed securities over all or any part of the company's property is not regulated by provisions contained in the instrument creating the floating charge or in any instrument altering it, the order of ranking is determined in accordance with the following rules: (a) a fixed security, the right to which has been constituted as a real right before a floating charge has attached to all or any part of the property of the company, has priority of ranking over the floating charge; (b) floating charges rank with one another according to the time of registration, floating charges which have been received by the

Registrar for registration in the same postal delivery ranking equally.

If the holder of a floating charge has received intimation in writing of the subsequent registration of another floating charge, the preference in ranking of the first-mentioned floating charge is restricted to security for the holder's present advances, future advances which he may be required to make under the instrument creating the floating charge or under any ancillary document, the interest due or to become due on such advances and the expenses or outlays which he may reasonably incur.

Agreed ranking: The instrument creating a floating charge or any instrument of alteration of a floating charge may contain provisions prohibiting or restricting the creation of any fixed security or any other floating charge having priority over or ranking *pari passu* with the floating charge: similarly there may be provisions regulating the order in which the floating charge shall rank with any other subsisting or future floating charges or fixed securities over the property or any part of it. Notwithstanding any such statement the priority of a fixed security arising by operation of law is paramount.

Alteration of floating charges: The instrument creating a floating charge or any ancillary document may be altered by the execution of an instrument of alteration by the company, the holder of the charge, and the holder of any other charge, including a fixed security, which would be adversely affected by the alteration. If the instrument of alteration prohibits or restricts the creation of any fixed security or any other floating charge having priority over or ranking *pari passu* with the floating charge, or varies, or otherwise regulates the ranking of the floating charge in relation to fixed securities or other floating charges, or releases property from the floating charge, or increases the amount secured by the floating charge, then the instrument of alteration requires to be registered with the Registrar of Companies.

Fraudulent preference: The common law of Scotland permits the challenge of fraudulent preferences on the grounds of insolvency no matter what time has elapsed since the preferences were granted. In the case of the granting of a floating charge a challenge of its validity on the grounds that it constituted a fraudulent preference may only be made within twelve months of its granting (s. 322, 1948 Act and s. 8).

Discharge of floating charges: The Registrar, on application being made to him on the prescribed form, and on evidence being given to his satisfaction with respect to a charge that the debt for which the charge was given has been paid, or satisfied in whole or in part, or that part of the property charged has been released from the charge, or has ceased to form part of the company's property, may enter on the register a Memorandum of Satisfaction, in whole or in part regarding that fact. When such a Memorandum of Satisfaction in whole is entered the Registrar must, if required, furnish the company with a copy of it.

There is provision that the Registrar will not be satisfied that a Memorandum of Satisfaction should be entered on the register unless the creditor entitled to the benefit of the floating charge or a person authorised to do so on his behalf certifies as correct the particulars submitted to the Registrar with respect to the entry on the register, or the court, on being satisfied that such a certification cannot readily be obtained directs the Registrar accordingly.

Rectification of the register: If a Court is satisfied that an omission to register a charge within the time required by the Act, or an omission or mis-statement of any particular with respect to any such charge or Memorandum of Satisfaction, was accidental, or due to inadvertence or some other sufficient cause, or is not of a nature to prejudice the position of creditors or shareholders in the company, or that on other grounds it is just and equitable to grant relief, it may, on the application of the company or any person interested, and on such terms and conditions as seem to the Court just and expedient, order that the time for registration shall be extended, or, as the case may be, that the omission or mis-statement shall be rectified.

Company's register of charges: Every company has to keep at its registered office a register of charges and enter therein all charges specifically affecting property of the company and all floating charges on any property of the company, giving in each case a short description of the property charged, the amount of the charge, and except in the case of securities to bearer, the names of persons entitled to the charge. In addition the company must keep at its registered office a copy of every instrument creating any floating charge requiring registration. The copies and the register of charges are to be open during business hours to the inspection of any creditor or member of the company without fee and to the inspection of any other person on payment of a fee, not exceeding 5p for each inspection.

CHAPTER TEN

CAUTIONARY OBLIGATIONS AND GUARANTEES

A BANKER making advances or loans or granting overdraft facilities may wish to reinforce in some way the promise of his customer to repay. The taking of security is one method of achieving this; a second is to seek a cautioner, a third party who promises repayment of the whole or part of what is outstanding should the customer fail to fulfil his bargain. Caution sometimes called guarantee or suretyship, may be taken in substitution for, or in addition to, security.

Bell[1] defines a cautionary obligation as 'an accessory engagement, as surety for another, that the principal obligant shall pay the debt or perform the act for which he has engaged, otherwise the cautioner shall pay the debt or fulfil the obligation'.

The parties: The party to whom the obligation is due is called the creditor; the person whose debt or performance is due is called the principal debtor, while the person undertaking the accessory obligation is known variously as the cautioner, the guarantor or the surety.

The obligation: The undertaking of the cautioner is that he will indemnify the creditor should the principal debtor fail to honour his obligation, which might be to pay a debt, either due or to become due, or to perform acts or services due under a contract. Caution must not be confused with delegation which is where the proposed cautioner assumes the liabilities of the debtor and the creditor releases the original debtor. If there is any doubt as to whether a particular undertaking is cautionary or constitutes delegation the presumption is that the undertaking is cautionary.

Caution is of its very nature an accessory obligation; it depends on the existence of a valid principal obligation. Thus, if the principal obligation ends or is null, the cautionary obligation is not enforceable; for example, if the principal obligation has prescribed before recourse is made to the cautioner, he will not be liable, or, if the

---

[1] Princ., para 235.

principal obligation is null through lack of capacity or illegality, the alleged cautionary obligation does not exist. It is, however, possible to undertake a cautionary obligation as accessory to an obligation not yet in existence; the cautioner is bound when the principal obligation is formed.

If, however, the principal obligation is unenforceable rather than null, the cautionary obligation may be exigible.[2]

An obligation is said to be null or void where, despite the appearance of an obligation, the obligation is denied effect by law; examples are agreements which the law demands should be in probative writing and which are not, and agreements by parties lacking the capacity to make agreements of that type. An obligation is unenforceable when it cannot be enforced against a party to it.

Constitution: A cautionary obligation must be in writing and shall be subscribed by the cautioner or by some person authorised by him.[3] By the Mercantile Law Amendment (Scotland) Act, 1856: 'all guarantees, securities, or cautionary obligations made or granted by any person for any other person, and all representations and assurances as to the character, conduct, credit, ability, trade or dealings of any person, made or granted to the effect or for the purpose of enabling such person to obtain credit, money, goods, or postponement of payment of debt, or of any other obligation demandable from him, shall be in writing, and shall be subscribed by the person undertaking or by some person duly authorised by him or them, otherwise the same shall have no effect.'

Whether this Act means that a valid cautionary obligation must be in probative writing has not been satisfactorily settled,[4] although an improbative writing will suffice if there have been actings on the strength of it.[5]

Ancillary agreements, or modifications of the written agreement, must themselves be in writing. In the usual case the caution is consituted by an offer by the prospective cautioner to act as cautioner on behalf of a debtor in respect of some loan or advance; a sufficient acceptance of such offer is the giving of credit by the creditor.[6]

---

[2] Gloag and Henderson *op. cit.* p. 220; Lillie *op. cit.* p. 221.
[3] Mercantile Law Amendment (Scotland) Act, 1856, s. 6.
[4] Gow *op. cit.* p. 304, where Professor Gow examines the ambiguity of this section of the Act. See also Walker *op. cit.* p. 919.
[5] *National Bank* v. Campbell (1892) 19 R. 885.
[6] *Wallace* v. *Gibson* (1895) 22 R. (H.L.) 56.

Occasionally, the cautioner will promise the debtor that he will guarantee his transactions with a creditor envisaged in the promise who has given credit in reliance on this undertaking.

Proper and improper caution: A cautionary obligation may be, in form, proper or improper. In proper caution the relationships of the parties—creditor, principal debtor and cautioner—are made clear by the instrument creating the relationships. In improper caution, the principal debtor and cautioner are bound as if they were co-obligants jointly and severally liable for the obligation.

Whether the caution is constituted as proper or improper has important consequences for the cautioner. If it is proper caution he is entitled to all the privileges of a cautioner; if, in form, the caution is improper, these privileges are open to him only if the cautioner can prove that the creditor was a party to the arrangement and knew that he was truly a cautioner.

Co-cautioners: Where there are two or more cautioners, each is bound only on the understanding that the other or others are also validly bound. It is the duty of the creditor to secure that all become bound and a failure to do so releases from liability any cautioner who has signed. Thus in *Scottish Provincial Insurance Co.* v. *Pringle*[7] an insurance company lent money on the condition that four other persons were to become jointly and severally liable with the borrower for its repayment and three of the four signed while the borrower forged the signature of the fourth. It was held that the creditor had failed to secure that all four had been bound and they were unable to enforce the bond against the other three. This does not apply in judicial cautionary.[8]

The liabilities of co-cautioners amongst themselves depend on whether the caution is proper or improper. In improper caution each is liable for the full amount, with rights of relief against his co-obligants. In proper caution a cautioner has a right of division unless this has been renounced. This means that if the obligation is divisible by its nature, e.g. an obligation to pay money, he is liable only for a *pro rata* share unless other cautioners are insolvent, in which case any insolvent co-cautioner is ignored in calculating the amount due.

Fraud and concealment: A cautionary obligation is not binding on the cautioner if his consent was obtained by the fraud or misrep-

---

[7] *Scottish Provincial Insurance Co.* v. *Pringle* (1858) 20 D. 465.
[8] *Simpson* v. *Fleming* (1860) 22 D. 679.

resentation of the creditor; but the principal debtor is not the creditor's agent in the matter and his fraud or misrepresentation will not permit the cautioner to reduce the contract as against the creditor.[9] Where a person signs a guarantee to a bank on behalf of someone else he is presumed to sign at the request of the debtor and not at that of the bank.[10]

Except where the honesty of a servant is being guaranteed there is no obligation on the creditor to disclose material facts—he is entitled to think that the cautioner is aware of the extent of the obligation he is undertaking, particularly where he is guaranteeing money debts—but he must not mislead the cautioner by making partial or untrue statements either spontaneously or in reply to questions. It can be said that the cautioner has a duty to inform himself regarding the matters material to the obligation he is about to undertake.[11] The cautioner will also be liberated if the creditor allows him to undertake the obligation in the knowledge that the cautioner is entirely mistaken about the facts.

The law on this matter was summed up in the case of *Royal Bank of Scotland* v. *Greenwood* thus: 'The only circumstance in which I can conceive that a duty of disclosure would emerge, and failure to disclose would be fatal to the Bank's case, would be where a customer put a question or made an observation in the presence and hearing of the bank-agent which necessarily and inevitably would lead anyone to the conclusion that the intending guarantor was labouring under a misapprehension with regard to the state of the customer's indebtedness. Nothing short of that, in my opinion, would do.'[11a]

In 1974 in an English case, *Lloyd's Bank* v. *Bundy*,[11b] it was held that a banker who was obtaining a guarantee from one of his own customers, who happened to be elderly, had an obligation to that customer to ensure that he understood what he was committing himself to do. This case has narrow application, turning as it does on the two facts, one, that the proposed cautioner was elderly, and, two, of great importance, that he was, himself, a customer of the bank.

Extent of a cautioner's liability: The obligation of the cautioner

---

9 *Young* v. *Clydesdale Bank* (1889) 17 R. 231.
10 Wallace and McNeill *op. cit.* p. 310.
11 *Cooper* v. *National Provincial Bank* (1945) 62 T.L.R. 36.
11a 1914 SC 258 PN Ld Strathclyde at p. 268.
11b [1974] 3 All E.R. 757.

is to be construed in the narrowest sense which the words will reasonably bear.[12] Apart from this general rule he can never be liable for more than the principal debtor, the limit of the liability being the sum outstanding, interest, and expenses reasonably incurred in enforcing the debt against the principal debtor. Thus in *Jackson* v. *McIver*[13] where a cautioner was bankrupt and had granted a blank promissory note to the creditor it was held that the creditor could not fill up the note for a sum greater than his advance to the principal debtor in the expectation that his dividend on the cautioner's estate on the note would produce the actual advance.

Where the cautioner limits the amount for which he undertakes his obligation, it is a question of construction whether, in the event of the limit being reached and exceeded, he remains liable for this sum or whether payments by the debtor to reduce his indebtedness are applied to the reduction of the guaranteed sum.[14] Where the guarantee was in respect of a current account there may be a presumption in favour of a continuing guarantee.[15]

The cautioner may also limit his undertaking as to time and is released at the expiry of the period; he is entitled to be relieved by the debtor of all liability under the obligation and to receive a discharge from the creditor. If he does not limit the duration of the obligation he may withdraw his guarantee, thus safeguarding himself against future advances and additional liability, but not, of course, relieving himself of liability for debts already incurred.

At any time a cautioner who is not committed for a specific period, may, upon reasonable notice, call on the debtor to relieve him of his liabilities and to deliver a discharge from the creditor.

Cautioner's rights

The rights of a cautioner are to relief against the debtor and any co-cautioner, to the benefit of discussion in certain circumstances, to the benefit of securities held by the creditor, and to an assignation of the debt, and a share in securities held by a co-cautioner. The specific right of benefit of division in proper caution has already been discussed.

Relief: The cautioner, on payment of the debt or part of it, is

---

[12] *Veitch* v. *National Bank* 1907 S.C. 554; *Harmer* v. *Gibb* 1911 S.C. 1341.
[13] (1875) 2 R. 882.
[14] Clayton's case, supra p. 24; *Scott* v. *Mitchell* (1866) 4M. 551.
[15] *Caledonian Banking Co.* v. *Kennedy* (1870) 8 M. 862 at p. 868.

entitled to relief against the principal debtor for the amount he has paid and any necessary expenses he has incurred. He is a mandatary of the principal debtor for payment of any due debt and can pay any sum due to end his own liability, thereafter looking to the principal debtor for reimbursement. He may also pay if the debtor is about to become insolvent. In any case in which he has paid, he can exercise the full rights of a creditor against the debtor; exceptions to this rule are when he has paid prematurely, when the principal debtor had a valid defence, and where the payment was for the cautioner's benefit.

Where there are co-cautioners jointly and severally bound, anyone who has paid the debt or performed the work at his expense is entitled to a right of relief against the co-cautioners for a rateable contribution. Co-cautioners who are insolvent are excluded in computing the amount due by each co-cautioner.

Benefit of discussion: Where there is express stipulation in the deed, the cautioner is entitled to demand that the creditor has done diligence against the principal debtor before calling on him.

This right, called the benefit of discussion, was implied in proper caution but now, under the Mercantile Law Amendment (Scotland) Act, 1856 (section 8), requires express stipulation. In the absence of this stipulation the creditor may proceed against the cautioner as soon as the principal debtor defaults. Although such stipulation exists there is no need to do diligence against the principal debtor before calling on the cautioner if the principal debtor's estates have been sequestrated, if he is outwith Scotland or if he has no estate subject to the jurisdiction of the Scottish Courts. The death of the principal debtor does not relieve the creditor from the obligation to discuss, unless he died insolvent.

Where the caution is in respect of an act to be performed by the principal debtor, the cautioner is liable only to make up the loss proved to have been caused by failure of the debtor.[16]

There is, of course, no place for the necessary stipulation in improper cautionry.

Benefit of securities: The cautioner who pays a debt is entitled to have assigned to him the debt, any securities held by the creditor and any diligences done by the creditor. This is to enable the

---

[16] Erskine III, 3, 62; Municipal Council of Johannesburg *v.* Stewart 1909 S.C. 860.

cautioner to seek his relief against the debtor or co-cautioners. This right is not enforceable to the prejudice of the creditor, so that the creditor need not grant these assignations unless the whole debt has been paid in full[17] or if such assignation would conflict with an interest of his own.

A cautioner can enforce securities only over the estate of the debtor; if securities have been granted by third parties the cautioner has no right to these.[18]

Share in securities: Where there are co-cautioners and one has been granted securities by the debtor, each (assuming each to have a right of relief) is entitled to share in these on the theory that the estate of the debtor is a fund in which all the cautioners have an equal right. If the securities have been granted to one cautioner by a third party the right to share is not applicable, nor is it applicable if excluded by the express agreement of all concerned. It is no defence that a co-cautioner claiming to share securities engaged as cautioner without securities.

Bankruptcy of debtor

If the debtor becomes bankrupt there is a danger of double ranking,[19] that is that both creditor and cautioner may attempt to claim upon the debtor's estate. As the estate is liable to pay only once in respect of a single debt it is a matter of circumstance who should rank. If the creditor ranks, receives a dividend on the sum due and then claims the balance from the cautioner, the cautioner cannot claim against the estate. On the other hand the cautioner may pay the debt, if liable for the whole amount, and rank on the estate in place of the creditor. If the cautioner has guaranteed only part of a debt it is a matter of construction whether he has guaranteed a specific part, say the first £500, or agreed to contribute up to, say, £500 of sums advanced. For example, if he is held to have guaranteed the first £500 of a £2,000 debt and the debtor's estate is paying a dividend of 50p in the £, he could pay the creditor £500 and rank for £500 and be paid £250 in dividend or, alternatively, allow the creditor to rank and receive in respect of the £500 a total dividend of £250 which the cautioner would then make up to £500. On the other hand if he is

---

[17] *Ewart* v. *Latta* (1865) 3M. (H.L.) 36.
[18] *Thow's Tr.* v. *Young* 1910 S.C. 588.
[19] *infra* p. 321

T

guaranteeing the whole debt with a limit of £500 the creditor will rank for £2,000, receive £1,000 and the cautioner will be liable for £500 with no claim to rank.

Ultimate loss clause: The ultimate loss clause is a clause common in bank guarantees (and indeed in other securities) whereby the cautioner forfeits his right to rank in the principal debtor's estate and remains liable, to the limit of his obligation, to the creditor for the creditor's loss after the creditor has ranked for the whole amount of his debt in the bankruptcy of the principal debtor.

Where, however, the guarantor has paid up the amount of his guarantee before the sequestration of the principal debtor, he can require the bank to assign to him the debt to the extent that he has paid it and can rank on the bankrupt estate for the amount that is contained in the assignation in preference to the bank. This is the case even when the amount paid is credited to a separate account and the guarantee was given up under reservation of the bank's whole claims against the principal debtor.

Revocation: A cautioner can revoke his obligation unless or until the creditor has relied on it; thereafter the undertaking is not capable of withdrawal. Such revocation has the effect of avoiding future liability only.

Discharge of cautionery obligations

A cautionary obligation is extinguished in the same ways as any obligation and also by the extinction of the principal obligation, by the death of one of the parties, by alteration of circumstances, by revocation or by limitation.[20]

Extinction of principal obligation: As caution is essentially a accessory obligation the extinction of the principal obligation implies the extinction of the cautionary undertaking. If the principal obligation is terminated by performance or by some other method, or if the principal debtor is discharged absolutely, the cautioner is liberated.

It is necessary that the principal debtor be discharged; an undertaking by the creditor not to sue the debtor for his debt[21] does not

---

20 *infra* p.
21 a *pactum de non petendo.*

discharge the cautioner who, if held liable, can proceed against the principal debtor.

Novation extinguishes the cautionary obligation; the debtor's new obligation must discharge the old. There must be substitution not addition.

Compensation [22] can be pleaded in partial or total extinction of his liability by a cautioner called on to pay in respect of any debt due by the creditor to the debtor.

The effect of the rule in Clayton's Case[23] should also be noted as the application of this rule may extinguish that part of a debt to which the caution applies.

Death of a party: If either creditor or debtor dies a continuing obligation of caution ends. Further advances are not covered by it—although the liability of the cautioner for obligations due at the time of death remains unaltered. It is important to notice that the cautioner's liability is not extinguished.

If the cautioner dies his liability transmits against his representatives. This is certainly the case for monies advanced before the death but there may be a right of revocation vested in the cautioner which is excercisable by the representatives. If this right does not exist—as in the case of a guarantee for a fixed period—the representatives will be liable even for acts after the death of the cautioner. Where there is a right of revocation the cautioner's representatives must inform the creditor of the death of the cautioner if they are to avoi-dsubsequent liability. If they do not know of the guarantee the creditor is under no duty to inform them of it,[24] although if he does not inform them and allows them to dispose of the estate he may be barred from pursuing them.[25]

Alteration of circumstances: A cautioner is entitled to rely on the whole circumstances as he knows them at the beginning of his undertaking being maintained. He is, therefore, liberated if the creditor changes these circumstances to his prejudice; for example, by giving up securities, discharging a co-cautioner, or extending the date of performance of the contract between him and the principal debtor.

The undertaking of a cautioner is accessory to the agreement as it

[22] *supra* p. 19
[23] *supra* p. 24
[24] *British Linen Co.* v. *Monteith* (1858) 20 D. 557.
[25] *Caledonian Banking Co.* v. *Kennedy's TRs.* (1870) 8 M. 862, at p. 868.

was at the time of his giving it; it is not accessory to an altered or amended arrangement.

Giving up securities: If the creditor holds securities in addition to the cautionary obligation for the due performance by the principal debtor, the cautioner has a right to the assignation of these securities if he is called on to pay. If, without the cautioner's consent, the creditor voluntarily gives up these securities the cautioner's rights are impaired and he is, therefore, released to the extent he is prejudiced, that is to the extent of the value of the surrendered securities. Similarly, if the creditor is bound to do something, e.g. registering a Standard Security in the Register of Sasines, to render a security effectual, and fails to do so, the cautioner is released to the extent of the value of that security.

If, by contract, the creditor is bound to avail himself of a particular security before having recourse to the cautioner, and gives up that security, the release of the cautioner is total.

Release of co-cautioner: Where co-cautioners are bound jointly and severally and the creditor, without the consent of the other cautioners, releases one, he releases all.[26] If each cautioner is bound for a specific sum this rule does not apply.[27]

Giving time: Where the creditor agrees with the principal debtor that he will not sue for immediate payment for due debt, he is said to be giving time. This is not simply a case of delay in enforcement; it is a variation of the original contract since the creditor, by depriving himself of the right to sue, alters the terms of the contract. There may be an express agreement, a bill taken by the creditor payable at a future date or an agreement whereby the debt will be payable by instalments. In each case the cautioner is liberated, for, as he can stand only in the place of the creditor, his right of relief against the debtor is altered. He need not show prejudice to repudiate.

Mere delay in enforcement is not giving time, a cautioner being able to pay a sum due and payable and demand an assignation. Nor is a *pactum de non petendo*, providing that in undertaking not to sue the principal debtor the rights of the creditor against the cautioner are preserved for the cautioner, having paid, can ignore this and thus loses none of his remedies.

Alteration of contract: While giving time is an alteration of the

[26] Mercantile Law Amendment (Scotland) Act 1956, s. 9.
[27] *Morgan* v. *Smart* (1872) 10 M. 610.

contract, the liberation of a cautioner may result not only from this but from any alteration in the principal contract which prejudices the cautioner. For example, where a cautioner guarantees the fidelity of a servant, he is released if the nature of the servant's duties are changed from those which he understood them to be at the time he assumed the obligation. This rule holds even where the change has no bearing on the loss.[28]

Where there is a cautionary obligation given to a firm or to a third party in respect of the transactions of a firm, any change in the constitution of the firm revokes the obligation as to future transactions unless there is agreement to the contrary.[29] A change in the constitution of a firm may be the retirement of a partner, the admission of one, or the registration by the persons comprising the firm of a limited liability company to carry on its business.

Revocation: It is not in every case that the cautioner has a right of revocation. For example, if he undertakes to guarantee the satisfactory completion of a building contract he cannot revoke before performance is complete. If he is free to revoke he may do so by giving notice to the creditor and will thus free himself from future liability. If liability has already been incurred he cannot escape this but may call on the debtor to relieve him of it by giving him reasonable notice that he must deliver to the cautioner a discharge from the creditor.

Prescription: By the Act 1695,[30] where the caution is proper or, in the case of improper caution, where the cautioner has obtained a separate bond of relief which has been duly intimated to the creditor, the cautionary obligation subsists for seven years from the date of the undertaking and is thereafter extinguished. It is essential that the caution was constituted in the same deed as the principal obligation or, if the cautioner is bound as co-obligant, his bond of relief is intimated to the creditor. The creditor's private knowledge of the true relationship is not enough.

If a cautioner entitled to the relief offered by this Act pays in ignorance of it, he is entitled to repayment.[31]

The Act only applies to cautionry for sums of money; a cautionary obligation for faithful service or for due performance of some

---

[28] *Bonar* v. *Macdonald* (1850) 7 Bell's App. 379.
[29] Partnership Act, 1890, s. 18.
[30] c. 5.
[31] *Carrick* v. *Corse* (1778) Mor. 2931.

act is not affected. Further, the limitation only applies where the debt was fully exigible at a definite time within the seven years.

By the Prescription and Limitation (Scotland) Act 1973 changes have been effected in the whole law relating to prescription in Scotland. As from 25th July, 1976, a cautionary obligation will expire by prescription in five years[32] unless during that time there has been a relevant claim under it or it has been relevantly acknowledged. A relevant claim is defined by the statute[33] as a claim made by or on behalf of the creditor for the implement or part implement of the obligation being a claim in appropriate proceedings, an action in a Scottish Court, an arbitration in Scotland or elsewhere if the award would be enforceable in Scotland, or where the creditor presents or concurs in a petition for sequestration, or lodges a claim in the hands of the trustee, or Sheriff or presses at any meeting of creditors in the course of a sequestration, including corresponding action in the winding up of a company. The execution by or on behalf of a creditor in any obligation of any form of diligence directed at the enforcement of the obligation is deemed to be a relevant claim.

A relevant acknowledgement as described by the Act is constituted where there has been such performance by or on behalf of the debtor towards implement of the obligation as clearly indicates that the obligation still subsists, or where there has been made by or on behalf of the debtor to the creditor or his agent an unequivocal written admission clearly acknowledging that the obligation still subsists.

Where there are co-cautioners bound jointly and severally, performance as would indicate the subsistence of the obligation by one is relevant acknowledgement as far as the liability of both is concerned but, where one co-cautioner gives written admission, that is not relevant acknowledgement as far as the liability of the other is concerned.[34]

As obligations constituted or evidenced by probative writs are excepted from the five-year prescription,[35] although cautionary obligations are specifically included and fall within it, special provision is made for the case where there is improper caution. The Act provides[36] that, where by virtue of a probative writ there are

---

[32] s. 6. and Sched I, i(g) and 2(c).
[33] s. 9(1).
[34] ibid. s. 10(2).
[35] Sched. I para 2 (c).
[36] Sched. I, para 3(1).

co-obligants in an obligation to pay money and they are jointly and severally bound, the obligation will be treated as respects the liability of each as if it were a cautionary obligation unless the creditor can establish that a co-obligant against whom he is proceeding is either truly a principal debtor or, if not truly a principal debtor, that the original creditor was not aware of that fact when the writ was delivered to him.

The five-year period is to be calculated from the date when the obligation became enforceable.[37] It is suggested that a cautionary obligation is enforceable from the date of its constitution unless there is stipulated delay during which the creditor's rights are suspended or unless the cautioner enjoys the benefit of discussion, which would mean that diligence would have to be done before the liability of the cautioner would emerge. The alternative possibility is that the starting point for the prescriptive period is the date of default of the principal debtor; this is based on the idea that, although potential liability emerges on the constitution of the obligation, the obligation is not enforceable until there is default. Under the previous law, however, the septennial prescription ran from the date of the undertaking, benefit of discussion or not, and until there is authoritative decision on the starting point prudence would demand bearing in mind the date of the execution, the less attractive from the point of view of the creditor, as the starting point.

[37] s. 6(3).

CHAPTER ELEVEN

THE LAW OF DILIGENCE

DILIGENCE is 'the legal process by which a creditor attaches the property or the person of his debtor, with the object of forcing him either (1) to appear in Court to answer an action at the creditor's instance, or (2) to find security for implement of the judgement which may be pronounced against him in such action, or (3) to implement a judgement already pronounced'.[1]

It is unnecessary to examine the enforcement of payment of debt by steps against the person of a debtor. Civil imprisonment is virtually non-existent in modern Scots Law, being available to, although rarely resorted to by, local authorities and the government in the collection of rates and taxes. Of great commercial significance are the legal processes which attach property, either heritable or moveable, for the purposes described.

Diligence against moveable property

Arrestment: Arrestment is the process by which moveable property, corporeal or incorporeal, due or belonging to a debtor but in the hands of a third party, is attached by a creditor; e.g. a creditor will commonly attempt to arrest balances due to his debtor by the debtor's bank. When effected an arrestment prohibits the third party from paying or handing over to the debtor, although the creditor needs to take further steps if he himself wishes to be paid or take possession of the subjects arrested.

The party in whose hands an arrestment is lodged is called the arrestee, the party using the arrestment the arrester, and the party against whom the arrestment is used the common debtor.

A debt, even contingent, or any type of interest belonging to the debtor, in respect of which the arrestee has an obligation to pay or account, or any moveable property, can be arrested. The arrestment may be used to found jurisdiction against the debtor in the Scottish

[1] Graham Stewart, *Diligence*, p. 1.

Courts, or to attach the property as security for a pursuer in an action, so that, should he succeed, he can seek satisfaction out of the subjects arrested; in this latter sense, he creates a right in security. More usually an arrestment is in execution, that is, used by a creditor who already has a Court decree against his debtor, and represents one method open to the creditor of securing payment of the sums due under that decree.

The arrestee must not pay or hand over the arrested property to the debtor, under pain of criminal prosecution and penalty of having to pay the creditor also. The effect of the arrestment is to create a right in security; it does not confer on the arrester a right of payment or delivery unless the debtor agrees or the arrester obtains a decree in an action of forthcoming, an action in which the arrester seeks a Court order against the arrestee demanding payment or delivery. An arrestee who obeys such a decree is freed from any claims against him from the common debtor.

The arrestment secures the property subject to it from claims of other creditors—where an arrestee is presented with several arrestments they take precedence in the order of their lodgement with him—but may be reduced in a question with a trustee in bankruptcy or a liquidator.[2]

An arrestee is entitled to see the warrant under which an arrestment is made and in one case,[3] where the Messenger-at-Arms who made arrestment did not have his warrant to do so in his possession, the arrestment was held to be invalid.

Arrestments are of four types. They are used in execution of decrees held; they are used to secure the retention of property on the dependence of an action raised by the arrester; they are used to found jurisdiction in Scottish Courts; and they can be used where a warrant has been obtained on a liquid document of debt such as a bill of exchange.

Arrestments in execution: An arrestment in execution is founded upon an extract decree of the books of a competent Scottish Court or an extract from the Books of Council and Session of a duly recorded bond or obligation which contains the consent of the debtor to the registration of the bond for execution and on an extract registered protest of a bill of exchange or promissory note.[4]

[2] *infra* p. 311
[3] *MacKillop* v. *Mactaggart* (C.H.), 1939 S.L.T. 65.
[4] *supra* p. 170

Arrestments on the dependence of an action: An arrestment may be made when there is contained in a summons or petition in an action a request by the pursuer that warrant to arrest upon the dependence of the action be granted and such warrant has been granted. If such arrestment is made the property will be held pending the outcome of the action and will be available to the pursuer in satisfaction of the award in the action should he succeed. Such an arrestment falls if the defender is not cited to appear in the action within twenty days after the date of the arrestment, or if the summons or petition is not called in Court within twenty days thereafter, or, when the Court is on vacation on the first day it sits thereafter, although a banker would not release funds merely on the belief or on the strength of a statement that citation had not been effected. Otherwise, an arrestment on the dependence of an action does not fall until the matter has been finally resolved by judgement in favour of the defender. Such judgement is not final until the pursuer has exhausted, or failed to utilise, all avenues of appeal which are open to him.

Arrestments ad fundandam juristictionem: The object of an arrestment *ad fundandam juristictionem* is to subject to the jurisdiction of the Scottish Courts, by holding within the jurisdiction his property, someone not otherwise be subject to that jurisdiction. The arrestment is based either on a warrant granted by the Sheriff or on what are called letters of arrestment. Any property belonging to the proposed defender can be arrested. The smallness of a sum due and arrested is no bar to the success of the tactic although things of no mercantile value, such as plans and documents,[5] will not be sufficient to establish jurisdiction.

Unlike an arrestment in execution, or one on the dependence, the purpose of such an arrestment is not to create a right in security in favour of the pursuer or creditor but merely to found jurisdiction. The arrestee in such a case is therefore faced with difficulty if the proprietor of the property demands its return to him. There is no authority on whether the arrestee should comply with such demand or refuse to do so. It is suggested that the prudent course for a banker who finds sums due to his customer have been the subject of such arrestment is not to release these sums to his customer without the consent of the arrester, or under judicial authority. There is open to

[5] *Trowsdale's Tr.* v. *Forcett Rlwy.* 1870, 9 M. 88.

the banker in such a situation the right to raise an action of his own accord requesting judicial direction as to what he should do with the funds and obedience to that direction will free the banker from claims from the party disappointed by the payment of the cash or by its retention.

In practice it will be found that where an arrestment to found jurisdiction has been successful and sums of significance are attached, it will be followed by an arrestment on the dependence of the action and in this case, of course, the banker has no difficulty; he must retain the funds until the outcome of the action is known.

Arrestment on warrant on liquid document of debt: Where a creditor holds a liquid document of debt, such as a bond or a bill of exchange not yet due, he can, if he can convince the Court this his debtor is insolvent or about to leave the jurisdiction of the Court, obtain a warrant upon which arrestments can be made. If an arrestment is made on the strength of such a warrant, the position of the arrestee is no different from any other cases.

Arrester's right to information: An arrester who has used an arrestment on the dependence is not entitled to know whether or not his arrestment has attached any funds. The arresting creditor who has used an arrestment in execution is entitled to be told if his arrestment has attached anything, as is the arrester on the dependence once he has obtained decree. The banker in whose hands an arrestment is lodged, when bound to disclose the success or failure of it, should reveal only as much information as will apparently cover the rights of the arrester under the arrestment, disclosing if a sum sufficient to meet these rights in full, or a lesser sum has been effectually attached.

Effect of arrestment: The effect of an arrestment is to attach in the hands of the arrestee either the property specified in the arrestment, if it be corporeal, or such sum as is specified in the arrestment, if the subject matter of the arrestment is money. Liable to be affected by arrestment are the whole personal debts or moveables in the hands of a third party, a servant, an agent, or anyone who is a custodier for, the common debtor. It is important that the arrestee should have a duty to pay, hand over, or account to the common debtor, as a debtor. Thus where a banker holds securities the revisionary interest in these may be arrested, and it is thought, items held in custody could be arrested.

There are important statutory limitations upon the liability of wages for arrestment. The first £4 and one-half of the remainder of wages is immune from arrestment. Further, an arrestment of wages can be in execution only and, when made is effective only for monies then due, it does not continue.

Sums attached should be due to the common debtor in the capacity in which he is described in the warrant although it has been held that an arrestment in the hands of a bank of funds belonging to 'A' attaches money deposited in the bank in name of 'A in trust', the beneficiary not having been specified.[6] It is a matter of fact at any given time the amount for which the arrestee is liable in account with the common debtor. Where money is the subject of the arrestment the warrant will normally specify a certain sum, the words 'more or less' being added after the sum named to meet any contingency, such as interest and expenses. The practical effect of the words 'more or less' is to stop payment by the arrestee of whatever sums he holds; thus if the sum held by the arrestee is in excess of the sum specifically stated in the warrant the excess should not be paid out to the common debtor except under judicial direction, or with the consent of the arrester. If it is decided to retain a sum sufficient to meet the arrestment and make the excess over and above that available to the common debtor any losses incurred by doing so to the arrester would require to be met by the arrestee.

There may arise the case where the cheques are presented for payment after an arrestment has been effected or the case that a further arrestment is received. As in each of these cases the effect would be to attach available sums, note will require to be taken that when the amount payable under the first arrestment has been ascertained any balance will require to be accounted for to those presenting cheques or subsequent arrestments in the order in which these appeared. The same applies should the original arrestment fall.

Loosing an arrestment: The common debtor may apply to the Court to have an arrestment loosened. Where the funds arrested are in excess of the amount due to the arrester, the Court will restrict the amount affected by the arrestment, or may, if the common debtor provides caution that the sums will be paid to the arrester, loosen the arrestment entirely. An arrestment will also be loosened if it can be shown that it was used oppressively, and in such case an arrester may be found liable in damages.

---

[6] *Union Bank of Scotland* v. *Mills* 1925, 42 S.L.R. 141.

A banker will normally treat an arrestment as loosened if he receives a letter from the solicitor or agent who instructed it confirming that the rights of the arrester are waived.

Actions of furthcoming: As has been noted the effect of an arrestment is merely to attach the debt or subjects of it. It does not operate as a transfer of the subject to the arrester nor does it give title to the arrestee to pay over or deliver what has been arrested. An arrestment is completed and made effective by the arrester raising an action of furthcoming in which both arrestee and common debtor will be called as defenders. When such action has been raised and decree pronounced the authority of the arrestee to make over the subjects of the arrestment is contained in the extract decree. The arrestee does not normally enter appearance in an action of furthcoming so long as the sum sued for is not greater than the amount in his own hands; if it is he will seek to have the decree restricted to that amount.

The decree will order the arrestee to pay the fund which has been arrested, or as much of it as will pay the common debtor's dues to the arrester. If there are competing claims the proper course for the arrester is to raise an action of multiple poinding and allow the Court to allocate the arrested subjects amongst the various claimants.

In any event it is in the interests of the arrestee to ensure that all is regular, thus guaranteeing that when he meets the decree of furthcoming by payment the matter is at an end.

Poinding

Poinding is a process which has the effect of creating a nexus over property, necessarily corporeal, in favour of the creditor. The effect of poinding is to this extent the same as that of arrestment, the differences between the two processes being: (1) that poinding is usually directed against property in the hands of the debtor himself, (2) that it is competent only in execution, that is in securing payment after a decree has been obtained, and (3) that it is normally necessarily preceded by a step of diligence known as a charge for payment.

The purpose of a poinding is to attach, and thereafter sell for payment, moveable property belonging to the debtor. It proceeds on a warrant to poind which is contained in extract decrees and deeds or protests registered in the Court books. By virtue of these decrees and deeds a poinding may take place, once the days of the charge for payment have expired and will affect the moveable effects of the debtor to an extent sufficient to cover the creditor's debts with interest and expenses. A poinding is carried out by a Sheriff Officer or Messenger-at-Arms and must be reported within eight days to the Sheriff, who will grant warrant to sell the poinded articles in accordance with the prescriptions of the law. If a sale is held the articles are exposed for sale at a price not less than the value put on them when they were poinded and if they fail to fetch this price they will be delivered over to the creditor.

No one must transact or carry off poinded effects, under pain of imprisonment until he restores the effects or pays double the appraised value.

Liable for poinding are the whole goods of the debtor, including those in the possession of the creditor, but excluding animals, the implements of a farm if the debtor has other effects and effects of which the debtor is only joint owner or in which he has only a qualified or temporary interest.

Poinding of the Ground: Poinding of the ground is a remedy open to heritable creditors, such as superiors, owners of ground annuals and creditors under a standard security. The effect of the action of poinding of the ground is to secure payment of the heritable debt over, not the heritable subjects themselves, but over moveable property situated on the ground. The subjects attached by a poinding of the ground are all moveables situated on the ground at the date of service in the action and belonging to the proprietor of the land, an exception being moveables belonging to tenants in so far as the value does not succeed rents due by them and unpaid. Where there is any competition between poinding of the ground and ordinary poinding or between different heritable creditor's poindings of the ground the following rules—based on the theory that a poinding of the ground is the 'crystalisation' of a prior charge—apply: a poinding of the ground of a superior for feu duty takes precedence; those of heritable creditors holding under deed are preferred amongst themselves according to the date of the constitution of the real right on which they base their claim; poinding of the ground is preferred to any ordinary poinding. In questions with a trustee in bankruptcy a poinding of the ground must be executed more than sixty days before the sequestration if fully effectual, although a poinding subsequent to this secures the current half year's interest and one year's arrears.

Diligence against heritable property

Adjudication: Adjudication is the diligence by which land and other heritable subjects are attached in satisfaction of debts. Any interest in heritable property may be so attached by the process of adjudication. An action to obtain adjudication is raised in the Court of Session, there being specified in it a particular piece of land or heritable interest. Such action proceeds on a decree or liquid document of debt and a notice of the summons, in statutory form, is registered in the Register of Inhibitions and Adjudications. The effect of such registration is to prohibit the debtor from making any voluntary alienation of the heritable interest within five years of the date of registration. When a decree in the action of adjudication is obtained and an extract recorded in the General Register of Sasines the rights in the land become the property of the creditor, the decree supplying in law the want of a voluntary conveyance from the debtor.

The right acquired by the creditor is not final. The right can be redeemed within ten years, a period known as the 'legal', by the debtor paying the sums due to the creditor. Thus the right which the creditor has during the 'legal' is not a right of property. The adjudication is not a transference of the property, but simply a step of diligence, which only creates a security for debt. On the expiry of the 'legal' the creditor seeks a court declaration of the expiry of the 'legal', and, this obtained, the right of redemption is extinguished, the redeemable security being converted into an absolute and irredeemable right of property.

When a notice of adjudication is registered the property is rendered litigious and thus cannot be alienated voluntarily by the debtor. Where there are several creditors seeking adjudication all those prior in ranking to the first effectual adjudgor and those who obtain adjudgement within a year and a day after the first adjudication is made effectual rank equally.

Inhibition

An inhibition is a writ prohibiting a debtor from alienating or otherwise affecting his heritable estate to the prejudice of the creditor who seeks the inhibition. It may be used in security of debts already due or of future debts. Letters of Inhibition follow a form regulated by statute and when registered such letters prohibit all voluntary alienations of, and all diligence against, the debtor's heritable estate for debts contracted subsequent to the date of the inhibition. An inhibition does not effect lands acquired by the person against whom such inhibition is used after the date of the recording of the inhibition. The diligence of inhibition, designed to protect the estate for the benefit of the creditor is personal against the debtor and prescribes in five years. An inhibition may be withdrawn by a voluntary discharge by the creditor or an order of Court recalling the inhibition.

CHAPTER TWELVE

BANKRUPTCY

THE ideas which lie behind the law of bankruptcy and the aims of this branch of the law may be stated briefly as the ensuring that each creditor of a man hopelessly encumbered with debt receives fair treatment and the liberation of that man from an impossible situation.

Historically these ideas and objectives developed late and then but gradually. Originally a man had to pay his debts and pay them in full. Failure to do so led to his imprisonment, his release depending on his ceding all his possessions to pay his debts. But when released, although he could not be imprisoned again for failure to pay in full the debts which he had incurred before his imprisonment, he was still saddled with the burden of debt. Further, it was for individual creditors to press their own claims at all stages; thus success in recovery was to the swiftest, the most cunning or the most fortunate creditor.

The first stages of development of the modern law of bankruptcy were enactments to render illegal attempts by a debtor to evade the claims of his creditors by giving away his property. Then came the idea that the creditors should be treated as a body and that the debtor's estate should be divided rateably and equally among them. An extension of this was the provision that the debtor might ultimately be discharged from his obligation to meet the claims.

The modern law of bankruptcy is to be found largely in the Bankruptcy (Scotland) Act 1913 which consolidated the law. This Act deals mainly with sequestration, the process by which the debtor's property is transferred to a trustee for management, realisation, and distribution among his creditors. But sequestration is a single use of the term bankruptcy, a word without technical meaning. Also covered by bankruptcy are insolvency and notour bankruptcy, two stages in the process of inability to meet obligations. All three terms have importance and must be examined.

U

Insolvency

Insolvency may be practical or absolute.

Practical insolvency: is a present inability to meet present debts.[1] It is of no importance that a man's assets, if realised, would cover his liabilities.[2] From the point of view of his creditors, whose interest is in procuring payment when due, their debtor's assets are of but passing importance; they are entitled to treat him as insolvent if he cannot, or will not, meet their due claims. Thus in the case of *Re Patrick and Lyon Limited*[3] the judge said: 'A company is not solvent unless it can pay its debts as they become due, and commercial solvency alone in the sense that assets exceed liabilities, is insufficient. Balance sheet figures do not count.' While in a later case[4] wilful refusal to pay a debt, although it could be shown that the debtor was perfectly able to do so from available assets, was held to constitute insolvency.

Thus the Sale of Goods Act 1893[5] permits treatment of a man as insolvent when he has ceased to pay his debts in the ordinary course of business or cannot pay them as they fall due.

Absolute insolvency: is when a man's liabilities exceed his assets.

When someone is absolutely insolvent and knows it his freedom of action with his own estate is reduced; he must act in the interests of his creditors, and is deemed to administer his estate on behalf of his creditors generally,[6] a rule which precludes his disposing of his property to the prejudice of the body of creditors as a whole.[7]

Notour bankruptcy

Notour bankruptcy is 'insolvency of a public or notorious nature'.[8] Formerly describing the state of the man who, to avoid imprisonment for debt, had retired to the sanctuary of the Abbey of Holyrood, the term now describes the man whose insolvency is public knowledge. What constitutes notour bankruptcy is laid down by the Bankruptcy (Scotland) Act 1913 (s. 5). It is constituted in any of the following ways: (*a*) by sequestration (in cases where notour bank-

---

[1] *Teenan Tr.* v. *Teenan* (1186), 13 R. 833.
[2] *Scottish Milk Marketing Board* v. *Wood* (1936) S.C. 604.
[3] 1933 Ch. 786.
[4] *Scottish Milk Marketing Board* v. *Wood, supra.*
[5] s. 62.
[6] *infra* p. 307.
[7] *infra* p. 306.
[8] Goudy on Bankruptcy (4th ed.) p. 63.

ruptcy is not a necessary prerequisite to an award of sequestration or the issuing of an adjudication of bankruptcy or the granting of a receiving order in England or Ireland or (*b*) by insolvency, concurring (*i*) with a duly executed charge[9] followed by the expiry of the days of the charge without payment; (*ii*) (where a charge is not necessary) with the passing, without payment of the days which must elapse before further steps can be taken to enforce a decree or warrant for payment of a sum of money; (*iii*) with a poinding or seizure of any part of the debtor's moveables for non-payment of rates or taxes; (*iv*) with a decree of adjudication of any part of his heritable estate for payment or insecurity; or, (*v*) with a sale of any effects belonging to the debtor under a sequestration for rent.

The importance of notour bankruptcy is twofold. One, it is a prerequisite in certain cases for the sequestration of the debtor and, two, diligence which has been done in a certain period prior to or following upon its constitution may be equalised.[10]

Reduction of gratuitous alienations

One of the early developments in the law regarding insolvency was to strike at endeavours by the debtor to defeat his creditors' rights by ridding himself of his property. Such attempts on his part to give away his property, called gratuitous alienations, can be rendered nugatory either at common law or under statute, the relevant Act being the Bankruptcy Act 1621.

Reduction at common law may be sought by any creditor, whether he was a creditor before the alienation or not, or by a trustee in the debtor's sequestration.[11] A gratuitous alienation in this connection is any alienation by an insolvent without his receiving valuable consideration for it. The challenger of the transaction must show that the alienation was non-onerous and to the prejudice of the creditors. Obviously a gift is a gratuitous alienation while a sale for real worth in money is not. If however the alienation was made to implement a prior obligation or a non-contractual obligation such as for aliment for a child, it will be deemed to have been made for true and just cause and it will not be reducible.

---

[9] i.e. a demand for payment formally made after a Court decree for payment has been obtained against the debtor. The debtor has a fixed number of days in which to comply with the demand.
[10] *infra* p.
[11] Bankruptcy (Scotland) Act 1913, s. 9.

The challenger must also prove that the debtor was insolvent—for this purpose absolute insolvency must be shown—when he made the alienation, or that the result of the transaction was to create insolvency.[12] Further, he must prove that the debtor is still insolvent at the time of the challenge.

Reduction under the Act of 1621; The Act, 1621, c. 18, deals with gifts made by insolvent persons to 'conjunct and confident' persons. Where the alienation was to a conjunct person, a relative or close friend, or to a confident person, anyone who stood in a confidential relationship with the debtor, the challenger has an easier task that at common law. He will have the transaction reduced by proving that he was a creditor prior to the alienation, that the debtor was absolutely insolvent when the action was raised, and that the recipient was conjunct or confident. This raises the presumption that the debtor was insolvent at the time of the alienation and that it was without just cause. The debtor must then rebut these presumptions if the transaction is to stand.

It must be noted that the easier task of the challenger under the Act is available to him only when conjunct and confident persons are involved.

Reduction of fraudulent preferences

Another early development in the law relating to debtors was an endeavour to secure equal treatment for all creditors to ensure that one would not be favoured by the debtor at the expense of the others. Such a preference shown towards one creditor by an insolvent is branded as fraudulent and is reducible once again either at common law or under statute.

Reduction at common law: An insolvent person will often carry on his business and may have to grant security for advances to be made to him. His insolvency is no bar to such a transaction.[13] He almost certainly will require from time to time to pay bills to his creditors, and again such a transaction is unexceptionable. What he must not do is to make over fraudulently,[14] any part of his estate to a particular creditor in satisfaction of or in further security for a prior debt.

---

[12] *Abram Steamship Co. Ltd.* (In liqun.) 1925 S.L.T. 243.
[13] *McInnes* v. *McCallum* (1901), 9 S.L.T. 215.
[14] *McCowan* v. *Wright* (1853), 15 D. 494.

At common law a challenge of such a transaction must show that the debtor was absolutely insolvent and was aware of the fact.[15] Further, it must be shown that the debtor 'intentionally and in anticipation of his failure' conferred on a favoured creditor a preference over the other creditors. If there is collusion between debtor and creditor, the reduction of the transaction will be secured more easily, but mere knowledge by the creditor of the insolvency does not make the payment or transfer collusive.[16] Exempt from challenge as fraudulent preferences are cash payments actually due to be made in discharge of debts justly due, transactions in the course of trade, and *nova debita* (new debts).[17]

Reduction under statute: The Act 1696, c. 5, was designed to ease the burden of the challenger of an allegedly illegal preference. This Act declares that all voluntary dispositions and assignations granted by the debtor at or after or within sixty days before his notour bankruptcy in favour of a creditor for his satisfaction or further security in preference to other creditors are null and void. The immediate effect of this is obvious. The challenger, who may be a prior creditor[18] or the trustee in the debtor's sequestration, need not prove knowledge of it or fraudulent intent; he simply points to the date of the notour bankruptcy and if the transaction is within the prescribed period before that date or is after it then it is reducible. The effect of the Act is to extend constructively the period of the bankruptcy.

The period of constructive bankruptcy was increased from the sixty days prescribed by the 1696 Act to six months by the Companies Act 1947.[19]

Exempted from the provisions of the Act are cash payments of debts due, transactions in the ordinary course of business and *nova debita*, unless fraudulent contrivance between debtor and creditor can be proven. What these terms encompass (and it will be recalled they apply at common law as well as under the Act) must be examined.

Payments in cash include payments by cheque although not, when usage in a particular trade allows such an arrangement, payment by

---

15 *McDougall's Tr.* v. *Ironside.* 1914, S.C. 186.
16 *Jones's Tr.* v. *Wesbter* (1886), 13 R. 1112, but see Gow *op. cit.* p. 622.
17 These categories of payment are recognised by the Act 1696 and are dealt with below.
18 Prior, i.e., to the transaction challenged.
19 s. 115.

indorsement by the debtor to his creditor of a cheque received by him from a third party.[20] The payment must be of a debt due—payment of a debt not due is not protected[21]—although proof of collusion between debtor and creditor to defraud other creditors will make the payment reducible.

Transactions in the ordinary course of trade include payment for goods supplied on credit and delivery of goods paid for[22] although if the delivery is not bona fide but an attempt to create a security it will be reducible. Thus in the case of *Striven* v. *Scott and Simpson*[23] invoices for the goods were delivered to a creditor, the goods themselves being retained by the debtor. Within the period of constructive bankruptcy the goods were delivered. It was held that this was not a delivery following sale but a grant of security for a prior debt, and as such was reducible.

The categories of payment in cash and payments in the ordinary course of business often have between them an indistinct or even invisible boundary line. They 'tend to merge and are usually pled together'.[24]

An example of an endeavour to create a preference which failed is to be found in the case of *Anderson's Tr.* v. *Somerville and Co. Ltd.*[25] In this case the law agents for a debtor indorsed in favour of a creditor a cheque payable to them representing the proceeds of the sale of some of the debtor's property. This was held not to be a cash payment in the ordinary course of business. In the case of *Craig's Tr.* v. *Craig*[26] a man who signed a promissory note along with his brother and gave the note to his bank sold some goods by auction and instructed the auctioneer to pay the amount of the note to the bank. The note had not matured. This was held to be an illegal preference in so far as it benefited the brother, who was ordered to repay the amount to the trustee in bankruptcy of his co-obligant. In the leading case of *Taylor* v. *Farrie*[27] an insolvent agreed to sell goods and was paid for them. During the period of constructive

[20] *Carter* v. *Johnstone* (1886) 13 R. 698; *Whatmough's Tr.* v. *British Linen Bank*, 1934 S.C. (H.L.) 51.
[21] *Blincow's Tr.* v. *Allan and Co.* (1828), 7 S. 124.
[22] *Taylor* v. *Farrie* (1885), 17 D. 639.
[23] (1871), 9 M. 923.
[24] Gow op. cit. p. 621.
[25] (1899) 1 F. 90.
[26] 1903, 10 S.L.T. 357.
[27] (1855) 17 D. 639.

bankruptcy he delivered the goods. This delivery was held valid as being an act which he had to do, it was not voluntary, and might also be justified as being in the ordinary course of business.[28] The question of compulsion is important. The Act does not mean that the debtor must not do what he might be compelled to do at law, but it does prevent him 'from entering spontaneously into some new transaction with a favoured creditor wherein in lieu of— or as a substitute for—regular payment of a debt in cash the debtor grants and the creditor receives a transference of some other funds or effects forming part of the debtor's estate'.[29]

'*Nova debita* include transactions where the bankrupt and the party whose right is challenged incur reciprocal obligations at the same time or with an interval so short as to admit of the application of the term *unico contextu*. To these, [transactions] though the party may have been insolvent at their date, or may have become notour bankrupt within six months thereafter, neither the common law nor the Act of 1696, as amended, constitutes any objection.'[30] Obviously payments for purchases made during insolvency or constructive bankruptcy will be protected as payments in cash or in the ordinary course of business. The type of transaction which is protected as *novum debitum* is where the debtor borrows money and grants security for it. The disposition of the security subjects is not an illegal preference. It need not be made at precisely the same time as the advance[31] but the promise to grant it must be unconditional; otherwise the ultimate granting is not mere completion of the transaction. Obviously no attempt to grant security to an existing creditor will be successful if challenged, as there is no new debt.

Equalisation of diligences

The date of notour bankruptcy is also important for fixing the period during which diligences done against the debtor's estate are equalised.

Diligence is 'the legal process by which a creditor attaches the property or person of his debtor with the object of forcing him (1) to appear in Court to answer an action at the creditor's instance or (2)

---

28 Gloag and Henderson op. cit. p. 718.
29 *Taylor* v. *Farrie, supra.*
30 Gloag and Henderson, op. cit. pp. 718–9.
31 *Cowdenbeath Coal Co.* v. *Clydesdale Bank* (1895) 22 R. 682.

to implement a judgement already pronounced'.[32] Of the various forms of diligence, the two which are most relevant in this context are arrestment and poinding.

Arrestment is a diligence attaching property of the debtor which is in the hands of a third party who must thereafter retain the property as security for the ultimate payment of the debt. The property will be released by the third party only when there is a judicial order authorising him to release it or when the debtor consents to it being delivered to the creditor. Poinding is a diligence by which moveable property in the hands of the debtor is attached. The effect of poinding is to immobilise the property and it may be followed by a judicially-ordered sale of the property for the purpose of paying the creditor from the proceeds. It will be appreciated that the creditor who has arrested or poinded property is in an advantageous position in questions with other creditors.

To offset the advantage to be gained by a creditor, the idea of equalisation of diligences has been developed. Now contained in the Bankruptcy (Scotland) Act 1913,[33] the law is that all arrestments and poindings effected within a period of sixty days prior to notour bankruptcy or four months thereafter[34] are equalised, that is, the creditors who have done diligence fall to be treated as equal claimants and the diligences rank equally among themselves as if they had been effected on the same date. Further, any creditor who within this period produces in Court liquid grounds of debt or a decree of payment is entitled to be treated as if he too had done diligence. This means that if sequestration occurs within the period the creditors who have arrested or poinded will be treated equally with all the creditors, as sequestration is equivalent to an arrestment on behalf of all the creditors.[35]

Diligences effected before the sixty days are not affected by this rule and the creditor who has used diligence outwith the period is preferred to the body of creditors whose diligences fall within the period.

Sequestration

The sequestration of a bankrupt's estate is the process by which

---

[32] Graham Stewart, *Diligence*, p. 1.
[33] s. 10, s. 104.
[34] For the significance of the period see *infra* p. 313.
[35] s. 104, *Stewart* v. *Jarvie*, 1938 S.C 30.

the bankrupt is judicially divested of his property which is vested in a trustee for the benefit of his creditors. The award of sequestration may be made by either the Court of Session, provided that the debtor is subject to its jurisdiction, or by the Sheriff Court under whose jurisdiction the debtor has resided or carried on business for the year preceding the petition.

Any person subject to the jurisdiction of the Scottish Courts may have his estates sequestrated; the estate of a party who has died may be sequestrated if he was subject to the jurisdiction at the time of his death.[36] Similarly, the estate of a partnership or a corporate body[37]—with the exception of a company registered under the Companies Acts for which a similar procedure known as liquidation exists—may be sequestrated; unincorporated associations are not liable for sequestration as they cannot be notour bankrupt.[38]

Petition for sequestration

Where the debtor is alive he may petition for sequestration himself. To do so he requires the concurrence of one or more creditors whose aggregate debt amounts to at least £50. Provided the Court has jurisdiction it must award sequestration in such a case.[39]

The petition may also be presented by creditors. Any creditor or group of creditors owed £50 or over may petition. The petition must show that the debtor is notour bankrupt and that within a year before the presentation of the petition the debtor resided in or had a dwelling house or a place of business in Scotland if the petition is presented in the Court of Session. If the petition is presented in the Sheriff Court the petitioners must claim that the debtor has resided or carried on business for a year within the jurisdiction of the Court.

The debtor may concur in the petition. If he does so the Court must award the sequestration. If the debtor does not concur, the petition must be presented within four months of his notour bankruptcy and the Court will order intimation to the debtor and advertisement in the *Edinburgh Gazette*. This order is called the 'first deliverance' and is of importance in so far as its date is held to be the material one for the commencement of the sequestration. If the

[36] s. 11.
[37] *Wotherspoon* v. *Magistrates of Linlithgow* (1863) 2 M. 348.
[38] *Pitreavie Golf Club* v. *Penman* 1934 S.L.T. 247.
[39] s. 28.

debtor does not oppose the petition, the award of sequestration will be made and that date of the first deliverance will be held to be the date of the sequestration.

If the debtor wishes to fend off the sequestration he must pay the debt in respect of which he was made notour bankrupt and those he owes to the petitioners or otherwise show cause why the order should not be made.

Where the debtor is deceased the petition may be made by a mandatary of the deceased or by qualified creditors, i.e. creditors owed at least £50. In either case the deceased must have been subject to the Court's jurisdiction at the time of his death. Where creditors petition, no award may be made until six months after death [40] although, if granted, it dates back to the date of the first deliverance. If, however, the debtor was notour bankrupt at the time of his death, or if his successors concur in the petition or renounce the succession, the award need not be delayed.[41]

The award of sequestration

The effect of an award of sequestration is to vest in the creditors the whole estate of the debtor. In practice the title to the property is that of the trustee under the sequestration when he is appointed. Until his appointment the property is in the debtor. All property to which the bankrupt has a beneficial right, with the exception of clothes necessary for himself, his wife and family, and working tools or implements necessary to enable him to earn a living, are affected by the award. If necessary before the trustee is appointed the Court can take steps to preserve the estate either on the application of a creditor or of its own volition by appointing a judicial factor[42] who will take care of the property. The Court may also order that money, bank notes, bonds, bills, cheques and other moveable property be put into safe custody or that the debtor and his premises be searched for moveable property. Any shop or warehouse of the debtor may be ordered to be put under lock and key.[43]

Publication: The award of sequestration is not fully effectual until published and recorded. The petitioners must within two days of the first deliverance present for recording an abbreviate of the

[40] s. 76.
[41] s. 13.
[42] s. 14.
[43] s. 15.

petition and first deliverance to the Keeper of the Register of Inhibitions and Adjudications and also insert a statutory notice in the *Edinburgh Gazette* within four days and in the *London Gazette* within six. The effect of the recording is to render the debtor incapable of granting voluntarily any deed or incurring any debt in respect of his heritable estate and also to render the heritable property litigious and incapable of attachment by any single creditor.

The affidavit and claim

A creditor who intends to claim in the estate of the bankrupt may or may not wish to participate in the management of the estate, even to the extent of voting on the election of the trustees. Whether he cares to do so or not, his entry as a creditor in the sequestration rests on his production of an affidavit and claim, a statement made on oath that a debt exists, accompanied by the account or vouchers of debt which support the deed. Such a statement is made before a judge, magistrate, justice of the peace, notary public, or commissioner for oaths, on oath. In the case of a corporation the oath is competently made by an officer of the corporation. In cases dealing with banks the oath of a country agent, the forerunner of the branch manager, has been held to be bad[44] and that of the assistant manager to be effectual.[45]

The penalties for falsehood in connection with the production of the affidavit and claim are severe; prosecution for perjury at common law is competent, while under the Act (s. 186) wilful falsehood under oath subjects the perpetrator not only to prosecution but, upon conviction, to liability to forfeit his whole claim on the estate.

Valuation of securities: If a creditor holds any security as at the date of sequestration[46] he must state this in the affidavit and claim and put a value on it; the extent of his voting rights is the net worth of his claim after deducting value of the security.

If a number of securities are held the Act (s. 55) provides that each must be valued separately, while if securities are appropriated to specific debts they should be valued against the particular debt to which they refer. A security which has been provided by a third party, not the debtor, is specified in the affidavit and claim for information but need not be valued or deducted.

[44] *Anderson* v. *Montheith* (1847) 9 D. 1432.
[45] *Dow and Co.* v. *Union Bank of Scotland* (1875) 2 R. 459.
[46] *Royal Bank of Scotland* v. *Millar's Tr.* (1882) 9 R. 679.

Contingency claims: When a creditor has a claim which is contingent, that is a claim the payment of which depends on the occurrence of some event which is uncertain, special considerations arise. An example is where a cautioner becomes bankrupt, the principal debtor remaining solvent; in such a case, the claim, not being immediately exigible, is contingent.

A contingent creditor is not allowed to vote or to draw a dividend in respect of his claim, but he may apply to the trustee, or to the sheriff if no trustee has been elected, to put a value on the claim. When this valuation, which can be appealed to the Courts, is made the creditor is entitled to vote and draw dividends in respect of that value.

Notice of an application for valuation must be given to the bankrupt and to any petitioning or concurring creditor. Any creditor may challenge the valuation.

If the contingency takes place before the debt has been valued, the creditor may draw dividends and vote in respect of the amount of the debt, but payment of any such dividend will not affect former dividends paid to other creditors. Once valuation has taken place, the claim of the creditor is restricted to that amount.

Valuation of claims against co-obligants: If there are co-obligants with the debtor in the claim the creditor for the purposes of voting, must in his affidavit and claim, disclose and put a value upon, and deduct, such value from his claims the obligation of any person he may hold bound with, but liable in relief to, the bankrupt to the extent to which the bankrupt has a right or relief. Any security he holds from a co-obligant or any security from which the bankrupt has right of relief is similarly treated. When the question of ranking on the estate is relevant such deduction is not made, the creditor is entitled to rank and draw a dividend for the full sum due to him. Where there is a bond promising repayment of a fluctuating amount it is usual to include in it a clause stipulating that the amount due at any time is conclusively shown by the certificate of a specified official or person. In such case the affidavit and claim will be supported by the production of the bond and a copy of the account duly certified as provided in the deed.

Where there is no bond the vouchers necessary for sums on an overdrawn current account are a Certificate of Balance or a certified copy account, stating at earliest from the last annual balance. There is weak authority that the dockets and the cheques should be produced but, probably, the case is met by having the account certified in the terms of the Bankers Books Evidence Act 1879, and, in any event, the practice of having accounts docketed has been discontinued and cheques are given up.

If the account has not been docketed, the whole account from the beginning must be produced; it is not sufficiently vouched if beginning with a balance either on the creditor or debtor side.[47]

The Trustee

Election: The award of sequestration fixes a day for a meeting of creditors for the purpose of electing a trustee. The meeting must be held not earlier than six days and not later than twelve days from the appearance of the notice of the award in the *Edinburgh Gazette.*[48] Entitled to attend this meeting are all creditors of the bankrupt; corporate creditors are represented by a mandatory, as any creditor may be. Creditors must produce at the meeting the affidavit and claim on which their claim to be entertained as creditors rests and upon which the voting rights of the creditors is based. It must be noted that voting is by value so that the larger creditor has more influence in the management of the sequestration than the smaller.

The first duty of the meeting is to elect a preses, or chairman, and clerk. There is provision in the Act[49] for the Sheriff presiding at this meeting and he must do so if requested by two or more creditors. This is a little-known procedure.

The trustee, usually an accountant, is also elected by the creditors. Ineligible for appointment are the bankrupt, conjunct and confident persons, anyone who has an interest opposed to that of the creditors as a whole,[50] persons not subject to the jurisdiction of the Scottish Courts, and minors. The result of the election is reported to the Sheriff who, assuming no competition or objection, will confirm it. The judgement of the Sheriff so declaring a person elected as trustee is final, although there is provision for the removal of a trustee either by a meeting of creditors or by the Court.[51]

---

[47] *Low* v. *Baxter* (1851) 13 D. 1349.
[48] s. 63.
[49] s. 64.
[50] Philip Wolfson Ltd. 1962 S.L.T. 252.
[51] s. 67.

Also at this first statutory meeting the creditors will elect commissioners[52] and examine the bankrupt's state of affairs.[53]

The trustee, once elected, will find caution, to a sum fixed by the creditors, and on his lodging his bond of caution with the Sheriff-clerk and having his appointment confirmed by the Sheriff he will be issued with an Act and Warrant.

The Act and Warrant: The Trustee's Act and Warrant is his authority to perform his duties under the Act and is evidence of his right and title to the sequestrated estate. Within ten days of the confirmation of his election the trustee must present an abbreviate of the Act and Warrant for recording in the Register of Inhibitions and Adjudications. It is also recorded in the register of sequestrations kept by the Accountant of Court who supervises all bankruptcies.

Visiting of the estate: The Act and Warrant vests in the trustee on behalf of the creditors the whole property of the debtor.[54] Both heritable and moveable property vest and subject to any preferable securities which existed at the time of the esquestration and which are not reducible, become the property of the trustee. However the generality 'the whole property' is restricted to property in which the debtor had a beneficial interest, so that property held on trust by the bankrupt for third parties is not affected[55] except for money which his wife has lent or entrusted to him or allowed to become inmixed with his funds.[56] Further, the property attachable for debt, which is the property described in the Act as vesting, does not include the necessary wearing apparel of the bankrupt and his family, working tools and the like, so these are excluded.

The trustee steps into the shoes of the bankrupt and takes no higher right in property than the bankrupt had; hence a right of property reducible on the grounds of the bankrupt's fraud could not be maintained by the trustee. Non-vested contingent rights under a will, marriage contract or other document of an irrevocable nature are[57] vested in the trustee, while alimentary provisions can be ordered by the Court to be paid to the trustee in so far as they are in excess of what the Court thinks suitable for the bankrupt.[58] Govern-

---

[52] *infra* p. 323.
[53] *infra* p. 319.
[54] s. 87.
[55] *Heritable Reversionary Co. Ltd.* v. *Mackay'sTr.* (1892) 19 R. (H.L.) 43.
[56] Married Women's Property Act, 1881, s. 14.
[57] s. 86.
[58] s. 92(2).

ment pay or pension may, with the sanction of the department concerned, be made available to the trustee.

Property acquired by the bankrupt between his sequestration and his discharge falls under the sequestration. The bankrupt must notify the trustee of any property he acquires, called *acquirenda*, to enable the trustee to seek a vesting order from the Court in respect of that property. Salary and wages are *acquirenda* but would be subject to a reasonable allowance to the debtor for maintenance.[59]

All rights of action which the bankrupt had[60] vest in the trustee who may pursue or raise actions for the benefit of the estate. Similarly he is entitled to adopt or contracts to which the bankrupt was a party, unless he is barred by an element of *delectus personae*, or he may repudiate the contract, thereby rendering the estate liable for damages for breach of contract. If he choses to continue a contract he incurs personal liability on it.

The duties of the trustee

The duties of the trustee,[61] which begin with the issue to him of his Act and Warrant confirming his election, are too numerous to list in detail. Broadly, he administers, realises and distributes the estate subject to the rules laid down in the Act. Some of his principal duties are:

Examination of the bankrupt:[62] Within eight days of the issue of the Act and Warrant the trustee must petition the Sheriff for examination of the bankrupt. The purpose of this examination is to ascertain the extent of the estate, where it is and what has been done with it. There is also provision in the Act[63] for examination on oath of the bankrupt's wife, family, clerks, servants, and agents and any other person who can give information regarding the estate. This examination may take place in open Court.

Statutory meetings: The second statutory meeting of creditors is convened by the trustee after the examination. The purpose of this meeting, notice of which will be given to the creditors in the circular giving them the date of the examination, is to allow the trustee to report as to the state of the bankrupt's affairs and to present an

---

59 *Caldwell* v. *Hamilton* 1919 S.C. (H.L.) 100.
60 Excluding those affecting his character, e.g. defamation, and his status e.g. divorce.
61 ss. 75–80.
62 ss. 83–89.
63 s. 86.

estimate of the realised value of the estate. The creditors may give directions regarding the administration of the sequestration.

There may be other meetings of the creditors for specific purposes mentioned in the Act. If there is a need for any such meeting it will be called by the trustee.

Adjudication of claims: The trustee has a duty to adjudicate the claims of the creditors. The creditors who wish to rank on the estate must lodge an affidavit and claim. As we have seen, the creditors will usually lodge such an affidavit at the time of the first statutory meeting, but there is no fixed time for lodging it, although participation in a dividend will depend on the claim being lodged at least two months before the dividend is paid. However, if the dividend is being paid sooner than necessary, the period is shortened to one month. A creditor who misses the first dividend by failing to claim timeously may be entitled to an equalising dividend later if funds are available.

To enable the trustee to investigate each claim he has powers to examine the bankrupt, the creditor and any other person relative to any claim. He will then notify the creditor whether he admits or rejects the claim, or, if he admits the claim, whether he is prepared to accord any preference to it. There is provision for appeal against the decision of the trustee.

Preferential claims: As well as the right to rank on the estate a creditor may claim a preference, i.e. a right to be paid in preference to the other creditors. Any such claim must be made in the affidavit and claim. Preferential debts[64] are the payment of the trustee and the law agent employed in the sequestration and, in the case of a deceased debtor, deathbed and funeral expenses. Thereafter, ranking equally amongst themselves but before all other claims, are claims for local rates and taxes due at the date of sequestration up to the amount of one year's assessment, national taxes to the extent of one year's assessment, wages and salaries for employees of the bankrupt up to a limit of £200 or four months' pay per employee. National insurance payments and monies deducted from employees are also preferred claims. It is for the trustee to adjudicate the validity of a preferred claim.

Secured claims: As noted earlier any creditor holding a security must state in his affidavit and claim that he does so and place a value

---

[64] s. 118, as amended.

on the security, deducting that value from the amount of his debt and ranking only for the balance. For the purpose of determining voting rights a majority of the creditors is allowed to compel assignation of such a security by its holder to the trustee at the value put upon it by the holder plus twenty per cent of that value. The creditor in question cannot vote in this decision which may be taken at subsequent meetings also. For the purpose of ranking for dividends the trustee may, with the consent of the commissioners, demand a conveyance of the security at the value put on it by the creditor which cannot be refused, or may reserve to the creditor the benefit of the security.[65] If the creditor is allowed to realise the security and if the proceeds of the realisation together with any dividend he receives exceed his debt he must account to the trustee for the excess. If the trustee is discharged he accounts to the bankrupt.[66]

Double ranking: Where the bankrupt had a co-obligant or cautioner his creditor must choose whether to claim a ranking on the estate and seek the balance from the co-obligant or cautioner, or to hold the co-obligant or cautioner liable and allow him to seek a ranking on the estate. What cannot happen is that the principal debtor and cautioner both rank, for that would constitute two claims against the estate in respect of a single debt. If both parties liable on a contract were bankrupt, their common creditor could rank on both estates but not to the extent of procuring payment beyond twenty shillings in the pound. There would be no recourse by one of the estates against the other.[67]

Management and realisation: The trustee must take possession of the estate as soon as possible after his appointment. He must proceed to manage, realise and recover the estate and convert it into money according to the directions of the creditors at a meeting or the advice of the commissioners.

Heritage is usually sold by public sale but may be sold by private bargain with the concurrence of a majority in number and value of the creditors and of the Accountant of Court.[68] Book debts cannot be sold within a year of the award;[69] attempts must be made to collect them.

---

[65] s. 61.
[66] *Kinmoun Luke and Co.* v. *Finlay and Co.* (1904) 6 F. 564.
[67] Bell's *Comm* ii 416.
[68] s. 111.
[69] *Stewart* v. *Crokkston* 1910 S.C. 609.

W

The trustee must keep accounts and sederunt book in which the affairs of the sequestration are recorded. He must lodge money he receives in a bank in his own name as trustee. He must not keep in his own hands more than £50; if he does so for a period of over ten days he may be liable for interest, dismissal from office and loss of his right to remuneration.[70]

The trustee is entitled to be paid, his fee being fixed by the commissioners prior to the payment of the first dividend, a decision which may be appealed by the trustee, any creditor, or by the bankrupt to the Accountant of Court.[71] From the Accountant a further appeal lies to the Court itself.

Distribution of the estate: The whole realised estate of the bankrupt falls to be divided among the creditors rateably according to their separate rights. Paid first are the preferred creditors, after whom, assuming that the funds are sufficient to meet their claims in full, payment will be made to the ordinary creditors. If the funds are not sufficient to meet the claims of the preferred creditors in full they are paid reateably. If the preferred creditors can be paid in full a rateable distribution of any surplus is then made among the ordinary creditors who had no claim for preferential treatment. A third class of creditors are the postponed creditors whose claims do not fall to be met until the ordinary creditors have been paid in full. Postponed creditors are: the bankrupt's wife claiming in respect of property which had fallen under the sequestration because she had lent or entrusted it to her husband or allowed it to become immixed with the funds,[72] and any person who has lent money to a firm, or sold the goodwill of a business, on terms which involve the receipt of a share in the profits of the firm's business or interest at a rate varying with the profits.[73]

Payment to creditors is by way of dividend, the right to claim which is constituted by ranking on the estate. There are normally several dividends; the first may not be earlier than four months from the date of deliverance.[74] The Act stipulates when subsequent dividends may be paid but any dividend may be accelerated or postponed. If there is no acceleration or postponement dividends are

---

[70] ss. 78–79.
[71] ss. 121, 222.
[72] Married Women's Propery (Scotland) Act 1881.
[73] Partnership Act 1890, s. 3.
[74] s. 130.

payable at six months from the deliverance, ten months from the deliverance and every three months thereafter.[75]

Discharge of the trustee: The trustee, when the funds are finally distributed and after a final meeting of the creditors, may apply to the Court for his discharge,[76] and is entitled to be discharged. The sederunt books and deposit receipts for any unclaimed dividends are lodged with the Accountant of Court. Any creditor may object to the discharge of the trustee on the grounds that there are still assets to be recovered.

Resignation: A trustee is not entitled to resign office unless, at a meeting called for that purpose, a majority in numbers and value of the creditors consent to his resignation.

Removal: A trustee can be removed from office by the Court on cause shown if the application is supported by one quarter of the creditors in value.[77] The trustee may also be removed by the Court by the petition of a creditor or of the Accountant of Court on the grounds that he has not made an annual return or when the Accountant reports on the complaint of a creditor that he is not faithfully and properly carrying out his duties.[78] Retention of money in his own hands [79] unless kept from innocent causes, is also grounds for his removal.[80]

Commissioners

At the first statutory meeting the creditors will elect, as well as a trustee, three commissioners of their own number. The general duty of the commissioners is to advise and assist the trustee. In certain actions, e.g. the declaration or postponement of a dividend[81] or the fixing of the upset price for the sale of heritable property, their consent is required. They also fix the trustee's fees and audit his accounts.

The office of commissioner is gratuitous and may be resigned. If a commissioner is a mandatary of a creditor his appointment as commissioner falls if his mandate is withdrawn.

[75] ss. 126, 128 and 129.
[76] S. 152.
[77] S. 171.
[78] S. 152.
[79] *supra.* p. 322.
[80] S. 79.
[81] Ss. 121, 127, 131.

The bankrupt

The bankrupt has duties imposed on him by the Act. He must make up and produce at the meeting to elect the trustee a full statement of his assets and liabilities, the names of his creditors and debtors and the rental of any heritable property.[82] He is also obliged to appear at his public examination and there answer, under threat of imprisonment for failure, all lawful questions. Further he must, throughout the whole conduct of the sequestration, give the trustee every assistance and all information necessary to enable him to carry out his duties. He must grant all deeds necessary for the recovery and disposal of the estate.

The bankrupt has no power to administer his estate without the consent of the trustee. Two exceptions to his lack of power are: where he sells goods to someone who is ignorant of the bankruptcy and pays for the goods, or is willing to do so, the purchaser gets a good title and where a debtor of the bankrupt pays him in ignorance of the bankruptcy he is not liable also to pay the trustee.[83]

The bankrupt is prohibited by the Act from seeking credit from any person for more than £10 without disclosing that he is an undischarged bankrupt. Breach of this rule is an offence punishable by imprisonment for up to two years. There are also certain disqualifications attaching to bankruptcy. Certain offices, e.g. membership of parliament or a local authority cannot be held by a bankrupt.

Discharge of a bankrupt

For the bankrupt discharge is a privilege, not a right. The effect of the discharge is to free the bankrupt from all his debts and obligations due at the time of his sequestration with the exception of debts due to the Crown[84] (unless the Treasury consent to the discharge).[85] The sequestration may not be completed when the discharge is granted and is not affected by the discharge.

It is for the bankrupt to petition the Court for his discharge. The conditions attaching to a discharge are: (a) that there must have been paid a dividend of not less than twenty-five pence in the pound or, if the amount paid is less than this, failure to pay this amount cannot be held to be the responsibility of the bankrupt and (b) the Court

[82] S. 150.
[83] S. 107.
[84] S. 144.
[85] S. 147.

must be satisfied that the bankrupt's conduct warrants his discharge. With the petition for his discharge the bankrupt must produce a report from the trustee on his conduct and attitude during his bankruptcy. A report that he has been dishonest or unco-operative will prevent his discharge.

The times at which the petition may be presented are stipulated in the Act.[86] If the bankrupt petitions within two years from the award of sequestration he will require the consent of creditors. The rules are that he may petition (a) any time after the second statutory meeting if all his creditors consent; (b) six months after the award if a majority in number and four-fifths in value of his creditors concur; (c) twelve months after the award with the concurrence of a majority in number and two-thirds in value; (d) eighteen months after the award if a majority in number and value concur. After two years the concurrence of creditors is not required, although a favourable report from the trustee is still vital.

Any preference shown or consideration given to any creditor in exchange for his concurrence to the petition will, if discovered, negate the bankrupt's chances of discharge for ever. The creditor loses his right to rank on the estate and will be required to pay to the estate twice the value of the illegal payment.[87]

Recall of the sequestration

The deliverance awarding sequestration is not subject to review. There is, however, procedure, by which a petition may be presented to the Court of Session for the recall of the sequestration. Authorised by the Act[88] to petition are the debtor, provided he did not consent to the sequestration, the successors of a deceased debtor whose estate has been sequestrated without their consent, provided that the sequestration was not sought by a mandatary of the deceased, and must be based on grounds which would have been grounds for opposing the application for sequestration. An obvious defect in the procedure of the sequestration will lead to automatic recall; otherwise the Court has discretion to award or refuse recall.

The forty-day period is not applied if the petition is supported by nine-tenths of the creditors. Nor does if apply where the application is by successors of a deceased debtor who were edictally cited. They

---

[86] S. 143.
[87] *Thomas* v. *Sandenma* (1872) 11 M. 81.
[88] S. 30.

may apply for recall at any time up to the advertisement for payment of the first dividend. Finally, the Accountant of Court or any other interested party may petition within three months of the award on the ground that the majority of the creditors in number and value reside in England or Ireland and that from the situation of the property the estate ought to be wound up under the laws of England or Ireland.

While a petition for the recall of sequestration is being considered the sequestration continues normally. Only when the recall is granted is the debtor re-invested in his estate. Any proceedings taken with the estate by the trustee before the recall are valid and binding on the debtor.

Deeds of Arrangement[89]

A deed of arrangement is a deed embodying an arrangement between a sequestrated bankrupt and his creditors which has the effect of nullifying the sequestration proceedings. The terms of the arrangement are decided by the bankrupt and his creditors, must be accepted at a meeting by a majority in number and three-fourths in value, and must be approved as reasonable by the Court. If the Court approves of the arrangement the sequestration is deemed to be at an end. The deed of arrangement will provide for the discharge of the bankrupt as there is no statutory provision for this. If the bankrupt fails to honour the deed of arrangement the original debts revive.

Composition Contracts[90]

Another method of superseding the sequestration is by composition contract. The debtor or his friends can at a meeting offer to pay each creditor a sum in full satisfaction of his claims. The bankrupt is virtually offering to buy the estate back from the creditors for the value that the creditors expect it to yield.

After the meeting at which the composition is offered and at which a majority in number and three-fourths in value resolve to consider it, the trustee must advertise notice of the offer, give notice of the offer to each creditor and call another meeting. If this second meeting resolves, again by a majority in number and three-fourths in

[89] Ss. 34–39.
[90] Ss. 134–142.

value, to accept the offer, the trustee reports the resolution to the Court for approval of the offer. The Court can either approve or reject the composition offer.

If the Court approves the bankrupt is discharged. He is liable, under contract, for the agreed amount of the composition but is re-invested in his estate. The acceptance of the composition discharges the original debts, the claims of the creditors being converted into claims for their share of the composition.

Summary sequestration[91]

The process of summary sequestration, introduced by the Act, applies to those estates where the total assets of the debtor do not exceed £300 in value.

The petition for summary sequestration may be at the instance of the debtor—the process does not apply to the estates of deceased individuals or firms—and he does not require the consent of any creditor. Alternatively, a creditor owed £10 may petition. Where the petition is presented by the debtor he must produce a state of affairs to show that his assets are under £300. In a creditor's application the first deliverance orders the debtor to lodge such a state of affairs in Court. The Sheriff is not bound to grant a summary sequestration; he may at his discretion order the sequestration to proceed as an ordinary one.

The procedure of the sequestration is simplified. There is no need to call a second statutory meeting immediately after the examination, as it is assumed that the estate will be realised, the dividend declared —by the trustee and commissioners—and distribution will be made speedily.

When the funds have been finally distributed the Accountant of Court will grant a certificate to the trustee that he is entitled to be discharged. After advertisement in the *Edinburgh Gazette* for objections the Sheriff will discharge the trustee.

If there are no funds to be divided the Sheriff may dispense with procedure and the bankrupt may apply forthwith for discharge without the concurrence of any creditor; otherwise his discharge is procured in the normal way.

[91] Ss. 174–177.

Extra-judicial settlements with creditors

To avoid the expense, publicity and social effects of sequestration a debtor may attempt to reach with his creditors some private arrangement. These have two common forms, the trust deed and the extra-judicial composition contract.

Trust deeds

A debtor may grant a trust deed conveying his estate to a named trustee for realisation and distribution among his creditors. There is no prescribed form for such a deed and to be effective it requires the consent of all creditors. If a single creditor does not agree to the arrangement, he can wreck the whole scheme.

A stubborn creditor might apply to have the trust deeds reduced as a fraudulent preference under the Act of 1696 if it were granted within six months of notour bankruptcy on the grounds that it provided further security for prior debts.[92] Alternatively he might apply for sequestration of the debtor and thus have the deed superseded. It is also open to him to do diligence, which would be unaffected by the trust deed, and to cancel which the debtor or other creditors would require to seek sequestration.

If however the creditors do accede to the trust deed they are bound by its terms. There is an implied term that all creditors will be treated equally and that all will succeed. If there is any preference shown to one creditor to procure his accession, or if any creditor does not accede, the others will not be bound by their agreement. It is also an implied condition that the debtor has made no mis-representation about his affairs.

The deed itself will contain the rules of ranking, usually those laid out in the Act. If it does not, the creditors are entitled to rank for the full amount of their claims and to realise any security they hold to add to their dividends. Non-acceding creditors are not bound by any rules of ranking in the deed although the trustee cannot ignore their claims.[93]

The rights and duties of the trustee depend on the deed. He does not have the privileges of a trustee in sequestration. For example, if the deed does not confer on him powers to challenge illegal preferences, he cannot do so. If he has such power he challenges as an

---

92 MacKenzie *v.* Calder (1868) 6 M. 633.
93 *Ogilvie* v. *Taylor* (1887) 14 R. 399.

assignee of an acceding creditor.[94] Further, he must take the
estate of the debtor by appropriate means of conveyance to protect
it from diligence by further or non-acceding creditors; he has no
Act and Warrant. The trustee must have his accounts audited and
his remuneration fixed by the Accountant of Court unless the deed
provides for these things to be done by a committee of creditors
which has acted.[95]

Extra-judicial composition contracts

Such a contract is one in which a debtor offers to pay and his
creditors agree to accept a composition on his debts in full and final
settlement. If the composition is with all his creditors it is known as
a 'general composition'; if with only some it is a 'special composition'.

There is an implied undertaking that the creditors are being
treated equally and that the debtor has not misrepresented his
estate. The debtor is not divested of his estate and may continue
to manage it.

Failure to pay on the contract revives the debts in full,[96] although
the contract itself may provide otherwise.

Common terms in a composition contract are—a time limit for
the securing of the consent of all creditors; the granting of a trust
deed to be effective should the composition not be paid; provision
for security for payment of the composition.

[94] *Fleming's Trs.* v. *McJHardy* (1892) 19 R. 542.
[95] S. 185.
[96] As opposed to the judicial composition contract p. 326 *supra.*

x

INDEX

Absolute insolvency, 306, 308
Acceptance, 22
 see also Bill of exchange, acceptance
Acceptor *see* Bill of exchange, acceptor
Acceptor for honour, 175
Accommodation, bill, 163, 164, 173-4
 party, 173, 174
Account
 see also Current account, Deposit
 account
 Books of, 107
 closing, 7-8
 payee, cheque, 188-9, 198
 payee only, cheque, 188-9
Accountant of Court, 17, 318, 321, 322, 323, 326, 327, 329
Accounts, combination, 18-19
 group, 108-9
Accumulation, income, trust, 256-7
acquirenda, 319
Act and warrant, trustee, 318, 319
Action of furthcoming, 297, 301
Actual, authority, 59, 161
 delivery, 260
ad factum praestandum, 270
ad fundandam juristictionem, 298
ad non executa, 236
ad omissa, 236
Adjudication, 219, 303, 320
 see also Diligence
Administration, estate, 235
Administrator-in-law, 31
Adopted as holograph, 207
Adult, 30
Advances, collation, 227
Adventure, joint, 69-70
Affidavit, 223
 and claim, sequestration, 315, 316, 317, 320
Against cheque, 147
Age of majority, 30
Agency
 see also Agent, Mandatary
 capacity, 54
 constitution, 53-54
 of necessity, 54

termination, 63-4
 notification, 64
Agent
 see also Agency, Mandatary
 del credere, 62
 duties, 56-8, 118, 161
 for foreign principal, 62-3
 mercantile, 61-2
 rights, 55-6
 transactions, 67-8
Alien, trustee, 247
Alimentary liferent, 243-4
Allocation, feu duty, 213-4
Allodial land, 211-12
Allonge, 144, 156
Alteration, bill, 165-6
 cheque, 181, 182, 187, 194
 will, 223
and co., cheque, 192, 193
and company, cheque, 192, 193
Annual, certificate, 89
 general meeting, 108, 110, 111-12
 return, 110, 116
Approbate and reprobate, 228
Appropriation of payments, 24-5
Arrangement, Deed of, 326
Arrestee, 296
Arrester, 296, 299
Arrestment
 see also Diligence
 ad fundandam juristictionem, 298
 cheque, 200, 300
 dependence of action, 298
 in execution, 297
 moveable property, 296-301, 312
 wages, 300
Articles of Association, 87, 88, 89, 90, 98-9, 107, 112, 118
Ascertained goods, 262
Assignation
 bill of exchange, 152-3
 life policy, 264-5
 liferent, 243
 partnership, 80
 security, 292
Assignee, 80

330